Developing a Sense of Place

Developing a Sense of Place

The Role of the Arts in Regenerating Communities

Edited by
Tamara Ashley and Alexis Weedon

First published in 2020 by
UCL Press
University College London
Gower Street
London WC1E 6BT

Available to download free: www.uclpress.co.uk

Collection © Editors, 2020
Text © Contributors, 2020
Images © Contributors and copyright holders named in captions, 2020

The authors have asserted their rights under the Copyright, Designs and Patents Act 1988 to be identified as the authors of this work.

A CIP catalogue record for this book is available from The British Library.

This book is published under a Creative Commons Attribution Non-commercial Non-derivative 4.0 International licence (CC BY-NC-ND 4.0). This licence allows you to share, copy, distribute and transmit the work for personal and non-commercial use providing author and publisher attribution is clearly stated. Attribution should include the following information:

Ashley, T., and Weedon, A. (eds). 2020. *Developing a Sense of Place: The Role of the Arts in Regenerating Communities*. London: UCL Press. https://doi.org/10.14324/111.9781787357655

Further details about Creative Commons licences are available at http://creativecommons.org/licenses/

Any third-party material in this book is published under the book's Creative Commons licence unless indicated otherwise in the credit line to the material. If you would like to reuse any third-party material not covered by the book's Creative Commons licence, you will need to obtain permission directly from the copyright holder.

ISBN: 978-1-78735-782-2 (Hbk.)
ISBN: 978-1-78735-776-1 (Pbk.)
ISBN: 978-1-78735-765-5 (PDF)
ISBN: 978-1-78735-788-4 (epub)
ISBN: 978-1-78735-800-3 (mobi)
DOI: https://doi.org/10.14324/111.9781787357655

Contents

List of figures viii
List of tables x
Notes on contributors xi
Foreword by Hedley Roberts xvi
Acknowledgements xxi

    Introduction: Sensing place, a moment to reflect   1
    Tamara Ashley and Alexis Weedon

Section 1: Case studies of place-making   17

1. Eastern Angles: A sense of place on stage   19
   Ivan Cutting

2. Lesson drawing and community engagement: The experience of Take A Part in Plymouth   35
   Kim Wide and Rory Shand

3. Raising the Barr   44
   Sanna Wicks

4. Interview with E17 Art Trail directors Laura Kerry and Morag McGuire   56
   Alexis Weedon

Section 2: Models and methods for developing place-making through the arts   **71**

5. A model for university–town partnership in the arts: TestBeds   73
   Emma-Rose Payne and Alexis Weedon

6. The Beam archive, Wakefield   84
   Kerry Harker

7. *This Is Not My House*: Notes on film-making, photography and my father   98
   David Jackson

8. Notions of place in relation to freelance arts careers: A study into the work of independent dancers   116
   Rachel Farrer and Imogen Aujla

Section 3: Multidisciplinary approaches to place and contested identities   **137**

9. Performing places: Carnival, culture and the performance of contested national identities   139
   Jonathan Croose

10. A sense of place: From experience to language, from the Polish traveller through a Spanish saint to an adaptation of a Zimbabwean play   162
    Agnieszka Piotrowska

11. The *EU migrant*: Britain's sense of place in English newspaper journalism   183
    Paul Rowinski

12. Rethinking the photographic studio as a politicised space   203
    Caroline Molloy

13. Creative routine and dichotomies of space   212
    Philip Miles

14. Doing things differently: Contested identity
    across Manchester's arts culture quarters   227
    Peter Atkinson

15. First, second and third: Exploring Soja's Thirdspace theory
    in relation to everyday arts and culture for young people   240
    Steph Meskell-Brocken

16. A sense of play: (Re)animating place through recreational
    distance running   255
    Kieran Holland

17. Shiftless Shuffle from Luton: An interview with Perry Louis   272
    Jane Carr

Afterword by Tamara Ashley and Alexis Weedon   286
Index   293

List of figures

Figure 1.1	The old horseman in *The Reapers Year*, 1994. Photograph by Mike Kwasniak, © Eastern Angles.	24
Figure 1.2	From *The Wuffings*, 1997. Photograph by Mike Kwasniak, © Eastern Angles.	27
Figure 1.3	*Parkway Dreams*, 2012. Photograph by Mike Kwasniak, © Eastern Angles.	29
Figure 2.1	Efford, The Capital of Culture for Plymouth Community Manifesto March Day with artists Rachel Dobbs and Hannah Jones of LOW PROFILE, 2012. © Dom Moore Photography.	38
Figure 2.2	Plain Speaking Tour of British Art Show 7 led by members of Efford Crazy Glue, 2011. © Gemma Ward Photography for Take A Part CIC.	41
Figure 2.3	Nowhereisland Radio, North Prospect Community Day, 2012, which involved the artists Hana Backland, Mark Vernon, Neil Rose, Sophie Hope and Jo Bannon. © Gemma Ward Photography for Take A Part CIC.	42
Figure 3.1	Barr Beacon War Memorial after restoration. © Daphne Ison.	45
Figure 3.2	Barr Beacon app. © Sanna Wicks, Treehouse Media Productions Ltd.	48
Figure 3.3	Barr Beacon app, augmented reality feature. © Sanna Wicks, Treehouse Media Productions Ltd.	49
Figure 5.1	Unveiling workshop in Luton Library. © Aleksandra Warchol.	79
Figure 7.1	Film still from *This Is Not My House*, HD video, colour, 2014. © David Jackson.	98
Figure 7.2	Portrait with broken arm, photograph by David Jackson from the series *So Blue, So Beautiful*, colour, C-type print.	100

Figure 7.3	The family album, photograph by David Jackson from the series *So Blue, So Beautiful*, colour, C-type print.	102
Figure 7.4	The wedding photograph, photograph by David Jackson from the series *So Blue, So Beautiful*, colour, C-type print.	108
Figure 7.5	Film still from *This Is Not My House*, HD video, colour, 2014. © David Jackson.	111
Figure 7.6	Film still from *This Is Not My House*, HD video, colour, 2014. © David Jackson.	112
Figure 9.1	'Devon' procession, Exeter, *Battle for the Winds*, 2012. Photograph by Jonathan Croose.	146
Figure 12.1	Transvisual studio wedding photograph. Created by Caroline Molloy. © Belda Productions.	208
Figure 14.1	Street art near Oldham Street, Northern Quarter, Manchester. © John van Aitken.	235

List of tables

Table 8.1   Pseudonyms and backgrounds of research participants   133

Notes on contributors

Dr Tamara Ashley has an MFA and PhD from Texas Woman's University in the United States. Her work there initiated a lifelong interest in the application of critical pedagogy, feminist practice and somatics to dance education. She coordinates the MA Dance Performance and Choreography programme at the University of Bedfordshire, and is the artistic director of The Ensemble, the MA performing group. She has published *Mapping Lineage Artist Book*, lineage maps of practice by dance improvisation artists (Institute of Applied Social Research, University of Bedfordshire, 2018), 'Improvisation and the Earth: Dancing in the Moment as Ecological Practice' in *The Oxford Handbook of Improvisation in Dance* (2019) and journal articles, including a special issue of the *Journal of Dance and Somatic Practices* on interactivity and embodiment, 8(1), 2016. tamara.ashley@beds.ac.uk

Dr Peter Atkinson is Senior Lecturer in Film, Media and Popular Culture, specialising in popular music and television in the northern region of England. Publications include 'The Contrasting Soundscapes of Hull and London in David Bowie's *Ziggy Stardust*', in *Sounds Northern* (Equinox, 2017); 'Producing Habitus: ITV Soap Operas and the "Northern Powerhouse"', in *Heading North* (Springer Nature, 2017); 'The Sons and Heirs of Something Particular: The Smiths' Manchester Aesthetic, 1982–1987', in *Regional Aesthetics* (Palgrave Macmillan, 2015); and 'The Beatles on BBC Radio in 1963: The "Scouse" Inflection and a Politics of Sound in Mersey Beat' (*Popular Music and Society*, 2010). pjatkinson1@uclan.ac.uk

Dr Imogen Aujla is course coordinator of the MSc Dance Science at the University of Bedfordshire. Her research interests cover both the optimisation of performance among elite dancers and the impact of recreational dance on the health and well-being of non-dancers. Her current research with Stopgap Dance Company and the Imperial Society of Teachers of Dancing evidences the value and viability of talent development pathways for disabled dancers. She is also working on projects that explore the impact of intergenerational arts projects. Imogen sits on the Publications Committee of the International Association for Dance Medicine and Science. imogen.aujla@beds.ac.uk

Dr Jane Carr is currently Head of School of Media and Performance at the University of Bedfordshire and previously worked to develop participation in dance at Morley College in south-east London. It was here she first came across UK jazz dancing, interviewing key practitioners to inform publications including 'Disrupting the Habitus: Improvisational Practices in Jazz Dance Battles' (in collaboration with the dancer Irven Lewis) in *The Oxford Handbook of Improvisation in Dance* (ed. Vida L. Midgelow, 2019) and 'Researching British (Underground) Jazz Dancing 1979–1990' in *British Dance: Black Routes* (ed. Christy Adair and Ramsay Burt, Routledge, 2017). jane.carr@beds.ac.uk

Dr Jonathan Croose is a practitioner-academic specialising in place-based performance cultures, outdoor theatre, site-specifics and cultural geography. He is Senior Lecturer in Contextual Studies at Arts University Bournemouth. Jon's ethnographic PhD exploring UK carnival (University of Exeter) followed a practice-led MA in Cultural Performance (Bristol University), in association with Professor Baz Kershaw and Welfare State International. His career has spanned participatory festival, drama in education, community theatre, intergenerational performance and processional crafts. Notions of 'place' are at the heart of Jon's practice. He performs regularly as a street musician, as a showman, and as an associate artist with Gobbledegook Theatre. jcroose@aub.ac.uk

Ivan Cutting is the artistic director and a founding member of Eastern Angles, a touring theatre company set up in 1982 and based at the Sir John Mills Theatre in Ipswich and Chauffeurs Cottage in Peterborough. He has directed much of the company's work as well as devising and writing many new plays inspired by East Anglia's rich heritage. Ivan led the Forty Years On project funded by the Heritage Lottery Fund, a three-year arts and archive project around the Peterborough Development Corporation. His most recent project is *Red Skies*, a play exploring a possible meeting between George Orwell and Arthur Ransome. ivan@easternangles.co.uk

Dr Rachel Farrer is Senior Lecturer in the School of Media and Performance at the University of Bedfordshire. Her research and teaching focuses on community arts and professional practice within the performance industry, including arts and health, freelance working, mentorship and youth arts engagement. Rachel has led on a number of externally funded research projects, publishing and presenting her work internationally. rachel.farrer@beds.ac.uk

Kerry Harker is Founder and Director (since 2017) of the East Leeds Project, situated at the intersection of debates on contemporary art, green and blue infrastructure in the city, and sustainability. She was previously Co-founder and Director of Project Space Leeds (from 2006); Co-founder and Artistic Director of The Tetley, a centre for contemporary art and learning in Leeds (2013–15); and interim Director of The Art House, Wakefield (2015–16). www.eastleedsproject.org

Kieran Holland is a PhD candidate and Associate Lecturer in the Department of Theatre, Film and Television Studies at Aberystwyth University. He is also the organiser of the department's guest-speaker seminar series, Performance, Media and Sport. Kieran's research currently examines how theatrical and performative perspectives can be used together to teach us more about identity formations in recreational distance-running cultures. His broader research interests relate to ideas of identity, power, space, place, theatricality, performativity, sport and popular culture. mkh5@aber.ac.uk

David Jackson is an award-winning photographer, film-maker and academic. His documentary film *This Is Not My House* was co-winner of the 2014 Hotshoe Photofusion Award and his debut feature film *Winterlong* premiered at the 2018 Edinburgh International Film Festival, where it was nominated for the Michael Powell Award for Best British Feature Film. He is currently Senior Lecturer in Film-making at Nottingham Trent University. david.jackson03@ntu.ac.uk

Steph Meskell-Brocken is an arts and heritage engagement specialist and researcher with a background in youth theatre. She has worked across the arts and cultural sector including running digital and heritage projects with children, young people and communities. Steph is based in Manchester in the UK and has been engaged in research since 2011, primarily focusing on youth theatre and the intersection of arts work and youth work. She runs an arts charity based in her native Cheshire and also works for Peshkar, a National Portfolio Organisation based in Oldham and The Met, an arts venue in Bury, Greater Manchester. stephbrocken@gmail.com

Dr Philip Miles is a cultural sociologist with specific interests in how culture is experienced and understood by individuals and groups in society via narratives of personal value, emotion, variables of geography and intrinsic sociality, and how these criteria may be utilised and maintained in meaningful ways in contemporary life. His academic career has included posts at the universities of Lancaster, Cambridge, Brunel and De Montfort. He currently lectures in Sociology and English Literature at the University of Bedfordshire. philip.miles@beds.ac.uk

Caroline Molloy is Programme Leader for Fine Art and Photography at UCA Farnham, alongside which she is a PhD candidate in the Centre of Photographic History at Birkbeck. She has an MA in Photography from the Royal College of Art and an MA from Goldsmiths in Visual Anthropology. Her research interests are centred around photography and visual culture, postcolonial discourse and reactivating archives. She has shared her research at a number of national and international conferences and regularly convenes research events with the Family Ties Network. She regularly writes about photography and culture for *1000words* magazine, *Photomonitor* and *Visual Studies*. carolinemolloy@hotmail.com

Emma-Rose Payne is the University of Bedfordshire's Arts and Culture Projects Manager. Having joined the university in 2017, Emma leads the arts and culture team, which aims to widen participation in the arts and enable artists in local communities to thrive. Emma has international experience in establishing socially engaged projects in partnership with educational institutions and creative organisations. Prior to this, Emma was Learning and Participation Manager at Trestle Theatre Company and Lecturer in Drama (MA, PGCE) at Middlesex University. In 2016, she was part of the All Party Parliamentary Arts, Health and Wellbeing SIG Group, supporting the Creative Health inquiry. emma.payne@beds.ac.uk

Dr Agnieszka Piotrowska is a film-maker and a theorist. She is Reader in Film Practice and Theory at the University of Bedfordshire and Course Leader MA/MSc Digital Film. She is the author of the monographs *Psychoanalysis and Ethics in Documentary Film* (Routledge, 2014), *Black and White: Cinema, Politics and the Arts in Zimbabwe* (Routledge, 2016) and *The Nasty Woman and the Neo-Femme Fatale in Contemporary Cinema* (Routledge, 2019) as well as being the editor of four edited collections. She is best known for her documentary *Married to the Eiffel Tower* and has recently made a number of acclaimed films in Zimbabwe. agnieszka.piotrowska@beds.ac.uk

Dr Hedley Roberts is an artist and academic. He is represented by a number of international galleries, including Galerie Wolfsen, Denmark, and PierMarq Gallery, Sydney, Australia. He has been active in the East London art scene since the early 1990s, and maintains a studio in Margate in the UK. His practice is mainly located in painting and print media. His 'non-portrait' paintings examine self-representation and personal relationships through social media and are exhibited internationally across south-east Asia, Europe and the USA. He was formerly Head of School of Arts and Design at the University of Bedfordshire. hedley.roberts@beds.ac.uk

Dr Paul Rowinski is Senior Lecturer in Journalism at the University of Bedfordshire and worked for the regional, national and transnational press for two decades, including as a central European correspondent. Paul co-edited *Br(e)aking the News: Journalism, Politics and New Media* (Peter Lang, 2013) and wrote *Evolving Euroscepticisms in the British and Italian Press: Selling the Public Short* (Palgrave Macmillan, 2017). He is currently working on another book: *Post-Truth, Post-Press, Post-Europe: Euroscepticism and the Crisis of Political Communication*. paul.rowinski@beds.ac.uk

Dr Rory Shand is Reader in Political Economy at Manchester Metropolitan University. He has published *Governing Sustainable Urban Renewal: Partnerships in Action* (Routledge, 2013), *The Governance of Sustainable Rural Renewal: A Comparative Global Perspective* (Routledge, 2016), *Retirement, Pensions and Justice* (with Mark Hyde; Palgrave Macmillan, 2017), *Sport, Community*

Regeneration, Governance and Development (Routledge, 2017) and *The Creative Arts in Governance of Urban Renewal and Development* (forthcoming, Routledge, 2020), as well as articles in journals such as *Political Studies Review*, *Policy Studies* and *International Labour Review*. He has worked on projects funded by the Economic and Social Research Council and the Higher Education Funding Council for England. r.shand@mmu.ac.uk

Alexis Weedon is UNESCO Chair and Professor of Publishing at the University of Bedfordshire. She supervised the evaluation of the EU-funded training for artists and small to medium-sized enterprises (SMEs) in the creative arts in 2007–8. She has since provided consultancy for SMEs in the fields of illustration, design and publishing. Her publications include *Victorian Publishing: The Economics of Book Production for a Mass Market* (Routledge, 2003), *Elinor Glyn as Novelist, Moviemaker, Glamour Icon and Businesswoman* (with Vincent L. Barnett; Routledge, 2014) and *History of the Book in the West* (Routledge, 5 vols., 2010). She is currently working on research on adaptation and transmedia storytelling. alexis.weedon@beds.ac.uk

Sanna Wicks is Assistant Professor in Film Production at Coventry University and Co-director of Treehouse Media Productions, the company behind the films and mobile phone app for the Raising the Barr project. Her research interests concern cultural heritage media, the use of film language in heritage interpretation and engaging audiences. ac1712@coventry.ac.uk

Kim Wide is Founder, CEO and Artistic Director of Take A Part CIC, an innovative and award-winning co-commissioning public realm curatorial process developed and managed by communities in an embedded and risk-taking way. Born and educated in Canada, Kim came from a heritage background into the arts and has always worked in the realm of engagement. kim@takeapart.org.uk

Foreword
Hedley Roberts

In 1992 I was a student at Central Saint Martins College of Art & Design, and based at the old Lethaby building on Southampton Row in Holborn. During my first year, we came out of the building and went west, towards Soho and Mayfair to go to clubs, galleries and events. We went there because that's where most of the art activity seemed to be.

Within a year, everything changed. We started to catch the bus for 25 minutes going east to Old Street, Hoxton and Shoreditch. Back then, it was still very much desolate and 'post-industrial'. The development of the M25 in the 1980s had taken both the industry and the traffic out of the city, most of the pubs and shops were closed at the weekend, and the buildings were still empty. However, within a short period of a few years, everything changed. Artists had started living cheaply in the big empty warehouse spaces that doubled as studios and party venues. The Bricklayers Arms was full of artists, motorcycle couriers and fashionistas every Friday and Saturday night, the Blue Note jazz venue was hosting legendary evenings on Hoxton Square, the London Apprentice became 333/Mother bar, and the Foundry hosted late-night events. Art impresario and curator Joshua Compton set up his gallery Factual Nonsense and organised the annual art party 'Fete Worse Than Death', which featured wild stunts by the Young British Artists Damien Hirst, Gary Hume, Gavin Turk and Tracey Emin. The area quickly became a Mecca for young creatives taking advantage of cheap rent and cheap space to work and party.

Within a very short time, black cabs ferried in cultural types from London's glitterati from the West End and hedge-fund managers from the City. Gallery goers, art dealers and people with money were clubbing with penniless artists and young ravers. There was a 'scene', and it was exciting. Within five years the real-estate agents and architects had moved in. The fortunate cashed in and boosted their careers onto the international stage. Tourists came to 'experience' East London with its curious mix of old London strip bars next to pop-up galleries and thrift shops.

By 2000, Jay Joplin had set up the beautiful White Cube gallery on Hoxton Square and on opening nights its patrons filled the square. We'd finish our night at the infamous Charlie Wrights International Bar and Grill in the early hours of the morning, moving on for bagels on Brick Lane, or sloping back to West London. By the time that the East London Line enabled people to get to Shoreditch easily, the energy and vitality of the scene had manifested itself as an intense concentration of creativity. Digital start-up companies, designers, architects, restaurants, bars, cool shops and designer-maker fashion stores were everywhere. Magazines like *Dazed and Confused* based their business there, and coffee shops hosted people tapping away on Apple PowerBooks writing their next blog entry or script. East London became the centre for creativity, and a world-renowned district of London. The explosion of street art heralded daily street art 'tours' and a place could be secured on an art tour that took in the more obscure galleries that opened late on the first Thursday of the month.

By the 2000s most of the artists from the 1990s didn't have studios in Shoreditch any more. We'd long since moved further east to Hackney Wick looking for cheaper rent. We'd been replaced by a new breed: the hipster. These people had connoisseur tastes, disposable income and a style that embraced irony as fashion. They revered craft and authenticity, but also liked technology and newness. They were entrepreneurial, and they invested in the 'cool' identity of the area. A day and a night in East London felt like a cross between a pastiche of old East London, like Guy Ritchie's film *Lock, Stock and Two Smoking Barrels*, and Charlie Brooker and Chris Morris's Channel 4 show *Nathan Barley*, a comedy that parodied the more dysfunctional traits of the hipsters. It was fun, but it was a theme park.

Fast forward to 2015, and I'm leaving Hackney for Margate. I can't afford to rent a studio and rent somewhere to live any more. Ten years of six-month tenancies mean that landlords put the house back up for sale and/or rent every six months as a method to get a new tenant at a higher rate without the trouble of a rent tribunal. Artist studios are being closed down, or now cost more than the equivalent residential space. The area that was Hackney Wick has been redeveloped as part of the Olympic Park in the run-up to the 2012 event, and the same kind of cultural redevelopment that happened in Shoreditch has made it fantastically cool and hip. Art tourists visit to see the legacy of street art and graffiti, eat artisan pizza and drink wonderful cocktails from ironic jam jars. Tourists enjoy the performance and showcase of London's fashionistas and culture-goers making the most of the extension of East London cool from Shoreditch to Stratford. You can make your way from Stratford to Margate on the Southeastern High Speed Line in a little over an hour, if you get the right train.

Margate's pivotal change in recent years, according to locals, wasn't the opening of the Turner Gallery, but the installation of the stepped sea defences that create an amphitheatre to the same sunsets that inspired the great painter Turner. There wasn't such a positive appreciation for the Turner Gallery when it first opened, but then the people started to come, the economics of local industries looked up and the Dreamland vintage seaside fair opened, attracting more visitors.

Winters are tough here, facing the North Sea, but the summers are glorious. There are miles of sandy beach, and on the best days you can spend time cheek-by-jowl with day trippers on Margate Sands, or lounging at the Tiki bar, or barbecuing next to families and friends with generators and portable sound systems on Walpole Bay, swimming in the tidal pool. Over the last five years, a wave of creatives have relocated here, in search of cheaper housing and a better pace of life. They seem to have brought an energy with them, and a sense of righteousness. They're renovating houses, setting up cottage industries, taking on the council for not looking after the heritage of the area.

There are projects that have found funding for conservation areas, for the redevelopment of the forgotten Margate Caves, and for Margate's Lido. In many ways it feels like both Shoreditch and Hackney did. The faded glory is there in the architecture, but it's broken down, waiting for repair. In Cliftonville, which was the luxury area of Margate for the Victorians, houses are huge and there are large plots where hotels used to be. Shops on Northdown Road are boarded up or seemingly abandoned. The streets have been forgotten by councils desperately struggling to manage high levels of social deprivation in temporary housing; most of the property has been split into houses of multiple occupancy. However, something is happening here. Those who were probably young hipsters in London in the 1990s and 2000s are making their homes here. They're having families, working to improve schools, standing for councils, and lobbying for change, conservation and heritage. They're entrepreneurial, opening shops, businesses and venues. They're taking on dilapidated buildings to create studios and workspaces. They work together, and they're employing each other and generating local business.

Even since 2015 it seems more affluent, less troubled, more resilient. I live in a street where the bins overflow because they're inadequate for the number of people living in the houses. At the end of the road is a pub, where most summer nights there's a fight. It's not gentrified yet. However, when I'm tending my front garden, people stop and talk to me. I help my Romanian, Polish and Kurdish neighbours' kids fix their bikes; their families look out for my dog when he escapes. Pete Doherty passes by on a bicycle, just like he did in Bethnal Green a decade ago. It's as if Hackney has been transported to the seaside.

I've moved a lot in my life, too many times to be sure of the exact number. However, I think I've always found my sense of place in areas that are in the first swell of a creative transition. Looking back, I think I actively sought out places to live and work where change was about to happen. When I think about a place, there's often some sort of big development that precipitated a move into the area: the M25 moving business traffic out of the city and Shoreditch to create a vacuum for artists to move in, the Tate Modern on the south side of London, the extension of the East London Line, the Olympic project in East London, the Turner Gallery and sea defences in Margate. With hindsight, these events could be thought of as a pattern: a single big development happens and then a whole series of smaller changes cascade sporadically, organically, until they coalesce into a big change. However, it doesn't feel like that at the time. It's more usually a hunch that an area is interesting, vibrant, tense and full of promise.

Luton, for me, is one of those areas that's on the cusp of change. Before I came to work here, a friend who grew up here referred to Luton as 'England's Detroit', an ironic reference to the demise not just of the car industry in the area, but of industry in general. It's easy to see what he meant. Much of the inner town inside the ring road is landlord-locked empty property and there are no luxury shops at all. The Mall that occupies the whole of the centre of town where the streets once stood now struggles to maintain enough trade for major department stores. The council struggles to cope with socio-economic deprivation. Nevertheless, the Mall is always full of locals, and the old market area still has strong business catering for the diverse ethnicity of the community of Luton. It reminds me of Dalston, Hackney, Peckham, Deptford: areas of London that successfully house very broad communities, which then enables new cultures to emerge in the gaps and crossovers.

For me, a place is most interesting when there's a temporary vacuum that opens up, and Luton has that. Despite the challenges that the Mall faces, there are major developments on the horizon: Luton Town Football

Club's recent revival, the site for the club's new ground in the centre of the town, and the development of Newbury Park all point to opportunities for economic revival. The airport continues to manage more passengers and grow its footprint, and secure public–private investment. The area next to the station that is referred to as the 'Cultural Quarter' is a mixture of hat-making industry heritage buildings that are ripe for development. There are strong key players in these communities lobbying for positive change, underpinned by entrepreneurs and businesses that see the possibility of creative regeneration for this town.

In the 1990s, we took a bus to East London. It took around 25 minutes from the centre. We went there for cheap rent and freedom to be entrepreneurial, and we built a world-renowned artists' community. That opportunity opened out East London all the way to Stratford and beyond. Luton is a vacuum of empty property, empty shops and land plots, just 25 minutes' train journey from King's Cross, one of Europe's biggest cultural redevelopments this century, with an international airport and a major motorway. It's also fringed by some of the most beautiful green belt that the Home Counties have to offer. If Luton can find a way to open up and provide opportunities that could benefit a wider creative community, it could just become one of the most important towns in the country again.

Acknowledgements

This book would not have appeared without the inspiration of the Centre for Academic Partnerships' innovative leadership of the TestBeds for artist development programme at the University of Bedfordshire, Luton, which is the creative motivation for this volume. The project has energised artistic endeavour within the town of Luton and beyond both regionally and nationally. Our particular concern has been with the effect of the university as a broker between the researchers and artists, and we have been influenced by the mutually intelligible meanings which have emerged. Many of these were first expressed in the TestBeds conference 'A Sense of Place' held in November 2017, convened by Professor Helen Bailey, and have subsequently been deepened and developed for publication in this volume. Our thanks to the organiser of that conference, Michaela Nutt, whose tireless work over those three days, and the months beforehand, brought together excellent art practice from the local community and beyond and researchers from the university. Her successor in the role, Emma-Rose Payne, also deserves much thanks for her unvarying positivity and commitment to this project, as well as for organising the second conference for the TestBeds project in March 2019, focusing on the role of the university in leading urban regeneration.

A book is always the effort of many people, and our thanks go to the contributors who have all been patient with our demands and silences, and to all the copyright holders of the photographs who have so generously given their permissions. Thanks too to the members of the Research Institute for Media, Art and Performance (RIMAP) who have supported the editing and production of the work. Over the years the research of RIMAP members has framed notions of place-making through the perspectives of dance tradition and local identity, the vocation of the freelance performer within regionals, and the effect of contested identities in postcolonial trauma and melancholia and in Britain's position in Europe, all of which has in various ways raised the intellectual debates within the institution and underpinned the practice of TestBeds. We are much indebted to Dr Chris Penfold and colleagues at UCL Press for their help and guidance in the production of this volume.

Final thanks to Dr Jane Carr, Head of Media and Performance, who is a multi-tasker par excellence, having given time to this volume alongside running a busy and successful School. She has taught Alexis, the non-dancer on the editorial team, to see the many strengths of tough, rigorous training in the consequent *esprit de corps*.

Introduction:
Sensing place, a moment to reflect

Tamara Ashley and Alexis Weedon

The chapters in this volume illustrate how place-making and the arts intersect civic, social and democratic life. Arts organisations and artists reveal how they work with sensitivity in regions, cities, towns and spaces to engage citizens in a deeper understanding of themselves and the places where they live. In a postmodern globalised world, where a sense of belonging to place is fragmented, disrupted and under continual redefinition, the opportunity to consider relationships to place through art-making, curated conversations and the bringing together of communities in a place is increasingly important in creating a sense of connection, well-being and understanding of how people are living together in the twenty-first century. Moreover, 'place-making' is a term applied by local authorities and developers to inform standards on the development of new places, which may or may not include specific arts and culture provision. The value of the arts and culture in terms of place-making is thoroughly explored in the *Culture and Local Development* background document (2018) prepared by the Organisation for Economic Co-operation and Development (OECD). The OECD propose the transformative role that culture can play in enhancing the economy and quality of life for a region:

> Cultural productions can contribute to the development of a territory by creating jobs and economic value, and by improving the quality of life. One of the drivers of local economic development is a positive image of a place or a region, by identifying and valorising own cultural assets. Whether urban or rural, culture can also contribute to a better living environment. Culture can re-activate decayed industrial zones of inner cities, breathing new

life into the dead infrastructures of factories and power stations, dockyards and tram depots, schools, barracks and banks. (OECD 2018, 22)

The OECD's vision of place-making includes arts and culture. In the UK, there is a commitment to making arts accessible to all communities: the government's white paper on culture states that 'Better collaboration between the cultural sectors, and between cultural organisations and their partners at a local, regional and national level will deliver the full benefits of culture for all our communities' (DCMS 2016, 34). However, in the context of funding cuts at national and local levels, such policies invite creativity, innovation and a tactical approach in order to create projects with genuine and meaningful impact. When discussing the UK context, Pritchard draws attention to the issues of gentrification and neo-liberalism, and argues that place-making is a deeply problematic project in that:

> creative placemaking is a state- and local-authority inspired policy wedded, via corporate partnerships, to neoliberalism: an approach that merges art with community and economic development at every level of society – from the global to the hyper-local. It suggests that creative placemaking thereby utilises Creative City and Creative Class models alongside New Urbanist principles and social capital theory to become an effective means of gentrification. (Pritchard 2019, 1)

Pritchard calls for artists to take on more grassroots and activist practices in order to resist gentrification. Other critics of place-making are also concerned with the superficial impact of projects and propose that many initiatives create more disparity through gentrification. For example, Kahne points out that, 'when places and amenities are "installed" in a community without genuine community input and a recognition of the specific needs and desires of that community, this kind of "placelessness" will inevitably result' (2015, 9). What does effective, inclusive and transformational place-making practice through the arts and culture look like? Chapters in this book offer national and international case studies from a range of arts practice – including theatre, film, creative writing, sculpture, storytelling, dance, photography and mixed media – that offer insight into successful as well as problematic projects. By analysing and documenting recent projects as well as offering a history of specific contexts and places, the book offers a useful insight into arts policy, practice and ambition for place-making in twenty-first-century Britain.

The term 'place-making' was first used by Jane Jacobs and William H. Whyte in the USA in the 1970s, and further elaborated upon in Whyte's book *The Social Life of Small Urban Spaces* (1980), which studied the use of city spaces, of which some 'work for people, and some do not' (p. 10). The book offers a detailed insight into people's behaviours in New York City, tracking patterns of use, social interaction and design decisions. The idea of participatory design with communities is seeded. The work of Jacobs and Whyte is continued by the Project for Public Spaces, who see themselves as 'the central hub of the global placemaking movement, connecting people to ideas, resources, expertise, and partners who see place as the key to addressing our greatest challenges' (PPS 2019). Focusing on a wide range of projects including urban regeneration, intervention and cultural practice, the Project for Public Spaces illustrates the varied and creative approaches to place-making that have emerged over the past 40 years.

Place-making and a sense of place are infused with tensions. The process of urban regeneration also signifies loss: a loss of what was there before, a loss of older architectures or empty spaces that, while derelict, may still hold cultural significance for many. One may witness the poetic representation of stark emptiness and abandonment of Potsdamer Platz in the iconic Wim Wenders film *Wings of Desire* (1987), or may have been in person to the vast emptiness of Potsdamer Platz shortly after German reunification. Later, perhaps one is not able to recognise the same location after its twenty-first-century regeneration into a sleek urban area of brand-new glass buildings, smooth concrete walkways and franchise restaurants. Tensions in desire and different agendas play out in architecture and in the apportionment of spaces for culture, commercial activities and living. In the UK, partnerships are across the private and public sectors. Urban planning is commissioned by local and city councils from private companies, while publicly funded arts organisations, schools and universities play significant roles in developing the cultural and social fabric of a place.

With so much at stake, participatory and community approaches to place-making and civic development have emerged over the past three decades. Since 2011, the Arts and Humanities Research Council's Connected Communities project has commissioned significant research into understandings of place-making across the UK. Significant to the development of cities in the UK has been the City of Culture programme, which has sought to bring urban regeneration through cultural programming. The long-term impact of City of Culture is yet to be measured and fully made sense of. However, the Creative Participation in Place-Making report found that a distinction could be made between the 'built environment' and the 'felt environment', and it is this felt sense of place that this book further explores, taking up the recommendation to investigate how 'participation in these broader conceptions of place-making can be facilitated at the local level' (Layard, Milling and Wakeford n.d., 2).

At the local level, a sense of place is about place, location, city, town and environment, and it is also about people, conversations and knowledges that arise through specific exchanges in specific places. The meeting between artists often represents a myriad of journeys, lineages and cultures. It can represent struggle and deep commitments to understand the different; to open the space for dialogue, transformation and exchange. In the first years of the twenty-first century, artists have used terms such as 'site-sensitivity' and 'site-responsiveness' when engaging with specific places to indicate a sensitivity to partnering with a place. Victoria Hunter points out that the artist ensures that 'the work develops in collaboration with the site as opposed to imposing itself upon it' (2005, 375). This key element of non-imposition is particularly important for artists to consider when working in diverse, hybrid and, sometimes, fractured communities. In the cultural agendas that have positioned artists as place-makers, the role of the artist as a positive force for creating community cohesion and community futures has been emphasised. While this agenda may be critiqued, Hunter goes on to explain how the artist can reveal elements of place through their work but stresses that the audience perceptions are key to creating the understanding of place through the experience of artistic work. Place-making through artworks comprises the specific meetings of artists, audiences, communities and points in space and time, thus creating an ephemeral and fleeting quality to the experiences of places and their meanings. Artistic practice offers opportunities to over and over again reconnect, reimagine and recalibrate relationships to place.

Context for each section

The recent Connected Communities initiative by UK research funders has led to a re-examination of the benefits of arts practice in urban and rural communities. Max Nathan (2016) talks of the political policy tremors and structural changes that have altered regeneration models in the last decade in 'Microsolutions for Megaproblems: What Works in Urban Regeneration Policy?'. He says that '[h]olistic neighbourhood-level regeneration has essentially ceased as a state-led activity' (Nathan 2016, 65; see also Florida, Mellander and Stolarick 2011). Central government has responded to the call for localism and devolved the activity, but due to austerity retrenchment in this sector it has become underfunded. Despite an increasing number of measures in place, the unevenness of urban renewal makes it difficult to assess regeneration and the picture is not clear. This hampers strategic interventions and progress in the sector. However, evidence-based evaluations show that local initiatives can work.

Case studies of place-making

In Section 1, on case studies of place-making, we give voice to the artists, curators and originators of projects which have been designed to enrich a specific locale or urban landscape. They cover different locations in the UK, from Norwich in the east to Plymouth in the west, and encompass an inner-city borough as well as a nature reserve. These histories are narrated by the people who made them and they come from a tradition of artistic intervention for community-building. Our case studies show an instructive range of techniques and link to the wealth of experience which the Connected Communities project brought together. Sanna Wicks's use of social media in 'Raising the Barr' draws on the potential of social media in a wildlife-rich habitat surrounded by, but away from, residential areas. It was used too in the 'Big Society' community project which engaged the local community in co-production. In their write-up in 'Contemporary Governance Discourse and Digital Media: Convergences, Prospects and Problems for the "Big Society" Agenda', Chris Speed, Amadu Wurie Khan and Martin Phillips show how their public art work involving a digital totem pole in Wester Hailes, Edinburgh, explored the notion of 'hacking'. They call for the embedding of a '"read-write" facility in public art to present possibilities for community engagement and regeneration' (Speed, Khan and Phillips 2016, 147).

The 'process of listening to stories and experiences and the potential truths they hold' was enabled by Steve Pool and Kate Pahl in their engagement with a group of young people to make a film to send a message to government (Pool and Pahl 2016, 89). Their belief in community co-production is taken forward in this volume in Kim Wide and Rory Shand's experience in the Take A Part community engagement. All of these artists testify to the importance of localism and show the need for policy-makers to 'direct their energies to creating the legal and funding framework to enable communities to achieve their preferred activities' (Speed, Khan and Phillips 2016, 159). How this is done through new forms of interactive governance and co-production with the community has been researched in Europe, and insights from the analysis of initiatives in Marseilles in France and Fieris Féeries in Belgium are relevant to the UK context. These are discussed by Bobadilla, Goransson and Pichault (2018), who evaluate the success criteria for urban planners opening a polyphonic dialogue between themselves, artists and the community, an idea we will return to when discussing the next sections.

In *Against Creativity* (2018), Oli Mould cites Sadiq Khan's 2017 launch of the 'London Borough of Culture' competition. The Mayor of London offered £1,000,000 of arts funding to a London borough that celebrated its creativity. In the narration of the promotional video, Khan said, 'Culture has the incredible power to transform lives, build new friendships, tell new stories and write new histories' (Mould 2018, n.p.). The competition was won in 2019 by Waltham Forest, in which Walthamstow's E17 Arts Trail resides, and Artillery CIC were heavily involved (Artillery's co-directors are interviewed by Alexis Weedon in this volume).

It is a testament to Artillery's inclusive approach and their sensitivity to the needs of the disparate groups within their community that Khan's award was for the community rather than the grand arts institutions, of which London has many. Their theme was 'Radicals, Makers and Fellowship', and there was a borough-wide collaboration between local residents, artists and creatives whose 'home' is in the borough. Mould's book of 2018 came at the beginning of the initiative and the author could not review the fruits of the competition. However, he reflects critically on the American example of Tony Goldman's 'outdoor street art gallery' in Wynwood, a small neighbourhood in Miami, Florida. Rather than developing a sense of place – it was not a place, Mould says; there was no place there – Goldman's company bought up buildings, whitewashed them and invited international artists in to paint murals to make a sense of place. It was, Mould observes, revitalisation as opposed to regeneration. 'It has been argued that Wynwood's by-the-book creative city development has been "post-race": it utilizes ethical and racial diversity as tools to promote cosmopolitanism (as per Miami's "global city" script), rather than to highlight racial and gender inequalities' (Mould 2018, n.p.). Mould's knowledgeable and insightful research into our changing cityscapes and deep concern over the superficiality of some interventions is evident in his article 'Tactical Urbanism' (2014). He points to the danger that short-lived, underfunded community co-productions can mask real problems, commenting that they represent 'the latest cycle of the urban "strategy" to co-opt moments of creativity and alternative urban practices to the urban hegemony' (Mould 2014, 537).

Models and methods for developing place-making through the arts

In our second section, on models and methods, we draw on research into how we sustain the creative sector. Rachel Farrer and Imogen Aujla's research into the freelance careers of dancers demonstrates the pull of the capital for those seeking to earn a living from their practice and the struggle within the regions. The 'London-centric skew of the wider creative economy is well established', say Jones, Long and Perry (2019, 224), citing Oakley (2006). Farrer and Aujla's qualitative interviews and quantitative approach raise important policy issues which must inform funding of the arts in Britain. They found that moving away from London led to dancers feeling that they had to start again on the career ladder and dual careers with secondary employment were common.

In 2016 Kirsten Forkert published the results of her interviews with 41 artists, intermediaries and academics in London and Berlin in 2008–10, comparing the ecology of the arts in the two cities. She found that high rents in London were a substantial drawback and as a result dual careers were common. In Berlin lower rentals enabled artists to support themselves on marginal part-time employment and identify as artists with a bohemian lifestyle which could be sustained with lower outlay. The issue Forkert identifies is the nomadic tendency of artists, who move to develop their practice and so may not act collectively to protect this loophole in affordable rents and protect the artistic careers of the next residents. The Canadian artist-researcher notes that in the UK pressurised careers resulted in 'slower processes of exploration and questioning' (Forkert 2016, 89). In Asia state-constructed solutions have had a beneficial effect: Lily Kong in 'Beyond Networks and Relations' observes that the artist cluster in Telok Kurau, Singapore, does have a sustaining momentum. Kong says that 'geographical propinquity does not in itself generate fruitful relationships amongst the artists' and for this community the answers lie in three factors: its reputation in attracting award-winning artists, an environment which is conducive to work, and cheap rentals (Kong and O'Connor 2009, 74).

Forkert (2016) notes that the culture of managerialism in arts funding, with its emphasis on measuring results in numerical terms, has similarly affected the depth of exploration that artists can sustain. Deriving from policy-led strategy, managerialism can veer towards short-term targets and meeting strategic measures of achievement rather than long-term goals which are outside the administration's lifespan. Kate Oakley concurs and observes that a mobile artistic community fuelling small to medium-sized enterprises in incubation offices and generating new industries has provided the good news that policy-makers and politicians crave (Oakley 2006, 2014). She is more critical of the influence in policy circles of Richard Florida's notion of a creative class and its impact on the economic health of our cities. Florida's methods of quantification have supplied numerical evidence that policy-makers have used in the allocation of arts funding. For example, Florida, Mellander and Stolarick (2011) surveyed 27,883 people across the USA on the effects of beauty and aesthetics on community satisfaction. They report that the four key attractions of a place were a solid economic foundation; the quality of schools; opportunities for social interaction and perceived ability to make and meet friends; and beauty and aesthetics. Less important were the colleges and universities, job opportunities, religious institutions, public transportation, climate, healthcare and cultural opportunities.

Oakley (2009) critiques this approach, arguing that is not transferable to contexts other than North America and presenting a UK perspective on the creative class. 'The degree to which economic needs, brought about by the global economic restructuring of the 1970s and 1980s, were the drivers behind creative industry and creative city strategies in the UK should not be underestimated,' she argues; and in response, regional cities offered 'a mix of subsidised workspace, job-training and support for intermediary networks in the creative industries, largely aimed at small firms' (p. 122).

More outspoken, Mould (2018) observes that the discourse of degeneration leads to regeneration, not to considerations of the more difficult topics to spin, those of redundancy or change of use. He marshals evidence to support this from Sir Peter Bazalgette's 2017 review of the creative industries, which states that '*emerging* evidence from place-shaping research indicates that growth in Creative Industries is enhanced when an area has a strong cultural, heritage and sporting offer, enhancing the attractiveness of locations to live and work and acting as an accelerator for regeneration' (emphasis original; quoted in Campbell 2019, 276). Such rhetoric suits political action, as Oakley comments: 'One of the attractions of the creative industries strategies adopted hitherto by UK cities was that they were seen as attempts to release talents and abilities of the local population' (Oakley 2009, 127).

The low entry barriers to freelance and micro businesses are attractive and they are seen as local cultural activity that offers 'an opportunity for places to negotiate a role within global flows of ideas, rather than simply be "subject" to them' (Oakley 2009, 127). Yet cultural workers offer a pragmatic and precarious entrepreneurship: 'They set up businesses because that is the easiest way to carry out their practice. They get premises because they need to work away from the kitchen table' (Oakley 2014, 145). Phil Jones, Paul Long and Beth Perry (2019) agree and question the utility of the Warwick Commission's (2015) ecosystem metaphor, which argues that the creative and cultural economy is an interdependent unit. Community artists, they say, have no real interest in making intellectual property out of their initiatives – that is not the purpose of their artwork. Their aims are vastly different from those of state-funded museums and galleries, which have different measures for their funding and outreach activities. So the purposes of their activity, their meaning-making, are poles apart. If they both have the same 'intermediary' function in society – to use Bourdieu's term – then their funding is competitive, argue Jones, Long and Perry.

The role of the university in Luton's regeneration project in preparing, training and paving the way for artistic intervention has developed in part from the University of Bedfordshire's previous EU-funded training for creative business entrepreneurs. It has been proactive in innovation zones, as well as regional and business leadership, as Payne and Weedon explain in this volume. Like many universities, it is thinking of how it can work best within and for its communities. Melhuish (2015) gathers prime case studies of university-led urban regeneration projects and their effect on the communities. These case studies, funded by UCL, have the practical aim of informing the university's redevelopment of part of Stratford's former Olympic grounds in London. In the foreword Ben Campkin says, 'We strongly believe there is a need for new ethical models of urban renewal – particularly in London – which are genuinely research-driven rather than misleadingly "evidence-based"'. The case studies include Durham University's redevelopment of Teesside in the 1990s through to the development of Queen's Campus at Stockton; Newcastle's Science Central site; and the development of Somerleyton Road in south London, where a university was the anchor institution. Another of the case studies, Cambridge University's development to the north-west of the city, used public art to get community engagement.

However, Cambridge is a unique place and what works in one urban culture may not work in another.

Bobadilla, Goransson and Pichault (2018) have observed that the capacity to use the engagement of the relevant stakeholders, artists, local government and citizens for any significant effect is a real challenge for developers. They witnessed, as the Marseilles development progressed, much disillusion amongst the participants, who saw their artistic involvement as a mere confirmation of the planners' aims. In Somerleyton Road in south London, the community involvement was measured and bottom-up, and expectations of its effect were more moderate. As in Fieris Féeries in Belgium, a more modest and equal partnership between listening and designing was more productive and longer-lasting. Perhaps another reason for the difference is that universities are familiar with developing infrastructures to build community and engagement with a nomadic population, as students flow through and go off to work elsewhere. As Robin Hambleton says, universities are the 'sleeping giants of place-based leadership' (quoted in Melhuish 2015, 9). Their commitment to such projects draws on the model of the 'engaged university' with its civic mission, service learning programmes, volunteering and widening access.

Multidisciplinary approaches to place and contested identities

In the third section, we draw from different disciplinary approaches to developing a sense of place. From an art and cultural studies background, Jonathan Croose's exploration of contested cultural identities and the Olympic Games shows some elements of 'tactical urbanism', which Oli Mould (2014) says is a 'popular movement for people who have a desire to change and reconfigure their city and do so without government involvement' (p. 529). Mould cites the example of Bat Yam, south of Tel Aviv, where in September 2010 the government ran a '72 hour Urban Action' event in which the community were given the tools and a small budget to build or create what they wanted. Examples included a children's play area in the community space of a residential tower block, a reflective garden and a pop-up market stall.

For Mould (as for Peter Atkinson writing on Manchester's arts culture in this volume), this artistic intervention organised and orchestrated by developers can be seen as 'artwashing', a cynical attempt to make the area suitable for the tastes of the creative class. Tactical urbanism is attributed to Mike Lydon, of the New York City 'Streets Olan Collective', but it is not new and, Mould says, is in danger of being a quick fix in budget-conscious austerity: '[T]his rhetorical world is just a pastiche of consumption, more often than not modelled on the consumption patterns of white, middle-class people' (Mould 2018, n.p.).

In Britain, yarn bombing (knitting round poles) and 'craftivist' interventions may be dubbed DIY and amateurish in nature, yet they can be a way into the community for people who do not consider themselves creative, as E17 Arts Trail has shown in this volume. A long-standing and by now accepted form of arts research is by practice: either based on the process of creative production or led by an understanding of art practice gained by the practitioner. Such research brings the affective knowledge of the artist into academe and also into the understanding of place-making at a community and personal level. Sarah Haynes's storytelling project, for example, developed a community memory of Liverpool from the perspective of the future, and engaged people in imagining their city, five, ten and a hundred years hence (Haynes 2017). They were able to articulate their fears and visions of their locale, which the author then edited into her science-fiction thriller.

More personally, David Jackson's exploration of his connection with his father in this volume touches on a relationship everyone can recognise as giving a sense of place and home. The relationship between father and son is something that Jackson has explored in his other photographic and film work located in Malta and along the English south coast (Jackson 2018). As an artist, he questions the emotional tug behind his father's return to a place where he had grown up but which was no longer the same. Through the empathy he builds between us and his inquiry, we delve deeper into our own private autobiographical narratives of home, growing up and the relationship with our parents. As our narrative becomes focused on the personal, we also resonate with the stories of others. Philip Miles points out in this volume that many of these are stories of migration and relocation where 'place' becomes somewhere to settle before becoming 'home'. As artist-researchers, Haynes's imagining of the future and Jackson's imaginings of a past draw us with them to view our present as our place in the continuum of existence.

Giddens's view is that 'modernity increasingly tears space away from place by fostering relations between "absent" others, locationally distant from any given situation of face-to-face interaction' (Giddens 1990, 18). Modernity's crime is multifold: it is in the trauma of the postcolonial encounter of the film-maker, in the journalist's 'othering' of migrants, in the youth's inability to find a free space within the cityscape, and in the black British dancer's desire to excel in an 'othered' form. In her chapter in this volume, Agnieszka Piotrowska views the other as a postcolonial object, drawing on feminist psychoanalysis, but explaining in lucid fashion how this theoretical lens has affected her work in theatre and film in Zimbabwe. She tackles her subject with personal courage as a Polish white woman in black Zimbabwe questioning its societal assumptions about the role of women. Her work can be framed within Kimberlé Crenshaw's legal challenge for racial justice, identity politics and policing in intersectionality (Crenshaw 1989). The articulation of a sense of place is much harder when the landscape of identity has been overplanted by other people's stories. There are parallels with the photographer Caroline Molloy's micro-analysis in this volume of a commercial studio within a Turkish community in London and the way it becomes a focal point for stories of reconnection and traditional cultural practices despite migration and relocation.

Different disciplinary angles on place-making show how we constantly redefine distance and nearness: Paul Rowinski uses discourse analysis to unpick the localism and tribalism embedded in newspaper journalism in community and national stories. Alternative media have been better at creating a sense of place and identity (Couldry and Curran 2003) and digital journals provide much more space for community news and information-sharing exchange (Hess 2013). For library and information scientists, everyday life information seeking (ELIS) has become much more of a concern 'because so much information is passively absorbed' (Williamson and Roberts 2010, 285). This is relevant in tourism studies, and the availability of ELIS is of special concern for local services (Franklin 2018).

Since Giddens, we have found vast digital spaces through which we can have face-to-face interactions and open up communication routes, exhibition venues and 'third spaces' – a term often used in human–computer design (Deuze and Prenger 2019). Even though we can 'hang out' in these spaces, they are not the first choice for many communities. This mix of spaces and places is evident in Wallis Motta and Myria Georgiou's investigation of the 'resources summoned, mobilized, and appropriated by locals in developing networks of communication' (Motta and Georgiou 2017, 183). They mapped the white British and black Caribbean residents of Haringey's use of hyperlocal online information, the Turkish community's use of the community centres, and black Caribbean participants' use of churches and mosques. In this volume, Caroline Molloy too traces the fusion of local and traditional spaces when rites of passage are celebrated by the photographer, and Kieran Holland relates how the lights of runners outlined the topography of Arthur's Seat in Edinburgh in an artist-inspired community event. Our notion of place has been changed by digital mapping technologies which overlay our landscape. They have an affectivity which Bradley L. Garrett talks of in relation to our heritage, how through exploring we create relationships with the immediate environment, making associations with places, sometimes with fearful, poignant, fight-or-flight reactions: 'These neurological responses create affective association with places, the sublime experience that explorers find difficulty in relaying' (Garrett 2015, 81). The educationalist David Gruenewald concurs: 'places make us: As occupants of particular places with particular attributes, our identity and possibilities are shaped' (Gruenewald 2003, 621).

Jane Carr, from a somatic perspective on dance and performance, aptly brings in the relevance of Maurice Merleau-Ponty (Carr 2014). Merleau-Ponty said in *Phenomenology of Perception* (1962) that our perception is inherently participatory. Place acts on the response, or beckoning, between the body and things; it has action, speech and something to say in the human–world relationship. Such reflections on the body and embodied experience are poignant for future investigations on place-making, and our sense of place. Senses are the experiential lens of the body–mind as one navigates the world. Moreover, in systems such as permaculture, practitioner Nala Walla points out that 'our bodies are the first units of localism from which homes, villages and communities are built' (2009, 1). Reflection is possible on how one lives in the body as well as how one lives in a particular place, and how the body is a place made, as much as a geographic location. The environmental crisis puts bodies at risk in terms of creating uninhabitable places and in terms of the health and well-being of the body itself. The crisis resonates at a cellular level. Living in the felt experience of the body, attending to the body, and thinking through its health and well-being in terms of place-making might give an ethical orientation to the future of place-making. Future place-makers might be tasked with innovative design that responds to rapidly shifting climates and migrating populations. The creativity of artists and cultural workers illustrated in this book shows how responsive and resilient approaches can be developed.

The artists and projects featured in this book show how those working in the arts traverse shifts in politics, funding and agendas with awareness, skill, insight, foresight and, sometimes, struggle. Considering a sense of place through the lenses of these contributors invites reflection upon the complex, hybrid and fluid knowledges that arrive in momentary meeting points of understanding. The notion of place as geographically anchored is under question and instead a sense of place is offered as just that: what is sensed in the moment as place, knowing, identity and meaning. In this book, places, architectures, locations, events and bodies are proposed as fluid, changing and responsive. Nonetheless, the case studies here illustrate the positive role that artists and organisations can play in curating and developing a sense of place with the people with whom they work: the felt and lived dimensions of place.

There is no doubt, reading through this collection, that a sense of place touches all of us and provides us with a sense of trust, security and identity. History tells us that we cannot simply build homes – we must develop place and that requires the expertise of a wide range of professions and academic disciplines. We must incorporate the wealth of knowledge which the arts and humanities bring to urban planning for our communities.

References

Bobadilla, Natalia, Marie Goransson and François Pichault. 2018. 'Urban Entrepreneurship through Art-Based Interventions: Unveiling a Translation Process', *Entrepreneurship and Regional Development* 31 (5/6): 378–99.

Campbell, Peter. 2019. *Persistent Creativity: Making the Case for Art, Culture and the Creative Industries*. Cham: Palgrave Macmillan.

Carr, Jane. 2014. 'Landmark: Dance as a Site of Intertwining', *Journal of Dance & Somatic Practices*, 6 (1): 47–59.

Couldry, Nick and James Curran, eds. 2003. *Contesting Media Power: Alternative Media in a Networked World*. Lanham, MD: Rowman and Littlefield.

Crenshaw, Kimberlé. 1989. 'Demarginalizing the Intersection of Race and Sex: A Black Feminist Critique of Antidiscrimination Doctrine, Feminist Theory and Antiracist Politics', *University of Chicago Legal Forum*: 139–67.

DCMS (Department for Culture, Media and Sport). 2016. *The Culture White Paper*. London: Department for Culture, Media and Sport. Accessed 15 October 2019. https://assets.publishing.service.gov.uk/government/uploads/system/uploads/attachment_data/file/510799/DCMS_Arts_and_Culture_White_Paper_Accessible_version.pdf.

Deuze, Mark and Mirjam Prenger, eds. 2019. *Making Media: Production, Practices, and Professions*. Amsterdam: Amsterdam University Press.

Florida, Richard, Charlotta Mellander and Kevin Stolarick. 2011. 'Beautiful Places: The Role of Perceived Aesthetic Beauty in Community Satisfaction', *Regional Studies* 45 (1): 33–48.

Forkert, Kirsten. 2016. *Artistic Lives: A Study of Creativity in Two European Cities*. London: Routledge.

Franklin, Adrian. 2018. 'Art Tourism: A New Field for Tourist Studies', *Tourist Studies* 18 (4): 399–416.

Garrett, Bradley L. 2015. 'Urban Exploration as Heritage Placemaking'. In *Reanimating Industrial Spaces: Conducting Memory Work in Post-Industrial Societies*, edited by Hilary Orange, 72–91. Walnut Creek, CA: Left Coast Press.

Giddens, Anthony. 1990. *The Consequences of Modernity*. Cambridge: Polity Press.

Gruenewald, David A. 2003. 'Foundations of Place: A Multidisciplinary Framewok for Place-Conscious Education', *American Educational Research Journal* 40 (3): 619–54.

Haynes, Sarah. 2017. 'The Memory Store, with John Moores University: Imagine the Year 2115 in This Writing Workshop'. Workshop, Tate Liverpool, 18 February.

Hess, Kristy. 2013. 'Breaking Boundaries: Recasting the "Local" Newspaper as "Geo-Social" News in a Digital Landscape', *Digital Journalism* 1 (1): 48–63.

Hunter, Victoria. 2005. 'Embodying the Site: The Here and Now in Site-Specific Dance Performance', *New Theatre Quarterly* 21 (4): 367–81.

Hunter, Victoria, ed. 2015. *Moving Sites: Investigating Site-Specific Dance Performance*. London: Routledge.
Jackson, David. 2018. *Winterlong* [film]. Edinburgh International Film Festival, 30 June.
Jones, Phil, Paul Long and Beth Perry. 2019. 'Conclusion: Where Next for Cultural Intermediation?' In *Cultural Intermediaries Connecting Communities: Revisiting Approaches to Cultural Engagement*, edited by Phil Jones, Beth Perry and Paul Long, 221–230. Bristol: Policy Press.
Kahne, Juliet. 2015. 'Does Placemaking Cause Gentrification? It's Complicated'. Project for Public Spaces blog, 2 November. Accessed 15 October 2019. www.pps.org/article/gentrification.
Kong, Lily and Justin O'Connor, eds. 2009. *Creative Economies, Creative Cities: Asian-European Perspectives*. Dordrecht: Springer.
Layard, Antonia, Jane Milling and Tom Wakeford. n.d. *Connected Communities: Creative Participation in Place-Making*. London: Arts and Humanities Research Council. Accessed 9 January 2020. https://ahrc.ukri.org/documents/project-reports-and-reviews/connected-communities/creative-participation-in-place-making/.
Melhuish, Clare. 2015. *Case Studies in University-Led Urban Regeneration*. London: UCL Urban Laboratory.
Motta, Wallis and Myria Georgiou. 2017. 'Community through Multiple Connectivities: Mapping Communication Assets in Multicultural London'. In *Communicating the City: Meanings, Practices, Interactions*, edited by Giorgia Aiello, Matteo Tarantino and Kate Oakley, 183–200. New York: Peter Lang.
Mould, Oli. 2014. 'Tactical Urbanism: The New Vernacular of the Creative City', *Geography Compass* 8 (8): 529–39.
Mould, Oli. 2018. *Against Creativity*. London: Verso.
Nathan, Max. 2016. 'Microsolutions for Megaproblems: What Works in Urban Regeneration Policy?'. In *After Urban Regeneration: Communities, Policy and Place*, edited by Dave O'Brien and Peter Matthews, 61–78. Bristol: Policy Press.
Oakley, Kate. 2006. 'Include Us Out: Economic Development and Social Policy in the Creative Industries', *Cultural Trends* 15 (4): 255–73.
Oakley, Kate. 2009. 'Getting Out of Place: The Mobile Creative Class Takes on the Local: A UK Perspective on the Creative Class'. In *Creative Economies, Creative Cities: Asian-European Perspectives*, edited by Lily Kong and Justin O'Connor, 121–34. Dordrecht: Springer.
Oakley, Kate. 2014. 'Good Work? Rethinking Cultural Entrepreneurship'. In *Handbook of Management and Creativity*, edited by Chris Bilton and Stephen Cummings, 145–59. Cheltenham: Edward Elgar Publishing.
OECD (Organisation for Economic Co-operation and Development). 2018. *Culture and Local Development: Background Document*. Paris: Organisation for Economic Co-operation and Development. Accessed 15 October 2019. www.oecd.org/cfe/leed/venice-2018-conference-culture/documents/Culture-and-Local-Development-Venice.pdf.
Pool, Steve and Kate Pahl. 2016. 'The Work of Art in the Age of Mechanical Co-Production'. In *After Urban Regeneration: Communities, Policy and Place*, edited by Dave O'Brien and Peter Matthews, 79–94. Bristol: Policy Press.
PPS (Project for Public Spaces). 2019. 'Our Mission'. Accessed 1 May 2020. www.pps.org/about.
Pritchard, Stephen. 2019. 'Place Guarding: Activist Art against Gentrification'. In *Creative Placemaking: Research, Theory and Practice*, edited by Cara Courage and Anita McKeown, 140–55. London: Routledge.
Speed, Chris, Amadu Wurie Khan and Martin Phillips. 2016. 'Contemporary Governance Discourse and Digital Media: Convergences, Prospects and Problems for the "Big Society" Agenda'. In *After Urban Regeneration: Communities, Policy and Place*, edited by Dave O'Brien and Peter Matthews, 147–62. Bristol: Policy Press.
Walla, Nala. 2009. *Body as Place: A Somatic Guide to Re-Indigenization*. BCollective. http://www.bcollective.org/essays/bodyasplace.ede.pdf.
Whyte, William H. 1980. *The Social Life of Small Urban Spaces*. New York: Project for Public Spaces.
Williamson, Kirsty and Julie Roberts. 2010. 'Developing and Sustaining a Sense of Place: The Role of Social Information', *Library and Information Science Research* 32 (4): 281–87.
Wilson, Kerry. 2012. *Connected Communities: Connecting Communities via Culture-Led Regeneration: The Cultural Cities Research Network 2011–12*. Swindon: Arts and Humanities Research Council.

Section 1:
Case studies of place-making

1
Eastern Angles: A sense of place on stage

Ivan Cutting

Eastern Angles has been producing theatre with a sense of place for over 35 years. Just like the national companies of Wales and Scotland, Eastern Angles has focused on subjects, characters and hidden experience that have a flavour of the area it serves: East Anglia. This chapter looks at the influential sources that have shaped the style and content of this work, including documentary, oral history and new writing, and also at how the venues Eastern Angles performs in contribute to the scale and direction of its annual programme. The chapter features specific examples around creating large-scale work and adapting to funding vagaries, new urban settings and the demographic changes in villages, and finally monitors the changes in the conception of 'heritage' over that period.

Beginnings

Eastern Angles is the regional touring theatre company for the East of England, although as the company's name suggests, its primary stamping ground is the largely rural region of East Anglia, an area with a nebulous identity shaped by a myriad of changing landscapes, from coastal/estuary areas (fishing and tourism) to high clay farmland (cereals and the bread basket of England), then the flat Breckland area (horses and turkeys), and finally its watery fens, which act as its protective moat. The area boasted a moveable population from several centuries BC but takes its title from the German tribes who settled here in the fourth to sixth centuries AD after the Romans left and whose King of the Eastern Angles, Raedwald, is believed to be buried at Sutton Hoo. The region lacks the strong loyalty (and accent) of other areas such as Yorkshire, Tyneside or the Scottish Highlands and is rarely featured in TV series and soaps. It tends to be bracketed with the south-east, yet its trade routes and levels of investment make it more connected to its western neighbour, the equally unprepossessing East Midlands.

The company was started in 1982 by five actors who saw a gap in the market and a job opportunity. At the time there were other companies in Northumberland, Oxfordshire, Herefordshire and in the south-west around Exeter. Their common denominator was touring to rural village halls with devised or commissioned shows aimed at local audiences, but East Anglia, apart from the Peterborough area (we'll come to that later), had no such provision. We offered to fill that gap and attracted funding relatively quickly from both local authorities and the Arts Council Regional Association, Eastern Arts.

Nowadays many regional theatres boast of their local significance and sense of place, even if few explore the deeper ramifications of that phrase: the local novel adaptation, the once-in-a-decade community play or a local writing workshop tend to be the limits of the alternatives offered in the annual artistic programme. Back in the 1980s this was even worse, and most seasons were permutations of dutiful and popular Shakespeare (for the schools), a classic like Gogol's *The Government Inspector*, an Alan Ayckbourn, the latest ex-West End release, a cheap farce and, latterly, a John Godber (John Godber Company 2020; Arts Council of Great Britain 1983). If our high streets gradually came to look the same, our theatres had beaten them to it.

But all was not lost. The counterculture of the 1960s and 1970s had set in train movements to challenge this monoculture and they were starting outside of London. Theatre in Education (TIE) was becoming a staple provision of regional repertory companies, often funded differently by local education departments; and the Manpower Services Commission (MSC) had helped establish a number of new endeavours in areas of low employment. TIE was an honest and proud achievement, although performers being what they are, they always had their eye on adult performance too and looked to flex their muscles outside of schools. These actors, directors and musicians were intrinsically opposed to what were called 'velvet spaces'[1] and large stages, so looked for alternatives and veered into more community spaces. Companies like Northumberland Theatre Company, Pentabus, Medium Fair and Peterborough's Key Perspectives joined the throng, nurturing writers like Charlie Way, Mike Kenny, Tony Coult and others, and found their métier in the more rural areas. Key Perspectives decamped to Mansfield in Nottinghamshire, and East Anglia was bereft. Even though Eastern Angles' own application to the MSC landed on the chancellor's desk the day he scrapped the scheme, there was enough evidence now that rural touring was an accepted concept and business model and should be adopted by any self-respecting rural county that valued the arts.

In 1982, Eastern Angles were relatively late arrivals to the scene, and the missionary purpose of rural touring – with its sometimes slightly patronising sense of not wanting to spook the horses – was starting to run out of steam. We needed a new source of energy and it came in the form of documentary theatre.

Documentary theatre

Documentary theatre has a long history that could claim 1930s German agitprop, US Living Newspaper groups, the work of Peter Weiss in *The Investigation* and even, it may be argued, the medieval mystery plays, which had a documentary element in their didacticism. In the 1960s, theatre documentary work reflowered in the work of Peter Cheeseman at Stoke, whose *The Knotty* I saw in the late 1970s. He acknowledged that he had taken the idea from the radio ballads of Ewan MacColl, Peggy Seeger and Charles Parker (Jones 1958). These exquisite slices of radio, both documentary and ballad in form, were a heady mix of actuality recordings, music and sound effects. MacColl's lyrics were perfect distillations of the oral history material, encapsulating industry dialect and work jargon like never before:

> In your dungarees, cleaning Super D's, you're a –
> Sweeper-upper, brewer-upper, shovel-slinger, spanner-bringer, steam-raiser
> Fire-dropper, general-cook and bottle-washer, learning how to keep 'em rolling
>
> Hey lad will you fetch me a bucket of red oil for a red tail lamp
>
> (MacColl *et al.* 1957)

Even the final piece of actuality clearly alludes to some poor innocent being sent on a pointless task on their first day at work, a classic staple of oral history interviews and subsequent stage scenes in documentary theatre.

Probably the most famous of the ballads was *Singing the Fishing*, about the herring season, which linked the north-east coast of Scotland with the great autumn 'hoom fishin'' of East Anglia (MacColl, Seeger and

Parker 1960). It was flawless radio and laid down the template for much of the travelogue, biopic and news programmes we listen to today, on both radio and TV.

Cheeseman took that idea and put it on stage. He had the advantage of an in-house company of actors who could go out and find material in libraries, record offices, newspaper archives and local museums, and from the people themselves who remembered working on whatever industry was being focused on: the railways before British Rail, the potteries or the coal mines. This was sense of place dug deep. Cheeseman's mantra was that there had to be a 'primary source witness' for anything he put on stage in a documentary. It could be a diary entry, a newspaper account (and the nineteenth-century newspaper is a wonderful source of verbatim accounts) or an oral history interviewee, but it had to represent an authentic account of someone who was there at the time. This was probably as far from Wikipedia as you could get. The shows were not written but edited and the content was shaped by the material offered. The only concoctions were the songs.

We took this idea and translated it to East Anglia with a series of shows about the agricultural worker, the herring season in Lowestoft, and life on the home front during the Second World War. With live music, good verbatim material and multitalented performers, the productions were very popular and gave us an audience. Quite simply, these productions established our reputation in East Anglia.

But they only got us so far, and gradually we realised that most industries had a similar story: advances in technology (sail to steam, horse to tractor) leading to record achievement followed by two world wars, unemployment between them and then an eventual massive reduction in manpower. The imprint of the twentieth century was so overwhelming that it meant we had to find an alternative structural device to tell our stories. This had two consequences: it solved the chronological problem but also prompted the urge to explore the inner world of our characters beyond the factual and the events. We now started to add in fictional material and to commission writers to explore the personal issues around each of the subjects. The story of the agricultural worker was structured around a single year's work from harvest to harvest, but now also included a play about an old horseman whose world is being overtaken by the tractor. Subsequent seasons included plays/documentaries about horse racing, brewing, lifeboatmen and changes to village life in the twenty-first century. This could also mean a fundamental shift in outlook. Whereas it's right that pure documentary must be shaped by the material – otherwise you end up looking for material to prove your point – writers choose their material according to character, plot and dramatic necessity.

In the meantime, we had already discovered that community audiences were no longer the assumed unsophisticated theatre-goers of before. The age of missionary work was over. Audiences were now familiar with actors doubling characters, switching character with a change of voice or hat, and with actors breaking the fourth wall to talk to them. Above all audiences were used to using their imaginations and filling in spare stage design. We never toured with a living-room-style set. They understood that a simple bentwood chair could be sat on at a table, in a taxi or in a helicopter, but could also represent a sheaf of corn or a plough. They also didn't need cheering up and were ready for something bleak. We looked to our old transcripts again.

The frog's bone

An example of digging deep from our point of view is the series of plays we produced about the 'magic' of the old horsemen in Suffolk who could 'jade' or freeze a horse so that it wouldn't move, a demonstration of their power over horses. I had read about it in the books of George Ewart Evans, another inspiration for the company's work, whose first book, *Ask the Fellows Who Cut the Hay* (1956), also triggered the use of oral history to get inside the forgotten experience of rural work practices. One old head horseman told me a story about a policeman arresting a horseman for being drunk and him asking to say goodbye to his horses before he was carried off to the cells. In the morning the police had to take him back to his horses as they hadn't been able to move them. The horseman 'went up to them and away they went'. I asked him what the horseman did and he said, 'Ah, them's old old secrets, that don't do to tell.' I hadn't got the heart to say that I knew what it was he did, involving the use of special oils that horsemen would mix in special ways: 'They used to get one oil from one chemist and one from another, so no one knew how they were mixed,' a blacksmith had told me (Blacksmith n.d.).

The oils were a physical cause, but I knew the horsemen also practised something else that was more bizarre. Again, I had to wait for someone to answer my question fully, and finally another old horseman in deepest Suffolk said, 'You have to get a frog what walk, not one that jump, one what walk, and you put that on a blackthorn bush to dry out, then in an antheap, and the ants eat off all the flesh. Then you take the bones and put them in a running stream, and there's one bone what will go contrary to the stream. You got to pick that bone out, if you dare, cos when you're there the devil's there too, and that's what will give you power over horses.'

I had read this before, but two other interviewees also told a similar story about the running stream and the frog's bone, sometimes to the concern of their wives, who knew nothing about it, and if they did, didn't like it. But it all fell into place when I realised that a horseman only has one chance when he steps into a field and has to draw his first furrow and any succeeding furrows. He can't turn around and start again or wipe away the first attempt. And what's more, his neighbours on a Sunday will turn out after the pub to inspect any recent 'bits of ploughing', and a kink in the furrow will be likely to invite mockery of the type, 'You'll find a dead rabbit in there in the morning, that'll break its neck trying to get round that corner!' The ploughman's dignity and reputation rested on a piece of work that was on public show for the rest of the year. It was essential that he had control over his horses. And he probably spent more time with his horses than he did with his wife. And he talked to them more too! It was not surprising then to find that the women didn't approve of this belief and felt it could take control of the men.

Eastern Angles produced three plays set in 1938, 1968 and 1998 with this as a background. The first, *The Reapers Year* (see Figure 1.1), set

Figure 1.1 The old horseman in *The Reapers Year*, 1994. Photograph by Mike Kwasniak, © Eastern Angles.

an old ploughman in the era of the arrival of the tractor, and marked a period when we realised we could challenge our audience with something darker, an old horseman in the throes of a breakdown; the second, *Days of Plenty*, was set in the world of the late 1960s and youth rebellion; and the third, *Bone Harvest*, embraced two time periods, harking back to the First World War and a more recent story of a young man who becomes an oral historian (Eastern Angles 2020).

These plays were some of the most popular we ever produced. They touched a nerve that can only be explored through drama and this could only have been achieved with a level of trust and loyalty from our audiences.

The Wuffings

A theme is developing here around secrets and burial. Rural areas are often noteworthy for things left unsaid and characters avoiding the kind of overemotional argument we associate with urban life. And in East Anglia the most hallowed site is that of Sutton Hoo, now recognised as the burial ground of kings but marked only by a series of low tumuli overlooking the River Deben at Woodbridge. The Wuffings were the royal house of the Eastern Angles, a tribe that over time had clearly proved themselves the most fearsome, clever and entrepreneurial. By 600 AD they were recognised as such and their king, Raedwald, was invited down to Kent to meet Augustine, an envoy of the Pope, who wanted to convert the pagan Anglo-Saxons to Christianity. Raedwald was inclined to agree, but his wife insisted on maintaining an additional pagan altar at their palace in Rendlesham, and when Raedwald died she ensured that, while his burial included Christian elements, the main thrust was according to Nordic custom, a ship burial in earth surrounded by his treasure and all the accoutrements to allow his safe journey to Valhalla.

Since the discovery of the famous treasure hoard in 1939 and its removal to the British Museum, the site has held a special place in the hearts of those that recognise a regional identity. We wanted to tease out these feelings, but we faced two problems: how to do it on a scale deserving of this epic event, and how to help our audiences understand who the Wuffings were in the first place. I was adamant that I wanted the road signs directing people to The Wuffings.

So, we looked again at the actual discovery of the treasure and found a story that had some of the features of an Ealing comedy: the little man, Basil Brown (the local archaeologist), teaming up with the wealthy widow and psychic Mrs Pretty (owner of the Sutton Hoo estate where the barrows lay). At a seance Basil was encouraged by a message from the spirit world to 'carry on digging' – a potential show title. But we settled on the more Ealing-like *The Sutton Hoo Mob* since Basil came up against the sharp-suited town museum curator from Ipswich, and then had to hold his own under the tutelage of the British Museum as the megalith-like academics from Cambridge muscled in to steal his thunder. Featuring songs of the period (*Why Does My Heart Go Boom?*), the show was a winner.

For the subsequent big show, *The Wuffings* (see Figure 1.2), we appealed for a place where we could have fire, water and a 400-seat auditorium. The local garden centre Notcutts offered their dispatch centre, a three-bay warehouse, and the Royal Shakespeare Company let us use their regional touring seating rig. Eight thousand people came to see the show, which featured a stage as wide as the Sutton Hoo boat was long (90 ft) and a cast of 16 performing on a stage made of 20 tons of sand, with braziers, running water and a scene that took Raedwald's wife into the underworld.

This success was an indication of something else, however. *The Wuffings* harnessed several sources of audience in one go: first of all, it brought in our village hall audiences – and in order to fund the project we had not produced a village hall show that year; second, since it was part of the Year of Opera and Music, which the Arts Council was promoting, it brought in the culture vultures; and third, it brought in a new heritage audience, just as the National Trust were moving to take over the Sutton Hoo site and turn it into the huge attraction it is now.

Peterborough

But *The Wuffings* was also an indication of how our villages were changing. Some Arts Council visitors to our village halls looked at the audiences and correctly identified that a good part of the audience probably also visited Norwich Theatre Royal or The Wolsey in Ipswich. Village housing was becoming desirable retirement homes. Add to this the fact that the new regional director of the Arts Council didn't like the word 'rural' and felt it was holding the region back in terms of arts investment, and our reason to exist was under threat. We were deemed subregional and any references to East Anglia in our grant applications were crossed out to be replaced by the East of England. So much for sense of place – an area with 1,500 years of history was being replaced with a designation barely 70 years old.

Figure 1.2 From *The Wuffings*, 1997. Photograph by Mike Kwasniak, © Eastern Angles.

In an odd about-turn, it was Arts Council Head Office that saved our bacon and we were offered the chance to include one of the new 'cold spot' designations in our brief. We chose Peterborough.

Peterborough has an odd history: a small city with a wonderful cathedral, it was also a railway centre and engineering hub. But in the mid-1960s its charismatic Labour leader, Charles Swift, allied with the Conservative leader, made a bold bid for New Town status and got it. The new Development Corporation was headed up by an equally charismatic Welshman, Wyndham Thomas, who brought in US-style parkways and shopping malls (though in the centre of the town). However, this 20-year period of fast growth from 1968 to 1988 was followed by a recession and then a lack of development so that by 2008, when we arrived in town, it was marked down as having a 'low cultural offer'. It was an old city that had become a New Town, but was struggling to become the new city it aspired to be. It was a centre for migration, which meant it had a very diverse population. Those new communities were very strong and welcoming, but the whole town was short of pride and ambition. In short, it had no sense of identity.

Is a sense of place in an urban setting different? We could create shows about rural life and tour them over 5,000 square miles and be confident they would appeal wherever we went. But Peterborough's experience, though sharing some aspects with other New Towns, was unique and its population had been transformed in the last 40 years. This wasn't just urban, it was also in flux! Could we apply the same techniques? Well, we'd soon find out.

We walked into the city's archives to ask where the stories were and they pointed to 400 boxes containing the records of the Peterborough Development Corporation (PDC). They had a plan for volunteers to catalogue them and an idea for an oral history project, but were struggling to demonstrate public engagement. We said we'd do some plays and the Forty Years On project was born. The Heritage Lottery Fund welcomed the idea and we fell into partnership with Vivacity, the new cultural trust set up to revitalise the city's cultural development.

Our first shows were short and contemporary, such as *Lincoln Road* by Danusia Iwaszko. This road, the focus for many of the diverse communities, was both the joy and shame of the city, depending on who you spoke to, but we asked Danusia to write a play about those communities coming together and trying to put on a joint carnival. Our most immediate success was a play about the local 'tramp' Nobby, who had lived in a bus shelter by local parkland, Ferry Meadows, and around whom several urban myths had developed. He was much loved by the city, given meals and golf clubs, and had recently been housed and disappeared off the streets. People came to see Kenny Emson's play *Our Nobby* as much out of care for him as curiosity.

We now started planning for our play for the Forty Years On project, which Kenny would write, following a family that moves from London to Peterborough. But it was when I realised the documentary element about town planning could just end up as a series of men in suits that I knew we needed something extra to lift a fairly intractable subject into the realms of entertainment. The period 1968–88 was probably the apogee of the TV quiz and entertainment show, from *Crackerjack* to *Blankety Blank* and *Take Your Pick* to *The Generation Game*. By making the TV quiz guests national politicians like the Minister for Housing, Michael Heseltine, along with local celebrities like Charles Swift and Wyndham Thomas, we brought together national themes and local issues. Songs like *It Never Rains in Queensgate* (the new mall) and *We're All Going on a – But It's Not a Holiday* (about the PDC's research trips to America) stitched a humorous thread into a political football. The most common reaction to *Parkway Dreams*, as we called it (see Figure 1.3), was 'I didn't think I'd like a play about town planning, but I loved it'. Subsequently the show toured other M25 New Towns as part of an Arts Council strategic tour.

Peterborough also offered the chance to focus on one place rather than always touring. We had always wanted to try our hands at the community play idea which Ann Jellicoe had pioneered in the south-west. Now we had the chance, performing *Dark Earth* by Forbes Bramble on the Flag Fen archaeological site, and exploring the local fen drainage history; and

Figure 1.3 *Parkway Dreams*, 2012. Photograph by Mike Kwasniak, © Eastern Angles.

then *River Lane* by Tony Ramsay in the Undercroft at the new shopping centre on the outskirts of the city, offering a personal view of the city's development from river crossing to local fishing mecca (Eastern Angles 2020). It's often difficult to interest younger generations in older history content, but add in the chance to perform and work with professional direction and they fly!

New writing

During all this time Eastern Angles' core touring activity had featured a consistent programme of new plays commissioned from writers who understood the nature of the productions we were asking for. In our world, new writing is what we have to do, because there are no plays already in existence. And although new writing is important for our Arts Council remit, the term is not necessarily used in our marketing. A sense of place in this context is different. No writer or artist likes to be told what they have to produce, and we don't expect to order up a play like a tailored suit. We want to encourage the full gamut of the writer's imagination and ability to create, so it's not just about giving out our measurements.

From the start, I tell aspirant writers that we are always more interested in the writer than the script that they have usually sent as their calling card. Once we have established a baseline not just of ability and interest, but also a shared notion of how a sense of place works, then we can talk about a specific subject, which might come from their own research or some of the areas of interest or events that have already been picked up on our radar.

These could be contemporary, like *Blending In* by Mary Cooper, commissioned to write about a black midwife in rural East Anglia who also sings barbershop; *Up Out O' the Sea* by Andrew Holland, linking a journalist's own tragedy with that of a lifeboat disaster; and James Vollmar's *Crossroad Blues,* pitching a serviceman's exploration of the slave trade into a modern American-themed diner.

Or they could be period: Peppy Barlow was commissioned to write *The Sutton Hoo Mob* to explore the background to the finding of the treasure; Alastair Cording to write *The Walsingham Organ*, a Hardyesque story of local village politics and a new vicar; and Polly Wiseman's *Somewhere in England* examined the consequences of a segregated US Army Air Force arriving in local villages in 1942.

Or quite often they could be both contemporary and period: Robert Rigby's *Peculiar People,* about the Essex religious sect that abjured doctors, covered two time zones, as did Tony Ramsay's *The Bluethroat*, comparing a nineteenth-century bird collector and a modern artist capturing the bird's likeness on paper. Later Tony Ramsay's *Bentwater Roads*, written for a former 1960s aircraft hangar, would go a step further by covering four periods: pagan, medieval, the Cold War and now. One of the wonderful things about theatre is its ability to integrate characters from different eras, allow them to share the same stage, and allow audiences to make connections of their own.

Occasionally a script comes in fully formed – like Alan Franks's *The Edge of the Land*, which achieved the high-wire act of dovetailing 1950s adoption procedures and sea defence management in the east, or Tony Coult's *The Devil On the Heath*, which poked fun at the local American airbases and the 'mutually assured destruction' doctrines of the time and had already been toured by Key Perspectives. But this is rare and most often we work with writers, emphasising the importance of producing scripts with our particular audiences in mind.

Sometimes we deliberately look outside the region for a play that will offer a counterpoint to our work and provide a parallel experience of, say, rural life. So, Charlie Way's *In The Bleak Midwinter* had fun with the Wakefield *Second Shepherds' Play* with Welsh sheep farmers looking for Bethlehem, a village in the Black Mountains; and Segun Lee-French's *Palm Wine & Stout* contrasted town and country in Nigeria when a mixed-race guy goes looking for his black dad with his white mum.

Most recently we have entered into a First Commissions project with HighTide, a national new writing organisation who, amongst other things, hold an annual festival in Aldeburgh, Suffolk. It's been fascinating posing questions about what sense of place means to young writers, some of them born and brought up in the East of England, others just having studied here or stumbled across the region through relationships or jobs. Those with a regional upbringing had often escaped to big cities but now relished the chance to re-examine their youth and the idiosyncrasies of place that had affected their rituals of growing up. So often the sirens of the outside world faded into the background when they were given the chance to explore their old stamping grounds, both physical and mental. They logged the sheer frustrations of a TV culture that has such a narrow vision of place and is straitjacketed in its soaps, serials and school or crime dramas. The best example of this was probably our commissioning of Joel Horwood's *I Caught Crabs in Walberswick*, a hit of the 2008 Edinburgh Fringe that ended up at London's Bush Theatre.

Heritage

'Heritage' is a contested word and needs some form of context as it appears more often in this story. If anyone had asked me 30 years ago if what we were offering was heritage, I'd have vehemently denied any such association, since back then heritage was National Trust gift shops selling decorated coasters and tea towels. However, over time that has changed and the term has been taken up by various industries, the government and other agencies. This is not the time to decide what the turning point was, but the arrival of the Heritage Lottery Fund and its support of activity projects beyond purely buildings played a major part. Its insistence on participation, engagement and heritage learning with the emphasis on activity and involvement chimes easily with our own outreach objectives. For me any notion of heritage has to include the past, the present and the future. Heritage that is only about the past is simple nostalgia and a passive consumption of what is little more than over-sugared tea. When it combines with the arts it has a double-pronged effect. Arts and heritage then becomes a concept that uses two powerful tools to pinpoint moments of reckoning and change, which like Harrison's famous clocks suddenly gives us access to vast new unexplored continents and trade routes. I would argue, for example, that Joel Horwood's contemporary play *I Heart Peterborough*, which tells the story of a transgender dad and his son as a metaphor for the city's confused identity, has strong elements of heritage in it.

Current projects to come under this 'arts and heritage' banner include contributions to the Harwich Surrender & Sanctuary project exploring the 100th anniversary of the surrender of the German U-boat fleet at Harwich and the 80th anniversary of the start of the Kindertransport. For the U-boat story, which is not about the military machinery, we will be using arts and heritage lab ideas to mix walks, lectures, discussions and workshops with actors, director and writers. This will explore further the issues regarding government food policy, which included debates around government intervention on rationing, distribution and control, but also about consumer issues, women's involvement and land use. We are also planning a wide-ranging project around the medieval theatre of East Anglia, which a recent US academic cited as 'the West End or Broadway of fifteenth- and early sixteenth-century England' (Scherb 2001).

The future

Eastern Angles, in its 37th year, is running a 10,000-square-foot venue in Peterborough and is planning to expand its Ipswich space to accommodate a new strand of work around arts and heritage, to include schools, the increasingly diverse community around the theatre itself, explorations around a narrative for Ipswich and the opportunity for large-scale events such as restaging the old medieval pageants of the town.

It feels like I should say something pithy about sense of place, but the term is like an eel continually slipping out of your grasp. Just as you feel you have a handle on something, other elements, thank goodness, creep in and twist it round.

All places need a past. It's the first thing residents of a modern housing development in Peterborough asked us for when we searched for their ambitions for the estate. The 'village' of Hampton (recalibrated from a township of the PDC era) is built on the old brick pits – plenty of history there, but they wanted something more imaginative. So we gave them a giant, Mavis, who lived in the Tump (a mound of earth spoil left behind following the development), and asked everyone to help her process down through the village.

Our current show, *Polstead* by Beth Flintoff, takes the 1827 murder of Maria Marten and, without disturbing the period details, gives it a modern context and all-woman cast. Over time the story of her murder has changed, from her being an innocent victim for 150-odd years, to a sassy seductress in the 1960s, and now to the victim of a controlling man and an example of domestic abuse, but still owning her own story. Each generation produces its own version. Sense of place is as much about sense as it is about place – it's a reaction to something first of all. As a result, theatre is ideally equipped to bring out the best in heritage and contextualise it in a way that gives new generations an alternative view of individuals, stories, buildings, events and industries. People often used to ask us, 'Won't you run out of subjects?' They don't any more.

Notes

1. A term first coined by Barry Rutter of Northern Broadsides and generally accepted now to refer to the old-style large theatre where seats, curtains and carpets were usually red velvet in look.

References

Arts Council of Great Britain. 1983. 'Ayckbourn More Popular than Shakespeare: New Plays Attracting Regional Audiences'. Press release, 2 November. Accessed 1 June 2020. http://biography.alanayckbourn.net/styled-5/styled-18/styled-24/ArtsCouncil.html.

Blacksmith. n.d. Sound recordings of Tuddenham man and blacksmith. In the oral history section of the Suffolk Record Office.

Eastern Angles. 2020. 'Eastern Angles'. Accessed 28 April 2020. www.easternangles.co.uk.

Evans, George Ewart. 1956. *Ask the Fellows Who Cut the Hay*. London: Faber and Faber.

John Godber Company. 2020. 'John Godber Company'. Accessed 28 April 2020. www.thejohngodbercompany.co.uk.

Jones, Dai. 1958. 'The Ballad of John Axon by Ewan MacColl, Peggy Seeger, and Charles Parker'. BBC Radio Ballads, 7 July. Accessed 8 January 2019. www.mixcloud.com/daijones77128/radio-the-ballad-of-john-axon-a-radio-ballad-by-ewan-maccoll-peggy-seeger-and-charles-parker/.

MacColl, Ewan, Peggy Seeger and Charles Parker. 1957. 'The Ballad of John Axon Lyrics'. Accessed 8 January 2019. https://genius.com/Ewan-maccoll-the-ballad-of-john-axon-lyrics.

MacColl, Ewan, Peggy Seeger and Charles Parker. 1960. 'Singing the Fishing'. BBC Radio Ballads, 16 August.

Scherb, Victor I. 2001. *Staging Faith: East Anglian Drama in the Later Middle Ages*. London: Associated University Presses.

2
Lesson drawing and community engagement: The experience of Take A Part in Plymouth

Kim Wide and Rory Shand

Take A Part Community Interest Company (CIC) is a grassroots arts organisation working with communities in areas of socio-economic deprivation to commission and develop arts projects that support themes of community regeneration. We make art that is long-term and process-based, bringing people together and giving the community a say in their area. The process of collective commissioning and decision-making means that ownership is high and that the projects reflect local desires and needs. The work is embedded in the community through co-commissioning and co-creating, using an Arts Action Group model of delivery (further described below).

Take A Part was started in 2006 as a series of pilot projects in the wider Efford neighbourhood in Plymouth to feed into the Master Plan process for the area.[1] Bringing artists into the conversations around ambitions for Efford attracted more people in the local area to engage. The process was highly successful: Plymouth City Council and Efford won a National Creating Excellence Award in 2010 for their work in engaging the community via the arts.

Because the pilot projects were owned and desired, in 2008 the local arts community formed a limited company, The Heart of Efford Community Partnership, to apply for further funding and appoint a dedicated community curator to work alongside the community to realise longer-term artistic ambitions. This became Take A Part (TAP).

Prior to these projects, the community in the Efford area had experienced attempts at regeneration which were not consultative or engaging:

> Too often in the past, Efford people had had things done to them, even for them – usually by well meaning 'officials' with the best of intentions – but not done by them or with them. Somebody else had always been setting the agenda. Here was a chance to get away from 'tick-box' clipboard questionnaires. No more 'consultations' simply seeking comments on plans, which had already been prepared. The hope was this time to embark on something different, to have a real say, for the first time, in the future of our neighbourhood. The role of artists was seen as an innovative means of achieving visual progress and change. At first, the question was being asked, why artists? But we began to realise that different people communicate in different ways. (Michael Bridgwater, chair of The Heart of Efford Community Partnership and local resident, quoted in Shand and Wide 2016, 32)

Such previous governance failures in design of regeneration projects in the area had failed to engage the community and had frustrated the progress of social and economic development in Efford.

TAP uses the Arts Action Group model of working. A curatorial and commissioning team of local residents, schools, council officials, police and health workers was set up to drive the process forward and ensure that the choice of artists and projects came directly from the community themselves. The group work collaboratively to devise project ideas, to write funding applications and artist briefs, to interview and select artists, to create the work with the community and to market and support the delivery of all projects. It is a ground-up approach that never selects projects or artists without the say of the wider community, ensuring that community ownership and voice are embedded from the beginning. The process is also transparent, with funding applications being made public via annual general meetings, and the payment of artists, staff and project costs being shared between The Heart of Efford Community Partnership, High View School, Plymouth City Council and other agencies active in the local area at the time, depending on the project and its audience.

As an organisation in the community, TAP's role is as broker. We are there to listen, to reach out to support networks in the city that may be of use, to support funding opportunities and to co-produce the work with the community. It is a long-term partnership way of working that is successful in that it works on trust-building and collaboration at all points.

TAP as a creative arts organisation has delivered projects and engaged with its local community in regeneration projects that target youth, health or social engagement, and that are engaged with governance mechanisms, through networks, and funding projects. TAP has been at the heart of community projects and participation, working with residents, the local authority, community groups and public-sector organisations such as schools. The community has been engaged in projects such as sculpture-making, performance and arts projects in schools.

TAP has become embedded in the local area and is currently expanding its work across other areas of the city. The role of community engagement is key to the success of TAP; and for regeneration initiatives, its degree of success or failure is dependent on community buy-in and visibility. In the case of TAP, the community has come to see the organisation as having a broader scope than creative arts: rather, it has become a means of engaging, in trying new activities and in realising potential – that is, the main means through which the governance of regeneration in the area has taken place (see Figure 2.1).

Ladder of participation

TAP applies the approach of Sherry R. Arnstein's 'A Ladder of Citizen Participation' (1969). The work of TAP is about doing with and not to. It is about partnership and delegated power within the Arts Action Group, ultimately leading to the ambition of a 'citizen power'. No one person in the Arts Action Group has the role of chair or leader. It is a flat system of partnership that exists around the shared aims of community involvement, ownership and decision-making. While Arnstein's ladder approach is simplistic and not subtle enough to represent the degrees of citizen power that are present in any collaboration between citizens and power holders, it does focus the work towards achieving, as best as possible, ownership and decision-making at a grassroots level.

As with any collaboration between communities, local authorities and institutions, there are limitations on all sides. There are paid and unpaid members; there are those representing authorities or special-interest community groups or indeed pocket corners of neighbourhoods that have differing approaches and agendas. With TAP, the aim is to work as far as possible in partnership and with delegated power to ensure that control is not in the hands of one particular power group.

Drawing on Arnstein's (1969) ladder of participation in community engagement, we can see that the community has progressed through

Figure 2.1 Efford, The Capital of Culture for Plymouth Community Manifesto March Day with artists Rachel Dobbs and Hannah Jones of LOW PROFILE,[2] 2012. © Dom Moore Photography.

the stages – or rungs – of the ladder through activities and engagement with TAP. First, as is evident from the discussion in the previous section, the community has moved from a **non-participatory** position to one of citizen power – driven by engagement, ownership and the sustainability of projects and community. Larger-scale regeneration projects often fall prey to didactic top-down targets or complex systems of delivery, and so while the community may be consulted at the implementation stage it is not engaged in design, co-production or co-commissioning of projects, reflecting Arnstein's **degrees of tokenism**: typically placation, consultation and informing.

However, through the accessible and consultative method of TAP, the community can be viewed as having reached **degrees of citizen power** – such as citizen control; delegated power; partnership engaged with the governance mechanisms and through networks, funding projects and the ways in which TAP as a creative arts organisation has delivered projects and engaged with its local community in regeneration.

Links to broader regeneration

TAP was born out of a pilot project to support Efford's Master Plan process and its series of themes for broader community regeneration projects, which relate to issues around health, opportunities for young people, sharing and developing new skills, supporting cohesion and physical improvements to place. Our approach is different from those in larger cities where power-based partners have vibrant ideas and projects that are developed, delivered to a place and to communities, and considered 'done'. In taking a long-term approach, we are very careful to bring the right partners around the table as much as possible. Often, we are approached by housing associations and large developers who want to 'artwash' their projects, seeing this as an appendage to their main work. The assumption is that involving artists in regeneration schemes as an add-on is a satisfactory way to be socially responsible. It is a thorny issue in any regeneration or neighbourhood planning scheme, as you need to collaborate to unlock funds and opportunities. To address this question, we can look back to Arnstein's ladder and consider the desires of the community for partnership. We have found that in almost all cases, the community refute the bolt-on approach and are empowered through the TAP model to address the developers from the very start with their overall ambitions for the area.

Communities are becoming more and more empowered to say no to add-on ways of working and to push developers into working in more collaborative ways. They access impact mitigation funding (Section 106) directly via Plymouth City Council partnerships and manage it on their own as part of the wider Arts Action Group fulfilling community partnership aims. For example, the North Yard Partnership Trust in Barne Barton secured 25 years of funding for community-chosen and -led projects that support local employment, education and sustainability.

How this could be rolled out

TAP's model of community-embedded social practice is a simple one. The Arts Action Group example can be rolled out as a process that can be replicated through nurturing and mentoring communities to take control in their own regenerative processes.

TAP are currently working with communities in Cheltenham, Exeter and Poole to help them think about long-term approaches, to model the Arts Action Group approach and to follow the process of committing to the long term. This is via the support of TAP acting as a catalyst and mentor for the work. But it is a slow process and needs careful brokering and use of soft skills to ensure that the work remains relevant. The process also needs to consider how succession is built in. With so many socially engaged regeneration projects, the largest question is one of when to let go. TAP in its first iteration was organic in how it grew, testing and developing its methods, and a firm concept of succession was not built in. Letting go in Efford has never been achieved and this may be due in part to being there too long. In other Arts Action Group communities, such as Ham Woods in North Prospect, a two-year project, prefaced with a statement that the process would be time-limited, resulted in the community understanding the role of the intervention and taking from it the tools and support they needed. They had the ambition to go on and self-fundraise and select artists in the Arts Action Group model far beyond the initial engagement of TAP.

In order to roll out a TAP model, most importantly, the right people need to be around the table. This includes the community, organisations and the local authority because each have their power bases and skills that are needed to ensure that the process of socially engaged projects in regeneration is realised. There is only so much that one player can achieve. Participatory projects in regeneration need all the players to drive high ambitions ahead.

Why is this example of TAP in Plymouth so important, and what does it tell us? Firstly, TAP is operating in a poor area, connecting residents and community groups to the creative arts, and widening access to these pursuits (see Figure 2.2). Key aspects in TAP's success in such endeavours are the visibility of the organisation and the accessibility of the art projects. Secondly, the success of TAP is not in the governance design: rather, it is in the relationship built with the community. TAP employs a more straightforward approach to community working rather than working with a raft of partners in a complex governance model. In addition to a range of activities in the community, such as running after-school clubs, TAP also commissioned a radio play in Efford that focused on the history of the area, showing an important aspect of partnership in working across delivery with the local authority, schools and the community.

Community engagement in driving regeneration in Efford is not a new idea. The roots of regeneration in the area go back to the 1980s, when local residents engaged with public services to discuss the issue of youth antisocial behaviour. By the 1990s there had been 'regular meetings of Efford ward councillors, open to all in Efford and Laira, to address individual concerns and wider neighbourhood concerns' (Shand and Wide 2016, 30). At the end of the decade, the Efford Ward Community Forum met with the Southwest Regional Development Agency (SWRDA) 'to discuss the possible investment in Efford of £100k "on a building for Community Forum use"' (Shand and Wide 2016, 30). The community group continued to work with both the local level and SWRDA in funding and driving forward regeneration projects.

Figure 2.2 Plain Speaking Tour of British Art Show 7 led by members of Efford Crazy Glue, 2011.[3] © Gemma Ward Photography for Take A Part CIC.

Why is what TAP do so innovative? There are several reasons. The role of TAP staff has been an innovative one as the visible force of change and progress in a disadvantaged area. They work with the community, not at the community. The engagement with the community necessitates trust-building and both short- and longer-term vision. In some cases, regeneration initiatives have been hard to navigate for communities due to changes in governance delivery, through cuts, austerity and the shift to business-led delivery. While budget cuts evidently presented large issues for TAP as a creative arts organisation, the broad range of projects was successful – such as running a radio station in the area, sculpture-making, schools projects and the crazy glue project, which aimed to reduce vandalism and graffiti in the Efford area by working with people in the community to produce street art and murals (they have not been vandalised since they were completed). This notion of community ownership, participation and identity is a key aspect of achieving success in regeneration and one which can work in other areas as well. (See Figure 2.3).

In any project which is consciously or unconsciously about regeneration and development, the role of engaging the community, and key individuals, is vital – it's very hard to achieve anything if the community,

Figure 2.3 Nowhereisland Radio, North Prospect Community Day, 2012, which involved the artists Hana Backland, Mark Vernon, Neil Rose, Sophie Hope and Jo Bannon.[4] © Gemma Ward Photography for Take A Part CIC.

or at least key figures in the community, are not open to your ideas. The role of TAP in Plymouth underlines the importance of three features: the participation of the community in Efford; the linkage with other organisations in the area; and the willingness to embrace local strengths, history and knowledge.

Notes

1. The Master Plan for regeneration was part of the Labour government's Building Communities Initiative and a partnership between Plymouth City Council and the local residents' association, The Heart of Efford Community Partnership.
2. LOW PROFILE's work is about not giving up, the impossible, the endless and the obsessive – our experiences of everyday life magnified and put on show. Their research and work has been concerned with the timely and persistent themes of survival and preparedness, alongside the perceived need for protection from others, the unknown and ourselves. Their work takes various shapes including live performance, video, installation, artists' ephemera, publications and bookworks.
3. Take A Part brought British Art Show 7 to Barne Barton, North Prospect and Efford to learn about what contemporary art was and to give people the confidence to have opinions about it and be able to talk about how the work in the show made them think and feel.
4. Nowhereisland was an island from the Arctic, created by artist Alex Hartley, which has been on a journey to south-west England in search of citizens. As an early part of the process, Take A Part worked with High View School's social enterprise Magic Hour and artist Hana Backland to produce a short film about what Nowhereisland is. This film is being used to raise awareness and understanding amongst other young people, particularly in Plymouth, about Nowhereisland. Take a Part have also enabled Magic Hour to take the film to other Plymouth schools, to share it and record creative writing in response to the content. The creative writing has been captured by our Take A Part reporters and is ready to be shared during the Nowhereisland Radio broadcasts in summer 2020.

References

Arnstein, Sherry R. 1969. 'A Ladder of Citizen Participation', *Journal of the American Institute of Planners* 35 (4): 216–24.

Shand, Rory and Kim Wide. 2016. 'Afterward: Take a Part Case Study'. In *Social Making: Socially Engaged Practice Now and Next, 28th and 29th April 2016, Plymouth UK*, 27–32. Plymouth: Take a Part. Accessed 23 April 2019. https://issuu.com/takeapart/docs/social_making_publication.

3
Raising the Barr

Sanna Wicks

In 2012 Walsall Council, in partnership with Barr Beacon Trust, received a grant from the Heritage Lottery Fund for a project called Raising the Barr to restore Barr Beacon local nature reserve and re-engage the community with the site. The project was led by Walsall Council with supporting partners, including the Beacon Trust, Birmingham and Black Country Wildlife Trust and the Collingwood Centre, as well as local schools, voluntary organisations, businesses and many volunteers. The grant was for a total of £485,838. The project ran for four years.

This chapter examines the meeting of digital media and heritage in this innovative case study. It will consider the challenges the project faced and the lessons that can be learned. As the project progressed, the media landscape changed, with technological advancement and with spreadable media (Jenkins, Ford and Green 2013) and participatory culture becoming more dominant cultural forms (Jenkins 2006). This required a transmedia strategy, the intentional creation of media for different platforms and the facilitation of online community participation. Raising the Barr was considered a 'wholehearted success' (NW Environmental Ltd 2016), but as always, lessons learned can be translated into models of working for new projects.

Project introduction

Barr Beacon is one of the highest points in the West Midlands, with panoramic views reaching to eleven counties on a clear day. The site offers various important habitats for wildlife, including lowland heathland, as well as being an important recreation site. The on-site heritage features include the war memorial, which is one of Walsall's most recognisable landmarks, a flagpole of rare design and the Sir Joseph Scott tree plantation.

The objectives of the Raising the Barr project were listed in a report as follows:

- To restore and improve Barr Beacon's historical features, including the war memorial, flagpole and Scott plantation;
- Engage with up to 120 volunteers;
- Improve interpretation across the site;
- Engage individuals and the community in the future management and development of the site;
- Deliver and establish ongoing events and an activities programme;
- Provide opportunities for community organisations to run their own events at the site;
- Provide training opportunities in specialist skills and crafts relating to the management of the site, archaeology and maintenance of structures.

(NW Environmental Ltd 2016)

The project saw the restoration of the nature reserve's heritage features: its war memorial, flagpole and tree plantation. The memorial had been badly damaged by weather, vandals and thieves, and its restoration was the most important achievement of the project (see Figure 3.1).

Figure 3.1 Barr Beacon War Memorial after restoration. © Daphne Ison.

It was carried out to a high standard in, at times, difficult circumstances with snow and high winds. It needed innovative techniques and materials to achieve a durable structure resistant to defacement and deliberate damage.

The grant was also used to increase the number of activities offered to help the community, visitors, schools and colleges make the most of Barr Beacon and take ownership of the site. Various events and activities, such as a forest school, an archaeological dig, a meteor watch, memorial services and the Bands on the Beacon music festivals took place over several years, with volunteers, community organisations and local businesses getting involved.

The interpretation of the site was another major aspect of the project. At the start of the project a 'stylebook' was created by an external agency to ensure a consistent branding across platforms and for different activities; this included logos, colourways, fonts, backgrounds and all design elements which could be used as part of interpretation across different platforms. This included digital interpretation – films, a website, social media channels and a mobile phone app – as well as more traditional leaflets, posters and on-site interpretation boards. The project attracted extensive press coverage, with various local press articles and a Central News report.

A website for Barr Beacon was produced as part of the project. This was originally meant to be developed by an independent production company and to be a stand-alone site for Barr Beacon. However, Walsall Council's IT department updated their policy on external sites and all council websites had to be developed using a specific web language, so staff were brought in to develop the website within the council IT team. While the design of the site was more constrained, being part of the council web umbrella will give the Barr Beacon site longevity, with the team being able to update the page without extra financial implications. Any new content and current news can be updated directly by the team, as can any council branding updates. This may be something other council teams should carefully consider when running their own projects.

During the four years, films were produced about different aspects of the project, such as the restoration, the remembrance services, the music festivals and the wildlife on the Beacon. Some of these films were uploaded onto the council's website. Shots of the lighting of the Beacon, which was part of the project launch event and the Queen's Diamond Jubilee celebrations, were included in an ITV Central TV news report. The films were also made into a four-part series and broadcast on the local TV channel Made in Birmingham.

Social media channels included 'Barr Beacon War Memorial' Facebook community page, which at the time of writing has 70 likes and 69 followers (www.facebook.com/BarrBeaconLNR). The dates of the posts range between 2009 and 2014. A twitter account, @BarrBeacon, was also created and while active had 425 followers, with the last posts being from 2015.

A free-to-download mobile phone app for both Apple and Android phones was produced as part of the project (see Figure 3.2). The app is intended to be both informative and fun, suitable for a wide range of visitors, including families. It includes two GPS-enabled trails: Habitats & Wildlife and Heritage & History. These trails take visitors around the site, with points of interest (POIs) being marked both on the GPS-enabled trail map and with physical waymarkers on site. At each POI, users are provided with a multiple-choice question relating to their trail and the location. Light-hearted hints and scores add extra interest. The app also includes further site information and an augmented reality feature (see Figure 3.3) that enabled the user to see what they were looking at in each direction from the Beacon, which has magnificent 360-degree views. Using an app allowed for user interaction, augmented reality and a GPS-enabled map – all impossible with traditional information boards.

Project context and challenges

Of the challenges the project team faced, the major one was the consequence of central government austerity measures, as Walsall Council was having to implement major cuts across its services (Elkes 2014; Walsall Council n.d.). This meant that the project was managed by a reduced team who had an increased workload. The media and communications officer job was cut, and two years into the project the project officer left and was not replaced. Instead the grant was extended by one year. Keeping project staff on fixed-term contracts is a challenge if there is no prospect of long-term employment. Losing these two key people meant that some of the strategic vision for media and communications was lost, community engagement was reduced both online and on site, and social media channels were no longer overseen by anyone but updated as and when. Fortunately, throughout these changing circumstances Jeff McBride remained as the project co-coordinator throughout the lifespan of the project; this consistency and Jeff's dedication to seeing the project through played a huge part in the project's successful outcome.

Figure 3.2 Barr Beacon app. © Sanna Wicks, Treehouse Media Productions Ltd.

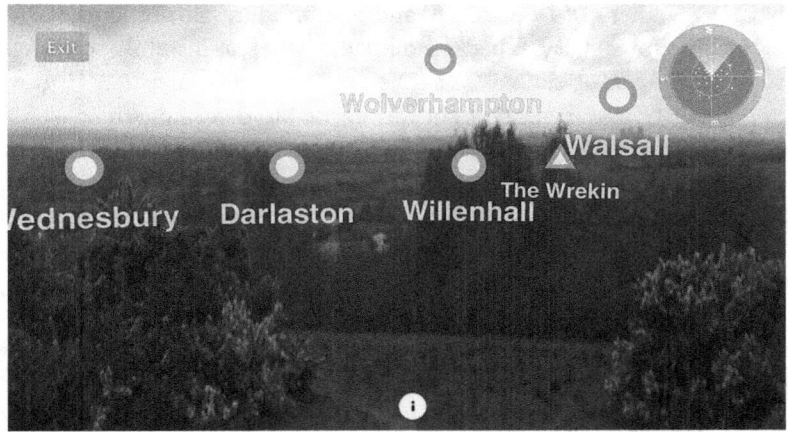

Figure 3.3 Barr Beacon app, augmented reality feature. © Sanna Wicks, Treehouse Media Productions Ltd.

Another challenge was the inflexibility of long-term projects to adapt to changing situations, and in the context of this chapter to a changing media landscape. The loss of the media and communications officer magnified this issue for Raising the Barr. Funding bids for large-scale projects are often written several years in advance of actually winning the bid and consequently of work starting. The Raising the Barr project bid writing started in 2009, before the grant application to the Heritage Lottery Fund was successful and the four-year-long project was launched in June 2012. This means the project was 'in the making' for seven years. Over this period much change took place in mobile media technology, affecting the way we use platforms and devices, as well as the way we consume content. The project, which was conceived as a multimedia one creating media for separate channels, needed to work hard to keep up with new ways of communicating across different media outlets. Not only does technology advance but the advance brings with it a change in culture. New media technologies bring with them a change in the way we behave, as Marshall McLuhan described so many years ago (1964). Technologies exist and make a difference in the context of the culture in which they are being used. 'It matters what tools are available to a culture, but it matters more what that culture chooses to do with those tools' (Jenkins *et al.* 2006, 8).

This change in the media landscape created significant uncertainties for a project team: for example, when the Raising the Barr project was originally conceived and planned, the council team were thinking of putting together a DVD as a record and possibly for resale purposes. As the project progressed, DVDs became outdated, whereas instantly accessible video-sharing sites, such as YouTube and Vimeo (Sweney 2017), grew in popularity, so further thought was needed to determine the purpose of the films and the best method of making them available. In fact many were uploaded onto a dedicated YouTube channel as the project finished.

Our experience suggests that project teams will need guidance to understand what direction technology is going in, how audience behaviour is changing and how both might impact the outputs they are planning to deliver. Many still choose to produce content *for* an audience, while as Alvin Toffler (1981) points out, audiences are now 'prosumers' – producers and consumers. Going further, Axel Bruns coined the term 'produsage' to describe a 'new hybrid form of simultaneous production and usage' in today's user-led online content creation environment (2007, 1). Users expect to be able to interact with content, share, repurpose and remix it for their own purposes in our participatory culture (Jenkins 2006). In participatory culture 'not every member must contribute, but all must believe they are free to contribute when ready and that what they contribute will be appropriately valued' (Jenkins *et al.* 2006, 7).

Social media is one of the easiest tools to enable and encourage audience involvement and participation. The use of social media was not part of the original bid to the Heritage Lottery Fund, but soon became a key tool in communicating and interacting with the community. The evaluation reported favourably on the project team's adoption of social media:

> Considerable effort has been made to promote the project through the media and the internet including the use of social media. The potential importance of this avenue may not have been fully realised in 2010/11 when the project was being planned, but it appears to have contributed to the project's success in raising awareness and understanding. (NW Environmental Ltd 2016, 5)

The use of social media is now a key part of advice given to current Heritage Lottery Fund grant winners for publicising their projects. The fund offers a selection of hashtags that project teams might want to use as part of their posts, such as #LoveHeritage, #HLFSupported and #ChangingLives (Heritage Lottery Fund n.d., 7). Lewi *et al.* (2015) argue that Facebook and other social media platforms offer a better solution compared to custom-built platforms for participation, requiring less moderation and easier maintenance with 'more likely longevity and support'. Importantly, in today's participatory culture, publicising the project is just the first step. Now projects need to consider other questions too, such as: How can we offer opportunities not just for physical, on-site participation, but for online participation? How can online communities be involved and engaged in our project via social media platforms?

In this new form of culture, 'the boundaries between amateur and professional, consumer and producer, grassroots and mainstream are breached, if not erased' (Leadbeater 2010, 46). Are project teams prepared to include both official and unofficial heritage on platforms they manage? Are they prepared to build new kinds of relationships with audiences (Giaccardi 2012, 4) and to some extent lose curatorial control and ownership? The term 'spreadable media' describes an 'emerging hybrid model of circulation, where a mix of top-down and bottom-up forces determine how material is shared across and among cultures in far more participatory (and messier) ways' (Jenkins, Ford and Green 2013, 1). In today's participatory culture, media producers and project teams need to reconsider the way they produce content and offer audience participation opportunities.

Raising the Barr was not merely a heritage interpretation project, but also aimed to engage the community as volunteers and encourage them to take ownership of the site. It could be argued that social media offer a valuable tool in strengthening a sense of place for projects such as Raising the Barr, as they offer project teams an opportunity of 'creating communication and interaction spaces capable of exploring and sustaining renewed forms of engagement with the physical and social settings of the heritage' (Giaccardi 2012, 8). Taking this a step further, it could be argued that Raising the Barr was also about place-making, about involving local people in making improvements to their community spaces (Anderson 2012). The goals of place-making, according to Anderson (2012), are 'to invite greater interactions among people and to foster communities that are more socially, physically, and economically viable'. When this activity moves online, it's called digital place-making. Although there is much enthusiasm for digital place-making, some research suggests caution in using information and communications technology to support community development activities. While it can 'amplify or catalyse activity' (Toyama, quoted in Matthews 2016), it's also 'likely to encourage a more mundane type of "cultural vernacular" of banal online interactions' (Matthews 2016, 421). So a balanced approach is required when considering how resources are spent on using social media as opposed to other means of audience and community engagement and digital place-making.

Today a co-ordinated or transmedia communication strategy is preferred by many companies and broadcasters (Jenkins 2006). The BBC, for example, broadcasts television programmes live, streams content and offers it for download via the iPlayer, and also offers a content-rich website and apps for mobile devices. BBC Worldwide publishes magazines about the TV programmes, runs events and much more. Many marketing companies promote a transmedia storytelling approach and it can fit well with heritage projects. 'A transmedia story unfolds across multiple media platforms, with each new text making a distinctive and valuable contribution to the whole' (Jenkins 2006, 96–7). The theory is that each bit of the 'story' or content is specifically designed for the platforms where it will be released, and works as a stand-alone, self-contained piece of content for audiences to engage with. Each platform will attract different audiences, and audiences experiencing stories across different platforms will have a deeper engagement and a fuller picture of the whole.

Raising the Barr received funding for specific purposes and the team commissioned stand-alone media components for various platforms, so its original approach was multimedia rather than transmedia. However, as the project developed there were opportunities to co-ordinate these components across media. The films were originally conceived to be mainly for archiving purposes, but as short-form film content is increasingly being used on social media platforms and by streaming providers to engage with audiences, they were later made available. It was perhaps due to the loss of the full-time project officer and the media and communications officer that these films were not regularly uploaded on to the council website, nor on social media, earlier in the project. Heritage Lottery Fund advice now includes: 'Images and film footage can make a social media post more interesting and encourage interaction from the public. Pick images that are bright and in focus' (Heritage Lottery Fund n.d., 7) and furthermore: 'Remember to send out any good quality photos and films relating to the project alongside your press release and upload them to your digital channels. Please send them to us too and we can share them on our website and social media channels' (Heritage Lottery Fund n.d., 9).

The mobile phone app is another component of the transmedia story of Barr Beacon. Mobile phone apps offer new ways of participating with the environment, and some, such as the Museum of London's Street Museum app, have been hugely successful. Apps have the 'potential to enhance the meaning and understanding of heritage and the cultural significance of place to clarify and explain the meaning behind the urban form and to form a better understanding of the place and its history' (Abdel-Aziz *et al.* 2016, 490–1). While there can be frustrations with technological and user experience issues, apps offer value by helping visitors find new information as well as offering enjoyable and engaging experiences (Wicks 2015). The aim of the Barr Beacon app was to provide an easy-to-navigate user interface, so as to offer an engaging and enjoyable experience for visitors, a way of finding new information in a fun way, as well as to enhance the sense of place. Abdel-Aziz *et al.* (2016, 491) argue that features offered by apps such as Street Museum 'contribute to enhance the "sense of place" and the attractiveness of public spaces which will increase the social interaction and the people attachment to their community'. The Barr Beacon app was offered on App Store and Google Play in 2015, but had only 186 downloads in the first seven months. It is unclear why the success of the app was limited, as no user feedback was collected, but the team's resources to promote the app were limited and there was no co-ordination across media such as a social media launch or follow-up, and the website was not online at the time of the app's release to promote it. In addition, the interpretation board that was meant to be installed on site, with a QR code link to the app, was not installed due to consecutive traveller encampments.

Nevertheless, a wide variety of media was produced, and in that way, together with the press coverage and the far-reaching community outreach that was carried out throughout the project's life, impact was created. Greater impact may have been possible with personnel in place to manage the media strategy but marketing and social media are time-consuming and require dedicated staff to manage them. Raising the Barr's experience suggests that in today's media landscape a transmedia strategy is required, including the intentional creation of media for specific purposes, particularly for online distribution via various platforms. These media could have spread virally within the surrounding community, in the wider area and among heritage enthusiasts. As it was, the various media were not strategically aligned – for example, the films were produced separately from the social media channels, rather than for them. On the other hand, one could argue that much was achieved, as evidenced by audience engagement on social media channels in the early years of the project.

Furthermore, the allocation of limited funding is always an issue. Project teams and funding bodies are always tackling questions about the most effective ways of spending finances. So they need to ask: is it worth spending funding on outside help to develop or manage an overall media strategy and to revisit it for longer-term projects, or is there a more cost-effective approach? And how much scope is there to change and amend plans as a project spanning several years progresses, so that funding is used in the most appropriate manner at the time, which is not necessarily as originally imagined?

Lessons learned

Raising the Barr can be considered a 'wholehearted success' (NW Environmental Ltd 2016). The main part of the project was the restoration of the war memorial and other heritage features, and this was done to a high standard, making a real difference to the site, which previously looked run-down and neglected. 'Both the Council and the local community can be proud of what has been achieved in turning battered, bedraggled, and largely forgotten features into a stunning new focal point for the public open space' (NW Environmental Ltd 2016, 19). The local community was engaged throughout the project, with local schools using Barr Beacon regularly for various activities, from forest school to memorial services, and volunteers taking an active role in various events, such as the archaeological dig. The interpretation, including digital media, was created to a high standard.

Nevertheless, lessons learned can be translated into models of working for new projects. The recommendations regarding digital media for heritage interpretation projects would be to ensure that a dedicated person is in place to be in charge of the media strategy – either someone in-house, with required support and training provided, or an external consultant or company who can devise a strategy together with the project team. In this way an overall media strategy could be devised and implemented, meaning that the media created would serve a clear purpose and be more likely to reach their target audience, thus promoting the purpose they were created for.

Here are some recommended steps to follow:

- Start with a clear media strategy which is coherent across all media platforms.
- If the project spans several years, make sure to revisit the strategy annually, either dedicating a project team member to do so or leaving funding aside to pay for an external provider.
- Be flexible enough to adapt your strategy if required. This may be due to a change in your own agenda as the project moves on, due to the feedback from your audience – the community you are trying to reach – or due to a changing media landscape.

References

Abdel-Aziz, Ayat Ayman, Hassan Abdel-Salam and Zeyad El-Sayad. 2016. 'The Role of ICTs in Creating the New Social Public Place of the Digital Era', *Alexandria Engineering Journal* 55 (1): 487–93.

Anderson, Eric. 2012. 'Placemaking: A Tool for Rural and Urban Communities'. Accessed 1 June 2020. https://community-planning.extension.org/placemaking-a-tool-for-rural-and-urban-communities/.

Bruns, Axel. 2007. 'Produsage: Towards a Broader Framework for User-Led Content Creation'. Paper presented at the 6th Creativity and Cognition Conference (CC2007), Washington, DC, 13–15 June 2007. Accessed 23 April 2019. www.cwanderson.org/wp-content/uploads/2009/08/Produsage-Creativity-and-Cognition-2007.pdf.

Elkes, Neil. 2014. 'Walsall Council Facing £86m More Budget Cuts', *Business Live*, 21 October. Accessed 28 May 2020. https://www.business-live.co.uk/economic-development/walsall-council-facing-86m-more-7969794.

Giaccardi, Elisa, ed. 2012. *Heritage and Social Media: Understanding Heritage in a Participatory Culture*. London: Routledge.

Heritage Lottery Fund. n.d. 'Promoting Your Project: Publicity Guidance for Grantees'. Accessed 23 April 2019. www.hlf.org.uk/running-your-project/promoting-your-project. No longer available online.

Jenkins, Henry. 2006. *Convergence Culture: Where Old and New Media Collide*. New York: New York University Press.

Jenkins, Henry, Katie Clinton, Ravi Purushotma, Alice J. Robison and Margaret Weigel. 2006. *Confronting the Challenges of Participatory Culture: Media Education for the 21st Century*. Chicago: MacArthur Foundation. Accessed 23 April 2019. www.macfound.org/media/article_pdfs/jenkins_white_paper.pdf.

Jenkins, Henry, Sam Ford and Joshua Green. 2013. *Spreadable Media: Creating Value and Meaning in a Networked Culture*. New York: New York University Press.

Leadbeater, Charles. 2010. *Cloud Culture: The Future of Global Cultural Relations*. London: Counterpoint.

Lewi, Hannah, Andrew Murray, Wally Smith and Sarah Webber. 2015. 'Some Implications of Digital Social Media for Heritage Practice'. Paper presented at the Australia ICOMOS Conference, Adelaide, 5–8 November 2015. Accessed 23 April 2019. www.aicomos.com/wp-content/uploads/Some-implications-of-digital-social-media-for-heritage-practice_full-paper.pdf.

Matthews, Peter. 2016. 'Social Media, Community Development and Social Capital', *Community Development Journal* 51 (3): 419–35.

McLuhan, Marshall. 1964. *Understanding Media: The Extensions of Man*. New York: Bantam Books.

NW Environmental Ltd. 2016. 'Raising the Barr: Barr Beacon HLF Project Evaluation'. Walsall Council, December.

Sweney, Mark. 2017. 'Film and TV Streaming and Downloads Overtake DVD Sales for First Time', *The Guardian*, 5 January. Accessed 23 April 2019. www.theguardian.com/media/2017/jan/05/film-and-tv-streaming-and-downloads-overtake-dvd-sales-for-first-time-netflix-amazon-uk.

Toffler, Alvin. 1981. *The Third Wave*. London: Pan in association with Collins.

Walsall Council. n.d. 'Budget Consultation'. Accessed 23 April 2019. https://go.walsall.gov.uk/About_the_Council/Consultation/Budget_Consultation.

Wicks, Sanna. 2015. 'The Value of Mobile Phones in Heritage Interpretation', *Furnace Journal* 2: 36–48.

4
Interview with E17 Art Trail directors Laura Kerry and Morag McGuire

Alexis Weedon

Background

Laura Kerry and Morag McGuire are co-directors of Artillery, an arts development organisation. Laura is one of the original co-founders of the E17 Art Trail while Morag leads on participation and development for the trail. They were interviewed by Alexis Weedon in August 2018.

    The E17 Art Trail is a festival produced by the people of Walthamstow in north-east London and coordinated by Artillery. In 2017 more than 7,500 painters, sculptors, poets, choirs, photographers, designers, ceramicists and dancers of all ages joined to welcome residents and visitors to exhibitions, performances and workshops in the studios and streets, parks and pubs, cafes and shopping centres, faith spaces and community places within their neighbourhood.[1] It is now a biennial festival. In 2019 the wider borough of Waltham Forest in which Walthamstow sits became the first Mayor's London Borough of Culture.

Interview

AW *When did it start?*

LK So the first E17 Art Trail happened in 2005 and was part of the Walthamstow Festival, a local predominantly music festival. They wanted to have a visual arts element to their programming. In the first year, we had 50 exhibitions in a day and there was a whole host of music stages down the High Street. We realised it deserved more than a day and, as it has evolved, it has got longer and longer and longer. It's now 16 days plus a press night and a launch, so 18 days of programme. We quickly became a festival in our own right.

AW *What is E17 Art Trail? Can you define it?*

MM We call it a festival now, though it took us time to have the courage to do so. The invitation is to anyone who wants to share their creative work, that they may do that within the E17 postcode boundary within the dates of the festival. The E17 postcode is the boundary for the town of Walthamstow within this borough: Waltham Forest.

LK We do make exceptions if people are taking us out of Walthamstow to the amazing green spaces around Waltham Forest. So if you want to take audiences to the marshes for an artist-led walk, or to nearby Hollow Ponds or Epping Forest, we will include that. Places just over the border have crept in because they are so fascinating we couldn't not include them – new ceramic studios, for example, or businesses that are just across the road that want to be involved – and we include online projects specially created for the E17 Art Trail in our 'off the map' section.

When we first began we imagined it as a visual arts trail but every conceivable art form has been programmed in the E17 Art Trail over the years: from bell-ringing to live tattooing, floristry, crochet, spoken word and to creative industries creating, for instance, bespoke furniture.

AW *What makes the E17 Art Trail different from other festivals you have been to?*

LK There is no selection process. Although that is quite a challenge for us in terms of reassuring funders and local authorities of its quality sometimes. There is that unfortunate assumption that community doesn't mean quality. But what we have found is that people individually are so ambitious that they just get better and better every year, and what they have achieved and the standard of what they are doing is incredible. Each year I marvel at how our participants strive to make it the best it can be: for instance, the design of artists' publicity materials is exceptional. Over the lifetime of the E17 Art Trail, technology has changed so much and become so much more affordable that the potential to publish and print has increased. In 2017 people produced their own catalogues for their exhibitions.

That investment of time and resources is an indicator of how artists value the E17 Art Trail. Added to that is all the extra expertise in social media that artists have been accumulating. People help each other to grow and that's the thing we love to see. So there is really no need for a selection process to determine quality and it means that for our audience there really will be something to delight everybody. The challenge now is helping audiences find *their thing*, as the programme is so huge.

The actual experience on the E17 Art Trail is meeting people in the street – you see them with the programme [called the E17 Art Trail guide][2] in their hand and you have licence to start a conversation with someone you don't normally speak to who is also excited about what is happening in their street or round the corner from where they work.

AW   How big is it now?

LK   It is quite difficult to calculate the actual number of events as it goes beyond what's in the programme. There is what we have on our map and then an overlay of events which go across it all. We have calculated that there are well over 7,500 exhibitors and performers, which is everyone from preschoolers to professional artists, hosting over 350 events. That is phenomenal.

MM   There are over 171 specific 'red spots' [on the E17 Art Trail map] indicating exhibition and event locations, all chosen by the exhibitors. And there are about 350 events happening. But there are different tiers of curation. While we support people with an infrastructure and some creative spark, there is a lot of curation by the individual participants or collectives giving rise to more things for audiences to encounter. These often evolve in the 12 weeks between submitting their exhibition or event listing and the opening of the E17 Art Trail.

LK   There was one particular event, 1000 Swifts over Walthamstow, which was a trail inside the trail, so there is another layer of 'spots' as it were that you can see as you go around.

AW   *I'd like to come back to 1000 Swifts as it intrigued me, but you said you provide an infrastructure – how is that done?*

LK   How do you manage that number of exhibitors when you don't know how many there will be or what their outcomes are? We have developed the tools from the beginning of the E17 Art Trail to manage that amount of information as accurately and as successfully as possible. We now use Google forms for people to submit their event listing to us, but originally we had paper forms that people would pick up in a pub and would get posted through our letter box with a tenner. Now we have online forms and invoicing systems. We have a whole series of networking meetings including our E17 Art Trail Idea Sparks talks, one-to-one meetings and different how-to meetings at different stages, so hopefully we can work with all manner of people whether they are individuals, professional artists, community groups, youth groups, faith groups. Working out the invitation is part of Morag's role.

MM At the heart of the E17 Art Trail is the invitation to be involved and in some communities and neighbourhoods we take more time to make sure that the invitation reaches everyone and offer some support for neighbours to co-produce something. Sometimes it is not Artillery doing this directly: sometimes other organisations or local collectives emerge to give residents the support, confidence and some resources to take part.

There is a locally driven, word-of-mouth, face-to-face ripple of invitations, resulting in people feeling that they know that they can take part. Sometimes that is through established existing services – for example, schools can connect us to whole communities and likewise faith communities and some local health services. These are particularly important ways of saying 'this is for everybody'.

We live in a dense urban area of Waltham Forest. And yet people don't necessarily feel connected. Much of our population is transient. There is a lot of tenancy 'churn' in private rented spaces which are not always well maintained. So residents may be unsure which street they will be in after their 12-month tenancy. By establishing this vast network – which we had no idea would evolve in this way when we started – residents have a positive reason to build connections with their neighbours, get to know each other better, and lasting friendships are made which survive even if they move elsewhere.

We use quite a lot of energy to make sure people feel invited to take part and understand what it is. Witnessing that excitement of ideas evolving out of conversations and our gentle proposals is incredibly rewarding. But I think it is one of the struggles of our work that we like to have an outcome that is genuinely co-produced and predicting what shape that might take is almost impossible. We know that people want to take part because now people tell us so in passing, but we never know who, how many or what until registrations complete in March, so there is always an incredibly uncertain element to what we do. That does not work well in a funding environment and we haven't solved that problem yet.

LK Different invitations go out to different organisations or individuals. So we have exhibitors' toolkits, business and venue information toolkits such as 'how to engage an artist' which has things you may not have thought about (e.g. are you prepared for them to turn up and drill holes in the wall of your cafe?). There are invitations to schools, and later there are invitations to come as [part of an] audience.

When we have had the funding and the time, we try and find out what bits of the curriculum exhibitions and events in the programme could complement and champion these to local schools. But it's all a bottleneck of deadlines: we have deadlines for registering, deadlines for the copy and pinpoints on the map, and whilst that is happening someone is interpreting what is behind each of these 300-odd listings and what is in it for a particular Key Stage.

There are bits of technology and tools we have had to learn to use to make it as successful as we can. We are not well resourced but we have learned by working on other projects that we are being as successful as we can with the resources we have.

AW So tell me about the resources you have – you have this building here, The Mill, which is what, a community centre?

MM We are tenants in it and have this office. This serves as a useful place to scratch our heads whilst preparing funding applications, for instance. We tend to use public buildings for network meetings, maybe libraries, maybe here [The Mill], maybe at Gnome House, which is a relatively new arts facility. This is not a perfect place for us to say 'hello, come in, drop in' – it's up a winding staircase, and it's quite a small office.

LK We do have people drop in, even to our homes. People feel able to do that because of the nature of the way this project has grown up. But we find it's more useful to host Idea Sparks meetings or 'how to' meetings rather than simply having the door open here all the time.

MM One of the useful things about having an office here is that there is a strong creative and exhibition programme at The Mill. They host Meet the Artist events with each of their exhibitions, and it is a space where artists can explore their ideas. They sometimes host up to eight exhibitions or events for the E17 Art Trail here. So they are very familiar with what we do. They are also very aware of how we complement each other's ambitions.

AW And you are Artillery? What is your involvement?

LK Yes, we are a Community Interest Company which we established after the E17 Art Trail because so much grew out of that project that we wanted to develop and deliver. Under the umbrella of Artillery we can deliver all that work, but the E17 Art Trail is our flagship project. Out of that festival have come art and food festivals: the Appetite Food Market, for example, came from us thinking about how can we work better with the food offer in venues – the cafes and restaurants. It is not easy to look at art across the heads of diners so we created more experiential events and we encouraged restaurants to pay performers and provide work for artists as food photographers or food writers. We moved artists from going apologetically to them and asking if they could be an exhibition venue to thinking, 'What can I do for your business and what can you do for mine?' – a professional exchange. There was a literature festival as well.[3] From there we became known for our model and were commissioned to do Cultivate, a borough-wide urban food-growing festival. So it may feel a bit of a departure but the networks are very similar – the food growers and the creatives.

MM The spaces we use for these different events and festivals are being changed, both inside and outside, but inviting people to participate is the same.

LK We find there is a lot of artist and business development in our work but that isn't a paid role and there is a tension there between offering a really good standard of advice – which takes time – while also having oversight of the bigger project for everybody. So that's why we have different ways of inviting people to manage that.

AW What does the E17 Art Trail offer from a community standpoint that other arts festivals don't?

LK I think you can see the E17 Art Trail model being adopted across the whole of Walthamstow's growing creative sector. When people organise events now, the nature of them and the invitation is very similar, because it's an understood approach locally, a trusted format. It is quicker to ignite a spark. People realise that they can make things happen; within the E17 Art Trail we see other networks forming, illustrators and designer-makers and photographers galvanising. More and more studios have opened and they are much more permeable than in other areas we have lived. They really enjoy being part of the E17 Art Trail because they get people who may not usually see their work; they value the Art Trail approach, and the non-hierarchical nature of it.

The E17 Art Trail invites every contributor to be the co-creators and co-authors of the festival programme on their own terms.

AW *To what extent was there a recognised 'need' when it started? And was there activism?*

MM Early on there was a desire that you, Laura, had and Chris had to show your work locally, and you found people expressing similar frustrations to you. Artists were really struggling to find spaces to exhibit locally. They thought they needed orthodox conventional art spaces, but really it was about encountering audiences and so the solution was discovering other ways to show work. And now people are thinking very creatively about finding ways to create work for the spaces that are available in Walthamstow and not necessarily choosing to show work that will be exhibited somewhere else. Each exhibition is interwoven into the existing infrastructure so that you could encounter it in a park or a street. It might be that it is shown on a lamp post, for example. We really quite enjoy unconventional spaces. They don't have an established sense of threshold that forces audiences to choose whether it is a space they feel comfortable entering or not. Coming across happenings in the High Street is accessible for everyone. There are encounters which surprise or shock or stimulate curiosity which don't happen in the same way in other spaces.

We are non-selective. Very, very occasionally, there are times when we might question whether somebody's work might be appropriate to be shown or whether it is strictly creative. If that is the case then often we can suggest they link with another participating group and deliver their contribution alongside that group's creative contribution.

LK The Mill is a very good example: you submit one piece to a group show and they have an artists' reception so you can be part of all those things and benefit from the support of their volunteer coordinators. On your own, that is an awful lot of work.

MM It is also good if you want to bring an issue-based talk or walk or similar to the programme. Local groups such as The Mill, The Hornbeam, Gnome House, Waltham Forest Cycling Campaign have their own set of guidelines. That way of segueing an issue that complements somebody's exhibition feels appropriate, rather than the trail becoming a festival of everything.

AW *What has been the impact of E17 Art Trail on Walthamstow since its inception?*

LK I was just looking back at the cultural landscape in 2005. There was the music festival that we were 'born in', there was a local arts club for the borough, a local arts council that was a way of holding the odd forum and giving small grants, there were a few clubs and societies such as the historical society. There was one artist that I knew of at the time opening her house every year – she still does. There was a small artists' studio building in the park, some gigs in a couple of pubs, a redundant disused theatre and cinema, a gift shop that would sell artists' work and that was it. Really quite barren. We had a central library and a couple of small libraries in Walthamstow and a local history archive. The William Morris Gallery, a museum which has since had Heritage Lottery funding but at the time needed modernising and updating to bring the collection to life. Nowhere was exhibiting art apart from the little gift shop[4] and occasionally the small gallery space[5] attached to the artists' studios in Aveling Park.

Because of the E17 Art Trail people kept on asking potential venues to exhibit their work, to the point that the local authority's museums and libraries had to put together their own submission process, and cafes and picture framers also had to do the same – and these places had to learn curatorship. We have one vicar, now a canon, who has learned to be a very good curator of his faith space and hosts some really challenging artists' work. He is prepared to hang it in the nave and sacristy, skilling his congregation and church wardens to welcome exhibitors to do that. It is really interesting seeing the skills and job roles people have found themselves having to adopt to be part of the festival.

AW *How has the E17 Art Trail changed the cultural landscape?*

LK The cultural landscape now is so dramatically different. We have regular designer markets and pop-up maker spaces and music festivals. This year [2018] we have seen two festivals of theatre in the last four months, there are window galleries year round, we have a theatre pub, many artist studio complexes and many more are planned, other art trails were established in the borough and numerous others are being developed. New creative businesses selling the work of local makers are opening where the business rates are lower, creating districts with distinct personalities. Other types of business employ local creatives to paint murals, design their branding, shop fronts and interiors. There are local culture publications: we have this amazing monthly magazine, *The E List*, which features artists, local creative heroes, and supports their business enterprise.

Contemporary craft skills are very visible on the trail: E17 Designers, which are designer-maker markets. And the knits! Dr Knit is a laboratory for experimental creatures that need some kind of perhaps surgery or care. Or enter a terraced house and there are whole entire underwater scenes crocheted and you come away with your own crochet jellyfish and there might be sharks' fins circulating on the floorboards. People take their craft skills to another space and it becomes an immersive experience or conceptual installation.

AW *So these things have sprung up independently of the E17 Art Trail?*

LK Yes, they have grown out of the relationships that people have made, the confidence that's been built, and the appetite for art. So that we now have, in 2019, Waltham Forest as the first London Borough of Culture. When this initiative was launched, Sadiq Khan said the borough that would win would be the one that demonstrated its residents wanted this the most. And I thought when he said that we had a real chance – it is local people who are producing culture here, even without traditional arts centres, a theatre or arthouse cinema or much resource. 2019 will be a really exciting time. It will be quite a challenge as it changes the goal posts because a lot of people will think there is money and it will shift people's expectations. When you are in a vacuum everything is a wonderful treat. It will be fascinating.

MM Our programme is repeating, but is episodic rather than year round as far as our audience offer goes. So it is interesting thinking about what the impact of a 12-month intervention will be, and the 'well, what next?' effect that follows it. There are those ambitions we have, we dream of, but they are always tempered by what is viable with the resources we have.

AW *You mentioned the episodic nature of E17 Art Trail and you have moved it from being annual to biennial – was there a reason for that?*

MM We gradually moved towards being biennial in 2014–15. First, in 2013, we rescheduled it to June from September which helped the new and developing artists to be able to take part, especially those in our schools and colleges.

LK We felt we were stretching resources too far to maintain the momentum annually for the size it was getting. We could not get more sponsorship than we were because of the financial situation nationally; we had the profile to get more sponsorship but people's marketing budget was gone. Funding streams were rapidly disappearing. It also felt that it was quite a challenge for artists to produce a new body of work within 12 months, even for a full-time artist. People were making art for the E17 Art Trail, testing it with this lovely supportive audience. Artists very much enjoyed the response they got: for example, in the case of a ceramicist we know, it helped in deciding what to send on to the Design Museum. They test things out, get this incredible feedback and go on to do other things. Two years gives them the space to do this.

LK People talk about 2013 as our year off but in 18 months we did four other festivals, three borough-wide and the fourth in Southwark. We learned so much realising ideas that had been bubbling away and we had the space to test those. It's really funny when people say you were having a year off as we were never so busy. That shift was crucial organisationally and for the participants.

MM There is still some debate about it.

LK There is: people miss the E17 Art Trail happening every year and organise their own trails in neighbourhoods now. There was a village trail, and studios link up when they are going to open. Which is great as we get to go and are not on duty. We can see how much more investment people make in a biennial art trail. They have got more ambitious. There is so much more year round.

AW *If someone from another community wanted to adopt your model, how would they start?*

MM We are trying to work out what it is that we have learnt, and if there is a way of supporting people in producing something in their community. We would love to see people flourish in what they do but don't think it is our place to say 'we are the people who can make this happen'. But we feel we can offer some initial workshops etc. to guide people towards finding what the resources are in their community to develop initiatives like the E17 Art Trail. By working in different places, starting from scratch, we keep learning strategies for mobilising creativity in neighbourhoods. But it does change depending on local things and the dominant agendas.

LK It is about people not about the place. It's about finding those instigators with the drive. Incredibly skilled people need permission sometimes: cooks, who wouldn't consider themselves an artist, or people who have skills they have lost touch with because they have had children, for example. They often need permission or to feel supported.

The physical geography does have an impact on how you feel about where you are but you can almost be more creative by pushing against the conventional perspectives of your place. It is not the defining factor in creating a sense of place at all. It's the people.

MM The biggest resource is the goodwill people show in sharing some sort of vision. It's our unlogged biggest bit of the accounts as it were.

LK Yes, if you added up the volunteer hours it would be a quarter of a million pounds in time easily, on a London living wage. What people seem to come away with, whether a visitor or a local, is the great art work right on your doorstep, and having spaces open that aren't normally. Demystify a local building that isn't used, or open the doors of a community building that you don't use, or mental health services that open their doors for a day or weekend. Seeing stuff spill out the door of a school on your way home. It's the sense that everything is open and welcome and celebratory.

AW What advice would you want to give the urban designers, art development managers, the readers of this book?

LK I really want local authorities and developers not to hear the words 'community art' and immediately dismiss it, to immediately assume how that will look, or undervalue the quality or opportunity. I think funders are beginning to respect the value of local expertise but have still to understand the resources needed to do it. When we consider how many agendas we meet – mental health, resilience, cohesion, all additional to culture – funders get a lot more for their money than you might with a more corporate outfit. Co-devising and co-producing arts programming in neighbourhoods results in a sense of collective ownership, something very different from bringing highly polished culture and 'renowned' artists to a neighbourhood. There is nothing to say you won't get innovation at a community-produced arts festival.

MM It [innovation] is what happens when we have an open-ended creative brief, outputs evolve and come to fruition very close to the delivery time, or sometimes you are witnessing it in progress. There are many people here who produce professional, highly polished work outside the area; some choose to do something else here, to invite their neighbours to create something together and be collaborative, and enjoy the shared achievement of that.

We briefly chatted about the shared space that people can use and adapt but for developers building new communities then it is about investing in people, and the different ways people can come together.

LK Just yesterday we were in a park; there is a small community space within the park. It is locked. No one quite knows how to access and use that space. So for developers and local authorities, they need to think about what they can do to resolve that. Obviously there are safeguarding issues and risk assessments, food hygiene ... but it's simple things that create opportunities – how can they get those keys? People want to create stuff: how can local authorities help make it happen? Make it feel like a space where you can make things happen – with a kitchen, facilities, toilets – those are really quite simple but not quite anyone's job. For us having spaces that residents can really feel are ours, that is what is happening on the E17 Art Trail, people are claiming it, they are demanding use of it, that window over there, that building that is not used.

AW *Does it happen because you have built up that expectation through the reputation of the E17 Art Trail? And therefore people can go to the council and say 'we are going to use this and develop this space for this activity'?*

MM Yes it does because there is already a 'we'. What is not always obvious is who you go to in the council to do this. Thinking back to your previous question, there need to be community development workers receptive to the wider impact of creative co-production. If you are moving into or part of very established communities, you will find the local offer that already exists very immediately to where you live. But in new developments that have flattened whole industrial estates and are going to be large conurbations there is no sense of 'local' yet and so you can't get together with your neighbour so easily and find a shared interest, because there are no shared spaces for meeting. Then there need to be community development roles.

We found this in a project that grew out of the E17 Art Trail. We made the assumption that there were housing officers and community development workers. Those roles changed in the time that we finalised the funding, and those people really don't exist in the same way. Those roles have gone in the past ten years or so and they can be the connectors that make some of the most isolated people feel confident that they can get involved.

LK There are really high expectations for art and culture right now locally and regionally I think, and what the outcomes can be. Because the bar is set quite high by some projects, there is the expectation that the arts can deliver on mental health, counselling, support, youth work. That's great but the partners that we usually work with have never been so stretched. Those organisations are our way in. We want to work with these partners to ensure the safeguarding for young people or build on the relationships that exist so that we don't need to start from scratch with the trust that service users already have with their worker. Now the post doesn't exist or they are so stretched that they can only do the immediate firefighting. So you have to urge the policy-makers and developers to invest in time and people. It's going back to people again, but I really feel so strongly about that. That's what makes someone feel safe. Not a gate but somebody to talk to about the breach of the gate.

AW *You mentioned earlier the 1000 Swifts as something that everybody, absolutely everybody, could take part in – how did this come about?*

LK You reminded me of what I wanted to say. Really that was an individual who lives on the edge of Walthamstow wetlands who saw the model [the E17 Art Trail approach] – she happens to have an arts background – and wanted to initiate a project about safeguarding the wetlands and it being a resource for everybody. So she wanted people to make and display swifts across town that highlighted the opening of the wetlands. It was a very instant tool, that anyone – you did not need to be an art-trail exhibitor – could just submit that you were going to exhibit your swifts in whatever fashion, drawings in a window, a welded sculpture or whatever suited you, and these would be mapped. There is an article about it in the 2017 trail guide. Over the years a lot of artists have led initiatives that are campaigning, that have become part of our programme. For us that is quite precarious because we are often trying to get funding from the people they are challenging. We have managed it by being quite neutral and being an umbrella for every voice but it is a tricky balance. A lot of those campaigns have been successful, such as fighting the height of certain buildings, and there was a 'culture bin' showing what resources were being lost and the fight to keep the William Morris collection – now the William Morris Gallery is described as a flagship venue.

MM It won the Art Fund Museum of the Year in 2013 and got a special status for its collection.

LK So we have come such a long way but that has been hard-fought battles of individuals and local campaigning groups. Now of course we have museums displaying exhibitions of protest as they feel confident to do so. We now see businesses co-opt our brand to further their aims and objectives as people want to be associated with the ethos of the Art Trail and they are making very sophisticated marketing campaigns about being part of the festival. We share the tools, we share the festival logo and it is there for anyone to use it.

MM The scale of sponsorship we ask for here from individuals, sole traders, small businesses is small. I think 98 per cent – can that be right? – of businesses in our borough are less than five people. So any bit of sponsorship is a cut into their income, let alone profit. We are very aware of that and very aware that the work we do is deliberately local.

AW *How do you find a particular focus or problem you are going to address? Your themes, for example: arts and sciences linking with STEAM [Science, Technology, Engineering, Arts and Media]?*

LK In 2017 we felt we had mapped so many of the creative brains locally we wanted to extend that to map some of the academic brains and broaden our audiences. Arts are being driven out of the curriculum so dramatically, we were thinking how do we ensure that schools can do exhibitions and fit it in? Arts and maths are interconnected – there is enough evidence to show this – so it made it easier to justify the time for what they are going to do as part of an arts festival. Personally I am excited about how these cross-disciplinary themes show that the arts are contributing to science – and doing it locally. You can see the influence of the local talks on their work. Many artists on the last art trail were inspired by mathematics.

AW *E17 defines a particular area – do you have any ambitions to grow it?*

LK The way we would expand on the E17 Art Trail model would be to deliver more focused and more sustained projects in the lead-up to the public events, which are the smallest part of it actually, when you see what you have achieved. But the building of that audience offer and the collaboration to make that happen is the most exciting aspect for us. Also, looking at cross-disciplinary initiatives between art, science and maths hopefully shifts people's perspectives and invites new audiences with different interests.

AW *You mentioned you did not intend to do it for this long when you started. Is it important to have that commitment for three, five or ten years?*

MM It has certainly helped to establish it locally and build participation. We have kept doing it in a way that we haven't been able to do with other projects when their funding has come to an end. That's because it's where we live. We could not do it if we didn't live here but there has to be the will to continue with it.

LK We give our time to it as the E17 Art Trail gives rise to so many ideas and it, quite democratically, informs our creative direction. My motivations over the years have changed: I started as an artist wondering where to begin and now I want my children to feel connected and that where they live is special.

Notes

1. At the time of interview, Artillery was preparing for the E17 Art Trail 2019 in which 8,500 people created a programme of 405 exhibitions and events.
2. See https://issuu.com/artilleryevents/docs/e17_art_trail_guide_2017 and https://issuu.com/artilleryevents/docs/e17_art_trail_guide_2019_web.
3. Words over Waltham Forest.
4. Penny Fielding's Beautiful Interiors.
5. Changing Room Gallery.

Section 2:
Models and methods for developing place-making through the arts

5
A model for university–town partnership in the arts: TestBeds
Emma-Rose Payne and Alexis Weedon

TestBeds is a project for artists' and creative practitioners' leadership and professional development in Luton. It is run by the University of Bedfordshire and is informed by the university's long experience of widening participation in education and of skills development for start-ups and small to medium-sized enterprises. The project applies this knowledge along with current thinking and practices in commercial start-up and entrepreneurship contexts to support the development of the arts and creative sectors in Luton and more widely in the county and region.

The fact that creative sectors are instrumental in achieving regeneration and economic growth in towns and cities is widely acknowledged. However, there have been few systemic programmes of business development for creative practitioners in the arts. Furthermore, even fewer skills development initiatives for local artists and arts organisations have been led by UK universities.

The TestBeds project harnesses the University of Bedfordshire's education mission in partnership with local, regional and national organisations and statutory bodies to support and develop artists and creative practitioners and the local creative ecology. This has direct benefits for local arts and creative organisations and businesses, but it also brings direct and lasting benefits to the university. By embedding the artist programme within a stable institutional environment, it is possible to broker alliances where the aims of the partners are cognate. For example, the jazz dancer Perry Louis contributed to the 'Creole Fest' conference on UNESCO's Convention on Intangible Cultural Heritage (Cuffy and Carr 2018) and appears in this volume interviewed as part of Dr Jane Carr's research into British jazz dance. Similarly, two artists have been working on the community radio station (Radio LaB 97.1fm and online) based at the university and run by students, and six more, inspired by the potential of the radio station, have incorporated working with it in their funding bids. Radio LaB's remit is to build links between the student population and the town, so having artists engage in programming fulfils its aim.

The fit with the university links the work of researchers and practitioners more closely with the community. Lecturer Noel Douglas's work on the imagery of protest art has been exhibited in the V&A and the Design Museum (Douglas 2001, 2018), while he bases his teaching and practice in the town and is involved in outreach events. The School of Art and Design in the creative quarter has run workshops in creative T-shirt making for children and adults. Some artists have given specialist talks through the 'Industry Wednesday' events at the School of Art and Design, while others, such as Gayle Storey and Oz Azubuine, have recruited students as interns. Nicola Moody has taken inspiration from the research ongoing at the university and partnered with academics in social sciences on an emerging project on sexual exploitation, while others have engaged in developing the co-curriculum. For example, the internationally renowned composer David Murphy taught leadership through music to MBA business students. He is now working with the department to co-develop a 'listening leaders' methodology.

Such collaborations provide mutual benefit: for the university in terms of the students' education, and for the artists in achieving a deeper engagement with audiences of this age group. The benefit to artists is also to ensure a 'step-change' in their own creative practice in terms of becoming increasingly interdisciplinary, and in enhancing their own sense of place in the town through stronger connections and collaborative partnerships with university staff that have the potential to increase the sustainability and competitiveness of their creative enterprises.

So what is TestBeds?

TestBeds is designed to offer support and training for artists at different levels of their careers. It comprises four strands of artist development, discussed below: Artist Accelerator, Catalyst Co-Lab, Arts Enterprise Zone and Arts Elevator.

Inspired by the tech industry start-up model, the Artist Accelerator is a year-long incubator for Luton-based early-career creative practitioners.

The programme of activity is formed of three phases: research and training, project development and bid writing, and outreach project development and delivery. The programme, in striving to be needs-led, is developed on the basis of each cohort's development needs, to which it continues to be responsive throughout the 12 months' duration.

Catalyst Co-Lab is for artists who are further on in their career. Artists on this research and development programme work in partnership with an academic department or research institute to explore their practice in the context of the artist as a catalyst for change, place-maker or global citizen. In addition to progressing through a process of academic collaboration, project development and leadership, the Catalyst artists are linked to an Accelerator artist, whereby the artist undertakes a mentoring role for the early-career artist, whilst the early-career Accelerator artist supports the Catalyst artist to become connected to, and invested in, Luton as a place. David Murphy, an Accelerator artist, created new work with a musician from Bangladesh and worked with schoolchildren, introducing them to the exhilaration of South Indian rhythm. He said that the 'process of defining core values' enabled him to see how sound was integral to everything he does and that 'exploring the common threads that run through our diverse experiences as artists' as a TestBeds cohort built resilience within the group (Murphy 2018).

In addition, Gayle Storey demonstrated a tangible progression route from the Artist TestBeds Year 1 cohort to acceptance as a Catalyst artist in Year 2. Through this two-year process, Gayle shares that:

> TestBeds provided a structured programme that equipped and facilitated me to understand the many different aspects to forge successful applications for funding. To illustrate this effective process, I have been able to achieve over £45,000 of funding through in-kind support and monitory contributions, bringing concepts into reality. TestBeds is an enriching experience as it offers access to facilities, academic departments, equipment and staff that help to build new dialogues which impact on all collaborators. (Gayle Storey, artist testimony at TestBeds 2019)

Alongside the Accelerator and Catalyst strands, there is a needs-driven programme of training and skills-development opportunities, Arts Enterprise Zone, designed to help people who work or volunteer in Luton in the arts, culture or creative sectors. This programme includes practical help in completing bids, building strategic partnerships and networks, developing professional resilience and diversifying income. Sessions are developed in response to artists' feedback, galvanised through partnerships with the Creative Forum (led by Luton Borough Council) and Revoluton Arts, Luton's Creative People and Places (led by Luton Culture).

All these three strands have been successful. In the first year, 2017, TestBeds artists bid for £292,406 and achieved £174,609, from six Arts Council England applications and one International Development Fund application. In 2018, TestBeds artists applied for £483,234 and achieved £184,129, with funds deriving from arts and non-arts funding. This included funding from the Aviva Community Fund, London Luton Airport, Creative Scotland and the British Council Quebec. Furthermore, in 2018 Luton Borough Council advertised five competitive artist commissions to lead on their Pilot Year of Culture programme, and three of the successful artists were TestBeds alumni from Accelerator and Catalyst Co-Lab project strands.

Luton is known as a culturally 'super-diverse' town (LBC 2020) and there has been an increase in success in application and progression onto the programme strands for BAME and disabled artists over the two years it has run. A new fourth TestBeds project strand, Arts Elevator, has built on this by targeting and encouraging involvement and participation in the arts by members of under-represented groups. For the consultation to develop Arts Elevator, the team either spoke to the group leaders or attended their community meetings and sought help from 22 grassroots groups or community organisations in the development of this strand.[1] In 2018, Arts Elevator successfully recruited six diverse artists and arts organisations, leading the cohort through a six-month process of intensive skills development activity, mentoring and bid-writing support. Each artist submitted a competitive project grant application to Arts Council England, the collective of successful applications totalling £142,734 for activity to take place across Luton, to the benefit of Luton's creative and non-creative communities. The projects included nationally significant partners, who were new partners for the artists. These included, but were not limited to, the following: the British Hat Guild and London Hat Week, Tamasha Theatre Company, Essex Cultural Diversity Project, Cultural Engine CIC, and the Festival of Norfolk and Punjab.

The level of activity so far has been rewarding. To put it into figures, over 2018–19 artists have held 75 exhibitions or performances nationally and internationally, secured 22 new national and international commissions, and engaged 14 sectors (including business, manufacturing, health, law enforcement, technology, science and construction). Activity has taken place across 50 local authorities, and engaged 14 different universities, including international higher education institutions such as the Valand Art Academy in Sweden. Across two years of delivery, 253 new partnerships were developed between artists and industry for Accelerator Artists, 234 new partnerships for Catalyst Co-Lab artists and 42 for Arts Elevator. More than 150 Arts Enterprise Zone workshops have been delivered in Luton to 3,138 local sole traders and small to medium-sized enterprises. This includes workshops relating to bid-writing for creative sector projects, creative and cultural sector evaluation, Arts Award/Artsmark, arts development one-to-ones and mentoring, and cross-sector networking. In 2018–19, 68 new industry partnerships were developed, representing 51 per cent growth in activity, and across TestBeds activity over £500,000 has been secured by artists for creative and cultural projects.

Artists' experiences

As a socially engaged artist, Nicole Mollett said that TestBeds Artist Accelerator 'widened her understanding of the discourse around creative community engagement', and helped her access funding for a graphic novel, a collaborative project based on real-life experiences of people who live in Luton, engaging communities and celebrating diversity (Mollett 2018). TestBeds connected artists with writers, composers and performers to develop collaborative projects. Even so, working within an institution whose main focus is the students and the service provision for those students has meant that there are time constraints which can become barriers. Access to the site of the STEM (science, technology, engineering and mathematics) building was necessarily restricted by health and safety concerns, for a 2017 Accelerator artist, a difficulty which was overcome by the time a 2018 Accelerator artist expressed a desire to engage with the construction site. Access to students was a more agile process and artists worked with students from a broad range of subject areas, including performing arts, dance, fine arts, psychology, science and business. In addition, artists undertook knowledge exchange and processes of observation in more empirical sites of research, including observing the use of space within the science laboratories to create an awareness of the communal and restricted places and spaces.

David Murphy said that the 'sheer number of face-to-face meetings with students, artists and community members facilitated by TestBeds' enabled him to develop strong relationships and a focused understanding of the diverse community for his project exploring protest and activism in

Luton: 'A network of strong relationships within the artistic community in a town results in highly charged artistic results.' David Murphy is Musical Director of the Luton-based international orchestra Sinfonia Verdi and developed a musical workshop curriculum for business designed to 'enable people to experience leadership and teamwork issues in their most primal form – without words'. This led to David collaborating with the university's Business School and delivering interdisciplinary music/business workshops to MBA students.

Similarly, in 2018 Andy Abbott worked with researchers across the university in media, computing and business to create an online video game which addresses the issue of a universal basic income (http://lutopia.co.uk). The content is user-developed and has emerged out of workshops in schools and community groups in Luton. Andy received Luton Arts Funding to extend the work and engage wider audiences, with support from The Mall, Level Trust and the university's Communications Team, and successfully became a lead artist for Luton's Pilot City of Culture programme. Lutopia is a virtual-reality video game in which you explore an alternate-reality futuristic version of Luton. With Sophie Gresswell, a TestBeds artist from 2017, Andy has offered the opportunity to reimagine Luton though live game play, where the players seek to improve the well-being of citizens though game-playing choices. The collaboration between Andy and Sophie is one illustration of the way in which TestBeds has provided an environment for artist collaboration, with partnerships growing across project strands and cohorts. This demonstrates the means by which TestBeds provides opportunities and forms of project and local sector sustainability through the development of an interconnected network of artists. Also in the town, Arts Elevator artist Alva Wilson partnered with Luton Culture to become the milliner in residence at Wardown Museum in March 2019. He worked with residents in sheltered housing on designing and making hats from sustainable materials and exhibiting them in London Hat Week. TestBeds training in planning, marketing and budgeting was crucial in the application for funding these initiatives.

Sophie Gresswell explained how 'my methods as an artist encourage people to research and learn about the space, the town, local history, people and a shared identity and in turn use that knowledge to create something in the public eye'. She designed and created murals and street art, film, animations and digital technology (see Figure 5.1), transforming hoardings, underpasses, libraries and walkways both temporarily and permanently: 'I have found this way of working allows for communities to get a deeper understanding of the place around them, and in turn the art opens up potential for dialogue between themselves,

Figure 5.1 Unveiling workshop in Luton Library. © Aleksandra Warchol.

the place and others who also use the space.' Catalyst Co-Lab artist Nicole Mollett reflected, 'I believe a sense of community can only be created by that community ... I think it is important that Luton is unique and experimental, and stays true to itself.'

The university–town partnership

TestBeds is one of four strands of activity in Luton as part of Arts Council England's Luton Investment Programme (LIP): Harnessing Momentum, As You Change So Do I, TestBeds and Imagine Luton were delivered by partner organisations Luton Borough Council, Luton Culture (now The Culture Trust Luton), the University of Bedfordshire and Watford Palace Theatre. In 2019 Luton Borough Council's People, Power and Passion celebrated the centenary of the 1919 riots in the city following widespread dissatisfaction over job losses by demobbed soldiers after the First World War. Running a five-month programme from 15 June 2019, it was Luton's Pilot Year of Culture to bring Luton's cultures and communities together. It ran a programme of associate artists and trainees who were involved in one of the five major events in the town. *Justice 39*, co-commissioned by Revoluton Arts and Luton Council, took the stories of the 39 people arrested in the peace-day riots in 1919 and through theatre and music explored the connection with local young people, asking what they would stand up for. The artwork on the hoardings announcing 'We stand up for Luton' formed an impressive backdrop to the performances. In *Riot Act*, Lutonians barricaded themselves in the Luton Council Chamber in a drama performance witnessed by councillors about the unseen or unheard jobless of Luton then and now. Children from Whitefield and Chantry Primary Academies designed the *Children's Peace Party* in Wardown Park in September 2019, a hundred years after a similar event took place there. Alongside the council's @getactive campaign providing greater access to sporting facilities, the events have stimulated pride in Luton more widely. It was notable that the Love Luton 10k and half-marathon run was oversubscribed in October 2019.

The People, Power and Passion programme has been criticised as an expensive addition to Luton's six other long-running events: St Patrick's Day, St George's Day, Carnival, Mela, fireworks and Christmas lights. Most are outdoor events as there is nowhere else to house them. But that can mean low audience numbers in inclement weather. David Murphy said there is a need to develop this as a feature of the town and provide 'flexible outdoor performance spaces with access to power supply (such as the raised stage area outside the Hat Factory and the Bandstand in Wardown Park)'. Moriam Grillo, another TestBeds artist, agrees on the importance of providing spaces 'beyond libraries and commercial ventures' for intergenerational activities and young people – 'neutral settings where different groups are invited to come to gather, create, explore, devise and witness', with artists working in the community for social change and community cohesion. But as Michaela Nutt, Luton Council's cultural enabler, says, 'We don't have a huge amount of private firms with lots and lots of money willing to give out sponsorship.' Luton Airport contributes to the six long-running events and there is also a Windrush event planned. Michaela adds that Luton 'can become known nationally as a centre for inclusive intercultural activities'. The branded events for the centenary were part of the Harnessing Momentum 2017–2027 'ten year strategic vision for the arts, cultural and creative industries … a vision that builds on the strengths of the local cultural scene and aims to make Luton an inclusive, flagship place of culture' (LBC 2017). The ambition is to apply for UK City of Culture in 2025.

As You Change So Do I was a contemporary public art project in Luton, kickstarting the strategy in 2017. The huge and inspiring artwork designed by the Luton-born Turner Prize nominee Mark Titchner was mounted on the wall of a building facing the station. Projection screenings and other works which are part of this initiative discussed Luton's heritage and cultural history. Projects in this thread included Storefront, which transformed an empty shop into an exhibition venue. Gayle Storey was one of many artists making use of the venue when she presented her TestBeds Darwin Bio Orchestra combining art, science and music. As part of this joint project, the junior students from the Royal College of Music (RCM) wrote compositions for 12 locations around Luton which were performed by the Bio Ensemble, and they premiered Simon Speare's composition *Turning towards the Sun* and a piece by RCM Junior Department composition student Alexia Sloane, entitled *Ricochets*. Gayle Storey took photographs of each location which were projected during the performances to give a sense of the place that was the inspiration for the music. Engagement with junior and senior students at the RCM and the Luton Youth Orchestra developed collaborative working practices between the two centres.

In a participatory event in the same year, Julia Cheng performed in the Imagine Luton festival in June 2017 which engaged musicians, dancers and audience in spontaneous performance. She became an artist on the Accelerator programme for a year and worked on two works: *Collision* and *HIVE 2018* with House of Absolute. Opening conversations and facilitating participation across generations and throughout the community has been a key message in these initiatives: Sophie Gresswell says, 'Local artists often know the community like no other and could be very useful in helping bridge the gap between authorities and communities.' The arts can often be a 'vital tool in allowing people to open up, discuss subjects, come together, explore new possibilities and even make money!'

Moriam Grillo's *Playing with Feeling* was a durational installation using 120 kilograms of clay on display for 120 hours in the campus centre at the University of Bedfordshire as social document. Grillo uses art therapy to encourage positive mental health and well-being based on psychodynamic theory. Her project used clay as a neutral material and platform for expression to explore thoughts and feelings while setting the scene for impromptu conversation between strangers, and in this manner she was able to document communal engagement. She urged planners to think how a sense of place is developed by integrating the 'weaving of difference with a thread of commonality'(Grillo 2018). The combination of TestBed's artist development and the cultural streams of As You Change So Do I and Imagine Luton has highlighted the investment within Luton in the arts venues, the refurbishment of the arts centre, and the provision of incubator spaces and galleries by Luton Culture and the Borough, all of which is having a profound effect on the town's sense of place.

So what next?

In March 2019 a conference, 'Harnessing Creative Collaboration: Strategic Partnerships with Universities', was held at the university's Luton campus to explore these ideas and take the project forward. Over the three days it was considered how to build on the work currently ongoing across both higher education and the national creative and cultural sectors. Day one provided a Sector Leaders Symposium that saw delegates travel to Luton from 109 UK towns and cities, with leadership representation from Arts Council England and their National Portfolio Organisations (NPOs), Creative People and Places projects (CPPs) and Bridge Organisations. From higher education, attendance derived from project managers, heads of department, deans, executive deans and vice chancellors from a wide range of UK universities, including the University of Newcastle, Sunderland, Edge Hill, Lincoln, Coventry, Staffordshire, East London, King's College London, Kent, Bath and Exeter.

Day two of the conference debated the potential for younger age groups to take cultural leadership roles as part of a town-wide arts and culture youth conference, which was open to secondary, college and higher education students. This was delivered in partnership with Royal Opera House Bridge, and Luton Borough Council's 16x16 programme. On the third day the local community came together in a diverse offering of performances and exhibitions by artists and creative practitioners as well as opportunities for creative freelancers to access information clinics of the Arts Enterprise Zone. Day three also provided a testing ground for artists and students to share academic thought-pieces that contextualised their creative practice in a university conference context.

Based on the outcome of the conference, and through the consideration of the impact data that the first two years of TestBeds provided, the university arts and culture team is currently applying for additional funding to extend and enhance the TestBeds project. This will see the project evolve in Luton, and extend across areas in Bedfordshire and the wider eastern region. Furthermore, the team has been successful in funding Luton's first Cultural Education Partnership (LCEP), which will enable skills development to extend to younger local audiences, with the added potential of aligning this cultural skills development agenda to the university's Access and Participation Plan (APP). Through growing and enhancing the TestBeds model, including through the inclusion of strategically aligned projects such as the LCEP, the team needs to see how TestBeds can be transplanted to other universities and their localities and test the potential to extend TestBeds' modules into national programmes of activity.

Acknowledgements

We would like to thank Sophie Gresswell, Moriam Grillo, Nicole Mollett and David Murphy for their contributions to this article.

Notes

1. The groups and organisations were as follows: the Ghana Society, Agency for Culture and Change Management UK, Carnival – LAM (Luton Association of Mas), Rampage CIC, Revellers Steelband, Polish – Polonia Polish Community Group, Sickle Cell & Thalassemia Care Forum, St Kitts & Nevis, Scandalous, St Vincent & the Grenadines, Asian – BP, OM Group, DJ Academy/Luton Sounds Forum, Aerial Arts, the Luton Training, Employment & Skills Fair: LET's Fair, Tokko, Youthscape and Dar Arminah.

References

Cuffy, Violet and Jane Carr (convenors). 2018. 'Creole Fest: Building Bridges Across Borders', conference held 9–10 November, as part of their research project 'Dominica as a Centre of Excellence for the Preservation & Celebration of the Creole Culture through Language, the Arts & its Indigenous Kalinagos', funded by the Arts and Humanities Research Council, AH/R004498/1.
Douglas, Noel. 2001. 'Our World is Not for Sale' (and other posters). Accessed 10 June 2020. http://collections.vam.ac.uk/item/O1276486/our-world-is-not-for-poster-douglas-noel/.
Douglas, Noel. 2018. 'Hope to Nope'. Exhibition held at the Design Museum, London, 28 March–12 August. Accessed 28 April 2020. www.noeldouglas.net/selected-exhibitions/.
Greswell, Sophie. 2018. 'Pride in Place and the T+ Space'. TestBeds blog, 18 February. Accessed 28 April 2020. www.testbeds.beds.ac.uk/blog/2018/t-space-luton-central-library.
Grillo, Moriam. 2018. 'Playing with Feeling'. TestBeds blog, 28 May. Accessed 28 April 2020. www.testbeds.beds.ac.uk/blog/2019/playing-with-feeling.
LBC. 2017. 'Harnessing Momentum: Making Luton an Inclusive, Flagship UK Place of Culture. A Strategic Vision for the Arts, Cultural and Creative Industries in Luton 2017–2027'. Accessed 26 May 2020. https://www.luton.gov.uk/Leisure_and_culture/Arts_and_culture/Pages/our-strategic-vision.aspx
LBC. 2020. 'Luton Borough Council Corporate Plan 2017–2020'. Accessed 26 May 2020. www.luton.gov.uk/Council_government_and_democracy/Lists/LutonDocuments/PDF/Policy%20and%20Performance/LBC-corporate-plan.PDF.
Mollett, Nicole. 2018. 'Graphic Novel for Luton'. Accessed 28 April 2020. www.nicolemollett.co.uk/graphic-novel-for-luton/.
Murphy, David. 2018. 'The Journey so Far'. TestBeds blog, 2 November. Accessed 28 April 2020. www.testbeds.beds.ac.uk/blog/2018/the-journey-so-far.
TestBeds. 2019. 'Harnessing Creative Collaboration', conference, University of Bedfordshire, 21–23 March. Accessed 26 May 2020. http://www.testbeds.beds.ac.uk/conference-2019.

6
The Beam archive, Wakefield

Kerry Harker

The arts charity Beam was founded in Wakefield, West Yorkshire, in 1986 under the name 'Public Arts', one that clearly situated them within a form of practice only then emerging as a distinct professional discipline. Operating today from the centre of the city which has been the organisation's home throughout those 34 years, Beam continues to work with artists and communities to enhance places through the development of creative arts projects (Beam 2020). Over the years, this has been done in partnership with multiple agencies including arts organisations, local and national government and regional development agencies, public funding bodies, and the built environment and culture sectors.[1]

In 2017, I was commissioned by Beam to respond to the organisation's extensive archives, as part of their ongoing Arts in Place project, funded by Arts Council England. This latest iteration aimed to expand on Beam's position as a catalyst for the involvement of artists in creating a sense of place, reflecting on the changing role of artists within this discourse over the last 30 years or so of its history. By exploring the advocacy and learning potential of the archive, Beam hopes to frame a series of research questions in order to better understand its own journey through the processes and practices of public art over this period; to reconnect with some of the participants in this journey (artists, communities and former staff); to explore opportunities for future partnership with the higher education sector; and to create opportunities for public engagement, enhancing access to the archive material.

To identify Beam's signature approach to developing a sense of place, Fran Smith and Kate Watson, Beam's principal consultants, and I elected to focus on key projects from Beam's history. Two of these projects, spanning a period of over 20 years, are considered here.

Choosing specific projects offered a way to navigate and find entry points into the large volume of material generated over such an extended timeframe – thousands of documents, images and objects, stored in both physical and digital form – but crucially also to connect our investigation to Beam's ongoing work today. As well as documenting the numerous individual projects undertaken by the organisation, the archive casts light on the evolution of public art discourse and practice, and the changing roles of stakeholders including artists, commissioners and funders in the endeavour that has increasingly become known as 'place-making'.

A curatorial approach

Still relatively unexplored, the archive, which has been accumulated organically but is well ordered due to the diligent efforts of staff, charts a major and possibly uniquely sustained commitment to the notion of art in the public realm. It acts, in effect, as a microcosm of the major developments within this area of practice, touching on artistic, curatorial and commissioning processes; the creation of identities in relation to place; the accelerated growth and role of new technologies in these practices; and shifting approaches to place-making and the creation of public space, from top-down narratives of master planning driven by centralised government or private development, to more participatory modes operating at the local level, among many other issues. With a particular richness in relation to these histories in the Yorkshire region, the archive also facilitates a reconnection with nationally significant moments in the history of public art initiatives in the UK, through major schemes such as The Northern Way, which I return to below.

As a curator, I am fascinated by many aspects of the archive: its materiality and the way it moves us through time from the analogue to the digital, from medium-format transparencies, 35-mm slides and handmade artistic techniques such as collage, to the sleek and seductive imagineering enabled by new technologies; how the use of the visual components of graphic design such as copywriting, photographic and digital imagery and typography and their combined articulations convey a changing approach to creating 'public art' as discourse and practice, and how this is positioned for different audiences. Of course it shows the central role played by artists in constructing, and sometimes challenging, the conventions and practices of public art itself.

But the archive, like any, holds challenges which are not limited to the daunting nature of its sheer physical mass, the fact that it is not yet adequately catalogued, or issues of its conservation. There is the danger of what Helen Freshwater refers to as the 'allure of the archive', of taking it at face value. She cautions, 'Without a continual awareness of the long association of archival research with a history of positivism, and a thorough understanding of our own investment in this form of research work, we may find ourselves reproducing discredited methodologies' (Freshwater 2007, 6). We cannot approach Beam's archive as a transparent window into the past, because it is constructed. It reflects a multitude of decisions made daily over numerous years about what to write and how to write it, and raises inevitable questions about who writes, and for whom they do so. Who speaks from the archive and who is silent? What is retained and what has been discarded?

In addition, I bring my own experiences to bear on this work, as a curator and now researcher active in the contemporary visual arts over the last 20 years, working primarily within artist-led, and artist-centric, initiatives. I inevitably bring my own interests with me. Any further analysis that Beam commissions in relation to its archive will necessarily need to ask questions of authenticity and authorship, and consider what agendas and frameworks have governed its creation. My methodology in this initial phase, which amounts to a scoping exercise, has therefore been to attempt to resurrect a sense of Beam's chronology (which was patchily understood across the entire span of its history) by putting in place the bare bones of a timeline of major projects, and to begin erecting some contextual scaffolding by connecting to the wider, changing picture of public art practice. Unashamedly, I also tune my ears and listen, as ever, for the voices of artists. This strategy has enabled me to gain some measure of what the archive contains and what it lacks, and to begin to formulate a set of research questions that may inform the next phase of Beam's enquiry – to seek to find answers to such questions as: what is at stake in the matter of embedding artists more fully in the processes of place-making, and what are the major challenges, possibilities, limitations and discoveries offered by the archive? How might this learning be applicable more widely across the sector? I return to these questions in my conclusion.

The arts in place and place as art: Wakefield Cathedral Precinct

Beam has long claimed a fundamental commitment to advancing the central role of artists in the practices of place-making. Further research is needed to evidence this claim and then to assess the value and impact of this ethos. The organisation has certainly worked with hundreds of creative practitioners over its long career, based in and beyond the UK. Projects documented in the archive allow us to revisit the work of well-established contemporary artists, designers and architects, among them Jan-Erik Andersson, Tess Jaray, Morag Myerscough and Luke Morgan, Richard Woods, David Mach and Michael Pinsky. We also encounter major international art world figures including Antony Gormley, Anish Kapoor, Jaume Plensa and Richard Wilson among others – astonishingly not a single woman artist among them – commissioned through Welcome to the North, at its time the largest public art project in the UK, and in which Beam played a leading role. Launched by the Blairite government in 2007, it formed part of the investment programme The Northern Way, an initiative of then-Deputy Prime Minister John Prescott, which brought together the three northern Regional Development Agencies in a bid to address the economic gap between England's north and its south.[2]

Welcome to the North sought to create iconic representations of northern identity at key gateway locations as a way to attract overseas investment and grow tourism to the region. In attempting to enhance local identities, and that of the north more broadly, the scheme clearly aimed to replicate the success of Gormley's *Angel of the North* of almost a decade earlier. Nearly 20 years later, this major project, which cost some £4.5m at the time, is ripe for re-evaluation. Although Beam's archive contains significant holdings on this, that fuller analysis is beyond the scope of this current enquiry. So too is the material on Public Arts' extended conversation with the late architect Will Alsop from 2003 onwards, regarding possible futures for the Orangery, Beam's home in Wakefield from 1997 to 2016, as a 'unique regional resource for activity in the arts, architecture and the public realm' (Powell 2004, 72), a vision that remained unrealised. A three-dimensional model, preserved in the archive, gives a tantalising glimpse of what might have been.

Despite the presence of these globally significant names in Beam's back catalogue, I have always been struck by the organisation's long-standing commitment to supporting emerging and established practitioners based locally and across the wider region, something I have experienced first-hand as a curator working primarily in neighbouring Leeds and periodically engaging with Public Arts/Beam through their public programmes. Again, the archive holds much relevant material on this and the ways in which Beam has contributed to supporting emerging practice in the Yorkshire region and across the north. Through a characteristically cross-disciplinary approach to collaborative working, Beam has therefore throughout its history to date demonstrably employed a working methodology which simultaneously embraces the hyper-local while seeking to connect its work to broader narratives and contemporary developments within discourses on place-making and the arts nationally. I want to turn now to a successful early project, still extant today, that encapsulates Beam's approach to embedding artists in place-making initiatives.

In 1989, the artist Tess Jaray, already known nationally for her work in painting and printmaking, as well as in the public realm, was commissioned jointly by Wakefield Metropolitan District Council and Public Arts, then in only its third year, to propose a scheme for the enhancement of its cathedral precinct.[3] The project was a contemporary and close comparator to Jaray's major commission for Centenary Square, Birmingham, completed just one year before, but sadly decommissioned in 2017, after 26 years, to make way for the redevelopment of the site to a scheme by Graeme Massie Architects. Other major public-realm works by Jaray include the concourse at Victoria Station, London (1985); Jubilee Square, at the Leeds General Infirmary (1999); and the forecourt of the British Embassy in Moscow (2000). As it does today, in the 1980s Wakefield Cathedral stood at the centre of the city, but was not at that time successfully integrated into the fabric of the modern retail core which had developed around it. Jaray's scheme, completed in phases from 1992 to 1994, incorporates hard landscaping in the form of brick paving laid in geometric patterns, street furniture including seating, lighting, bollards, litter bins and planters, as well as the natural planting itself. Described by the journal *The Planner* in 1992 as 'a bold and imaginative city centre landscape' and 'a new public space of distinction and quality' (quoted in Darwent et al. 2016, 50), it has matured remarkably well, and represents an early example of innovative partnership working between an artist and local government departments.

At the time, Andy Kerr, the principal design engineer for Wakefield Council, was quoted as stating, 'I feel it is important to introduce an artist at the earliest opportunity so that their input can have an effect on the whole of the project' (Public Arts 1996, n.p.). The Wakefield project does seem to have been characterised by a close and fruitful collaboration, remembered affectionately by the artist, between her and Public Arts, the Cathedral, and various departments of the local authority, including its Engineering, Transportation and Waste departments. In hindsight, the scope of Jaray's commission was extraordinary, with the artist in effect proposing and designing all aspects of an entire civic realm. Her role seems, in its articulation of disparate elements into a whole to encourage dialogue between them and the production of new meanings, to have been a curatorial as well as artistic one. This goes far beyond more conventional notions of public art as an element applied to a ready-made space at the end of the process. In Jaray's approach there is no arbitrary separation between 'place' and the 'public art' produced for it: the two are indivisible from one another and arrive concurrently. The experience is akin to stepping inside one of her geometric canvases, brought to life in three dimensions, albeit rendered here in a sensitively muted palette that distinguishes it from some of her more exuberant paintings.

Speaking about her work for a 2017 exhibition at London's Marlborough galleries, Jaray stated, 'My use of geometry has more to do with the relationships between people or things, rather than anything mathematical' (Marlborough 2017). This humanistic philosophy clearly governs her approach to the public realm as well as to the creation of paintings and prints. As Charles Darwent notes, 'Jaray's artworks, on the scale of a painting or of a piazza, in printer's ink or brick, are always intently the same,' and unusually this works against the trend to separate the work of artists who work in both the public and the private (gallery) realms (Darwent et al. 2016, 8).

My exploration of the Beam archive has to date revealed little relevant material on this commission, although happily one of the primary sources for revisiting this work, Jaray's unpublished, handmade and ring-bound proposal document, is preserved there.[4] It provides a fascinating insight into the artist's methodology, as well as the tools then available for artists thinking through place-making. Dated September 1989, it sets out the artist's vision for the Wakefield site – to open up areas between the cathedral and adjacent shopping streets and to unify the entire precinct, thereby creating the sense of 'city centre' that was then felt to be sorely lacking. In doing so it would create a 'national model in its approach to pedestrianisation' (Jaray 1989, 1). Previously dislocated elements of existing cityscape were reunited through the installation of a bank of sandstone steps to the south of the cathedral, placing it properly in context with the city and creating an extension to it in the form of a 'natural amphitheatre' that the artist proposed be used for 'sitting, observing, and participating in city life generally' (Jaray 1989, 5).

The new space thus created was paved with blocks in a limited colour range specified by Jaray and laid in a recurring series of graphic patterns which effect an extension of her studio practice, again within a limited visual lexicon. The overall effect of Jaray's choreography is a scheme of remarkable coherence and deceptive simplicity which not only thinks through the daily activities and requirements of the end users, the people of Wakefield, with great sensitivity, but also exists on a human scale, pre-empting debates on human interaction in the urban sphere later brought to the fore by the Danish architect Jan Gehl in his 2012 film *The Human Scale*. However, the proposal document makes clear Jaray's understanding of the needs of other stakeholders too, as she offers her thoughts on how the scheme will enhance civic identity, increase the city's tourist appeal, attract trade and commerce, and act as a conceptual and physical node in a trajectory linking Wakefield's history to its future. The artist writes, 'Through this enhancement of its environment, to help create confidence in its future development, and thereby a bridge to Europe and the 21st century' (Jaray 1989, 1).

While these sentiments lodge in our perception today in ways marked by Brexit that Jaray could not possibly have foreseen, her intent is conveyed with great clarity: Wakefield's way to the future is as a modern, European city, proud of its heritage but striding confidently towards a reimagined future in which the arts and culture are placed centre stage. It is a vision that the city has continued to embrace, notably in its more recent creation of The Hepworth Wakefield, an internationally significant space for modern and contemporary art, housed in a David Chipperfield-designed building, which opened in 2011. Some 20 years earlier, and enabled by Public Arts, Jaray's design for the cathedral precinct was already laying the foundations for an ambitious civic approach to the arts in place and the transformative potential of artists. The organisation's contribution to preparing the ground for this later fuller expression of the city's cultural ambitions must be acknowledged. The 30th anniversary of Jaray's proposal offers just such an opportunity, but can Beam convincingly tell the story of its own effectiveness here?

This takes us back to the point about archives and silences, with implications for how Beam, and all other publicly funded arts organisations, ask questions, gather data and approach evaluation of their own work. If we look for external validation, we might start with the final report of the Arts and Humanities Research Council's Cultural Value Project, published in 2016. This questions the trend for sinking millions into flagship cultural venues, finding evidence instead to support the claim that, 'Far more significant might be the effect of small-scale cultural assets – studios, live-music venues, small galleries and so on – in supporting healthier and more balanced communities' (Crossick and Kaszynska 2016, 8). It is within this context of the small-scale and the locally embedded that Beam needs to situate its contributions to the arts in place.

Jaray's wonderful project, still very enjoyable today, stands for me as a counterpoint to the excesses of some rather more muscular, object-based public art, typified by a number of large-scale sculptures realised through The Northern Way, with their clear alignment to an international art market. The Wakefield project's lack of showy visibility and of an obvious authorship, indeed its near-disappearance into the cityscape, is one of its most successful aspects. The *Tenth Anniversary Calendar* which Public Arts published in 1996 quotes Jaray's aspirations for her design thus: 'I hope the final design would fit so perfectly with its surroundings that people would say, "what a beautiful city", not "what a beautiful design"' (Public Arts 1996). Jaray's sensitivity to the task can be clearly appreciated in the pages of her proposal, a document put together from photocopies of photographs the artist took herself on the street, on top of which she has then hand-coloured and collaged other elements, with additional annotations and sketches overlaid on these. The facture of this predigital, handmade approach allows the artist's voice to emerge differently from the page, enhancing the accessibility of her thoughts and working processes. It is evident that the artist has stood in this place, observing for herself human interactions with and within it. She utilises the proposal document to convey her investment, her engagement with the granular detail of the city's fabric. Her achievement is, in fact, to see the city and its people *as artwork*, continually remade through the performance of the everyday upon a bespoke stage she has provided.

Changing practices: The 'public' and 'art' of public art

The Wakefield Cathedral Precinct project and Welcome to the North demonstrate quite differing approaches to making places, and to working with artists. If the latter now seems rather anomalous with the longer trajectory of Beam's more locally embedded work, they are nonetheless united in illustrating how the organisation has effectively operated over time as a nexus for the various stakeholder groups with an interest in how places develop, from local artists and cultural organisations, communities and commissioners, to funding bodies, agencies and specialist sector professionals operating at the national level. This role is enhanced by Beam's ongoing participation in local and national networks including the Wakefield Arts Partnership and as coordinators of the national Arts & Place Consortium. The convening of this group, emerging from the Farrell Review of Architecture and the Built Environment in 2014, has led to the production of a *Manifesto for the Arts in Place* (Place

Alliance 2018), also informed by Graham Henderson's essay 'Putting Soul in the City – Towards a Manifesto' (n.d. [2015]). Both documents continue to urgently make the case for new approaches to public art, and are in favour of more meaningful engagements with the arts and culture in the design of places. The *Manifesto* states:

> Artists, performers and cultural practitioners can contribute creative thinking and design and placemaking skills; help engage people of all ages and backgrounds in debating, understanding, planning, and designing the public realm; help animate and enhance a meaningful sense of place through their individual vision and working with communities. (Place Alliance 2018)

Beam has been central to these discussions and to production of the *Manifesto*, and I want to argue that rather than approaching its archive as a linear series of discrete projects unfolding chronologically in time within the niche discipline of 'public art', we might view it as representative of a still-unfolding 30-year conversation that continues to create a community of interest around the central question of the relationship between place and the arts, with a particular focus on artists themselves, and shaped by the accumulated skills, knowledge and experiences of all those who have passed through its doors and connected with its work.

The archive, thought of in this way, and approached thematically, allows us to trace a trajectory in thinking about art in the public realm since the mid-1980s. If the earliest of Public Arts' projects maintained the traditional dominance of a model based on the classical relationship between object and plinth (its very first commission was the bronze statue of J. B. Priestley by Ian Judd, erected in Bradford in 1986), its approach was to evolve rapidly thereafter. Unveiled two years later, Charles Quick's celebrated and widely known *A Light Wave* was commissioned by the British Railways Board and Public Arts for the main Leeds–London platform at Wakefield Westgate station, where it remained until it was decommissioned around 2009.[5] This piece moved the debate away from the figurative and commemorative towards a large-scale, rhythmic series of repeated geometric arcs, formed from lengths of stained wood and dramatically spotlit from below at night. Quick, who lived in Leeds and was later to become chair of Public Arts for a time, worked on the major commission for two and a half years, and it gave the young artist a national platform in the field of public art, then still in its relative infancy. He consulted with the people of Wakefield in shopping centres and commuters at the station, demonstrating his intention with the aid of an illuminated maquette. He also worked closely with the British Rail architects, local engineers and station staff. Public Arts ran an associated education programme. The opening was marked by community celebrations and an evening gathering on the platform for all those who had been involved, ending with a congregation in a local pub. The process and resulting work engendered a strong sense of ownership among the local population, a sense of ownership which the artist perceives as having been even 'greater than [that of] British Rail perhaps'.

Expanding on the crucial importance of creating meaningful conversations on art in the public realm with local communities, as exemplified by the collaborative and thoughtful approach to both the cathedral precinct and Westgate station commissions, Beam's archive documents the organisation's numerous initiatives, through training, discursive events, summer schools and other schemes, designed to enhance the skills and confidence of local communities, including young people, in equipping them to approach these debates. Such projects include People Making Places, a wide-ranging programme of people-oriented built environment and place-making awareness-raising funded by the Commission for Architecture and the Built Environment, Arts Council England, Yorkshire Forward and the European Regional Development Fund, which ran from 2002 to 2009; and the Partnership Skills Programme, funded through Yorkshire Forward from 2005 to 2009, which supported citizens to influence vision and development in a dozen Yorkshire towns. There is still much to do to chart the changing fortunes of public art practice in the eyes of major funding and policy bodies nationally, as this narrative could, in part, be reconstructed from projects documented in the Beam archive.

Conclusion

During Beam's lifetime, there has also arisen a very significant area of artistic practice which has sought to expose and critique the negotiated relationships, power dynamics and flows of capital at work in processes of culture-led regeneration, where 'public art' has historically most often found itself situated. Recent controversies have brought to the fore urgent questions of public goods and private ownership, our shared urban heritage, and the dangers for artists of apparent complicity in processes of displacement and gentrification. The concepts 'public' and 'art' that make up 'public art' are in themselves hotly contested, and our understandings of both have been largely reconfigured since Public Arts' founding. They intersect and conflict over issues such as the trend, under austerity, towards the sale of hitherto public assets and their re-emergence under private ownership as pseudo 'public' spaces, newly adorned with artwork. The implication of art and artists within these processes of privatisation and its effects have recently come to be known as 'artwashing', representing a significant challenge to artists and organisations interested in working in the public realm.

In response, some of the most progressive recent thinking on public art is emanating from hitherto unexpected places – Eastside Projects in Birmingham, In Certain Places in Preston, Lancashire, and In-Situ in Pendle, also in Lancashire, are just three examples of critically engaged organisations, led by artists and academics, incubating new approaches to practice and partnership in this field, rewriting the rules on public art both implicitly and explicitly. Eastside's ongoing project Park Life seeks, for example, to change the way that art is commissioned for new housing developments in the UK, challenging public art's decorative function. When Eastside Projects argues, 'however we think that art should be useful and that artists can be innovative urban planners as well' (Eastside Projects n.d.), this actually serves as an apt descriptor of Jaray's role within the regeneration of Wakefield's cathedral precinct nearly 30 years ago.

Such activities hint not only at the expanding civic role of galleries and arts organisations and the imperative to widen inclusion, or simply at the continuing erosion of boundaries between the discrete specialist realms of public art as opposed to other forms of visual arts production, but also at the still-evolving role of the artist and the rise of social, or socially engaged, practices. The practice of public art itself has simultaneously diversified, its definitions expanding and its boundaries becoming increasingly blurred, moving far beyond the traditional triangulation of commissioner, specialist public art organisation and specialist public art practitioner that characterised its early iterations in the 1970s and 1980s in the UK. In her foreword to *Desire Lines*, Vivien Lovell traces the origins of public art practice in Britain back to Victor Pasmore's role in the controversial design of Peterlee new town in 1955. She says it was 'the main precedent for an artist's vision informing the wider environment' (Darwent *et al.* 2016, 6) before its migration and promotion as a managed form under the auspices of the Arts Council of Great Britain, and from there to the regions, from the mid-1970s on. By the early twenty-first century, this form of practice was ripe for re-evaluation, which is not to suggest that its more traditional tendencies no longer exist – in fact they can be seen to be continuing everywhere – but to say that the leading edge of these debates has moved on considerably in parallel.

Public Arts' change of name to Beam, in 2007, is not only indicative of its understanding of its own changing remit at that time, but was also an acknowledgement of the wider changes in thinking on the relationship between art, artists and the public realm, to which there was an imperative to respond. Conceptually the new name moves the emphasis from something historically associated with static, object-based practices, to a new identity that emotively invokes the qualities of something as intangible and ephemeral, yet aspirational, as a beam of light. These qualities align the organisation far more effectively with radically new thinking on these issues: when the Bristol-based organisation Situations published its highly influential 'New Rules of Public Art' in 2013, this list of twelve provocations advocated for the introduction of temporality, co-production, risk-taking and local distinctiveness, against the authoritative certainties of the past, as ingredients essential to the future of public art practice. The 'New Rules' also strongly advocate on behalf of artists and the idea of taking a leap of faith with them in the creative process: 'Public art is neither a destination nor a way-finder. Artists encourage us to follow them down an unexpected path as a work unfolds. Surrender the guidebook, get off the art trail and step into unfamiliar territory' (Situations n.d. [2013]). I would argue that we can see such a leap of faith at work in Tess Jaray's Wakefield Cathedral Precinct commission, enabled by the positive and open approach adopted by its commissioners and collaborators.

This unique approach, developed over 30 years, is at work within Beam's thinking today, as the organisation continues to undertake ambitious programming such as the nascent 25-year plan for a public art strategy for City Fields, a major new development to the east of Wakefield city centre. We can also locate research material which illuminates the challenges and opportunities relating to art in the public realm more broadly – from best practice in community engagement, to the roles of key stakeholders, notably that of artists as place-makers, the impact and appropriateness of funding streams, and the longevity of approaches and methodologies whose legacies can now be reassessed 10, 20 or even 30 years later. What works in the long term? How can we build sustainability into place-making initiatives, and particularly the role of culture within these, when the funding landscape for public art is a constantly shifting terrain of agencies, bodies and strategies vulnerable to the changing ideas of national government? Beam's projects over the years cover the arrival and subsequent dissolution of initiatives such as the regional development agencies and the Commission for Architecture and the Built Environment, and evolving attitudes to supporting public art within the work of Arts Council England. How can these debates impact on future policy development?

In conclusion, this initial reappraisal of the work of Public Arts/ Beam, through material held in its archive, would suggest that its most successful projects embrace the simple but effective principle of embedding artists within place-making initiatives and teams, from as early in the process as possible. Its major contribution, therefore, has been to shift the centre of gravity in the discourse of public art, reorienting the debate towards that unexpected path. The challenge now is to hone this core research question and embed it within processes and partnerships still unfolding today, with funders, policy-makers, communities and artists themselves. Clarity of intent and appropriately designed methodologies are required in order to frame the right questions, and to gather compelling evidence. Partnership with a higher education institution is key to realising this goal. The findings may be of value right across the sector, for all those engaged in making creative places that are fit for the challenges of today, and which acknowledge the major debates on cultural value, social inclusion and sustainability. Only in this way can we adequately respond to the central question of *how we know* about the value of involving artists in place-making, and from there continue to make the case for support for another 34 years to come, and beyond.

Acknowledgements

The author wishes to thank all current and former staff, directors and trustees of Public Arts/Beam, as well as the artists, who have taken part in this research to date.

Notes

1. The organisation is housed today within the workspaces of The Art House on Drury Lane, opposite Wakefield Westgate station and the beautiful eighteenth-century Orangery which was its former home.
2. The information on The Northern Way and Welcome to the North is drawn from unpublished material held in the Beam archive.
3. My thoughts here are formulated from material in the Beam archive, a conversation with Public Arts' then-director Graham Roberts, and email correspondence with the artist. Jaray worked in association with Tom Lomax. Assistance, models and consultation were by Martin Creed, Louis Nixon and Georgia Vaux.

4. Jaray's designs for Wakefield are reportedly held in the Arts Council Collection (Wakefield Express 2008).
5. My notes here are formulated from material held in the Beam archive, and from email correspondence with the artist.

References

Beam. 2020. 'What We Do'. Accessed 28 April 2020. http://www.beam.uk.net/what-we-do/.

Crossick, Geoffrey and Patrycja Kaszynska. 2016. *Understanding the Value of Arts and Culture: The AHRC Cultural Value Project*. Swindon: Arts and Humanities Research Council.

Darwent, Charles, Doro Globus, Tess Jaray and Vivien Lovell. 2016. *Desire Lines: The Public Art of Tess Jaray*. London: Ridinghouse.

Eastside Projects. n.d. 'Park Life 2016–2020'. Accessed 28 April 2020. https://eastsideprojects.org/projects/park-life/.

Freshwater, Helen. 2007. 'The Allure of the Archive: Performance and Censorship', *Moveable Type* 3: 5–24.

Henderson, Graham. n.d. [2015]. 'Putting Soul in the City – Towards a Manifesto: Using Public Art to Transform the 21st Century Urban Landscape'. Accessed 25 April 2019. www.beam.uk.net/wp-content/uploads/2016/05/Putting-Soul-in-the-City-Essay-Towards-a-Manifesto.pdf.

Jaray, Tess. 1989. Proposal for Wakefield Cathedral Precinct. Unpublished item in the Beam archive.

Marlborough. 2017. 'Tess Jaray: Into Light, in Collaboration with Karsten Schubert'. Accessed 25 April 2019. https://www.karstenschubert.com/exhibitions/192/.

Place Alliance. 2018. *A Manifesto for the Arts in Place*. London: Place Alliance. Accessed 25 April 2019. http://placealliance.org.uk/wp-content/uploads/2018/06/BEAM003-Manifesto-A3-ISSU-ART.pdf.

Powell, Robert, ed. 2004. *People Making Places: Imagination in the Public Realm*. Wakefield: Public Arts.

Public Arts. 1996. *Tenth Anniversary Calendar*. Wakefield: Public Arts.

Situations. n.d. [2013]. 'The New Rules of Public Art'. Accessed 25 April 2019. https://studiotosituation.files.wordpress.com/2015/01/the_new_rule_of_public_art.pdf.

Wakefield Express. 2008. 'Gallery's Grand Designs'. Accessed 25 April 2019. http://www.wakefieldexpress.co.uk/news/gallery-s-grand-designs-1-964971. No longer available online.

7
This Is Not My House: Notes on film-making, photography and my father

David Jackson

Family photographs are about memory and memories: that is, they are about stories of a past, shared (both stories and past) by a group of people that in the moment of sharing produces itself as a family.

– Annette Kuhn, *Family Secrets*

This Is Not My House is the title of a film I made in collaboration with my father to accompany an exhibition of photographs I had made previously

Figure 7.1 Film still from *This Is Not My House*, HD video, colour, 2014. © David Jackson.

with him, following my mother's death. After she died my father was left alone in the house he had shared with her for nearly 25 years. The house, nestled on the corner of Carlo Manche Street in Malta (a small ex-British colony which lies in the middle of the Mediterranean between Libya and Sicily), had previously belonged to my maternal grandmother. The resulting creative project – a portrait of my father in still and moving images – mixes photography with film, film with photography. It is both a personal visual record and an emotional inventory, documenting, as it does, an intimate familial exchange between father and son, framed by the immediacies of the Mediterranean not only as a place of lived, everyday experience on the part of my father, but also as a projected space of home and belonging for both of us. This research project – part-biographical, part-ethnographic – is a journey simultaneously of the head and the heart, a journey which draws on stories from my own life about my own family and my shared past with them.

Whilst the project began creatively as an act of mourning in response to my mother's death, it also emerges as a project made within a university environment when I taught film-making as a full-time academic at the University of Bedfordshire. Given the project's development in an academic setting, it would be fair to say that it has also been a creative testing out and thinking through of ideas about how I might fit into the academy as a film-maker and, more specifically, of the idea that an arts practice might be a form of research.

Smith and Dean, the editors of *Practice-Led Research, Research-Led Practice in the Creative Arts*, argue that there has been a turn to creative practice which they regard as 'one of the most exciting and revolutionary developments to occur within the university over the past two decades' (2009, 1). As defined by Smith and Dean, practice-led research refers both 'to the work of art as a form of research and to the creation of the work as generating research insights which might then be documented, theorised and generalised' (p. 7). Importantly, they regard these latter elements – the documentation, generalisation and theorisation of the artwork – as 'crucial to its fulfilling all the functions of research' (p. 7). In response to the myriad forms of academic research now conducted within the university, they have constructed a useful model of creative arts and research processes and the overlapping and interconnected patterns between theory and practice which they call 'the iterative cyclic web' (p. 8). This model, they suggest, accommodates the different forms of research currently being conducted across the arts and humanities, and includes traditional academic research, practice-led research and research-led practice. Their model reflects what they regard as the complex overlapping and alternations between the two modes (practice and theory) in the research process, and central to the model is the concept of 'iteration' which, they argue, is fundamental to both modes: 'To iterate a process is to repeat it several times (though probably with some variation) before proceeding, setting up a cycle: start-end-start' (p. 19). Smith and Dean's model seems to me an accurate reflection of the conditions of production of my own project, as it recognises the fluidity and cyclic alternation between the two modes of practice and research. In their model the two approaches are woven together, inseparably intertwined, each being continuously shaped by the other, an observation my (still unfinished) project would endorse.

Family photography and cultural memory

This project, then, uses autoethnographic memory work with family photographs; in other words, it seeks to put memory to work by using material objects such as family photographs as prompts in

Figure 7.2 Portrait with broken arm, photograph by David Jackson from the series *So Blue, So Beautiful*, colour, C-type print.

the remembering of personal stories. In doing so, the project explores the ways in which memory – that is, 'the activities and the products of remembering' (Kuhn 2000, 179) – can bring together the personal, the social and the historical. By telling stories about my own family's past, I'm looking to find new ways of understanding my father's biography: in particular his feelings of postcolonial displacement as a widowed British expat now living alone, and the ways in which his personal story criss-crosses and intersects with broader historical narratives linking the distant southern shores of the Mediterranean to the northern shores of the United Kingdom via post-war migration and back again. Key to this research is a practical use of film and photography in a sensory, affective register – both separately and together – to demonstrate memory's complex role in making identities 'that place us as members both of families and of wider communities – communities of class, gender, nation, for instance' (Kuhn 2000, 179).

Much of the flourishing research on cultural and social memory across the humanities and social sciences over the past two decades has sought to enhance our understanding of how personal memory operates in the cultural sphere and to inquire how, where and when memories are produced, and how people make use of these memories in their everyday lives (Kuhn 2007, 283). The cultural theorists Marianne Hirsch and Annette Kuhn, in particular, have been formative in situating my own practice within this research field; by practice I mean to encompass overlapping kinds of activity which include cycles of thinking and making, reflecting and writing. In asking how personal memory figures and shapes the social world, both Hirsch and Kuhn point to the importance of photography – especially ordinary family photography – in the production of memories about our own lives and how these memories are bound, more broadly, to cultural memory. Annette Kuhn's theoretical excursions in this field have been ongoing for the last 20 years or so, beginning with the publication of *Family Secrets: Acts of Memory and Imagination* (2002), a collection of essays she describes elsewhere (Kuhn 2000, 179) as autobiographical case studies in a revisionist mode, and continuing with further refinements and clarifications of key concepts and methods in other occasional essays (Kuhn 2007, 2010).

In *Family Secrets*, Kuhn makes imaginative and creative excursions into her own past by examining her own private family photographs and the memories associated with them. The autobiographical trajectory she enacts, though, has a decidedly political intent since her project aims to find new ways of conceptualising the ways personal memories 'relate to, intersect, or are continuous' with shared, collective and more public forms

Figure 7.3 The family album, photograph by David Jackson from the series *So Blue, So Beautiful*, colour, C-type print.

of memory. Photography as a medium is intimately entangled in the production of memory, both personal and collective. A photograph, suggests Kuhn, is a form of evidence, but not in a directly mimetic sense of mirroring the real or even in a self-evidential relationship between itself and what the photograph may show (2002, 13). Making a photograph yield its possible meanings is not a transparent proposition; paradoxically, she observes, the more closely you look at a photograph, the less you will see: look closely with a magnifying glass and all the photograph will reveal is grain and blur and light and dark patches. The photograph, she argues, will yield nothing to this kind of scrutiny: 'to show what it is evidence of, a photograph must always point you away from itself' (p. 13). Whilst photographs may act as prompts to producing personal memories, these memories may well not have anything to do with what is actually in the photograph. 'Memories evoked by a photo', she writes, 'do not simply spring out of the image itself, but are generated in a network, an intertext of discourses that shift between past and present, spectator and image, and between all these cultural contexts, historical moments' (p. 14). What matters here is putting memory to work in a productive sense with the photograph.

Kuhn defines the concept of memory work as 'an active practice of remembering which takes an inquiring attitude towards the past and the activity of its (re)construction through memory' (2007, 284). Importantly, Kuhn wants to short-circuit assumptions about transparency or authenticity or even the 'truth' of what is remembered. Memory work should challenge the 'taken-for-grantedness' of memory. Instead, she argues, memory work should seek 'a conscious and purposeful staging of memory' whereby cultural material is rigorously interpreted, interrogated and mined (p. 284). Memory work, as a working concept, is developed in *Family Secrets* as a specific mode of inquiry embodying a number of methodological assumptions which she develops into a four-pronged approach to the study of a single photograph. First, Kuhn says we need to consider the subject(s) of the photograph. She suggests starting with a simple description, and then moving into an account in which you take up the position of the subject. Using the third person, she claims, is useful at this point. Second, she asks us to consider the photograph's context of production: where, when, how, by whom was the picture taken? Third, she urges a consideration of the context in which the image was made: here questions of photographic technology, aesthetics and conventions are raised. Finally, she says we need to consider the contexts of reception: who was the photograph made for? Who has it now and where is it kept? Who saw it then and who sees it now? (2002, 8). As an exercise, the aim of this methodology is to develop a radical approach to reading a photograph. To this end, Kuhn quotes John Berger, who advises that 'a radial system has to be constructed around the photograph' (Kuhn 2002, 9). This interpretive method needs to incorporate the personal with the wider political, historical and economic layers in which everyday memory and experience are necessarily woven.

Family photographs are particularly useful prompts as material for the interpretation of cultural memory. As we experience them in our daily lives, photographs of this kind have a special place in our own lives and carry a powerful affective charge, and yet are virtually invisible as objects in all their everydayness. It is exactly this line between the visibility and invisibility of these seemingly transparent domestic objects that has brought family photography to the attention of contemporary theorists, critics and artists (e.g. Hirsch 1999; Spence 1986; Batchen 2008; Bourdieu 1990; Kuhn 2002; Berger 1980). Taking an array of interdisciplinary perspectives, these various writers and critics attempt to deconstruct the myth of family, pointing to the rigid conventions of family photographs and the limited, rule-bound representations they give rise to. Similarly, many of these writers have devised radical reading practices that scrutinise and critique photography's perceived role as an instrument of familial ideology. Marianne Hirsch, in particular, seeks to interrogate, question and contest what she perceives as the complex interactions between family and photography. In *Family Frames* (1997) and *The Familial Gaze* (1999), she strives for what she terms a 'resistant reading' when she poses the following questions: what can we learn from family snapshots or more formal portraits; and, as inscriptions of family ties, what stories does the family album ultimately tell? (1999, xvi). Hirsch argues that the family album is the main problem because it consists of photographs that convey the romantic ideal of family life rather than the messy reality. She writes:

> This myth or image – whatever its contents may be for a specific group – dominates lived reality, even though it can exist in conflict with it and can be ruled by different interests. It survives by means of its narrative and imaginary power, a power that photographs have a particular capacity to tap. (Hirsch 1997, 8)

One way of looking at the narrative power of family photographs, Hirsch contends, is to locate them in the contradictory space between the myth and lived reality of familial relations. As such, one possible way of destabilising the myth of family is to create new narratives around old family photographs.

According to Hirsch, the individual subject is constituted in the space of the family through looking, or what she terms 'the familial gaze'. Hirsch defines the familial gaze as 'the conventions and ideologies of family through which they see themselves' (1999, xi). This distinctive form of looking within the family, she suggests, is both 'affiliative and identificatory': as I look, I am always also looked at (Hirsch 1997, 9). It is in this sense, then, that we can say that familial subjectivity is constructed relationally and entails relationships of power, domination and subjection. What we need, Hirsch insists, 'is a language that will allow us to see the coded and conventional nature of family pictures – to bring the conventions to the foreground and thus to contest their ideological power' (1997, 10).

Refocusing the familial gaze

One such project is Sultan's *Pictures from Home* (1992). The photographer and writer Larry Sultan spent over a decade photographing his parents in their home in Southern California. *Pictures from Home* is a collection of carefully staged choreographed portraits of his mother and father, Irving and Jean. The intimate photographs he made evoke the mundane togetherness of a long marriage and the optimism and frustrations of family life in the wealthy suburbs of the San Fernando Valley. In the photographs we see his mother, Jean, preparing a Thanksgiving turkey; Irving, his father, sitting on the edge of the bed, formally dressed in his dark blue office suit; Jean in the garage about to get in a car for a meeting; and, most famously, Irving practising his golf stroke in the living room while watching daytime television. Interwoven with these lush, beautiful pictures are snapshots taken from the family album, blown-up printed strips of 16-mm home-movie footage, and a first-person narrative that serves as an ongoing commentary on the project over time. When all these layers are read together, *Pictures from Home* reveals the multiplicity of looks that circulate between the son, the mother, the father, the husband and wife, and underscores the complex negotiation of roles involved in familial interaction as individual, personal identities encounter one another across the span of a lifetime (Hirsch 1999, xi).

The project began as a portrait of Sultan's father. After a long career at the Schick Safety Razor Company, Irving had recently been forced into early retirement after enjoying corporate success as a vice-president. Sultan's manifest intention was to show what happens when companies discard their unwanted elderly workers in favour of younger ones. At first Sultan thought he was interested in how his father's resulting feelings of powerlessness and resentment might show themselves at home with family. However, as he began to make the pictures, 'deeper impulses' Sultan was 'unaware' of came into play. In his commentary, the photographer writes: 'I can remember the peculiar feeling I had looking at the first pictures that I made of him. I was recreating him and, like a parent with an infant, I had the power to observe him knowing that I would not be observed myself' (1992, 10). Usually it's the parent who does the looking, who takes the picture, who tells the family's story by constructing a family album. But the opposite is the case in *Pictures from Home*. Instead, Sultan's images subtly and unexpectedly reverse the conventional familial relationships.

In his published essay about the project, Sultan gives an account of a telephone conversation with his mother over a picture he took of her for the real-estate section of the *LA Times*. His mother, a highly successful real-estate saleswoman, was so 'miserable' with the photograph that she refused to tell anyone her son, a highly regarded professional photographer, had taken it, claiming she had to hire a 'hack' to do the job instead because he wasn't available. 'Who would buy a house from someone who looks so severe?' she asked her son. 'It doesn't even look like me. I hate that picture' (Sultan 1999, 8). Sultan reports that his father shared similar misgivings along with his mother about many of his photographs. 'I just don't know what you're doing,' his father told him; 'I don't know what you're after.' The exchange that followed is highly revealing of the deep, generational chasm between them:

> [Son:] 'All I know is that every time I try to make a photograph, you give me that steely-eyed look. You know it: penetrating but impenetrable, tough and in control. [...] It's like you're acting the role of the heroic executive in an annual report, or in a diorama on success. Maybe you're looking for a public image of yourself and I'm interested in something more private, in what happens between events – that brief moment between thoughts where you forget yourself.'
>
> [Father:] 'All I know is that when you photograph me I feel everything leave me. The blood drains from my face, my eyelids droop, my thoughts disappear. [...] All you have to do is to give me that one cue, "Don't smile," and zap. Nothing. That's what you get.'
>
> [Son:] 'No. What I get is an image of you that you don't like. Doesn't it come down to vanity and power? A question of how you look and who determines that, who's in control of the image?' (Sultan 1999, 8–9)

The dispute between father and son over the photographs poses a crucial question here about the familial gaze: for who does the looking in *Pictures from Home*? And what might be at stake in this looking? At any instant we can see a number of looks and gazes intersecting across the photographs. First there's an exchange of looks between the camera/photographer and the subject; then there are the looks between subjects within the photographs, the look of the viewer which, in itself, as Hirsch notes, 'is an infinitely multiple and contradictory series of looks', and, finally, 'the external institutional and ideological gazes in relation to which the act of taking pictures defines itself' (1999, xvi). The child photographing his parents is a reversal of the norm here; it challenges our accepted representations of the family. *Pictures from Home* quietly and steadfastly refocuses the familial gaze, changing our way of seeing family life and familial relations. Irving Sultan saw himself as a successful American businessman, albeit retired. His son disagreed and made some photographs as evidence to the contrary. However, in the process of making the pictures, Sultan expressed a deep sense of unease about his situation and questioned why he was back in his parents' house with a camera. In his journal he writes:

> Sitting finally on the couch in the dark living room, I begin to sink. My body seems to grow smaller, as if it is finally adjusting itself to the age I feel whenever I'm in their house. It's like I'm inflating the air from an inflatable image and shrinking back down to an essential form. Is this why I've come here? To find myself by photographing them? (Sultan 1992, 10)

I understand Sultan's predicament and share many of his feelings regarding my own endeavours to create a portrait of my father. After the fact of my mother's death, I knew I would have to photograph him. I had no plan, had no precise idea what this would mean, only the certainty of an obligation, which began to impose itself on me. One day, I found myself alone in my parents' house whilst my mother was ill in hospital, and I spent the afternoon aimlessly rummaging through drawers and boxes of discarded memories. In one drawer I found my mother's bus pass. I held it a moment and glanced at her name below her picture: Vincenza Carmela Giuseppa Jackson. It occurred to me suddenly that I had never known her full name before. Of course, I knew her first and last name, but not the middle ones. How could this be? How could I possibly not know my own mother's full name? My father always used a strangely anglicised version of Vincenza: Tina. And, growing up, she was known to us as Tina Jackson. I realised that in the story of her name, née Darmanin, was the story of her passage from one shore to another, through her marriage to my father. On my father's side there had always been a reluctance to recognise her Mediterranean otherness and this was always a source of familial tension. On reflection, I began to realise that my own story, the story of my own identity, was deeply entangled in the story of my mother's Mediterranean crossings. Likewise, to encounter my father to make my photographs and film was also to encounter my*self*. I knew, like Larry Sultan, that returning to my father's house to photograph him, and later to make a film, was also an attempt to find myself and my own sense of place.

Between island and empire

There's a framed photograph that used to hang on a white wall above my father's desk in his house in Malta. It hung next to an assortment of other family photographs. To be truthful, I never paid much attention to this photograph in the 20 or so years it hung there: it was just a family photograph, the same as any other. The photograph was taken in St Joseph's Church Hall in Southsea, Portsmouth, on Saturday, 31 March 1962, the day of my parents' wedding. At the centre of the picture are my father, aged 22, and my mother, aged 19. I found myself looking at this photograph over and over in the two weeks I spent with my father after my mother's death. When I asked my father about it, he told me it was taken by Kenneth L. Guy, a local professional photographer. The photograph had cost 15 shillings for 'a half plate mounted' and the photographer's fee for attending the wedding was one pound (my father still has the receipt from Mr Guy with his address and telephone number: 78 Middle St, Southsea, 27061).

When we buried my mother, it fell upon me as the eldest to make a final address. Standing at her graveside, in the shadows of the cypress trees, suspended between light and dark, close to the invisible boundary between life and death, I wondered about the multiple and mutable meetings, crossings and journeys evoked in the wedding photograph that had led us all to this place. For me, the photograph was more than

Figure 7.4   The wedding photograph on the wall, photograph by David Jackson from the series *So Blue, So Beautiful*, colour, C-type print.

a document of the ceremonial meeting between my mother and my father; it also reverberated with the silent passages made by people whose stories lay outside the frame, passages between north and south, between island and empire, between past and present. The cultural critic Iain Chambers invokes the 'many voices' of the Mediterranean when he writes:

> There is the Mediterranean, the sea itself, not so much as a frontier or barrier between the North and the South, or the East and the West, as an intricate site of encounters and currents. It immediately invokes the movement of peoples, histories, and cultures that underlines the continual sense of historical transformation and cultural translation which makes it a site of perpetual transit. (Chambers 2008, 32)

Perhaps it is in this sense, as 'a site of perpetual transit', that my parents' wedding photograph can be most productively read. For I read this photograph not only as an instrument of a family history but also as an act of cultural memory; for it tells a story, a story that inadvertently evokes the unspoken passages between the shores of the English Channel and the more distant shores of the Mediterranean.

In *Mediterranean Crossings,* Chambers aims to reconfigure previous understandings of any single definition of the Mediterranean by proposing a 'multiple Mediterranean' open to 'other voices, other bodies, other histories' (2008, 388). According to him, 'the Mediterranean' as a category and as an object of study is fundamentally the product of modern geographical, political, cultural and historical classifications. 'It is a construct and a concept', he writes, 'that linguistically entered the European lexicon and acquired a proper name in the nineteenth century' (2008, 12). As he rightly reminds us, it is during this time, of course, that the cartography of much of the Mediterranean and North African coastline and beyond was 'elaborated and divided' by the imperial foreign policies of Britain, France and Italy to encompass Egypt, Algeria and Libya, respectively. In the wake of colonial expansion, argues Chambers, we need to adopt a more fluid geography of the Mediterranean, whereby its boundaries are made vulnerable to the cultural and political importance of discontinuity in the telling of its history. Such a fluid and open-ended understanding, he suggests, will seek to interrupt and disturb 'the discursive desire for transparency', reconfiguring our historical conceptions of the past in order to dissect the present (2008, 387).

This image of the Mediterranean Sea as an open-ended flow that continuously interweaves multiple histories and cultures is a useful trope when it comes to considering not only the photographs I have made with my father, but also photographs I have found in our family archive. In these photographs taken as a whole, the sea is the thread of a narrative, which, even in its absence, pulls together the fragments to produce a family story. The photographs *are* the telling of our story. They serve as literal and metaphorical reminders of the proximity and distance that separates me from my father, as well as stark signs of his emotional displacement and dislocation in the Mediterranean. Looked at together, they are archival and poetic evidence of the vulnerable encounters opened up across distant shores between a group of people I call my family, and affirm the spatial and temporal relationships that give this story its past and present tense. As images on paper, the photographs are also material reminders of the free flow, drift and circulation of memory itself, recording the trace of places near and far. This narrative, then, is still unfolding: unfinished and unresolved.

Five years after I made the photographs, I received an email from my father with the word 'house' in the subject line. He wrote: 'Well the deed is done. I have signed the contract to sell the house and now there is no going back. […] I have arranged for mums grave to be kept clean until they remove her in five years time anyhow. Lots of love dad.' When we talked over his decision to sell his house, he told me that was the end of the story. But it didn't seem like the end of anything to me – more a case of one door closes, and another opens. Indeed, this circular, repetitive movement echoes Smith and Dean's (2009) iterative cyclic web model for creative practice and research mentioned earlier. According to this cyclic model, my initial ideas had been pursued as research and realised through various outputs and/or public outlets: in this instance, photographs, exhibitions, photobook. The 'formulation and theorisation of ideas, processes and techniques which have developed through the creation of the published artwork' may, in turn, Smith and Dean suggest, 'also be published and/or else applied to the generation of future creative works' (2009, 21). And now I was back at the ideas stage: I had made the photographs and had theorised some of the ideas around them, which, in turn, opened up further creative possibilities: this became a film which I called *This Is Not My House*, a title I borrowed from Larry Sultan.

What does home mean? According to Blunt and Dowling (2006), the notion of home as a sense of belonging or attachment is a complex and multi-layered concept. Taking a geographic perspective, they identify two key elements as unique to the idea of home. Home, they suggest,

Figure 7.5 Film still from *This Is Not My House*, HD video, colour, 2014. © David Jackson.

is a *place* we make meaningful and significant to ourselves. We imbue home with feelings, and these feelings, they argue, are 'intrinsically spatial'. In their terms, home is 'a social imaginary', or in other words, a space in which we make an emotional investment. Home is thus 'a set of intersecting and variable ideas and feelings, which are related to context, and which construct places, extend across spaces and scales, and connect places' (Blunt and Dowling 2006, 2).

So I returned to Malta. One evening I sat with my father up on his roof drinking cold beer after dark. We talked about his decision to sell the house. He said he wanted to go home. I asked him where he thought home was. Portsmouth, he replied, the place he was born and had grown up. In this respect his answer was similar to the experience of many migrants who identify with their place of origin many years after they have left. We talked some more; I wasn't convinced his plan was a good idea. When we eventually went back downstairs, he complained of a headache and asked if I had any aspirin. I said I didn't. He went to his kitchen window, leant out and smoked a cigarette. His next-door neighbour, Laurie, was leaning out too. My dad mentioned his headache. Laurie popped inside and returned with a pack of aspirin, which he passed over in a kids' fishing net. When my father stepped back inside, I remarked on what I had just witnessed: how could he possibly not feel at home here? After all, he had lived in this house with my mother for nearly 25 years, he knew all his neighbours, and was surrounded by friends who loved and cared for him. This, I told him, *was* his home. He didn't agree.

Figure 7.6 Film still from *This Is Not My House*, HD video, colour, 2014. © David Jackson.

From analogue photography to digital film

My film, *This Is Not My House*, extends the memory work of the photographs, and documents my father's house as inhabited space: in other words, his home. The story of what happens to my father and his home is neither here nor there; the narrative itself is of minimal interest and acts only as a frame for some of the depicted events. Instead of a story, *This Is Not My House* sets out an intimate understanding of my father's everyday reality by taking the ordinary seriously, and stitches together sounds and images into a loose montage of closely observed vignettes in which I ask my father to re-enact aspects of his everyday life before the camera. What matters here, what most concerns me as a researcher, is a question of approach, of method, of form: how best to conjure my father's world into being, how best to understand his experiences, his identities, his way of life?

In making the photographs I used a solely analogue process, from start to finish. I chose a fully manual medium-format camera, a Mamiya RB67, and shot on 120 negative film. Each and every image was purposefully staged and I would more often than not move the camera several times before I was happy with the composition (much to my father's exasperation). Everything about the process was slow. Deliberately so. When it came to making the film, I wanted to ensure my slow working methods continued. My preference initially was to shoot analogue 16-mm film with a Bolex camera, but the costs of the stock, processing and printing were prohibitive. So I shot digital video instead and kept the slow working method of making photographs. Each camera setup, each shot, was considered in much the same way: from choice of lens to composition, and, in this case, duration of the shot. Interestingly, what is most remarked upon about the film is its photographic quality: how each shot, each image, has the aesthetic quality of a photograph. What I'm trying to do here is place film and photography – still and moving image – into a dialogue with one another as spatial practices.

The difference between a fragment of film and a photograph lies in the specific capacities of still and moving images to give form to a passing moment of lived time as different temporalities. What I mean by this is best illustrated by a short sequence in the middle of the film where my father sits on the edge of his bed and browses silently through photographs in family albums. As he turns the pages, we have, I think, an opportunity to rethink the differing temporalities of the image, in how the moving image depicts stillness. Still images (photographs) are seen throughout the film. We see them in family albums, or hanging on walls, or stored on his computer. My father's identity is bound by the abundance of photographic images he lives with. By asking him to look at his family albums, I am trying to foreground the embodied aspect of photography as a staged act of memory, or in Kuhn's formulation, 'an enacted practice of remembering' (2000, 186). And as we see him leafing through the family album, we not only see the differing temporalities but also *feel* the simultaneous surging capacities of still and moving images to affect and be affected by each other. In this short simple sequence, I am trying not only to draw attention to family photography as a social practice, but also to make visible what we take for granted in everyday life: the passing of time.

Making the film was a struggle, not just technically, but also emotionally. Put simply: my father doesn't like being my subject. My project is a reversal of the usual means of familial looking: I'm the son looking at his father. Framing him as an image is not a straightforward matter. It's complicated for both of us. The entire 10 days of filming was fraught. My father had made himself vulnerable by selling his house with no real plan and here I was, probing his vulnerability with a camera in hand, looking at him, without blinking. And the film, I think, is a document of the tension between us. What is it to be a father, a son – let alone a good one? I'm not sure what the answer is, but I can see now that each frame, each scene, pulses with our habits of relating that reach back deep into our shared past and experiences, which is why I chose to put myself in the picture with the scene of the two of us on the roof. I come out badly: the reluctant son playing up for the camera. Again.

Endings ... and beginnings

In the moment of the click of a shutter: the relation between looking and being looked at has been central to my encounter with my father. I have felt acutely aware that whenever I look at him through the camera I am framing him as an image. Once he asked me what he was supposed to be looking at when he gazed into the camera: I laughed and replied, 'eternity'. This journey has been difficult and painful. From the outset I wanted the project to be a collaboration between us, to bring us closer together. But he found the process of shooting too cumbersome, too long. Looking back, I'm not sure what the point was. More often than not we completely failed to understand each other. At the airport when I left, I asked him if he'd enjoyed what we'd done together. He replied he'd liked my company but not the film-making.

So what drove me to carry a digital camera and tripod 3,000 miles to film him? Larry Sultan asked himself a similar question about his portraits of his own parents. He thought it difficult to name, but suggested 'it has more to do with love than sociology' (1992, 18). I understand this: *This Is Not My House*, too, is a work of love. On reflection, I am reminded of Jean-Luc Nancy's extraordinary ontological affirmation of the most ordinary aspects of our existence when he writes: 'What is a singularity? It is that which occurs only once, at a single point (out of time and out of place, in short) that which is an exception' (2004, 41). There were moments in my encounter with my dad where I would look and just have to stop, simply stunned: this *is* my father. I am astonished that a photograph, or a fragment of film, is able to capture the single point of this moment and make it an exception. It is precisely the camera's capacity as 'a clock for seeing' – to use Roland Barthes's incisive formulation (1981, 15) – which makes remarkable things that, at first, would appear to be apparently insignificant.

I recognise that whilst the story of my relationship with my father is unique to me, it is also deep-rooted as common, shared experience: we all have knowledge of familial relations, one way or another, whatever they may be. By putting the emphasis on how life takes shape and meets with the ordinary, my film and photographs give creative expression to everyday routines and encounters without definitive interpretation. I am saying: here is my encounter and here is its representation as *affective* experience: this is what the encounter *feels* like for me, for my father, depicted in sounds and images. Here, then, is my own attempt to arrest time for the briefest of moments, to show my father as remarkable by highlighting his apparent insignificance. By narrowing the focus to his house, I am trying to understand his intense feelings of dislocation about his own sense of place.

Indeed, making the film is also a reckoning with the question I posed earlier about finding my own place within the academy as a filmmaker, about how my creative practice might fit the demands of research. *This Is Not My House* begins and ends with the image of a door opening and closing, a cyclical looping which seems to me entirely appropriate as a way to describe the iterative process and interaction between creative practice and research. Rather than closing anything down, the project has achieved the opposite: practice and research are inseparably intertwined, each continuously shaped by the other. In this instance, one thing really does lead to another. *This Is Not My House* is not the end of the story but rather the opening up of other possibilities, other ways of telling about place and how we may make sense of it.

This Is Not My House is available to view online: https://vimeo.com/110994606.

References

Barthes, Roland. 1981. *Camera Lucida: Reflections on Photography*, translated by Richard Howard. New York: Hill and Wang.
Batchen, Geoffrey. 2008. 'Snapshots: Art History and the Ethnographic Turn', *Photographies* 1 (2): 121–42.
Berger, John. 1980. *About Looking*. London: Bloomsbury.
Blunt, Alison and Robyn Dowling. 2006. *Home*. London: Routledge.
Bourdieu, Pierre. 1990. *Photography: A Middle-Brow Art*. Cambridge: Polity Press.
Chambers, Iain. 2008. *Mediterranean Crossings: The Politics of an Interrupted Modernity*. Durham, NC: Duke University Press.
Hirsch, Marianne. 1997. *Family Frames: Photography, Narrative, and Postmemory*. Cambridge, MA: Harvard University Press.
Hirsch, Marianne, ed. 1999. *The Familial Gaze*. Hanover, NH: University Press of New England.
Kuhn, Annette. 2000. 'A Journey Through Memory'. In *Memory and Methodology*, edited by Susannah Radstone, 179–96. Oxford: Berg.
Kuhn, Annette. 2002. *Family Secrets: Acts of Memory and Imagination*. New ed. London: Verso.
Kuhn, Annette. 2007. 'Photography and Cultural Memory: A Methodological Exploration', *Visual Studies* 22 (3): 283–92.
Kuhn, Annette. 2010. 'Memory Texts and Memory Work: Performances of Memory in and with Visual Media', *Memory Studies* 3 (4): 298–313.
Nancy, Jean-Luc. 2004. 'Banks, Edges, Limits (of Singularity)', translated by Gil Anidjar, *Angelaki* 9 (2): 41–53.
Smith, Hazel and Roger T. Dean. 2009. *Practice-Led Research, Research-Led Practice in the Creative Arts*. Edinburgh: Edinburgh University Press.
Spence, Jo. 1986. *Putting Myself in the Picture: A Political, Personal and Photographic Autobiography*. London: Camden Press.
Sultan, Larry. 1992. *Pictures from Home*. New York: Harry N. Abrams.
Sultan, Larry. 1999. 'Pictures from Home'. In *The Familial Gaze*, edited by Marianne Hirsch, 3–13. Hanover, NH: University Press of New England.

8
Notions of place in relation to freelance arts careers: A study into the work of independent dancers

Rachel Farrer and Imogen Aujla

In the UK, self-employment is almost three times higher among cultural workers than in the general workforce (Robinson 2018). The project-based nature of many arts sectors means that practitioners are responding to varied working conditions, and regularly adapting and applying their skills and knowledge in different contexts. In a survey undertaken by Art Works in 2014, 47 per cent of artists described their practice as 'happening across multiple different settings', commonly taking on different roles in relation to artistic practice, education, community work and social engagement. As a result, artists' work can be difficult to categorise or quantify. The most recent Arts Council England evidence review (BritainThinks 2018) reported that artists found peer networks to be crucial for artistic development in terms of both developing practice and discovering opportunities, indicating that artists rely heavily on informal exchange to support their work. These conditions create a particular set of challenges for artists, in relation to their place both within a geographical community and within established sectors of the arts. The aim of this chapter is to explore how notions of place can be understood in relation to these kinds of working conditions. It will consider how factors such as geography, networks, relationships and perceptions of different arts sectors affect those working in freelance capacities. The chapter draws upon a recent study into the UK dance sector (Aujla and Farrer 2016) as a case study that will evidence how these themes are understood and addressed by self-employed dance artists, and highlight the models of practice they engage with that might be relevant to other arts sectors.

Background: The UK dance sector

It has been estimated that around forty thousand people work in the UK dance sector, but the varied and ad hoc nature of their roles makes it challenging to quantify and describe the workforce accurately (Burns and Harrison 2009). The sector operates within a mixed economy, relying on significant funding from Arts Council England, as well as investment from other sources including private-sector funding, local authorities, trusts and foundations, and earned income. There is a network of 64 dance-specific organisations that receive regular funding from the Arts Council and work across the UK supporting individuals and smaller organisations. Individuals and organisations who do not receive regular funding can apply for Arts Council England's National Lottery Project Grants scheme for amounts of between £1,000 and £100,000, for projects of up to three years, in addition to many non-arts-specific funds which support other dance-related agendas. Geographically, the sector has been notably London-centric, with the last large-scale study reporting that 48 per cent of dance artists were based in London and the South East (Burns and Harrison 2009). There have been attempts to address this concern through recent investment in dance hubs in Birmingham and Leeds and the relocation to Birmingham of One Dance UK, a consortium of leading dance organisations.

A large majority of those working in dance do so as freelance or self-employed individuals, and the term 'independent dancer' is commonly used to describe these practitioners. The previously described sector conditions mean that self-employed dancers operate in a largely project-based capacity, moving between different modes and conditions of employment, roles, locations and rates of pay. This approach to work means that dancers engage with a range of dance communities, geographically and artistically, developing and applying diverse skills, and collaborating with multiple partners in wide-ranging locations and settings. The varied nature of their roles means that dancers are no longer bound by single labels, such as 'performer', 'choreographer' or 'teacher', and instead work across these roles in more fluid and horizontal ways.

Although dancers work independently in terms of their employment status, their work is extremely collaborative as it involves group dance-making, performance and teaching. Dancers therefore rely on their ability to build effective relationships and networks in order to both find and sustain employment. Recognising the support needs of this particular artistic community, Independent Dance, which was established in the early 1990s in the UK, was one of the first organisations to respond to this way of working. They describe themselves as 'an artist-led organisation working responsively to support and fuel dance artists in all roles, at all stages of their career, and of all physicalities' (Independent Dance 2020). *Supporting, Stimulating, Sustaining* (2007), a report written by the late Gill Clarke, who was an influential dance activist, summarises their approach to working collaboratively with and for artists in terms of 'the generosity of mutual support; the communal and cooperative engagement; a flexibility and readiness to lead or follow that flows naturally from improvisational practices and an embodied understanding that giving is also receiving' (Clarke 2007, 2).

Independent dancers identify with this ethos within many different roles and contexts, sharing their skills and knowledge across horizontal networks with a focus on community and support for each other. They are further supported by an infrastructure of dance agencies that operate regionally across the country, funded by Arts Council England's National Portfolio Organisations programme. These organisations, alongside many other independent arts organisations, provide development opportunities, resources and a sense of community for many freelance dancers. They create a network of practice that individuals can engage with, underpinned by shared values of collaborative and communal working.

Although the UK dance sector has a strong infrastructure, there remain many challenges for dancers working in freelance contexts, including the inconsistency and uncertainty of their employment, the informality of their working conditions, and the often low rates of pay they experience in relation to long and unsociable hours. In the past there have been several reports published about the independent dance sector (Clarke 2007; Clarke and Gibson 1998) as well as interviews published with renowned independent dancers (e.g. Rubidge 1993) that provide an insight into these working conditions. However, with the industry developing so rapidly, these sources are no longer current. There is a lack of up-to-date knowledge about the UK independent dance sector, meaning that this dynamic and mobile force still 'works in relative invisibility' (Clarke 2007, 2). Therefore, the study reported on in this chapter appears timely in order to provide current information about independent dancers and how they negotiate such a varied and challenging career. It focuses particularly upon how the nature of the contemporary dance sector today creates complex conditions under which dancers have to establish their sense of place within a heavily saturated and often product-driven market. Many of the conditions identified here in relation to the dance sector are highly applicable to other artistic communities such as those of theatre, music and visual art, which operate under similar self-employed conditions and report similar challenges in terms of navigating career pathways and seeking out professional networks to support their work (BritainThinks 2018; Cox and Crone 2014; TBR 2018). This study will consider how insights into the practices of independent dancers could be used to identify approaches to negotiating place that can be adopted by others.

Method

To examine this area of practice, a constructivist methodology was adopted to gather data about experiences of working as an independent dancer. Constructivist research assumes that there are multiple realities, each one being unique to the individual participant depending on his or her background and social context (Lincoln, Lynham and Guba 2011). In order to understand these multiple realities, the researcher creates knowledge interactively with research participants. To this end, in-depth, semi-structured interviews were conducted with independent dancers working in the UK, which provided rich narrative accounts of conditions in the sector. The experiences of these participants were analysed to identify contributory factors which shed light on the work of independent dancers, and how such an understanding might be used to support others working in the sector.

Participants

A total of 14 dancers, 11 female and 3 male, volunteered to take part in the study. The participants were recruited using a web call-out from an independent dance organisation and defined themselves as independent dancers. They were varied in terms of both their age (while the mean age was 32.4 ± 6.05 years,[1] the range was between 22 and 42 years) and their background in dance. Ten of the dancers had taken relatively conventional routes into the profession via university or vocational dance training programmes; the remainder had pursued a career in dance at a relatively late age having undertaken non-dance-related training or worked in different careers. As a result, although the dancers' mean number of years' experience in dance was 20.79 ± 7.58 years, the amount varied greatly depending on their background, age and stage of career. Participants reported working in a range of roles, including dancer, choreographer, community dance artist, teacher and director. They were based in different geographic locations, with the majority working in London (seven) or the South East (four), and the remaining three working in the North West, East Midlands and South West. Their pseudonyms and backgrounds are detailed in Table 8.1 in the appendix to this chapter.

Procedure

Once ethical approval had been received from the University of Bedfordshire Research Ethics Committee, the participants were sent information sheets detailing the aims and procedures of the research, and returned consent forms prior to taking part in the project. An interview guide was developed based on the aims of the study and gaps in the literature, and was trialled in two pilot interviews and refined accordingly. The interview guide was semi-structured in format and addressed several broad categories: general background questions pertaining to training and transitioning into the profession; demographic information on working hours and roles; motivation to work independently and the advantages and disadvantages of such work; perceptions of success; and factors that facilitated success. The flexibility of semi-structured designs enables researchers to use probe questions to generate greater detail on particularly pertinent topics (Patton 2015).

Participants were invited for face-to-face interviews with the first author at a mutually convenient time and location. In three instances where this was not possible, the interviews were conducted via Skype. Participants were recruited and interviewed until theoretical saturation was reached (i.e. no new information from the interviews was emerging; Patton 2015). Interviews lasted between 35 and 70 minutes and were digitally recorded, then transcribed verbatim.

Analysis

The transcripts were uploaded to NVivo 10 qualitative analysis software, and read and reread for familiarity before being coded by the first author into meaning units. The coding was inductive in nature, to allow meaning units to emerge from the data itself rather than use predetermined codes (Kvale 1996). The second author independently coded 15 per cent of the transcripts to ensure agreement between the researchers and thus enhance trustworthiness (Creswell and Miller 2000). Once meaning units were agreed upon, they were arranged into a hierarchy of lower- and higher-order themes representing relationships between each theme and the overarching area of research interest. This process was initially undertaken collaboratively by the researchers, before reviewing the themes and hierarchy independently to further explore and debate the findings. The nascent themes were discussed with two objective industry experts as a form of peer debriefing, and member checking was conducted by inviting the participants to an informal focus group (Creswell and Miller 2000). These processes ensured an informed and accurate interpretation of the themes and provided additional contextual understanding. Finally, we have balanced thick, in-depth description of the findings with quotes from the participants to illustrate the themes and allow readers to form their own interpretations (Sparkes 1998). Participants, are referred to by pseudonyms.

Results and discussion

The study yielded a large number of findings, including on the role of mental skills in successful negotiation of the dancers' careers, and the characteristics of different career stages in the independent sector, the details of which can be found in the research report and journal articles (Aujla and Farrer 2015, 2016; Farrer and Aujla 2016). For the purposes of this chapter, findings pertaining to working conditions, hierarchies, establishing an identity, and the role of networks and relationships are reported on in detail in relation to notions of place.

Working conditions for independent dancers

Supporting the evidence shared in previously published literature about the sector (Clarke 2007; Clarke and Gibson 1998; Rouhiainen 2003), participants described their work as being multifaceted, with dancers initiating their own work in a variety of contexts simultaneously. They described themselves as having portfolio careers or 'wearing different hats' (Mary). The formal roles that the participants assumed included choreographing, performing, teaching, examining, facilitating projects and arts management. Although evidence from Aujla and Farrer (2015) suggests that variety is generally considered a positive aspect of freelance work, some dancers raised concerns about how sufficiently they could fulfil so many roles:

> Lecturer in HE, primary school, I deal with dance management, I perform, I run like a local dance community group ... Am I happy to be all of those things? I enjoy each of them but then it's unsettling

that so many people know me as a different thing ... How do I bring these things together? (Mary)

The participants also spoke about less formal activities that still contributed to their careers, but which usually took place outside of paid work time, such as administration, budgeting and accounting, continued training and physical conditioning, networking, finding work and funding opportunities, application writing, auditioning, planning, marking and evaluating. While a number of sources have previously described independent dancers' work as 'varied', there is no existing research that specifically addresses this range of informal roles (Clarke and Gibson 1998; Rouhiainen 2003). Furthermore, many participants identified such informal activities as happening during their 'time off' or 'down time,' indicating that dancers are not being sufficiently recognised or supported for the informal work they undertake:

> I was really good, in my what I'd say, in my time off to actually technically still be working ... I'd be doing administration, applying to auditions, making contacts, perhaps being involved in a pre-project, going to a residency, all those kind of things. (Alice)

As well as describing a range of different dance-related roles, the participants also spoke about other disciplines they had engaged with in order to find work or pursue particular interests. Some worked collaboratively with other art forms or had undertaken projects within different industries to enhance their skills. Similarly, the participants also recognised the value of taking on unpaid work if they felt it would satisfy their artistic needs, enhance self-development or lead to other opportunities:

> I did an unpaid job with a choreographer and she didn't really know me at the time and she had like four of us dancing but I made sure I made an effort to talk to her and I would volunteer to do stuff and then a few weeks later I got a phone call saying I'm doing another project do you want to be involved. (Sally)

Despite the range of activities that dancers spoke about, they sometimes still had to take on extra non-dance-specific work that they would have preferred not to do, in order to support themselves. In some instances these work commitments were undertaken solely to provide financial support; however, some participants undertook arts-related positions that fed into their artistic roles.

Hierarchies

Perceptions of success

One of the key findings from the study was the extent to which perceptions of success influenced the way that the sector operated. There appeared to be a set of pervading hierarchies that, although not always endorsed by individual practitioners, impacted upon how they undertook their roles and how they felt about their place in the industry. The self-employed, project-based nature of most work in dance means there is less of a sense of formal hierarchy compared to that of an organisation with pay scales and management structures. Many dance practitioners transition between teaching, performing and making roles, indicating that the skills needed within each role are transferable. Despite this, and the growing body of research highlighting the positive contribution that different roles within the dance ecology make, participants in this study still described feeling governed by an implicit hierarchy that valued roles differently (Butterworth 2004; Tambling 2015; Roche 2011; Farrer 2014). Many of the dancers interviewed spoke about there being an unofficial career ladder which they felt they ought to respond to, and which valued community practitioners and teachers the least, followed by paid performers, and then choreographers and directors, who were perceived as the most 'successful' in their careers.

In a performance context, many of the dancers reinforced this hierarchy by describing a motivation to work with high-profile choreographers and companies, even though some participants acknowledged that this did not necessarily live up to expectations:

> When I first got the job, it was like 'wow' this was a massive tick off my ambition list. Fantastic! And it was a great experience in some ways, but then in other ways it made me realise actually it wasn't what I wanted to do. (Anne)

Some of the participants recognised that although they felt a desire to work with high-profile names, they also valued the work of more small-scale practitioners which challenged their perceptions and made them rethink their own definitions of success:

> I think I'd always have liked to have worked a bit more with people like [high-profile choreographers] but when I actually think of the reality of that I kind of go ah … I mean who is successful? Is it the people who dance in good companies? Yeah, they are successful

> or you could look at somebody amazing like [well-known community artist], who works in Oxford and has done for years and does amazing things in the community. (Jane)

Several participants stated that they had ambitions to create their own work, start their own projects and have successful funding bids in order to do so. This appeared, hierarchically, to be considered the most successful role within dance as it meant they were leading or taking responsibility for a project. Again, however, several participants commented that they did not feel comfortable assuming this position and that it created a lot of pressure that detracted from the enjoyment they found in their work. One participant felt disheartened by the fact that they had put so much effort into pursuing one avenue of their career as a performer, and now felt pressure to change it:

> I've put all of my work so far into developing myself as a dancer and I don't know whether ... maybe I've not got enough energy or will, or kind of life sacrifice to do that as a choreographer, I mean I might do, but at the minute I'm thinking, actually no, I'm really happy with how things are going here. (Anne)

Generally, the participants appeared to be torn between a pressure to pursue this apparent hierarchy of success in dance, and the desire to continue working in a way that enabled them to feel satisfied and motivated (Aujla and Farrer 2015). Many of the participants reported measures of success that related to their personal needs and development. Specifically, feeling fulfilled in what they did was a key factor, and many dancers described their work as enjoyable, making them feel 'inspired', 'happy' and 'interested'. Some participants discussed this in relation to the financial instability often associated with the work and expressed that their passion for the job outweighed any financial difficulties. For those in the later stages of their careers, there was also a sense of satisfaction that came from supporting others, with several of the participants describing how they wanted to leave some kind of legacy through the projects they establish or the work that they produce, to have an impact on others:

> Leaving a legacy that increases not only your reputation but the reputation of dance practice ... You help create opportunities to network, share resources, share experiences, support each other and find ways of acknowledging what you've done in some ways. (Louise)

Indeed, the participants felt highly motivated by the collaborative nature of their work and the opportunities it created for them to work with different people in order to share and exchange skills and knowledge:

> Advantages are the diversity of people that I have worked with and continue to work with, in terms of stimulation and creative growth. (Louise)

As a result, some dancers were less inclined to want to pursue their own projects as a singular director or choreographer, as they felt this meant they were less supported:

> I find that it's hard to think that you're an independent dance artist when you actually want to dance on project-based stuff, for other people. I suppose you could apply for funding as a collective, and get choreographers in. (Leigh)

Despite Clarke and Gibson (1998) calling for hierarchies and career ladders to be dismantled, this discussion demonstrates how particular attitudes and perceptions inform how the sector values different roles. These concerns have been raised in relation to choreography by Farrer (2014) and Roche (2011), who both argue that the dancer's contribution to choreographic practice should be recognised and valued more. Similarly, Pauline Tambling has written about what she describes as the split between 'superstar' artists and 'low paid practitioners' (2015, 11), which sees a disproportionate amount of artistic and financial value associated with these two sides of the industry. Interestingly, many of the dancers in this study appeared to have an awareness that pursuing roles that were perceived to be more successful could put unnecessary strain on their work and detract from some of the things they enjoyed about their own particular practice. They valued the supportive and sharing environment often cultivated within the independent dance sector, which created opportunities for them to support and nurture others, rather than assert their own success. These findings indicate that more horizontal networks of activities that bring dancers together on equal levels would better support the way independent dancers engage with the industry, and reflect the ethos that attracts them to pursue these kinds of careers. Valuing the varied skills and expertise that independent dancers bring with them to each project they undertake would enable dancers' sense of place within the dance sector to remain fluid, rather than responsive to a vertical hierarchy that serves to promote the competitiveness more common in private enterprise (Paramana 2017).

Location and training
Several of the participants felt that being in London increased their ability to find work successfully. Although those who were based in other regions noted it was easy to set up networks and achieve success, there remained an emphasis on the capital being the most relevant and current place for the dance industry, and thus it appeared to be viewed by many dancers as the most desirable place to find work. The factor of location also related to the idea of training, as some of the participants commented that training at a contemporary, vocational school (of which most, but not all, are based in London) was viewed by others as an indication of your success:

> I think London is a little fixated with technique, not in all areas of dance, but there is a big thing about where you trained. You know it's the first thing that people ask you and if you were at a vocational school, then oh that's great you can tick that box. And if you look at the dancers that are dancing they are predominately from [London dance school], well at least at companies I would like to work for. (Stephanie)

The participants recognised that establishing networks and building relationships with other independent artists was important for enabling them to find and manage their work. Some cited geographical location as an important factor, with London being a particularly desirable place to work:

> I feel in London it takes maybe a bit longer but once I'm there, up there, as a choreographer and people know my name it will be easier to do everything. (Robert)

However, others contrasted with this by explaining that they were able to build effective professional networks in other cities or smaller communities:

> Once I moved home [Derbyshire] and started to get back into contact with people involved in dance regionally and involved in community dance and dance in education, I started to realise that actually, there were lots of great things going on in the arts. (Alice)

In both instances local networks were a crucial element of the participants' employment. Existing literature suggests that regionally based arts organisations or dance agencies support such networks and provide 'specialist and coherent year-round programme[s], offering opportunities to share practice and exchange information, to deepen enquiry, enhance skills and acquire new knowledge' (Clarke 2007). Such support is a vital part of independent dancers' careers as it enables them to sustain and hone their physical abilities as well as providing opportunities to meet and work with new people. Having the opportunity to connect with like-minded people and form a community of practice enables dancers to further establish their own place within a particular location and its artistic community.

Several participants commented upon how the networks they established were important for finding new work. This often happened through casual communication and word of mouth:

> I get all my work and most of my enjoyment as well, just from talking to people, finding out what's going on. (Mary)

Many of the participants felt that these kinds of relationships were more valuable in terms of finding future employment than attending formal auditions or interviews, as they allowed them to get a better understanding of the work they were likely to undertake. They also provided potential employers with an insight into the participants' practice and personality that they felt could not be expressed through a CV. Therefore, in their view the strength of the dancers' local networks and social support was critical in their career success and progression.

Establishing an identity

When describing the early periods of their careers, most of the participants said that they were open to taking on as many roles as possible and were 'applying for everything' in order to ensure they found work. As a result, they found it challenging to articulate their own position in relation to the wider dance sector, or to know how to label their role. However, as the participants became more confident with their roles, they also appeared to develop more of a sense of identity about who they were as artists. They felt clearer about the kind of work they wanted to do and why:

> I wouldn't work for anybody now. I am going to be really, really selective. (Stephanie)

The dancers also appeared to develop more of a sense of ownership over their work:

> I'm not so interested in performing work for other people where I feel like the work itself doesn't have a lot of integrity or where I feel very much like a kind of tool ... it's not so interesting to me to simply replicate, necessarily, every time I do performance work. (Louise)

The sense of confidence and ownership over their work that they described was clearly a positive development within the participants' careers. However, with increased success and experience came new pressures and concerns. Some of the dancers commented that as they got more work they found it increasingly difficult to manage their time and keep up their networking and self-development opportunities. Some dancers felt that this also led to them feeling 'pigeonholed' (Alice). As they established success in one area of their practice, it sometimes led to employers assuming this was their sole skill or interest. This seemed to be particularly prevalent among emerging practitioners who initially engaged largely in teaching work, but still wanted to pursue performance or choreographic roles.

A further problem may occur when dancers move to a new location. Despite their previous career experiences and successes, being new to an area and lacking a local reputation may mean that dancers feel they must 'start again'. One dance artist, in a recent panel presentation as part of the research project (Farrer, Aujla and Drew 2017), explained her difficulties in moving to Birmingham, having worked previously in London, Israel and Leeds:

> At this point, I'd been teaching dance for 10 years, I'd been working really hard for 10 years, and I felt like an undergraduate when I came back to Birmingham. It was really demoralising because I've done a lot of courses, a lot of training, a lot of teaching, and I suddenly had to volunteer all the time, just to get my name known ... It took me two years in Birmingham to get known.

This dancer found that local networks were somewhat 'closed' and competitive, and that by creating new networks she was better able to support and promote herself. Thus, even well-established artists may struggle to find their place in the local workforce initially in new locations.

The role of networks and social relationships

As well as building networks to seek employment, the participants also discussed how they developed working relationships to support them in other ways. Several participants described some kind of mentorship that had helped develop their careers. In some instances this was through a formal mentorship programme set up by organisations or individual practitioners looking to support others, but in most cases it involved dancers informally seeking advice or support from people they were working for and felt comfortable with:

> It's recognising someone that I feel I have an affinity with and then seeking out their opinion on certain things when I can. (Jenny)

In the past, the *Independent Dance Review Report* called for more structure and distinction to ensure mentorships are mutually beneficial and effective (Clarke and Gibson 1998). Although this argument is well founded and could improve development opportunities within the industry, the findings from this study also demonstrate the importance of informal mentorship.

As well as building relationships with more advanced practitioners, participants found support from their peers highly valuable, explaining that being around dancers in a similar position could be just as beneficial as seeking advice from someone with more experience. The findings further echo Farrer's (2014) work on how dancers learn tacitly from peers that they trust and share mutual cares and concerns with. These relationships appeared to be vital in combating the sense of isolation or loneliness that some participants described when working independently:

> I think it's bringing those networks of people around you that can support your career. I think that's the most important, you know even though I work independently, on my own a lot, the people I ring are in the same boat as me. And they're all artists; they're all dancers actually. And they get it. So I don't feel on my own. (Jane)

Some of the participants also described sharing resources and coming together with other artists to 'play'. By sharing their time, skills and ideas during informal creative encounters, or 'playing' without the pressure of working towards producing a performance product, dancers are able to work collaboratively for artistic development. This coming together of individuals is important in enabling the sector to develop with limited resources. Dancers are able to recognise their own currency and can exchange their skills and knowledge with others.

Finally, some participants spoke about the importance of their social or family networks. Some commented generally upon how relationships informed their approach to work, and others had made clear decisions about their careers in response to their home lives:

> I did make a pact when I was 26, 27 – I am not working weekends any more, this is ridiculous, I need to see people and have a life. (Jeanne)

As well as shaping the way the participants engaged with their work, the support that friends and families provided also extended to particular skills that were helpful for their careers. Some participants spoke about instances where friends or family members had advised them on issues such as finance, business and organisational skills. This concern is increasingly raised within the arts, where entrepreneurial thinking and business acumen is called upon to support the artistic practice of such workers who have to manage their own projects (Aujla and Farrer 2015; TBR 2018). The findings from our study, together with previous research, indicate that because participants were relying on informal and social networks to support these areas of their work, skills like finance, marketing and business planning may not be provided sufficiently by the sector or by dance training.

Implications and applications

The results of this study suggest that notions of place related to both geographical location and perceptions of success in tacit hierarchies are important aspects of the working lives of independent dancers. Support from those both within and outside of the sector helped dancers to navigate this unpredictable career. While the majority of the participants lived and worked in London, several were working successfully in other locations; however, changing location came with its own challenges in terms of how dancers established themselves and found work.

The study further highlighted the benefit of professional infrastructures that support those working as independent dancers, to provide hubs of activity and meeting points for workers. It is recognised that the profession has a particularly strong network across the UK with dedicated dance agencies in each region. Although there is inconsistency in terms of what they offer, the connectedness of these organisations provides a valued sense of structure for those working independently. Furthermore, the propensity for group working and collaboration, which was highlighted throughout this study, is a special and highly valued aspect of the dance sector. In the field of dance scholarship, researchers have articulated the economic and political benefits that this commons-focused approach to working creates (Burt 2016; Paramana 2017). By valuing resources, knowledge and the knowledge production that takes place through shared practice, dancers working independently avoid some of the competitiveness commonly associated with private enterprise (Paramana 2017).

Although not all art sectors share the kind of collaborative and group-based conditions experienced by dancers, they may benefit from the kind of horizontal exchange that this approach to working creates. By valuing their individual skills and knowledge as a form of currency that can be shared and exchanged with others, artists can work together collaboratively to develop their creative ideas and knowledge of the sector in informal settings such as dance classes or 'play' sessions, or even in conversation over coffee. They learn from each without the pressure of having to produce a performance or creative product and, in turn, further establish their own position within the sector by recognising how they support others. These approaches to continued development and networking rely on little support from external organisations but appear to play a significant part in underpinning the success of the freelance dance sector. This way of working could enable artists from a range of practices who work in freelance capacities to share their experiences in order to feel more connected to and established in their place of work.

Another significant feature of independent dancers' work which is pertinent to the wider arts sector is how they negotiate and navigate their multifaceted roles. Across art forms it is commonly recognised that artists engage in multiple sectors, and work in community, participatory and socially engaged settings to both support and grow their artistic practice (Cox and Crone 2014; Aujla and Farrer 2016). It is also well recognised that there is a lack of parity in how different roles are valued and financially rewarded (Tambling 2015), which resulted in some of the dancers in this study feeling a pressure to seek out particular kinds of work, even if they were not personally fulfilling. Furthermore, in the study by ArtWorks into employment of artists in relation to community practice (Cox and Crone 2014), 36 per cent of respondents strongly agreed that engaging with participatory projects had changed their practice, despite only 7 per cent saying that they produced an artistic product from it. It appears that much like the dancers in this study, artists working across disciplines are able to recognise and value their engagement with different roles and how it contributes to their careers, despite a lack of wider recognition. They adapt their practice in different situations to support the needs of different projects spanning education, health, social mobility, tourism and heritage, whilst finding ways to experience personal development and artistic growth. Further evidence of the contribution that artists can make in different areas of society would enable artists' sense of place within their communities to remain fluid whilst being valued and recognised.

Conclusion

This chapter has highlighted the experiences of a group of dancers working in the contemporary dance sector. It has shown how they draw upon – and in many instances create – structure, support and opportunities for sharing that enable them to establish their sense of place within the sector and experience rewarding careers. Despite many positive and rewarding features, there remain significant challenges to working in dance; in particular, the hierarchy of roles which seems to pervade the sector prevents some dancers from feeling established or valued by their place within it. The results of this study indicate that further strengthening of social networks, both regionally and nationally, to provide more formal networks and mentoring opportunities may help to address these career challenges. Continued discussion and dismantling of the pervading hierarchies around career success, location and training may also benefit dancers who work in multiple ways. Finally, better recognition of the contribution that dancers make to their communities through their varied practices could enable them to feel more valued and supported in their work.

The findings can be compared with those for other art forms such as theatre, music and visual art, for which similar concerns have been raised (BritainThinks 2018; Cox and Crone 2014), to consider how the nature of their disciplines informs artists' abilities to connect with and find support from others. The notion of place is complex for self-employed artists who rely on varied conditions of work and networks of practice to support their careers. Thus, this chapter may drive new ways of thinking about how location, identity and relationships can be understood flexibly to support the UK arts sector.

Appendix

Table 8.1 Pseudonyms and backgrounds of research participants

Pseudonym	Age	Background	Current role(s)
Robert	31	Undertook dance training at a university in Germany and experienced working in dance theatre.	Working to establish himself as a choreographer in London.
Louise	30	Undertook contemporary dance training at a vocational school.	Works across disciplines, often collaboratively with other artists or organisations in a range of movement-based roles, e.g. movement director or dramaturge. Based in London.
Jenny	22	Undertook contemporary dance training at a university.	Trying to establish herself as an independent artist engaging with small choreography and performance projects and undertaking teaching roles. Based in the South East.
Mary	27	Undertook contemporary dance training at a university.	Works part-time lecturing at a university and part-time within freelance teaching and performance contexts. Based in London.
Anne	31	Undertook contemporary dance training at a university and vocational settings.	Had previously worked freelance, predominantly as a performer, and now had a fixed-term performance contract with an integrated dance company. Based in London.
Sally	26	Undertook contemporary dance training at a university.	Works in a freelance capacity for several choreographers and has had (?) her own choreographic projects funded. Based in the North West.
Jane	40	Undertook contemporary dance training at a vocational school.	Had previously worked as a performer for professional companies, and undertaken her own project work as a choreographer. Based in the South East.

Table 8.1 (continued)

Pseudonym	Age	Background	Current role(s)
Jeanne	46	Undertook contemporary dance training at a university.	Runs an arts organisation as well as undertaking project roles as a choreographer and teacher, and is undertaking an MA. Based in the South East.
Aiden	30	Undertook training in commercial dance at a vocational school before taking an apprenticeship with a major contemporary company.	Works as a choreographer as well as performing for other companies. Based in London.
Leigh	27	Undertook vocational training in a range of dance styles including contemporary and commercial.	Works predominantly as a performer for other choreographers, and undertakes some teaching roles. Based in the South East.
Patrick	41	Undertook vocational contemporary dance training and experienced working full-time in a professional dance company.	Had previously worked as a performer for professional companies, and now undertakes own project work as a choreographer. Based in London.
Stephanie	34	Trained to be a primary school teacher at a university before undertaking a vocational MA course.	Works predominantly in an education setting and undertakes small performance projects when able to. Based in London.
Claire	42	Undertook contemporary dance training at a university. Experienced working with a circus group in early career.	Has her own children's theatre company as well as working freelance on other projects. Based in the South West.
Alice	36	Undertook contemporary dance training at a university.	Worked predominantly as a performer with small companies. Had recently taken time off work to have a baby. Based in the East Midlands.

Notes

1. We use ± to indicate standard deviation.

References

Aujla, Imogen and Rachel Farrer. 2015. 'The Role of Psychological Factors in the Career of the Independent Dancer', *Frontiers in Psychology* 6, Article 1688: 1–13. Accessed 2 May 2020. http://dx.doi.org/10.3389/fpsyg.2015.01688.
Aujla, Imogen and Rachel Farrer. 2016. *Independent Dancers: Roles, Motivation and Success*. Luton: University of Bedfordshire. Accessed 2 May 2020. www.beds.ac.uk/media/242947/final-report.pdf.
BritainThinks. 2018. *Next Ten-Year Strategy: Evidence Review*. London: BritainThinks. Accessed 25 April 2019. www.artscouncil.org.uk/sites/default/files/download-file/ACE_10YSEvidence%20Review_July18.pdf.
Burns, Susanne and Sue Harrison. 2009. *Dance Mapping: A Window on Dance 2004–2008*. London: Arts Council England.
Burt, Ramsay. 2016. *Ungoverning Dance: Contemporary European Theatre Dance and the Commons*. New York: Oxford University Press.
Butterworth, Jo. 2004. 'Teaching Choreography in Higher Education: A Process Continuum Model', *Research in Dance Education* 5 (1): 45–67.
Clarke, Gill. 2007. *Supporting, Stimulating, Sustaining*. London: Independent Dance. Accessed 25 April 2019. www.independentdance.co.uk/rsc/SupportingStimulatingSustaining.pdf.
Clarke, Gill and Rachel Gibson. 1998. *Independent Dance Review Report*. London: Arts Council England.
Cox, Tamsin and Stephen Crone. 2014. *Paul Hamlyn Foundation: ArtWorks Evaluation Survey of Artists*. Birmingham: DHA.
Creswell, John W. and Dana L. Miller. 2000. 'Determining Validity in Qualitative Inquiry', *Theory into Practice* 39 (3): 124–30.
Farrer, Rachel. 2014. 'The Creative Dancer', *Research in Dance Education* 15 (1): 95–104.
Farrer, Rachel and Imogen Aujla. 2016. 'Understanding the Independent Dancer: Roles, Development and Success', *Dance Research* 34 (2): 202–19.
Farrer, Rachel, Imogen Aujla and Tori Drew. 2017. 'The Impact of Location for Freelance Dancers'. Paper presented at the 'A Sense of Place' conference, Luton, 3–5 November 2017.
Independent Dance. 2020. 'Welcome to Independent Dance'. Accessed 2 May 2020. www.independentdance.co.uk/.
Kvale, Steinar. 1996. *InterViews: An Introduction to Qualitative Research Interviewing*. Thousand Oaks, CA: SAGE Publications.
Lincoln, Yvonna S., Susan A. Lynham and Egon G. Guba. 2011. 'Paradigmatic Controversies, Contradictions, and Emerging Confluences, Revisited'. In *The SAGE Handbook of Qualitative Research* (4th ed.), edited by Norman K. Denzin and Yvonna S. Lincoln, 97–128. London: SAGE Publications.
Paramana, Katerina. 2017. 'The Contemporary Dance Economy: Problems and Potentials in the Contemporary Neoliberal Moment', *Dance Research* 35 (1): 75–95.
Patton, Michael Quinn. 2015. *Qualitative Research and Evaluation Methods*. 4th ed. Thousand Oaks, CA: SAGE Publications.
Robinson, Mark. 2018. 'Provocation from Mark Robinson, Founder, Thinking Practice'. Accessed 9 June 2020. https://www.nesta.org.uk/feature/experimental-culture-provocations/mark-robinson/.
Roche, Jenny. 2011. 'Embodying Multiplicity: The Independent Contemporary Dancer's Moving Identity', *Research in Dance Education* 12 (2): 105–18.
Rouhiainen, Leena. 2003. 'Living Transformative Lives: Finnish Freelance Dance Artists Brought into Dialogue with Merleau-Ponty's Phenomenology'. PhD thesis, Theatre Academy, Helsinki.
Rubidge, Sarah. 1993. 'Gill Clarke: Dancer and Campaigner', *Dance Theatre Journal* 11 (1): 6–8, 52–5.

Sparkes, Andrew C. 1998. 'Validity in Qualitative Inquiry and the Problem of Criteria: Implications for Sport Psychology', *The Sport Psychologist* 12 (4): 363–86.
Tambling, Pauline. 2015. 'What Are the Future Employment Opportunities for Dance?', *Animated* 13: 10–12.
TBR. 2018. *Livelihoods of Visual Artists: 2016 Data Report*. Accessed 9 June 2020. https://www.artscouncil.org.uk/sites/default/files/download-file/Livelihoods%20of%20Visual%20Artists%202016%20Data%20Report.pdf.

Section 3:
Multidisciplinary approaches to place and contested identities

9
Performing places: Carnival, culture and the performance of contested national identities

Jonathan Croose

In 1988, the geographer Peter Jackson suggested that carnival, as a place-based cultural performance, was a 'culture of resistance' that expressed 'competitive social relations, physically inscribed in space' (1988, 222–4). Carnival, Jackson suggested, offered 'a test case for exploring the intersection of culture and politics in the creation of a specific geography'. My aim in this chapter is to revisit this observation and to apply the insights gathered from my own research into the cultural performance of place-identity, in order to explore the theory, ethics and politics of state-funded, place-based arts practice.

This chapter draws on the field of cultural geography for much of its theoretical insight. Geographical notions of 'place' encompass concepts as varied as topography, landscape, architecture and spatial planning, heritage, economic, industrial and agricultural practice, and the spatialities of sociocultural communities and networks. For the cultural geographer, these concepts find expression through cultural practice, in a range as diverse as performing arts, painting, sculpture, procession, poetry, fiction, festival, gardening, graffiti, music, walking, skateboarding and a host of other iterative cultural performances, each of which casts a particular 'place' in a different light. Study of what Abrahams (1983, cited in Jackson 1988, 224) refers to as competing 'symbolic landscapes' within place-based arts practice therefore allows us to frame place-identity as a contested performativity, building on Cresswell's conceptualisation of place as 'constructed space' or 'space invested with meaning in the context of power' (2004, 12) and on Harvey's articulation of the 'social process of place construction' within 'cartographies of struggle, power and discourse' (1996, 293).

In cultural archaeology, Tilley's phenomenological approach considers how space/place is embodied during cultural practice according to specific sociocultural instrumentalities, and how the weave of physical movement, symbolism, history and ritual 'socialis[es] the landscape and react[s] meaning in it' (Tilley 1994). Doreen Massey's progressive theorisation of place sees it as an inherently plural, dynamic *locus* of meanings, which are drawn from a variety of physical locations, yet expressed within a particular geographic spatiality (Massey 1997). Place, by this critique, is *itself* a carnivalesque, performative concept. Place-based art and performance therefore sit firmly within a cultural politics that chimes with Jackson's theorisation: as 'contested social event[s] whose political significance is inscribed in the landscape' (1988, 213).

Key questions arise, within this theorisation of a plural, socially constructed and contested notion of place, when it comes to the performance of place-based arts. Whose 'version' of place is being performed? Furthermore, what is the effect on vernacular culture of the inevitable imbalance in cultural and economic capital that exists between local, marginalised or grassroots place-cultures and professionalised, state-funded, place-based arts practice?

Between 2010 and 2012, I conducted ethnographic research as a street performer within the London 2012 Cultural Olympiad and the *Battle for the Winds* performances that launched the Olympic sailing at Weymouth, exploring how processional performance was used as spectacle to promote a specific set of local and regional place identities. At the same time, I was embedded within two local community carnivals, conducting interviews and participating in their preparations and processions. This allowed me to consider how an alternative sense of place was expressed through their vernacular processional practice during the Olympic period (Croose 2014). In Rio de Janeiro in 2016, I conducted three weeks of fieldwork during the 31st Olympiad, where I attended cultural events and conducted interviews with arts activists, transgender artists, black artists, street performers and countercultural visual artists, as well as with Olympic cultural producers, tourism officials and artists involved in the official ceremonies. This process allowed me to explore local opinions about how Rio/Brazil was represented in the Olympic Opening Ceremony and, by contrast, how vernacular art and cultural performance expressed alternative notions of community, place and identity. This research exposed the considerable tensions between state-funded place-making and the vernacular practices of local people in both settings.

Our aim, then, is to consider together the implications of relative cultural power with regard to place-based arts and performance, in order to observe 'who travels confidently across [these] borders, and who gets questioned, detained, interrogated, and strip-searched' (Conquergood 2002, 145). In terms of cultural capital, the ethical and political implications of these questions are significant for any artist working with notions of place and community, and for any official seeking to influence public engagement with place-identity through the arts. The insights gathered permit a critique of how place-based arts currently constitute an increasingly 'official feast' (Bakhtin 1984) within contemporary culture, as institutional actors seek to exert aesthetic and symbolic control over the performance of place-identity through professionalised community arts practice. At the same time, I suggest, vernacular practice is increasingly subjugated and restricted within public space. Following Edensor *et al.* (2010, 11), this discussion therefore distinguishes between 'productive' arts practice, which is embedded within the cultural, social and economic instrumentalities of the state or other governance organisations, and 'vernacular' practices, which locate as 'local' cultural performances of place and identity *outside* such processes.

These distinctions allow us to frame the development of productive state-sponsored vocabularies that were designed to articulate preferred 'Jurassic Coast', 'South-West' and 'Olympic' place identities in the UK between 2007 and 2012, and their equivalents in Rio in 2016. In 2012, these 'symbolic landscapes' were performed in the *Battle for the Winds* Olympic street carnival at Weymouth, and in the Jurassic Coast-themed *Moving Tides* procession that was part of the Olympic Torch Relay. In Rio, the Olympic Opening Ceremony offered an equivalent symbolic framework for the productive representation of the city as the progressive host of the 'Diversity Olympics', for the regeneration of the city's port area, and for the rebranding of Rio as a go-to centre for economic neoliberalism in South America. At the same time, Rio was in the midst of a period of social, economic and political turmoil, which featured a presidential impeachment, the social 'cleansing' of favelas, and significant artist-led, anti-government and anti-Olympics protests that led to violent clashes between protestors and police. 'Official' vocabularies for arts-based place-making, then, usually reflect a productive, (inter)nationally driven set of policies towards the performance of preferred symbolic landscapes. These operate as a driver of economic investment and as a cultural public-engagement framework for processes of post-industrial regeneration, global inter-place competition and remedial political communitarianism: the creation of new social constituencies, often under the banner of 'social inclusion', through which place-based policy values might be 'created' or 'learned' by people through arts practice.

By contrast, two key narratives presented in this chapter articulate the effect that these policy-led vocabularies may have on the vernacular culture: on the Weymouth Town Carnival prior to the 2012 Olympics, for example, and on the creative responses of marginalised artists in Rio. Later, I briefly describe how vernacular community carnivals in East Devon and Dorset challenged Olympic place-hegemonies through their popular aesthetic and progressive participatory structures. Finally, I describe a vernacular dance performance in the Maré favela and how it revealed the 'other' Rio during the 2016 Olympics.

The clash between cultural democracy (grassroots artistic agency, identity and genuine participation) and the democratisation of culture (hierarchical, remedial notions of 'great art for everybody') therefore lies at the heart of this debate (Kershaw 1992, 184–5). As a result, we are encouraged to reconsider the ethics of our own work as place-based, community-focused artists, and the politics of the representations we create as a part of our creative public engagements with 'place'.

Whose place? Developments in cultural policy

Cultural policy with regard to art and place is often about building 'affective' (emotional) rather than 'cognitive' (informational) public engagement with places, in order to facilitate the ideological recruitment of local people to external policy goals of post-industrial regeneration, national identity and environmental or landscape conservation (Carter and Masters 1998). From 1990 onwards, UK cultural policy steadily steered publicly funded, place-based arts practice firmly towards these instrumentalities, within a framework that revitalised the constituency-forming traditions of early to mid-twentieth-century historical pageants (Croose 2014). Over the same period, the UK vocabularies of diasporic Caribbean and South American carnival coalesced with the participatory methods of theatrical street procession that were developed from the 1960s to the 1990s by 'alternative theatre' companies such as Welfare State International to form the preferred style of many Arts Council and local authority-funded, place-based arts programmes in the UK today, while at the same time experiencing a reduction in their countercultural politics.[1] The ability of processional forms of place-based performance in particular to cross borders of race, class and location and to open up new methods of public engagement meant that Arts Council policy began to validate their cultural role in processes of urban regeneration, multiculturalism and 'community cohesion'.[2] These historical developments increasingly formulate the role of place-based spectacle in particular within publicly funded, professionalised, ideological recruitments to preferred notions of local, regional and national identity (Croose 2014).

At the same time, local, vernacular cultural access to public space is increasingly limited, due to the impact of excessive legal requirements, such as licensing, stewarding, compulsory insurance, vehicle restrictions and community management of road closures without commensurate public funding (Croose 2014). 'Unofficial' busking and street arts culture in the UK is increasingly restricted by Public Space Protection Orders and the privatisation of outdoor cultural spaces, with local authority 'licensed-only' performance schemes now in force in many town centres. With spontaneous, large-scale vernacular festivity also rendered illegal by the 1994 Criminal Justice Act (Bucke and James 1998), place-based arts practice in the UK appears now to be firmly established as an 'official feast' (Bakhtin 1984).

Cultural tensions in UK carnival: A key narrative

One particular narrative emerged during my research which highlighted the problematic subjugation of a vernacular arts-culture as a result of institutional efforts to exert aesthetic and symbolic control over the performance of a particular place-identity. For more than 50 years the annual Weymouth Carnival has involved a sea-front community procession of decorated, lorry-based floats, followed by an air-show and fireworks. This community-funded procession raises money for local charities and draws on working-class, seaside popular culture for its aesthetic. In 2007, the voluntary Round Table Town Carnival Committee announced it was handing over to new leadership. Organisational responsibility devolved to the Weymouth Community Volunteers (WCV), a community development charity supported by the local authority. The WCV soon found itself caught between competing public agendas, within which the carnival's function as a cultural representation of the town was judged to be in need of change.

Research interviews revealed how the traditional form of Weymouth Carnival was seen by local authority partners to be lacking the 'right kind' of creativity with regard to its aesthetic content and systems of community engagement. Its working-class, seaside aesthetic was considered 'brash' and 'tacky', and was described by one arts professional as 'the antithesis of everything I would want to see in a carnival'.[3] Wider policies also came into play, following the designation of Weymouth and Portland as sailing venues for the London 2012 Olympics, and the establishment of the nearby Jurassic Coast as a World Heritage Site. Cultural change was on the agenda for Weymouth, within a process which would ultimately lead to its Olympic rebranding.

With their funding conditional on local authority partnership, the WCV came under pressure to change the procession. These changes, which prompted significant local conflict, reflected a wider policy context wherein carnival had become a focus for community engagement across a host of public-sector agendas. As a result of new environmental sustainability targets for local authorities, the lorry-based community floats were banned from the parade. The WCV were encouraged to organise carnival workshops, run by a professional carnival arts company, which drew on Caribbean and South American 'walking' or *mas* vocabularies. Courses in carnival making and design were established at the further education college in response to the designation of the Jurassic Coast World Heritage Site, in order to generate a site-specific iconography of ancient ichthyosaurs and marine creatures for the carnival. This artistic shift sought to replace the event's traditional aesthetic, which was drawn from TV, film and popular culture.

The new carnival ran for one year in this radically altered form. However, these changes were fundamentally disconnected from the town's existing carnival communities, and, in banning the lorries, the WCV and its partners had publicly rejected the communities' aesthetic forms and structures of participation. As a result, the new carnival met with public opposition. The WCV found themselves caught in a bitter conflict between carnival traditionalists and an agency-led effort to change its form, purpose and structure. A vitriolic local press campaign demanded the return of the carnival to 'community' control, and in 2010 the WCV gave way to a new, community-led committee. The lorry floats were immediately reinstated. The state-funded institutions that had instigated the disruptive changes immediately withdrew their financial support and created *Moving Tides*, an artist-led procession for schoolchildren which ultimately became a well-funded part of the Olympic celebrations.[4] The carnival therefore lost the successful funded workshop programme which had supported its walking entries during 2008–9.

The Weymouth example reveals how the 'vernacular' mode of place-based arts practice is in increasing conflict with 'official' performances of place that consider it inconvenient in aesthetic and policy terms. The following section seeks to describe the symbolic construction of the preferred, 'productive' Olympic and 'Jurassic Coast' place identity for Weymouth during 2012, which was performed through carnival and procession during the Games.

Symbolic geographies of an Olympic carnival: *Battle for the Winds*, 2012

The following report captures the cultural, inter-place competition which arose during the 2012 Olympiad in Weymouth:

> A 'Battle for the Winds' erupted in Weymouth Bay on Saturday as an anarchic troupe of acrobats, actors and dancers fought to banish the doldrums on the eve of the Olympic sailing regatta. Not to be outdone by London's spectacular opening ceremony on Friday, the English seaside town, that along with its near neighbour Portland is hosting the world's best sailors, staged its own extravaganza. At the end of the 'Battle for the Winds' the waters of Weymouth Bay were set alight as 2,012 people waded into its murky depths holding flaming torches above their heads. Thousands flocked to the beach to catch the show, which included disabled performers from Britain and Brazil and captured some of the carnival atmosphere more typical of Rio de Janeiro than the cooler waters of England's south coast. (News report: 'Sailing – Battle of the Winds bodes well for sailors', Reuters, 28 July 2012)[5]

The *Battle for the Winds* street parade along Weymouth Esplanade featured seven processional episodes from the county areas of the south-west UK[6] that characterised the region in terms of its urban multiculturalism and the natural and historical 'rootedness and authenticity' of its rural places (Relph 1976). Each episode was led by a 'Wind Vessel' carnival float which reflected an explicit place-iconography, including representations of the Severn Bore (Gloucestershire); a 100-year-old rowing gig (Cornwall); a human-powered industrial vessel evoking Brunel, accompanied by *mas* performers from the St Pauls Carnival (Bristol); a parade of waitresses serving gigantic cream teas (Devon; see Figure 9.1); an agricultural vessel from the Somerset Levels; a Jurassic

Figure 9.1 'Devon' procession, Exeter, *Battle for the Winds*, 2012. Photograph by Jonathan Croose.

Coast-themed Wind Vessel (Dorset) and a rolling sound system evoking the nightclub and urban circus cultures of Swindon (Wiltshire).

Battle for the Winds was also part of a wider process of 'official' regional place-making. The designation of the Jurassic Coast World Heritage Site in 2001 generated a public engagement strategy that used place-based arts to raise awareness of local geology and to redefine the area's international place-significance.[7] Jurassic Coast place-identity was also asserted through the iconography of the *Moving Tides* children's procession within the 2012 Weymouth Olympic Torch Relay celebrations, which featured 'Jurassic sea creatures, ammonites ... microscopic sea creatures ... seabirds, frogs, [and] shells'.[8]

This strategy reflects what the social geographer David Harvey describes as a 'discursive construction of affective loyalties': a constituency-forming process that was driven by 'particular imageries of place [and] environment', and through the creation of processions that were designed 'to celebrate and become symbolic of some special place' (1996, 323). *Moving Tides* and *Battle for the Winds* offered distinct, official articulations of place, set within an assertion of 'south-west' identity that was itself part of a broader performance of 'British' place-meaning, projected internationally through the globally televised performances of the Cultural Olympiad.

The (non?) art of vernacular carnival and its performance of 'place'

This research uncovered the cultural competition that existed between official and vernacular performances of place during this period. In interviews, arts professionals tended to devalue local, vernacular carnival and to denigrate its popular 'mass' culture aesthetic, which they felt conflicted with cultural policy aims, represented local places in a poor light, discouraged middle-class tourism or hindered economic and cultural regeneration (Croose 2014). A value distinction between professional 'art' and vernacular 'creativity' was used to deny access to state arts funding for vernacular practice and to establish the professional creative class as cultural gatekeepers to preferred symbolic landscapes, as evidenced by the interview comments below:

> ... there is a creative element to [community carnival] ... whether they create dance for majorettes or whether they, you know, interpret the *X Factor* on the back of a float, that's creative in a sense. But it is difficult to say why that is creative but we don't like it, if you like, in a rather kind of arty way, and why something else is better. (Arts professional, 27 October 2010)

> Because we are funded by the Arts Council, I suppose we have to ensure that we are meeting their idea of art ... It is about quality and how do you assess quality, and what we see as quality. (Arts professional, 27 October 2010)

These comments reveal how policy-driven practice can result in the creative class 'crowding out the community' (Evans 2010, 20). The public space available to vernacular participatory arts practice comes under pressure, because of its 'lack of fit' with the preferred aesthetics and place-identities of funded policy. In fact, vernacular creativity within community carnival often represents a cultural *resistance* to this aesthetic hegemony. Vernacular expressions of 'place' through carnival practice in the south-west UK are generally *non*-site-specific in their symbolism, preferring popular culture as a source of satire and inspiration and using a 'bricolage'[9] of popular forms. In vernacular settings, 'place' is, therefore, often symbolised through performed community memberships; linked to notions of 'club', 'home' and 'town' rather than through site-specific iconography. In terms of south-west carnival practices, place is also demonstrated through the physical procession of a performed 'local' identity at other circuit events in the wider region.

In 2012, the popular, seaside, film- and TV-inspired aesthetics of vernacular carnival were in clear tension with the 'official' site-specific performances of regional place identity that were articulated by *Moving Tides* and *Battle for the Winds*. However, as Doreen Massey states: 'If it is now recognized that people have multiple identities then the same point can be made in relation to places' (1997, 321). Vernacular carnivals may here be seen to act as a cultural resistance to institutionally preferred processes of local, regional and national place-making, through their presentation of alternative versions of place that are 'out of place' in prevailing cultural policy terms (Cresswell 2004).

Rio 2016

The published aims of the Rio Negocios 2016 Tourism and Branding Conference, an international seminar held during the Games, offer a useful summary of how Olympic mega-events reflect Harvey's notions of inter-place competition:

> [A focus on] the international development of the Rio brand and its potential as a tool to attract investment ...
>
> [We must] take advantage of the new face of Rio ...
>
> [Our aim is to] develop the image that Rio de Janeiro wants to sell to the world ... (Rio Negocios 2016)

At the conference, Vinicius Lummertz, President of Embratur, the Brazil Ministry of Tourism, stated that:

> [The Olympic Opening Ceremony] reset our minds at the level of symbols ... This is the City of Rio. It was a symbolic reinvention. Looking at the images on TV, people thought: 'This is what we are'. (Lummertz 2016)

Daniel Alencar, Director of the Future Brand consultancy, added:

> What the world perceives as the definitive qualities of a place ultimately influences its ability to attract investment ... Everything is a brand ... There is no 'reality,' only perception. (Alencar 2016)

This symbolic reinvention of Rio's place-identity was a distraction from the social realities of the time. Rio 2016, billed as the 'Games of Celebration and Transformation' and the 'Diversity Olympics', offered a set of idealised symbolic landscapes that were firmly geared towards attempts to effect a 'transformation' of Rio's place-identity (Schausteck de Almeida, Marchi Júnior and Pike 2014, 284). As Vinicius Lummertz also stated:

> The second tier [after the ceremony] is the legacy. We want to internationalize our economy ... Brazil has the most important national potential in the world for tourism ... But there is too much red tape ... The system hinders development ... We need concessions and public-private partnerships, and after the [presidential] impeachment we will push this forward. (Lummertz 2016)[10]

A key part of the Olympic transformation of Rio was the gentrification of the downtown Zona Portuária and Porto Maravilha areas to create a new cultural quarter that included the Boulevard Olímpico, the Museum of Art and the Museu do Amanhã (Museum of Tomorrow). This regeneration involved a slew of economic deals between the Rio Prefeitura and international hotel chains, urban infrastructure and property development interests, many of which led to multi-million-dollar corruption charges against senior local government officials.[11] Another key plank in the transformation was the controversial clearance of 4,000 favela residents at Vila Autódromo at Barra da Tijuca to make way for the Olympic Park and Athletes' Village (Talbot and Carter 2018). A further 'invisibilisation strategy' served to preserve the preferred place-identity that institutional actors in Rio wished to present to the world, by screening favelas from public view along major Olympic tourist routes behind new concrete walls up to three metres in height (Steinbrink 2013, 137).

The Rio 2016 Olympic Opening Ceremony was, therefore, part of a cultural spectacle that recruited national and international TV audiences into an affective ideological community that would accept an aspirational, neoliberal 'version' of Rio as a centre of harmonious urban diversity, culture, business and progress. The ceremony was part of a place-making process that presented a progressive vision of a rainbow nation overcoming its colonial past to embrace a futuristic, scientific and environmentalist future, while simultaneously facilitating significant systems of urban restructuring in the host city. The official ideology of the performance was best summarised by local arts and culture professionals in interview and during the Rio Negocios conference proceedings, who said, variously:

I think this [was] *gambiarra* from the beginning, because what is *gambiarra*? It is to make something out of nearly nothing ... (Anon. Olympic Ceremony artist)

The world loves Brazil, the world loves Rio. It is the iconic city, the gateway to the country and it is a melting pot city ... And I think this ceremony was a way of showcasing that ... The opening ceremony was wow! Beautiful! (Cristina: cultural producer, Rio)

The brand is built day by day, with each experience, contact, picture, news article. It all builds a perception of the city of Rio ... Everything people see and listen to: fashion, violence, natural beauty, cuisine, all of that contributes to perception ... [We must] organize public policies, private investments, initiatives in communication, in order to create a relevant and consistent perception of the place for stakeholders. (Alencar 2016)

The themes of the ceremony – 'Reinvent, Rejoice, Replant' – also expressed this sense of urban transformation. The event presented a series of preferred local *carioca* identities[12] alongside a display of historical, national and regional place-cultures.[13] An introductory film montage focused on Rio's beaches and urban sports cultures, juxtaposing its urban spaces with the green of the rainforest, as a prelude to the historical pageant that followed. The opening sections, *Pindorama (Land of the Palm Trees)* and *The Birth of Life*, linked Brazil to notions of the Garden of Eden, presenting Brazil's indigenous people as a feature of nature and as the 'earth's natural caretakers' (Chisholm 2016, 526), supported by 72 indigenous dancers from Parintins, Amazonias.

This representation of indigenous culture reflected Gilbert's assertion that indigenous performers tend to appear in Olympic ceremonies as exoticised peoples who are 'set apart from the real sphere of contemporary indigenous politics' (2014, 158). The international TV audience would have been unaware of the controversial role that the Olympic Maracanã stadium complex itself had played in recent indigenous politics in Rio de Janeiro. In the early 2000s the Aldeia Maracanã, an indigenous community of people from the Apurinã, Guajajara, Pataxó and Tukano tribes, moved from the Amazon Basin to the grounds of an abandoned mansion adjoining the Maracanã, in search of healthcare and education. In 2013 the community was forcibly evicted to make way for construction projects for the 2014 World Cup and 2016 Olympics (Chisholm 2016). The vernacular Museum of Indigenous Culture that the community had established on the site was shut down, and was patrolled by armed police throughout the 2016 Olympics to prevent reoccupation (Kon 2016). Gilbert further suggests that in 'New World' contexts:

> carefully choreographed Olympic performances [reflect] an elite investment in casting the conquest ... of original peoples as a generative process that culminated in the birth of the modern mestizo nation. The violence of colonial subjugation [is] elided from that vision, along with the ongoing reality of indigenous impoverishment. (Gilbert 2014, 161)

This 'elite investment' was characterised in the pageant section entitled *Here in Brazil, We Mix*, which re-enacted the arrival of a fleet of Portuguese caravels in 1500. This section depicted a meeting of indigenous people and Portuguese colonists, but gave little sense of the violence of conquest or the contemporary position of indigenous people in Brazil. Rather, this representation, and the depictions of enslaved Africans that followed, were a prelude to the dramatisation of what Gilbert describes as 'the coming together of many different cultures in a folkloric celebration that enact[s] a semblance of the nation's pluralism' (2014, 163).

This national *mestizo* ideology continued in the section entitled *Geometrization: Arrival of The Africans*, in which the experience of 400 years of colonial slavery was represented by a parade of shackled African slaves. Sugar cane plantations and field systems emerged in the projected floor cloth, before the pageant moved on to represent successive waves of immigration: groups of nineteenth-century Syrian and Lebanese immigrants carrying wire suitcases, and the red banners and wire coolie hats of Japanese arrivals in the early twentieth century. These symbolic landscapes of Africa, Syria, Lebanon and Japan were mixed with Afro-Brazilian *Maracatu* folk dancers from Pernambuco, *Bate Bola* carnivalists from the Baixada Fluminense suburb of Rio de Janeiro, and the 'fire sword' battle of Cruz Das Almas, in the state of Bahia. At its peak, and as a prelude to representations of 'modern' Brazil, the super-model Gisele Bündchen performed a catwalk out of the melting pot, to the tune of *Girl from Ipanema*.

Many interviewees were positive about this attempt to show Brazil's place-identity in all its diversity, and were highly respectful of the progressive credentials of the director, Fernando Meirelles. One cultural professional said: 'it was black, it was poor, it was trans ... it went back to being the Brazil I know, people loving and accepting each other'.[14] However, representations of indigenous and Afro-Brazilian cultures in the ceremony were problematic for most indigenous and Afro-Brazilian interviewees, who found the 'melting pot' idealisation highly ironic given the social realities affecting black, immigrant, indigenous and transgender Brazilians:

> [It was] a Brazil of mixed cultures, of mixed races, creating a nation in the middle of the jungle ... And it was very ironic when the symbol of national beauty actually arrived as a white, blonde woman walking down the stage [Gisele], as if everything has happened for her to be born ... the centre of all attention. What Brazil really wants to sell is that skinny, blonde, white woman ... The world saw a pacified Brazil, [but Brazil has] so many monstrous, latent, cultural, ethnic and social differences. If you can find a *barraco*[15] built against a mansion wall, how can that be peace? How is it possible that, in some places in town, if you walk the wrong way you die? You get shot? ... Brazil really does sell itself as a product. It adjusts the packaging and that's it, but when you read the ingredients you see how it was really made. (Gilberto, 'Black Rock' musician)

A significant focus of Olympic critique during the Games was the Ministry of Culture (MINC) Occupation protest at Canecão. A development of the 2013 Movimento Reage Artista, which demanded '[more] pluralistic and democratic policies in arts and culture' (Schneider Alcure 2017), the occupation was a reaction to the impeachment of President Dilma Rousseff and the 'coup' which brought Vice President Michel Temer to power. Following a 73-day occupation by artist-activists of the MINC regional office in Rio, riot police expelled the protestors, who then occupied a former university concert hall at Canecão and organised a cultural programme of art, music, theatre, debate and alternative education, much of it with an anti-Olympics slant. Reacting to the ceremony's depiction of a progressive, *mestizo* place-identity, Canecão activists Ana and Dione stated:

> It was a mask, it represented the reality of very few people. It's the black population that suffers from virtual genocide here in Brazil, right? Every day there's death in a favela, every day the black youth is dying. (Ana, arts activist)

That was an origin myth, it's the 'Brazilian races' myth: very romanticised, right? [That] there are the Indians, the black and the white and that has bred a culturally happy, balanced nation. That is a dated idea, it does not correspond anymore to what we are, right? So obviously it's a spectacle, anyway, done to please, like, to impress and such ... we *are* mixed, but this mixture also causes a lot of oppression ... (Dione, arts activist)

The transgender actress and model Lea T led the Brazilian team in the athletes' parade at the Opening Ceremony. Dandara, a transgender theatre artist, added:

[Lea T] represented all trans people with the talent, beauty and tenacity of an empowered woman. [But Brazil is] still a transphobic country ... Religion and politics get very mixed, and our main executioners are the politicians. Transvestites and transsexuals are marginalised, and stripped of rights, for example the right to a formal job. As a consequence over 90 per cent of Brazilian transvestites are in prostitution. [However,] art has a strong power of transformation, and to have a transvestite actress as a protagonist [in the ceremony] is a very powerful symbol in the fight against prejudice, and it evidences this marginalised group. (Dandara, transgender theatre artist, Rio)

Representations of favela place-identities also featured prominently, with representations of funk and passinho dances and a reconstruction of favela architecture and people. The *Voices from the Favela* segment culminated in a reconstruction of the *Baile Charme* open-air street dances of the Madureira zone of North Rio, described by Cecchetto, Monteiro and Vargas (2012, 459) as 'a cultural space where a black aesthetic is given positive values, allowing social recognition'. However, as Penglase observes:

The city's favelas – symbols of poverty and crime – have been subjected to the most intense interventions ... The UPP[16] policy is designed to 'rebrand' Rio [in preparation for the 2014 World Cup and 2016 Olympics] ... Rio's favelas had come to be seen as a prime symbol of the city's insecurity: zones which existed beyond the state's control, areas where the rule of law did not apply. ... When the police occupy a favela, they often hoist the Brazilian flag, as if until that moment favelas had been part of a separate nation. (2016, 254–82)

On the street, wrapped in a banner and on her way to a pre-ceremony protest at the Maracanã, where police used tear gas to disperse hundreds of protestors,[17] Inês, an art student and anti-Olympics activist, said:

> Eleven thousand people were relocated from their homes in order to build the Vila Autódromo, and the Olympic Park. A lot of police went up those hills two or three months ago and they killed a lot of people ... That's why we say these are the Exclusion Games, that's why we call them the Murder Olympics. (Inês: street interview, Rio)

On the Rua Sacadura Cabral, Telma, an artist with the radical Saracura Artist Collective, described the tension between downtown Olympic gentrification and the lives of local street people, and how this had been transformed into creative, place-based practice:

> The Boulevard Olímpico is one street away. In Brazil, [building] materials are always over-calculated because of corruption ... [so] they just left them in piles along the street and they didn't come back to collect what was left over ... So, looking from a critical Olympic point of view, I built some ovens with the bricks that they left behind ... I made just a structure, very ephemeral, putting some bricks up ... and I used the pallets to burn and make a fire ... and I made four ovens. I brought a pan, I boiled some water and I made meat soup, some people came and the people living in the street brought macaroni ... And somehow this was an Olympic sculpture. How do you say? An Olympic torch? (Telma, artist, Saracura Collective, Rio)

Later that evening, other hidden, vernacular place identities expressed themselves through art and performance. In the Complexo de Maré favela, a sprawling 'unofficial' community of more than fifty thousand inhabitants, an alternative performance of Rio's favela identity took place. At the Centro De Artes De Maré, an abandoned factory repurposed as a vernacular community arts space, the Lia Rodrigues dance company, born, bred and trained in the shanty town, performed *Para Que O Ceu Não Caia: We Dance so the Sky does not Fall in*. Inside, strip lighting and seating made from wooden pallets adjoined the dance space, below a high-arched roof with ventilation fans that turned in the slight breeze. The bare auditorium was hung with black drapes, around a raised black dance floor. The Lia Rodrigues company draws its performers from the

Maré Dance Free School that is based in the building, and *Para Que O Ceu Não Caia* was devised in conversation with favela residents. The show turned the hopes, energies, fears, tragedies and determinations of the favela community into kinetic movement for a local audience, beyond the view of the Olympic TV cameras, as the following research fieldnote reveals:

> The company entered: men and women of all races, who faced us and slowly stripped naked. They scattered coffee grounds on the floor, rubbing the brown dust into their faces, torsos, breasts, legs and feet. Their bodies were of all types and ethnicities; muscular, lean, and hungry. They knelt, and then crawled to where we sat, coming close, making steady eye contact and holding it; crouching as if baptized in the dirt and dust of the favela streets, and doused in the brown gold of coffee, Brazil's great commodity. (Fieldnote, Centro De Artes De Maré, 4 August 2016)

The Centro De Artes De Maré is part of Redes da Maré (Maré Network), a vernacular social justice and education organisation which was founded by favela residents in 1997. Redes da Maré has the stated aim of promoting 'the social role of citizens [and] their collective actions' (Redes da Maré n.d.), and at the centre of its mission within the 16 separate communities that comprise the Maré favela lies a 'respect for differences and diversity, as well as the critique of social inequalities currently existing in Brazil and in Rio de Janeiro' (Redes da Maré n.d.). While firmly vernacular in its organisation and constitution, the Centro was also part of the *Ponto de Cultura* (Points of Culture) programme, established between 2004 and 2010 by Gilberto Gil, Brazilian Minister for Culture, and Celio Turino, his Secretary of Cultural Citizenship. As Heritage explains (in Turino 2013, 6–24), *Ponto de Cultura* briefly offered a radical programme of recognition for vernacular, place-based arts practice. The policy deliberately directed state funding and support into the hands of existing, grassroots, vernacular arts groups, rather than undermining these cultures by creating a 'radical monopoly' of top-down models of professionalised, place-based art (Kelly 1984). The eventual swing of Brazilian politics to the far right meant that *Ponto de Cultura* was a short-lived left-wing experiment in cultural democracy. Nevertheless, it offers an influential model that challenges the neoliberal instrumentalities of state-funded attempts to articulate a sense of place through community arts practice, as Heritage explains:

> The challenge is to create public policy that can maintain, develop and celebrate the 'imperfect mosaic' that is Brazilian culture ... a way of celebrating and developing that diversity against opposing forces that seek to limit the ways in which Brazil sees and shows itself ... By supporting and developing what exists, and, even more importantly, by refusing to define what is art and what is not, the state has been able to align itself with forces that are potentially in creative, critical dialogues with what is both local and also tuned to influences from outside. (Heritage, in Turino 2013, 15)

In his introduction to Turino's writings about the *Ponto de Cultura* approach, Heritage outlines its fundamental attempt to contest the cultural hierarchies that prefer certain forms of aesthetic expression over others. This is particularly important with regard to the 'performance' of place identity, as we saw in the Weymouth Carnival example earlier in this chapter. In the Brazilian context, Heritage points out that 'when popular culture has been favoured ... it has been within structures that sought to domesticate or pacify anything subversive or politically challenging' (Heritage, in Turino 2013, 10). Hence the difference between the commodified favela representations of the Olympic Opening Ceremony, which sought to reinforce the idealised place-identity of Rio de Janeiro as a positive melting pot of cultures, and the favela dancers of the Centro De Artes De Maré, whose performance was rooted in social reality, as the following fieldnote reveals:

> The dance built into anguished crawling, the dancers' heads covered like torture victims, their torn tee shirts and trousers pulled over their naked torsos, their red makeup like stab wounds or bullet holes ... Their stamps were like the beat of police rotor blades or the marching of pacifying boots, like a warning code tapped through the walls of favela houses to raise the alarm ... By the end, the dance whispered the early mortality of many in the Maré. Saffron powder, the third mask applied, turned them into holy corpses, disappearing at the end to leave just scuffs in the dirt, beneath a sky full of street lights and stars. They left in darkness: in-place and out-of-place; part of the city, yet excluded from it. (Fieldnote, Centro De Artes De Maré, 4 August 2016)

This analysis of the links between art, economy, politics and place-making in the context of the Rio 2016 Olympics benefits in many ways from the extreme sociopolitical conditions that were prevalent at the time, and which threw the general conflict between neoliberal instrumentality and cultural democracy into sharp relief. In 2018 Brazil shifted further to the extreme right, with the presidential election of the white supremacist, homophobic, anti-indigenous former paratrooper Jair Bolsonaro, who favours a return to military dictatorship. Nevertheless, these extreme conditions offer a framework for considering the general ethics of our own work as place-based, community-focused artists, and the politics of the representations we create as a part of our creative public engagements with 'place'. As Turino explains:

> Democracy will only exist when we have polyphony. Social groups, any groups, need and want to look at themselves in the mirror and know that the image reflected is the one they want to see and to show. This is what it means to become the protagonist. Much of the social maladjustment and violence that we experience in big cities is the result of the vast majority of the people being prevented from seeing themselves and being seen. (Turino 2013, 29)

Conclusions

This chapter has explored how official, state-funded processes of place-making through cultural performance often reflect a neoliberal agenda based on inter-place competition. Olympic festive practices in particular are tuned towards the cultural idealisation of places in the service of hegemonic interest, and vernacular creative identities which contest 'official' aesthetic values, or offer a grassroots challenge to preferred notions of place, are often subjugated as a result. This discussion also raises ethical questions about the instrumentalities of state-funded arts practice within city-regeneration strategies and the role of place-based arts and cultural performance within wider academic discourses of 'creative and cultural economy' (Landry and Bianchini 1995; Landry 2000; Florida 2002). It reminds us that when producing cultural performances of place, we must be alert to the degree to which the 'official' may obscure the 'vernacular' culture, and that we must be equally prepared to embrace and support 'inconvenient' place-cultures within systems of funding and spaces of public representation, in the interests of cultural democracy.

Massey's (1997) principle, that place is a *locus* of diverse meanings and social experiences that resists a unique definition, prompts a democratic view of the diversity of place-identity that may be expressed within any given geographical spatiality. The benefits of respecting this principle are that, alongside institutional programmes of place-making, vernacular arts cultures might thus also receive levels of unconditional support that have hitherto been denied to them. 'Free public space' should be maintained, in order to protect vernacular street arts cultures and to provide room for iterative vernacular cultural performances and festivals. Edensor *et al.* (2010) rightly point out that the challenge for the professional arts sector is, therefore, to recognise that:

> an understanding of vernacular and everyday landscapes of creativity honours the non-economic values and outcomes produced by alternative, marginal and quotidian creative practices, and has the potential to move us toward more holistic, diverse and socially inclusive creative city strategies. (Edensor *et al.* 2010, 1)

Finally, Miles's concept of 'radical vernacularism' offers a rallying call to organisations involved in place-based arts development practice:

> A radical vernacularism would involve artists, like radical planners, handing over the means of production to participating groups and individuals whose tacit and intellectual knowledges are given equal status to those of professionals. (Miles 2010, 59)

It is my hope that the qualitative understanding which arises from this discussion will prompt the renewal of processes that bring place-based arts practice and cultural democracy together. Let us imagine processes that complement, support and reveal diverse vernacular expressions of place and festive culture, rather than competing with or obscuring them, and that thereby develop 'a concept of vernacular art whereby we respond continually to local demand … generating a social poetry of a high order within a very specific community context' (J. Fox, in Kershaw 1991, 249).

Acknowledgements

This chapter is derived in part from an article published in *Social and Cultural Geography* (2017), copyright Taylor and Francis, available online: http://www.tandfonline.com/doi/abs/10.1080/14649365.2017.1362587?journalCode=rscg20.

This work was partially supported by the Arts and Humanities Research Council under Grant Number AH/H035230/1, Collaborative

Doctoral Award: *The Practices of Carnival: Community, Culture and Place.* CDA Partners: University of Exeter, UNESCO East Devon and Dorset 'Jurassic' Coast World Heritage Site.

This work was also partially supported by the award of an Arts University Bournemouth Research Fellowship, 2015/16.

Notes

1. See D'Cruz 2005; Mason 1992; Mascia-Lees 2011; Kelly 1984; Kirshenblatt-Gimblett and McNamara 1985; Fox 2002.
2. See Croose 2014 for an overview of policy development. See also Hall 2002; Micklem 2006; Arts Council England 2008, 2015.
3. Interview, arts professional, Weymouth.
4. http://www.maritimemix2012.co.uk/event/6/Moving-Tides,-part-of-London-2012-closing-celebrations/
5. http://www.reuters.com/article/2012/07/29/us-oly-yach-opening-day-idUSBRE86R12M20120729.
6. Gloucestershire, Bristol / West of England, Somerset, Devon, Dorset, Cornwall and Swindon / Wiltshire.
7. JCAP (Jurassic Coast Arts Programme) 2007a, 2007b, 2008, 2010a, 2010b.
8. Interview, arts professional, 31 October 2011.
9. See Croose 2014; Edensor et al. 2010.
10. Brazilian President Dilma Rousseff was removed from office immediately after the Olympics in August 2016 on corruption charges, and replaced by Michel Temer in what many arts activists described as a coup.
11. https://www.theguardian.com/sport/2017/apr/23/brazil-olympic-world-cup-corruption-bribery.
12. *Carioca*: deriving from Rio de Janeiro.
13. This pageant of local and regional folk culture was also reflected in the *Patrimônio Imaterial Brasileiro* and *Brasil Junino* exhibitions at the Casa Brasil pavilion on the Boulevard Olímpico.
14. Aurea, cultural producer, Rio.
15. A *barraco* is a shanty house, generally built within a favela.
16. UPP is an acronym for the Unidades de Polícia Pacificadora (Police Pacifying Units) programme of favela intervention that began in 2008 and was closely tied to preparations for the 2014 World Cup and 2016 Olympic Games.
17. Maracanã protest, 5 August 2016. See: https://www.independent.co.uk/sport/olympics/rio-2016-olympic-protesters-tear-gas-police-brazil-a7175271.html.

References

Abrahams, Roger D. 1983. *The Man-of-Words in the West Indies: Performance and the Emergence of Creole Culture*. Baltimore: Johns Hopkins University Press.

Alencar, D. 2016. Conference address, Rio Negocios Tourism and City Branding Conference, held at Casa Rio, Espaço River, Olympic Boulevard, Tuesday 16 August.

Arts Council England. 2008. *New Landscapes: Outdoor Arts Development Plan 2008–2011*. London: Arts Council England.

Arts Council England. 2015. *Ambition for Excellence*. London: Arts Council England. Accessed 9 June 2020. https://www.artscouncil.org.uk/search/ambition%20for%20excellence.

Bakhtin, Mikhail. 1984. *Rabelais and His World*, translated by Helene Iswolsky. Bloomington: Indiana University Press.

Bucke, Tom and Zoe James. 1998. *Trespass and Protest: Policing under the Criminal Justice and Public Order Act 1994*. London: Home Office.

Carter, J. and D. Masters. 1998. 'Arts and the Natural Heritage', *Scottish Natural Heritage Review* 109.
Cecchetto, Fátima, Simone Monteiro and Eliane Vargas. 2012. 'Young's Sociability, Color, Gender and Sexuality on the Charm's Ball in Rio de Janeiro', translated by David Coles, *Cadernos de Pesquisa* 42 (146): 454–73.
Chisholm, Jennifer. 2016. 'Forced Evictions and Black-Indigenous Land Rights in the Marvelous City', *Brasiliana: Journal for Brazilian Studies* 4 (2): 513–49.
Conquergood, Dwight. 2002. 'Performance Studies: Interventions and Radical Research', *TDR: The Drama Review* 46 (2): 145–56.
Cresswell, Tim. 2004. *Place: A Short Introduction*. Malden, MA: Blackwell.
Croose, Jonathan Freeman. 2014. *The Practices of Carnival: Community, Culture and Place*. Doctoral thesis, University of Exeter, available at https://ore.exeter.ac.uk/repository/handle/10871/15833.
D'Cruz, Corinne. 2005. 'An Open Letter to Participants, Münster, Internationale Street Arts Konferenz'. Accessed 8 February 2011. www.open-air-theater.net/htcms/de/konferenz-2005/feedback.html. Online source no longer active.
Edensor, Tim, Deborah Leslie, Steve Millington and Norma M. Rantisi, eds. 2010. *Spaces of Vernacular Creativity: Rethinking the Cultural Economy*. London: Routledge.
Evans, Graeme. 2010. 'Creative Spaces and the Art of Urban Living'. In *Spaces of Vernacular Creativity: Rethinking the Cultural Economy*, edited by Tim Edensor, Deborah Leslie, Steve Millington and Norma M. Rantisi, 19–32. London, Routledge.
Florida, Richard L. 2002. *The Rise of the Creative Class*. New York: Basic Books.
Fox, John. 2002. *Eyes on Stalks*. London: Methuen.
Gilbert, Helen. 2014. '"Let the Games Begin": Pageants, Protests, Indigeneity (1968–2010)'. In *The Politics of Interweaving Performance Cultures: Beyond Postcolonialism*, edited by Erika Fischer-Lichte, Torsten Jost and Saskya Iris Jain, 156–75. New York: Routledge.
Hall, Felicity. 2002. *Strategy and Report on Street Arts*. London: Arts Council England.
Harvey, David. 1996. 'From Space to Place and Back Again'. In *Justice, Nature and the Geography of Difference*, by David Harvey, 291–328. Malden, MA: Blackwell.
Jackson, P. 1988. 'Street Life: The Politics of Carnival', *Environment and Planning D: Society and Space* 6 (2): 213–27.
Jackson, Peter. 1992. 'The Politics of the Streets: A Geography of Caribana', *Political Geography* 11 (2): 130–51.
JCAP (Jurassic Coast Arts Programme). 2007a. *The Jurassic Coast Arts Project (2008–11)* ACE, Grants for the Arts Project Proposal.
JCAP (Jurassic Coast Arts Programme). 2007b. *The Jurassic Coast Arts Strategy*.
JCAP (Jurassic Coast Arts Programme). 2008. 'How to Get Involved'. Accessed 17 March 2011. www.eastdevonaonb.org.uk/.../HowToGetInvolved_JurassicArts_jul08.doc. Online source no longer active.
JCAP (Jurassic Coast Arts Programme) 2010a. *Planning a Festival of Carnivals*, agenda document.
JCAP (Jurassic Coast Arts Programme) 2010b. *Planning a Festival of Carnivals*, break-out group notes.
Kelly, Owen. 1984. *Community, Art and the State: Storming the Citadels*. London: Comedia.
Kershaw, Baz. 1991. 'King Real's King Lear: Radical Shakespeare for the Nuclear Age', *Critical Survey* 3 (3): 249–59.
Kershaw, Baz. 1992. *The Politics of Performance: Radical Theatre as Cultural Intervention*. London: Routledge.
Kirshenblatt-Gimblett, Barbara and Brooks McNamara. 1985. 'Processional Performance: An Introduction', *TDR: The Drama Review* 29 (3): 2–5.
Kon, Luke. 2016. 'Aldeia Maracanã Fights for Indigenous Museum Next to Olympics Opening Ceremony', *RioOnWatch*, 4 August. Accessed 9 May 2020. www.rioonwatch.org/?p=31291.
Landry, Charles. 2000. *The Creative City: A Toolkit for Urban Innovators*. London: Earthscan.
Landry, Charles and Franco Bianchini. 1995. *The Creative City*. London: Demos.
Lummertz, Vinicius. 2016. Conference address, Rio Negocios Tourism and City Branding Conference, held at Casa Rio, Espaço River, Olympic Boulevard, Tuesday, 16 August.
Mascia-Lees, Frances E. 2011. 'Aesthetics: Aesthetic Embodiment and Commodity Capitalism'. In *A Companion to the Anthropology of the Body and Embodiment*, edited by Frances E. Mascia-Lees, 3–23. Chichester: Wiley-Blackwell.
Mason, Bim. 1992. *Street Theatre and Other Outdoor Performance*. London: Routledge.

Massey, Doreen. 1997. 'A Global Sense of Place'. In *Reading Human Geography: The Poetics and Politics of Inquiry*, edited by Trevor Barnes and Derek Gregory, 315–23. London: Arnold.

Micklem, David. 2006. *Street Arts Healthcheck*. London: Arts Council England.

Miles, Malcolm. 2010. 'Art Goes AWOL'. In *Spaces of Vernacular Creativity: Rethinking the Cultural Economy*, edited by Tim Edensor, Deborah Leslie, Steve Millington and Norma M. Rantisi, 46–60. London, Routledge.

Penglase, Richard Benjamin. 2016. 'Pacifying the Empire of Love: Security, Sport and Scandal in Rio de Janeiro', *Brasiliana: Journal for Brazilian Studies* 4 (2): 254–82.

Redes da Maré. n.d. 'Quem somos – nossa história'. Accessed 9 May 2020. http://redesdamare.org.br/br/quemsomos/historia.

Relph, E. 1976. *Place and Placelessness*. London: Pion.

Rio Negocios. 2016. Opening presentation, Tourism and City Branding Conference, held at Casa Rio, Espaço River, Olympic Boulevard, Tuesday, 16 August.

Schausteck de Almeida, Bárbara, Wanderley Marchi Júnior and Elizabeth Pike. 2014. 'The 2016 Olympic and Paralympic Games and Brazil's Soft Power', *Contemporary Social Science* 9 (2): 271–83.

Schneider Alcure, Adriana. 2017. 'Art and Insurgency in Urgent Times', *Theatre Research International* 42 (2): 212–16.

Steinbrink, Malte. 2013. 'Festifavelisation: Mega-Events, Slums and Strategic City-Staging: The Example of Rio de Janeiro', *Die Erde: Journal of the Geographical Society of Berlin* 144 (2): 129–45.

Talbot, Adam and Thomas F. Carter. 2018. 'Human Rights Abuses at the Rio 2016 Olympics: Activism and the Media', *Leisure Studies* 37 (1): 77–88.

Tilley, Christopher. 1994. *A Phenomenology of Landscape: Places, Paths and Monuments*. Oxford: Berg.

Turino, Célio. 2013. *The Point of Culture: Brazil Turned Upside Down*, edited by Paul Heritage and Rosie Hunter. London: Calouste Gulbenkian Foundation.

10
A sense of place: From experience to language, from the Polish traveller through a Spanish saint to an adaptation of a Zimbabwean play

Agnieszka Piotrowska

In a volume about 'developing a sense of place', this is an essay which questions the enterprise, in agreement with the philosopher Michel de Certeau, who advocated the notion of a space rather than a sense of place, and furthermore advocated that placeness as a site of freedom (Certeau 1984, 131). Theoretically, the notions of a 'place', and therefore 'placeness', are contested ideas (see, for example, Freestone and Liu's edited 2016 volume *Place and Placelessness Revisited*). Here I pose some questions relating to the notion of translating physical experience which connects to a place but becomes something different and more complicated. This will include a linguistic translation of a bodily and physical experience into words that can then be shared by a community and indeed develop a sense of communality of a kind. My starting position is therefore to reject the physical in favour of the metaphorical, not to say metaphysical, hoping, after Certeau, that this will become an essay about a sense of freedom and fidelity, in translation but also in life. In this essay, therefore, I will attempt to hold in one space different notions of a translation of the experience of a place and placeness using three very different examples: a novel about travelling, St Teresa's visions and my own adaptation of Stanley Makuwe's play *Finding Temeraire*.

Olga Tokarczuk's 'novel essay' – or essay novel – entitled, in English, *Flights*, won the International Booker Prize in 2018. The book, as its blurb on the back page says, is about 'travel in the twenty-first century and human anatomy, broaching life, death, motion and migration'. The volume, initially published in Polish in 2007, was translated into English by Jennifer Croft, who shared the award with the writer. As a scholar and a creative person whose first language is Polish, I have to admit that I have found some of the translating solutions used in the novel challenging, despite the excellent voice of the work's English version. I have found it curiously 'straightening' of Tokarczuk's convoluted and ambiguous language at times. Maybe it makes it even 'better' or more accessible to an English reader.

For a start, the work's Polish title, *Bieguni*, feels very different from *Flights*. 'Bieguni' is not a proper word in Polish, or at least not a word anybody would know in Poland (Tokarczuk explains in the novel that 'bieguni' is the name of an ancient nomadic tribe, which may or may not be the case, but in any event, I have never heard of it and neither has anybody I have spoken to). 'Bieguni' sounds as if, etymologically, it has something to do with 'running' ('biegac') but also with the word 'poles' as in 'the North Pole' ('bieguny' would be the plural of 'the Pole'). The title therefore sounds strangely uncanny, foreign, exotic, and yes, evokes a sense travel of the kind Tokarczuk writes about that is not easily definable – the very title immediately suggesting something out of the ordinary. 'Flights' on the other hand – well! 'Flights' just sounds like 'flights' – to do with a journey but of an ordinary kind, to do with planes, and airports, and maybe flights of fancy, and maybe even escapes, but the word is just an existing word and has lost the connotations of strangeness that the original title had.

This chapter will not critique that award-winning translation of the award-winning novel. Instead, it will reflect on the nature of words and what they can describe and what they cannot describe, trying to think through some of the relationships between places, emotions and translations. In connection with this, I will also briefly examine my own experience of attempting to evoke a sense of place by adapting the play *Finding Temeraire* by the Zimbabwean Stanley Makuwe, about life in a colonial mining settlement, Mashava, in Rhodesia and in the early independence years of Zimbabwe. Mashava exists as an actual historical place but the intense engagement of the two characters in the play and in my film is of course fictional. Makuwe's writing choice included placing a female character at the heart of the piece with sparse descriptions of the place. The play, and later my adaptation of it, becomes also a mythical space in which the grand political narratives play out as the background to the profound intimate dramas in the foreground; the play is therefore about how the political and the historical affect the personal in the particular place. In this specific case it was not an issue of an adaptation to screen – although it was that too – but rather, I would argue, it was indeed a translation, not just from the play onto the screen, but rather, from one semiotic system to another, from one way of thinking about the place and its meaning to another.

There have been very many works on cinema and adaptation (e.g. Andrew 1984; Cohen 1979; Corrigan 1999; Stam 2000), but here I am trying to focus in particular on the process of 'describing' and 'naming' a particular place and what it might mean in terms of some kind of notion of accuracy, both historical and geographical, and epistemological truth. I am also interested in the ability of writing to describe physical experience as an enabling procedure – enabling knowledge but also facilitating deep enjoyment, or psychoanalytical *jouissance* (of which more later). As we will see directly, there is controversy about the above and the question is indeed: is it true that writing and naming enhances experience? Or does it take away from it, making it too concrete and obvious?

The case study of my own work that I am using here is just one example but the questions asked have broader significance, also in terms of establishing the relationship between the experience and the description of it, and here the particular translation that occurs between the two, between the author (and therefore the reader and the viewer) and the place and the experience described. I will also briefly offer a few reflections on what psychoanalysis might have to offer and contribute to this conversation. Before I proceed, however, I need to make a disclaimer. I will be mentioning here the thinkers and writers whose work I have found useful for this discussion, regardless of gender, but I will be purposefully favouring female voices in the discussion.

A relationship between bodily experience and speech was of course crucial at the outset of psychoanalysis. In *Autobiographics in Freud and Derrida* (1990), Jane Marie Todd makes a connection between a bodily symptom and an autobiographical statement: 'the hysterical body is a text, in fact, an autobiographical text. Every symptom tells a story about the patient's life, or rather several stories' (Todd 1990, 5). Todd further points out that the work of a psychoanalyst is really that of a 'translator', a translator of symptoms: 'It is the task of the psychoanalyst to work with the patient, to collaborate on a *translation* of this secret and motivated language of the body into the conventional language of the words' (p. 5; my emphasis). Freud calls this collaboration, this task of translation, 'an analysis'. Todd further glosses 'analysis' as the name given to 'an autobiographical practice whose principal purpose is neither to testify nor to confess (one's sins or one's devotion), though both modes may be part of an analysis. The work of analysis is autobiographics as *cure*' (pp. 5–6).

One could take issue with the above, or with many other matters – one of these being Freud's at times patriarchal attitude to females, which I have discussed elsewhere (Piotrowska 2019). I am putting a marker here but bracketing the discussion in order to focus on another question: is translating one's experience into words always therapeutic? It is interesting to note the moment of 'translation' from bodily experience to language which, psychoanalysts believe, has a curative effect but could also have other effects if that 'translation' enters a public space: psychoanalysis names (artistic) sublimation as a way of channelling (indeed translating) one's frustrated sexual energy into a creative activity. Lacan famously took away the 'frustrated' element and suggested that there is enjoyment (*jouissance*) in talking and writing which is equal to sexual satisfaction. In the introduction to her recent book on sex, Alenka Zupančič argues: 'The point that Lacanian psychoanalysis makes, however, is more paradoxical: the activity is different, yet the satisfaction in talking is itself "sexual"' (2017, 1), meaning further that it need not have roots in its 'sexual origin'. She says further that it is narrating the experience that makes it special and not the other way around: 'the satisfaction in talking contains a key to sexual satisfaction (and not the other way around)' (Zupančič 2017, 1).

Freud and those who followed certainly wanted to relieve the symptoms of his suffering patients, but the main objective of psychoanalysis has been for more than a century the project of gaining knowledge, in terms both of self-knowledge on the part of the patient/analysand and also of the knowledge which can then be shared with others *through language* in order to advance our collective knowledge – or non-knowledge – of who we are, as humanity or perhaps as merely Western civilisation. That was emphatically not Lacan's idea, not at the moment of enunciation and even less so towards the end of his life. In addition, Zupančič and other members of the Slovenian school of psychoanalysis and philosophy have emphasised the profound links between psychoanalysis and philosophy, the inherent contradictions notwithstanding (Zupančič 2017, 2). Jacques Lacan, of course, by pronouncing that 'the unconscious has a structure of language', did in some way inadvertently confuse the issue, as the phrase was promoted by structuralist thinkers (including structuralist film theorists), who focused on languages as a system of signs, ignoring the body and its experience.

Nonetheless, there is much we can learn from semioticians. Umberto Eco in *Experiences in Translation* (2001) reminds us that in order to translate anything from one system of meaning to another there must be at least some points of convergence, some mega-system of meanings that is accessible by all despite different ways of expressing it. He therefore makes the following point:

> If, in order to translate a text α, expressed in a language A, into a text β, expressed in a language B (and to say that β is a correct translation of α, and is similar in meaning to α), one must pass through the metalanguage X, then one is obliged first of all to decide in which way α and β are similar in meaning to a text γ in X and, to decide this, one requires a new metalanguage Y, and so on *ad infinitum*. (Eco 2001, 12)

Roman Jakobson (1971, 261) identified the type of translation that Eco discusses as interlingual translation ('an interpretation of verbal signs by means of some other language'), which he distinguished from intralingual translation ('rewording [...] of verbal signs by means of other signs of the same language') and intersemiotic translation ('an interpretation of verbal signs by means of signs of nonverbal sign systems' – in which we can include the translation of experience into language). The terms 'intralingual', 'interlingual' and 'intersemiotic' will be useful in the following discussion of translation.

Flights

This seems simple enough but the narrator of *Flights* creates a meta-system of meaning significantly different from the obvious ways of thinking about links between experience and its physicality and language. Tokarczuk early on puts a curious disclaimer into her novel – which, as I have mentioned, is all about travel. Sensationally and provocatively, she believes that the translation between experience and language fails.

In the English paperback the book is over 420 pages long; some of its sections are almost baroque in their richness and curious phrasing, despite the translator's valiant efforts to make the language 'straighter'; and yet the female narrator (who incidentally is never named and has many similarities with the author, although is not the author) questions the whole project of actually 'describing' things through language. She says the following:

> Describing something is like *using it*[1] – it destroys; the colours wear off, the corners lose their definition, and in the end what's been described begins to fade, to disappear. This applies most of all *to places*.

> Enormous damage has been done by travel literature – a veritable scourge, an epidemic. (Tokarczuk 2018, 75; my emphasis)

Tokarczuk's narrator then goes on to confess that she too 'in her youthful naivete, once took a shot at the description of places' (p. 75) but discovered soon enough that they never worked, that they always betrayed the experience. She bemoans: 'The truth is terrible: describing is destroying', and then elaborates:

> Which is why you have to be careful. It's better not to use names: avoid, conceal, take great caution in giving our addresses, so as not to encourage anyone to make their own pilgrimage. After all, what would they find there? A dead place, dust, like the dried-out core of an apple. (Tokarczuk 2018,75)

To Tokarczuk's narrator, the (intersemiotic) translation of an experience always fails.

In order to avoid this danger, therefore, in a book about travel and different places, the narrator focuses on people and stories and *not* the places in which they happen. She mixes fiction and facts, and real places with made-up ones. Her aim is to disturb the viewer, and maybe to inspire, but not to convey any concrete knowledge. The narrator of course at times offers brief locators but her main effort is descriptive and non-linear. In addition, the narrator/storyteller of *Flights* offers airports as liminal spaces in between concrete destinations of travel. Rather than being a nuisance, and dreaded terminals that most passengers would prefer to avoid, in Tokarczuk's novel they begin to become mythical places where one meets extraordinary people, including philosophers, attempting to direct the weary traveller to a way of thinking about the world which might avoid the constant disappointment built into any journey.

One such mythical group comprises travel psychology scholars who are somewhat related to psychoanalysis ('travel psychology has not cut all ties with psychoanalysis'; Tokarczuk 2018, 81). A certain young female lecturer attempts to interest airport passers-by in her lecture address, and the superiority of motion and fluidity over constancy, consistency and stability which in any event are but an illusion related to fear. As this becomes a spontaneous airport conference, she explains that travel psychology 'studies people in transit, persons in motion, and thus situates itself in opposition to traditional psychology, which has always investigated the human being in a fixed context, in stability and stillness – for example, through the prism of his or her biological constitution, family relationships, social situations and so forth' (p. 80). The narrator's key philosophical point is that if a translation of the experience is bound to fail, you might just as well abandon any attempt at fidelity to it and instead have fun in creating – well, enjoyment. She does not use the word *jouissance*, of course, but we are clearly in the same territory as Zupančič's postulates.

Tokarczuk sows more seeds of confusion. In *Flights* the lecturer goes on to say that the fundamental concept in travel psychology is desire which lends 'movement and direction to human beings' (p. 81) and that the destination is never reached (nor is the desire, of course). It is clear here why the reference to psychoanalysis was introduced into the discussion, for 'desire' is the very basis of psychoanalytical thinking. I shall return to this later in this chapter.

In *Flights* another lecturer – this time male – at the same ad hoc airport symposium offers further insights to the way this novel-essay or a fragmentary narration is constructed. Tokarczuk makes the reader 'listen' to his presentation, which insists that it is impossible to build 'a consistent cause-and-effect course of argument or a narrative' (p. 83), and which suggests instead that in order to reflect human experience more accurately it might be necessary 'to assemble a whole, out of pieces of more or less the same size [...]. *Constellation*, not sequencing, carries truth' (p. 8; my emphasis).

This thought seems to be a key idea of the whole book – things do not come in a sequence, they come and go, feelings come and go and impressions come and go. Life and the world are fluid – experience is transient. Even though actual physical places might appear constant, they are far from it; they are in constant flux, which is why any attempt to describe them with words will fail miserably. The unsaid theme of the book is also its anti-establishment stance, anti-stability, anti-coupledom, anti-predictability of any kind. Its anti-description stance is indeed a stance against translation as an epistemological project.

Soon after the beginning of this airport presentation, the narrator of *Flights* gets bored, decides that the lectures are too long and walks off, to find her own adventures which she then retells us as a series of short stories, without particularly describing in any detail the physical locations where they occur, but rather focusing on the curious characters and events which surround them – with no sequencing and no chronology. She uses what traditional theories of narration might call 'flashbacks', but she returns to the stories at times with no warning and no special reason. There are 116 stories in the book, and they are at times overindulgent and clearly luxuriating in the pleasure of writing, perhaps more so in Polish than in English.

What the writer does structurally, therefore, is indeed a kind of constellation of storytelling (rather than the established 'fragmentary narration'), in which she undermines the process of 'describing' at the outset but then, as a writer, has no option but to describe something – moments, characters – even if she tries to undermine the importance of writing. The language persists and she states that she detests that it does – but of course that very annoyance at it is the source of her *jouissance* too.

To my mind, it is most interesting that Tokarczuk mentions the notion of 'describing' as 'destroying' and then mentions psychoanalysis. In the systems of the latter, the process of describing/naming/writing is, as previously stated, of crucial importance: without it the psychoanalytical subject cannot come into being at all, and is stuck in the non-linguistic hell of the Real. To even evoke psychoanalysis in a work so angrily dismantling any logical systems is perhaps a signal to the reader that not everything is what it seems. The narrator of *Flights* is not exactly an unreliable narrator – she is very reliable in her method, which is quite perverse since, in a very long book devoted to travel and the places one visits during these travels, she appears to insist on undermining her own project; but she is a sort of constellational unnamed narrator – the author sticking at least to her dislike of naming places and things.

The stories told by Tokarczuk's narrator span centuries and have something important in common, namely their attention to the body. Whilst the blurb for the book speaks about anatomy, and there are indeed some gruesome stories about obtaining and preserving body parts, the main striking qualities of *Flights* are its reflections about bodily experiences, bodies perishing or being preserved, bodies of potential lovers being replaced or at least replaceable, bodies of unborn infants being wrenched out of the bodies of their mothers and then kept in jars with chloroform.

The narrator, after a hundred-page interlude of adventures and reflections, gets back to the airport travel psychology-cum-philosophy lectures, just in time to confirm the importance of the body, in case the bewildered reader has missed what else is at stake here – and what is at stake is the very sense of the place which is our existence on this planet:

> Once the gods were external, unavailable, from another world, and their apparent emissaries were angels and demons. But the human ego burst forth and swept the gods up *and inside* [...] Only in this way can the gods survive – in the dark, quiet nooks of *the human body*, in the crevices of the brain, in the empty spaces between the synapses. This fascinating phenomenon is beginning to be studied

by the fledgling discipline of travel psychotheology. (Tokarczuk 2018, 181; my emphasis)

The sudden mention of theology in Tokarczuk's constellatory narrative is unexpected. The narrator makes a leap and the reader is purposefully confused yet again and realises that the journey is after all not in the physical world alone. If the describing of physical places is hopeless and impossible, language may still have a role in describing the fleeting moment of defining who we might be on the one hand, and commenting on our clumsy communications, on the other.

St Teresa: *Jouissance* through language

A conversation about the body and language often becomes a conversation about God, it seems, which brings me to the psychoanalyst and philosopher Julia Kristeva's peculiar novel *Teresa, My Love: An Imagined Life of the Saint of Avila* (2014), which is not a project entirely dissimilar to *Flights* in so far as it was written by a female author, it focuses on a lone female narrator (and indeed the main protagonist is a single woman), and it consists of fiction and philosophical sections. It is also very long. Therein the similarities end. Whilst the unnamed narrator of Tokarczuk's novel repeatedly states her suspicions vis-à-vis language and states that it must be used only as a gesture of despair (in order to share and despite knowing that it is a failed project), Kristeva's main notion is that St Teresa's complicated life, her suspected epilepsy, her mental health issues, her problematic relationships with others in her daily life and, finally, her deep pain and pleasure, her *jouissance* (as Lacan described it in Seminar XX), come only because of her writing and through it. The experience is secondary – the writing is primary. Meaning can only come through writing. Without the description, the interpretation, the creation of the narratives, not only would Teresa of Ávila have been totally forgotten *after* her lifetime, but also, and importantly here, she would have lost this precious *jouissance* in her lifetime. Her experience was not enough to make her happy or make sense of her life; it was the writing, the description of it, that made it become real at all. Kristeva's argument, and her thesis, is therefore exactly the opposite to that of Tokarczuk: whilst the latter says that experience is always superior to its narrativising, the former praises the process of writing:

> And so I arrived at this conclusion: Teresa's ecstasy is no more or less than a writerly effect! Spinning-weaving the fiction of these

ecstasies to transmute her ill-being into a new being-in-the-world, Teresa seeks to 'convey', to 'give to understand' the link with the Other-Being as one between two living entities: a tactile link, about contact and touching, by which the divine gifts itself to the sensitive soul of a woman, rather than to the metaphysical mind of a theologian or philosopher. To sense the sense, to render meaning sensible: in Castilian, Teresa's writing and her ecstasy overlap. (Kristeva 2014, 105)

Teresa of Ávila in her writings, which she began to carry out only at the behest of her male confessors, in order to help her soften her pain and improve her health, describes a variety of *places* she visits during her ecstasies and which she perceives as actual and not imaginary. There are other interesting things to reflect on also as the times of St Teresa were brutal. This is sixteenth-century Spain with the accusations enunciated by Luther and the Reformation against the Catholic Church on the one hand, and the threat of the Illuminati on the other. According to Kristeva, Teresa of Ávila was lucky in so far as she had the protection of her priestly father confessors, who supported her and understood that she was sailing quite close to the winds in a political climate that forbade certain forms of mysticism. Those could even be seen as heresy and lead to severe repercussions. On the other hand, the Roman Catholic Church at the time did need something different and attractive to hold on to the congregations shaken by the Reformation. In the misfortune of her bad health, Teresa was therefore very lucky to have met some people (men) who would support her and it was very lucky indeed that she was able to write. In other words, she was in a position to intersemiotically *translate* her bodily and spiritual experience into words.

The places she describes are gardens and castles of her body and there was a real danger that her descriptions would be considered both too sensuous and too mystical at the same time, heretical in short. The Holy Inquisition did take some interest in her visions but her writing, interpreted by the father confessors, convinced them she was not one of the Illuminati but a legitimate visionary who could document her experiences in her writing to the benefit of the Church. But the truth appears quite different: Teresa translates her deep *autoerotic* enjoyment, her *jouissance*, into words and that saved her. Kristeva sees this process of translation as crucial:

Hunting for the mots justes, for an exact image of the touching-touched body thrown open to the plenitude of Other-Being, Teresa adds to the water fiction of the Life and later works of fiction of *overlapping dwelling* places inside *a castle*: heaped, penetrable, ostensibly numbering seven but consisting of a host of doorless rooms and cellars, porous spaces separated as if by the stretches of translucent film. (Kristeva 2014, 106; emphasis in the original)

Finding Temeraire and *Repented*

If St Teresa in Kristeva's book could inhabit one of the stories told in *Flights*, so could Primrose, the main character of Stanley Makuwe's play *Finding Temeraire*, which premiered first at the Harare International Festival of the Arts in May 2017 (directed by me) and was then performed in New Zealand, where the Zimbabwean author now lives (directed by somebody else). In an act of intersemiotic translation, I then adapted it to the screen as a medium-length experimental film entitled *Repented* (2019). Here the issues were plentiful, for a male Zimbabwean author wrote a strong female character and asked a European female director (me) to direct it. Makuwe wrote a very powerful female voice and asked me to direct the play in order, he said originally, to give the play the right emotional engagement with the material. The play was written in English, and not Shona, the initial process of translation taking place in the writer's mind – as the characters lived in colonial times, it is possible that English was indeed their main shared tongue. Nonetheless, in my experience of Zimbabwe in contemporary times, people would mostly speak Shona to each other in intimate circumstances, despite English being one of the legal languages. Stanley Makuwe takes pleasure in his mastery of the English language.

Of course, I was excited and flattered to be asked to direct the play; nonetheless, I was aware of some of the difficulties, which can be spelled out as follows. In his Introduction to *Orientalism* (1978), Edward Said discusses one particular scene, from the French writer Gustave Flaubert, which symbolises the encounter between the West and the subaltern, and in broader terms, the encounter between the coloniser and the colonised. The scene features the Egyptian courtesan Kuchuk Hanem, who may have been Flaubert's lover too. Said comments: 'He was foreign, comparatively wealthy, male, and these were historical facts of domination that allowed him not only to possess Kuchuk Hanem physically but to speak for her and tell his readers in what way she was "typically Oriental"' (Said 1978, 6). Said goes on brilliantly to construct an argument, used in due course by Spivak, and employing some of Gramsci's ideas, on hegemonic forces in culture and society, ascertaining that West–East and West–South relations at that point in time rested on a strategy of 'flexible *positional* superiority, which puts the Westerner in a whole series of possible relationships with the Orient without ever losing the relative upper hand' (Said 1978, 7; emphasis in the original). Rereading the above quote today, what is very clear, almost embarrassingly blindingly clear, is that the colonisation taking place in the encounter between the prostitute and Flaubert is not only a colonisation of a subaltern non-Western subject by a dominant Western one, but it is also, or perhaps primarily, an inter-gender encounter of an all too familiar kind: a man buying a woman, penetrating a woman, taking things from her that he needs, including her voice, which he then makes his own. Said's poignant point *equates* in some way a woman and the subaltern in the colonial encounter: and perhaps it is also true that a non-Western woman has been the most likely object of such a colonisation.

In regards to *Finding Temeraire*, a male writer wrote a voice for a subaltern woman (an inter-gender, interlingual translation) and asked a European woman director to translate it for stage and film (an intersemiotic translation). I was slightly anxious, but I considered the situation and was seduced by the beauty and strength of Makuwe's work, so I put other doubts aside. Between us, Stanley and myself that is, I think we managed to subvert and circumvent the inter-gender and intralingual issue of the female voice being written by a man.

Finding Temeraire takes place in a former mining village called Mashava. The play is a two-hander, consisting of a woman visiting an ex-lover for revenge. Primrose carries on long monologues about the past, before actually revealing her own identity as that of Temeraire's former lover and the mother of his son. Faced with his coldness and the indifference of the world, she has had a psychotic breakdown, murdering her baby soon after his birth. The play's construction works in a way which in part is indeed similar to Tokarczuk's 'constellation' in so far as the main character retells a number of short stories of their life in pre-independence Mashava. Without actually describing the settlement, she offers vignettes which give the reader (or the theatre-goer) a sense of the place. These vignettes include stories of the whites-only club they all visited despite not being white, a story of a prostitute calling herself Dolly Parton who was the reason a great fight broke out in the club, the bizarre colonial couple Baas and Madam Clipston (who had a large dog Madam Clipston got too fond of so that Baas Clipston shot it), and other episodes.

These stories evoke the sense of the precolonial settlement with roles assigned and with no possibility of any fluidity whatever of the kind that Said (to name but one) and Tokarczuk ask for. In the play the stories have the role of preparing both the viewer and Temeraire for the revelations to come. Temeraire does not recognise Primrose as his former lover in the first instance – some 20 or even 25 years have elapsed since they were lovers and she has spent that time in prison, plotting her revenge. Even though Temeraire is the reason for her action and the core of her being, his role in the play is that of a listener and a passive responder; he too is a shadow of his former self. The play, like *Flights*, opens with a description of loneliness which leads into a story. The arrival of the woman is an intrusion, an unwanted visit – on the surface – but in another way this is a deeply yearned-for interruption of the loneliness. Temeraire, who remains silent for most of the play, begins it this way:

> I am Temeraire, once the plumber of Mashava. It is like this. I am killing cockroaches when this woman comes to my house. At that time the afternoon sun is hot but not too hot. […] It is a long time since I spoke to someone who knows the people and the places I knew, so I just talk to her like I know her and I don't have to ask her who she is or where she came from. (Makuwe 2017, 1)

The stage direction after the first short introduction is 'a crumbling house', and the very first words uttered by Primrose relate to the settlement's state of decay – 'the Compound', she calls it, now infested by cockroaches:

> PRIMROSE
>
> When did cockroaches start coming to Mashava?
>
> TEMERAIRE
>
> Every year they keep coming. We have seen more this year than any other time.
>
> PRIMROSE
>
> There were no cockroaches in Mashava. Not in Westernlee. In the Compound one all the houses would be scrubbed and sprayed.
>
> (Makuwe 2017, 1)

In the initial scenes, we also learn that his garden has grass and no flowers, as flowers are harder to grow 'and need a lot of water', continuing the theme of abandonment and decay. We also learn that many houses are empty – in the Compound, which presumably means where the white people used to live. Primrose asks straight out: 'where are all the white people?' and Temeraire just says, 'They left.' But this is all the description Makuwe gives us about the actual physical place in which the dramas unfold: that the houses were cleaned and scrubbed under colonial times and that now they are infested and neglected. I will come back to the cockroach presence in the play, but for now let us just consider the character of Primrose and her long monologues both before she physically overwhelms Temeraire and afterwards. Her stated plan is revenge. Once she has tied him and gagged him, she appears to be preparing to hurt him further ('She circles him, like she wants to tear him apart'; Makuwe 2017, 11). She enjoys taunting him too: 'Tell me, Temeraire. Are you afraid to die? Are you afraid of death? Do you fear hell?' (p. 11), although she also appears to still be considering whether torture might be enough. ('Not so fast. Your type dies better in a slow cooker'; p. 11). And then: 'Temeraire, I am not here to kill you. I'm here to piss in your face' (p. 13).

Crucially, before any of her torture can take place, she demands that he talk to her – for it appears he never really talked to her in the past:

PRIMROSE

You don't want to talk.

She sharpens the knife.

PRIMROSE

Ooh, today you will talk. I swear, you will talk.
(Makuwe 2017, 14)

The story Primrose tells Temeraire (as well as the audience) is that of an almost classic subaltern woman not only not being listened to by anybody but also really not knowing how to *translate* any of her experiences or emotions into words. She describes how in the past, as a very young woman, she never learnt how to find pleasure in talking (never mind writing). This is reminiscent of (post)colonial melancholy, as Ranjana Khanna (2003) would say, and its 'metaphorisation', that is indeed the ability to describe emotions, being the negative ones, which will lead to violence (of which I have written extensively elsewhere, for example in Piotrowska 2017). The only *jouissance* Primrose knows is a simple bodily pleasure – which, when corrupted, turns into a full psychotic episode and physical violence. There is nowhere to go and when she is abandoned by all with her unwanted baby son, she first strangles him with a scarf she shows Temeraire and then drowns him in the white men's sewage pond.

Somehow through the journey of describing, for the first time perhaps, her emotions and her suffering, Primrose arrives at a point where she is able to move beyond her despair and her fury – and eventually forgive Temeraire. Despite Tokarczuk's mistrust of descriptions and naming, of emotions as much as places, the naming does work. When Primrose leads Temeraire to the sewage pond to look for their son buried there 25 years ago, clearly a metaphorical gesture of despair, she demands that he name him. Naming is crucial after all, for without naming, the experience is meaningless and does not last. Words do matter:

> Do you have a name for your son, Temeraire? […] Name him. Name him now so that we call him by name. (She waits. He says nothing.) When you call someone you call them by name. You can't just say, 'hey you, hey you,' as if you are one of those white people whose shit swallowed your son's dead body. There has to be a name, Temeraire. This is your son, not your garden boy. You are the father. Name him. (Makuwe 2017, 22)

Temeraire, who by now has totally lost the power of speech, fails to name their dead son, and the word he eventually enunciates is the one word which by now really matters to him: her name, 'Primrose'. In the epilogue, we learn that he found other words in the end, words of love, and that somehow, Primrose and Temeraire are together again.

'Found footage' in translating, adapting and betraying

In her review article 'The Politics of Translation' (2018), Marina Warner argues that translation has always been a political issue, in terms of decisions made but also, more simply, who translates whom and why. She reviews a number of contemporary volumes on translation, including Mark Polizzotti's *Sympathy for the Traitor: A Translation Manifesto* (2018) and Mireille Gansel's *Translation as Transhumance* (2017). In general terms, Warner points out that:

> Two fundamental quarrels run through these books: the first over claims about fidelity and felicity, the second over cultural appropriation and consequent monolingualism (the continued expansion of the Anglosphere). How to honour the character of the source of the language and its relation to cultural difference? Should a translator respond like an Aeolian harp, vibrating in harmony with the original text to transmit the original music, or should the translation read as if it were written in the new language? (Warner 2018, 22)

Certainly Croft's translation of *Bieguni* makes it very English, without losing the work's inherent curiosity, although a native speaker like myself might have some issues with its tone at times. Perhaps to object is irrelevant, for the gain is so much greater than any potential and perhaps questionable loss. I cannot comment on the translation of Kristeva's novel, as my French, whilst good, is not native at all, so I do not hear the dissonances in the same way, but it seems to be closer to the original. Inside that work, of course, there are Kristeva's translations from the Castilian Spanish of Teresa's writing. An adaptation is a different matter, although perhaps not entirely different: we are still looking at two semiotic systems that need translating. Umberto Eco's most basic point of the possibility of a translation at all is relevant here, for adaptation in Jakobson's terms is intersemiotic.

Robert Stam, in his classic work on adaptation, quotes the author Salman Rushdie to define his own position: 'an adaptation is [...] less a resuscitation of an originary word than a turn in an ongoing dialogical process. Intertextual dialogism, then, helps us transcend the aporias of "fidelity"' (Stam 2000, 64). Later in the volume, in his discussion of *Robinson Crusoe*, Stam celebrates 'hybridity, impurity, intermingling, the transformation that comes of new and unexpected combinations of human beings, ideas, politics, movies, songs', and concludes, 'artistic innovation [...] occurs on the transnational borders of cultures and communities and discourses', and 'it is only in the eyes of another medium [...] that a medium reveals itself fully and profoundly' (Stam 2000, 362, 364–5). It is beyond the scope of this chapter to review critiques of Stam's view and my case is very different – it was a collaboration with a Zimbabwean writer which in some ways was simple and respectful to the original. In other ways, particularly in the screen version, my work did take Makuwe's play in a slightly different direction, I hope without changing the spirit of his work.

My main innovation regarding the theatre production of *Finding Temeraire* was nothing out of the ordinary regarding the writer–director collaboration. Amongst other things, I lowered the ages of the main characters for reasons of my own – the actors Charmaine Mujeri and Eddi Sandifolo are my trusted collaborators and I had confidence they could pull off the difficult parts. I also thought it was possible to imagine the characters from 20 or 25 years ago as young rather than already middle-aged then – and in fact questioned the initial suggestions of their ages as written by Stanley Makuwe. My vision was that Primrose would have been a very young woman indeed, naive in her infatuation with Temeraire.

The key issue of the adaptation/translation of Stanley Makuwe's play was indeed the addition of another level of intertextuality to the piece – and that was through the use of black and white archive footage not necessarily directly linked to the proceedings, or rather linked thematically and conceptually but not in any way actually connected to the physical place of Mashava. This seems a very simple idea now, and almost obvious, but it was neither of these two things when I presented it as a plan to the film's editor, Anna Dobrowodzka. We then experimented with introducing split screens to the film, in order both to offer different perspectives on the narrative and also to translate the historicity of it onto the screen, at times alongside the live action of the drama between the two main characters. All of the footage we used would have been shot during colonial times in Rhodesia and in South Africa by those who were either supporting the oppressive regime or directly hired by representatives of it to obtain relevant footage. We felt that the introduction of the split screens, with the archive footage not directly linked to the place in which the action occurred, offered in fact *more* of a sense of place than any literal or faithful use of the actual footage could do – notwithstanding the fact that there was not any footage directly linked to Mashava. In addition, and very importantly, the colonial archive as 'found footage' in conjunction with the words uttered by Primrose was more successful at 'translating' her experience, which is only partially spoken about in the play, namely the experience of a young black woman whose only currency is her bodily beauty and affective labour. The concepts of intersectionality (Crenshaw 1989, 139)[2] come to mind here also, as within the hierarchy of the women in Mashava, and in many other colonial settlements, a woman like Primrose was really at the very bottom of the pile.

The final element of this discussion of translation is the notion of ethics and fidelity regarding using the archive as 'found footage' and also, more generally, the freedom a translator might have. Thomas Elsaesser in his essay 'The Ethics of Appropriation' (2015) reminds us:

> the origins of found footage films, as opposed to compilation films, are usually located within the Marcel Duchamp tradition of Dada and conceptual art, of Surrealism and the *objet trouvé*, the found object. The point of such a stranded object, left behind by the tide of time, is that it is made beautiful and special by the combination of a recent loss of practical use and its perishable or fragile materiality. (Elsaesser 2015, 32)

The situation here is both different and similar: different because the archive and the split screens have a direct role to play in the film, which is not to do with beauty but rather to do with truth and knowledge – and indeed the writing and describing of what life may have been like in the past. However, this appears to be only a part of the story: the characters of the play *Finding Temeraire* remember *the place* of Mashava as a good place. True, it is to do with them being young at the time, but there is also a certain ambivalent and ambiguous nostalgia which they both seem to evoke and which Makuwe has captured in his play. The nostalgia might indeed be for the rigid, predictable and fixed, as opposed to the independence which has brought with it cockroaches – a most bizarre image in Makuwe's play which resonates uncomfortably with known colonial insults towards the local population. Now, they stand for a dirty mess and lack of order – even though the order of the past was a denigrating and, in the end, a hated order. In our appropriating of the archive footage we also wanted to convey what was being missed – as it was not just the profound injustice and oppressiveness of the place, it was also parties and dances and fun, almost as a gesture of defiance on the one hand but also, painfully, a re-enactment of the systematic inequality, some of it perhaps again in the vein of Elsaesser:

> Appropriation, as the ambiguous name of a certain kind of love that raises issues of ownership, is perhaps most tersely expressed in the title of Eric Lott's study of how immigrant – mainly Jewish and Italian – entertainers from Europe appropriated African-American folk music, comedy routines and blackface minstrelsy: Lott called his book *Love and Theft: Blackface Minstrelsy and the American Working Class* (1993) and this is indeed the terrain of affective-emotional ambivalence, within which appropriation becomes so seductive, also in the cinema. (Elsaesser 2015, 32)

Finally, then, we can dismantle Tokarczuk's early despair over an inability to describe anything faithfully, or somehow, over one's lack of skill to be faithful to experience when one attempts to translate it. Polizzotti (2018) is adamant that it is good to abandon any idea of faithfulness to the 'original' or originating work: 'A good translation', he writes, 'offers not a reproduction of the work but an interpretation, a re-representation, just as the performance of a play or a sonata is a representation of the script or the score, one among many possible representations' (2018, 53).

Marina Warner reminds us further that 'many émigrés have performed acts of translation themselves, going into voluntary exile from the demands – the oppression – of the mother tongue' (Warner 2018, 23). Was this also Makuwe's decision? Perhaps the fact that his beautifully written work was written in the language of the colonisers has given him a sense of power, in a way not dissimilar to our use of the 'found' footage and split screens. The philosopher Jacques Derrida in *Monolingualism of the Other* (1998) observes the power of language and reflects on his own position in it as a stranger and a master at the same time. He also brings forth the notion of the importance of language as the carrier of the law. His own position is precisely that of a colonised subject and as such he states that:

> all culture is originarily colonial. [...] Mastery begins, as we know, through the power of naming, of imposing and legitimating appellations. [...] First and foremost, the monolingualism of the other would be that of sovereignty, that law originating from elsewhere, certainly, but also primarily the very language of the Law. [...] The monolingualism imposed by the other operates by relying upon that foundation, here, through a sovereignty whose essence is always colonial, which tends, repressively and irrepressibly, to reduce language to the One, that is to the hegemony of the homogeneous. (Derrida 1998, 39–40)

Derrida writes here as somebody whose supreme power of expression lies in the language which is in fact the language of the coloniser, as he was an Algerian child in Algeria going to a French school, and then higher edcation in France. There is no other language that he could in fact call his own any more, at the time of writing the words quoted or at any other time – French was not his mother tongue and his mother tongue was lost to him forever. His ability to write and name both his thoughts and ideas and also very much his emotions was his strength and our gift from him. As for the search for truth, the psychoanalyst Jacques Lacan, who was Derrida's friend and an intellectual sparring partner, maintained that we cannot help but lie in our various translations in the name of the search for truth, and that the harder the story, the better it is to tell it as fiction for 'truth has a structure of fiction' (Lacan 2006, 684).

Any adaptation is a translation from one semiotic system to another and indeed any creative work at all is a translation of kinds – of physical and bodily experience, of places we visit, people we love and histories we try to tell, looking for our place in the world.

It is the following thought that might be appropriate to conclude these reflections with: language might be inadequate to describe experience but it is the only thing we have at our disposal. It gives us an opportunity not only to record a sense of place, actual and metaphorical, but also, if we are very lucky, to create a tremendous enjoyment, *jouissance*, out of it – for those who write and for those who read.

Notes

1. Here 'using it up' might be better.
2. Kimberlé Williams Crenshaw, an African-American lawyer and thinker, in the late 1980s and 1990s famously pointed to the ineffectuality of Western (white) feminism and stressed different forms of discrimination converging often in a multi-fronted prejudice against women of colour in particular (Crenshaw 1989, 139). Prejudice is constituted by mutually reinforcing vectors of race, gender, class, ability and sexuality, and intersectionality has emerged as the primary theoretical tool designed to combat (feminist) hierarchy, hegemony and other forms of exclusivity and dominance.

References

Andrew, Dudley. 1984. 'Adaptation'. In *Concepts in Film Theory*, by Dudley Andrew, 96–106. New York: Oxford University Press.
Certeau, Michel de. 1984. *The Practice of Everyday Life*, translated by Steven Rendall. Berkeley: University of California Press.
Cohen, Keith. 1979. *Film and Fiction: The Dynamics of Exchange*. New Haven: Yale University Press.
Corrigan, Timothy. 1999. *Film and Literature: An Introduction and Reader*. Upper Saddle River, NJ: Prentice Hall.
Crenshaw, Kimberlé. 1989. 'Demarginalizing the Intersection of Race and Sex: A Black Feminist Critique of Antidiscrimination Doctrine, Feminist Theory and Antiracist Politics', *University of Chicago Legal Forum*: 139–67.
Derrida, Jacques. 1998. *Monolingualism of the Other; or The Prosthesis of Origin*, translated by Patrick Mensah. Stanford: Stanford University Press.
Eco, Umberto. 2001. *Experiences in Translation*, translated by Alastair McEwan. Buffalo: University of Toronto Press.
Elsaesser, Thomas. 2015. 'The Ethics of Appropriation: Found Footage between Archive and Internet'. Keynote address at the Recycled Cinema Symposium DOKU.ARTS.
Freestone, Robert and Edgar Liu, eds. 2016. *Place and Placelessness Revisited*. Abingdon, Oxon.: Routledge.
Gansel, Mireille. 2017. *Translation as Transhumance*, translated by Ros Schwartz. New York: Feminist Press.
Jakobson, Roman. 1971. 'On Linguistic Aspects of Translation'. In *Selected Writings, Volume 2: Word and Language*, by Roman Jakobson, 260–66. The Hague: Mouton.
Khanna, Ranjana. 2003. *Dark Continents: Psychoanalysis and Colonialism*. Durham, NC: Duke University Press.

Kristeva, Julia. 2014. *Teresa, My Love: An Imagined Life of the Saint of Avila*, translated by Lorna Scott Fox. New York: Columbia University Press.
Lacan, Jacques. 2006. *Écrits*, translated by Bruce Fink. New York: W.W. Norton.
Makuwe, Stanley. 2017. *Finding Temeraire*. Unpublished script.
Piotrowska, Agnieszka. 2017. *Black and White: Cinema, Politics and the Arts in Zimbabwe*. London: Routledge.
Piotrowska, Agnieszka. 2019. *The Nasty Woman and the Neo Femme Fatale in Contemporary Cinema*. London: Routledge.
Polizzotti, Mark. 2018. *Sympathy for the Traitor: A Translation Manifesto*. Cambridge, MA: MIT Press.
Said, Edward W. 1978. *Orientalism*. New York: Vintage Books.
Spivak, Gayatri Chakravorty. 1988. 'Can the Subaltern Speak?'. In *Marxism and the Interpretation of Culture*, edited by Cary Nelson and Lawrence Grossberg, 271–313. London: Macmillan.
Stam, Robert. 2000. 'Beyond Fidelity: The Dialogics of Adaptation.' In *Film Adaptation*, edited by James Naremore, 54–76. London: Athlone Press.
Todd, Jane Marie. 1990. *Autobiographics in Freud and Derrida*. New York: Garland Publishing.
Tokarczuk, Olga. 2018. *Flights*, translated by Jennifer Croft. London: Fitzcarraldo Editions. Originally published in Polish in 2007.
Warner, Marina. 2018. 'The Politics of Translation', *London Review of Books*, 11 October. Accessed 3 May 2020. www.lrb.co.uk/the-paper/v40/n19/marina-warner/the-politics-of-translation.
Zupančič, Alenka. 2017. *What is Sex?* Cambridge, MA: MIT Press.

11
The *EU migrant*: Britain's sense of place in English newspaper journalism

Paul Rowinski

Britain's sense of place has come to be understood for many through its Euroscepticism, pervasive in English society and articulated and constructed further by its press. This is a reaffirmation of self through differentiation from Europe – the Other. This post-war trajectory has now reached its zenith, with immigration and the presentation and coarsening of media discourse, presenting EU migrants in a pejorative light. This hostility by some journalists and politicians alike was used to justify what became a popular refrain: 'We Want our Country Back'. Britain has left the EU. This will have a bearing on whether England continues to see its sense of place as articulated through Euroscepticism – or, in fact, rows back and reappraises its role outside of the EU – and indeed how it now views its fellow Europeans.

Linking to Molloy's analysis of the ethnic and cultural practices in the photography studios in her area of London (Chapter 12 of this volume), this chapter explores the textual discourse in the media about the *EU migrant* which has emerged from London-based mainstream national newspapers (I use italics to indicate my focus on the phrases used within the discourse). This discursive construction of England defines Englishness against its Other: Europe. This is not new: Eurosceptic English discourses in the mainstream media are decades old. But their intensity and amplification in our post-truth digital age are not (Curtis 2016; Solon 2018).

In 2016 'post-truth' became the Word of the Year. The Oxford Dictionaries website said:

> The concept of post-truth has been in existence for the past decade, but Oxford dictionaries have seen a spike in frequency this year, in the context of the EU referendum in the United Kingdom and the presidential election in the United States. It has also become associated with a particular noun, in the phrase *post-truth politics*. (Oxford Dictionaries 2016)

Oxford Dictionaries define 'post-truth' as: 'relating to or denoting circumstances in which objective facts are less influential in shaping public opinion than appeals to emotion and personal belief'. I argue that the mainstream media are not just giving a platform for post-truth politicians, but constructing a post-truth rhetoric of their own. This paper shows how this is often achieved by the construction of discourse blaming *EU migrants* to justify the need to leave the EU. At present this is a constructed sense of place in relation to the Other: Europe.

I will demonstrate that there was an absence of EU migrant voices before the referendum and that some British national newspapers are utilising post-truth language, as well as providing a platform for politicians to do so. If the language of post-truth was indeed manifest in copy produced by UK national newspapers ahead of the vote, it could have had implications for corroboration and veracity at a vital moment in national history. There are also the wider implications of post-truth emotive rhetoric for the quality of journalism and its ability to hold politicians to account.

Britishness and the European Other

Gifford (2016) has argued that the distinction between anti- and pro-European arguments is not sufficient for understanding Eurosceptic Britain. Euroscepticism has become fundamental to constituting Britain and Britishness in the post-imperial context, *despite* EU membership. Anderson and Weymouth (1999) debate Euroscepticism in Britain and the perception of continental Europe as an external Other, and refer to its manifestation in the British press and a deliberate exaggeration of the principles, beliefs and intentions of the EU. Morgan (1995) evidenced a Eurosceptic inflection often added by London-based editors for the public, when they thought it necessary. Garton Ash (2005, 31, 271) evidences how three out of every four UK national newspaper readers 'pick up a daily dose of Euroscepticism'. Mainstream media are now competing with other voices in a crowded online marketplace (Kueng 2017).

This chapter seeks to establish whether the run-up to the EU referendum also saw a more emotive, post-truth rhetoric beyond Eurosceptic persuasion and evidence-based argumentation in the British press. It looks for any patterns to *EU migrant* post-truth discourse reflected in the language used and asks what the *EU migrant* has come to mean. Finally it explores how this has affected our sense of place (Rowinski 2016, 2017).

Previous work on this topic by Calcutt (2016) and A. C. Grayling (Coughlan 2017) argues that postmodernism and relativism are at the roots of post-truth. As part of that relativism, journalists followed academics in rejecting objectivity in the mid-1990s (Calcutt 2016; Gaber 2011). At that time, Baudrillard suggested: 'we live in a world where there is more and more information, and less and less meaning' (1994, 79). There is what Curtis (2016) calls the 'filter bubble' of contemporary mediated digital content and its influence on forming and entrenching opinion (Krasodomski-Jones 2016). As Laybats and Tredinnick argue: 'The filter bubble of social media is perhaps only a mirror of the filter bubble that individuals have always created for themselves by choosing to prioritise relationships and to consume information content that reinforces their existing values, opinions and beliefs' (2016, 4).

The difference is perhaps the scale, amplified very quickly, so 'where information proliferates freely, inevitably, so also do untruths' (Laybats and Tredinnick 2016, 4). A. C. Grayling (Coughlan 2017) concurs, arguing that circumstances have resulted in a coupling of the 2008 economic crash and the anger and disaffection people feel. Social media channel that fury, with what he calls the 'I-bite', where strong opinion overshadows evidence, eclipsing the sound bite.

Epistemic competition is as much about choosing which facts to use as about 'which claims can be considered true and false, and these choices have important consequences' (Sismondo 2017). Objective facts may be less influential, so which facts are actually included in a story is of even greater salience. Post-truth may mean that journalists reaffirm national, Eurosceptic perspectives and *certain* national truths, while sidelining others in what Nietzsche described as 'active forgetting' (Heer and Wodak 2008, 4), constructing a sanitised narrative, reaffirming how the reader understands Britain and its relationship with the EU. Lewis (2016, 2) also noted that the US national context which saw Trump victorious was 'characterized by competing sets of facts'.

In Britain public concerns were fed by the post-2008 economic downturn (Coughlan 2017) together with a preoccupation with immigration (Springford 2013; Taggart and Szczerbiak 2004; Gifford 2016; Garton Ash 2005; Rowinski 2017). Diamanti and Bordignon (2005) found that immigration was the argument most utilised by Eurosceptic parties, and that there was a correlation between fear of immigrants and falling support for EU integration. They also found a rise in xenophobia, alongside increasing distrust of institutions. Ipsos MORI conducted a poll in 2015 asking what percentage of the population people thought were immigrants. In the UK people thought 24 per cent. It is 13 per cent. Immigration was the key focus in UK newspaper coverage just before the British referendum (Deacon *et al.* 2016).

Assessing the prevalence of post-truth rhetoric in mainstream journalism

'Post-truth' has become associated with a particular noun in the phrase 'post-truth politics' and with the rise of Eurosceptic populist politicians tapping in to the British public psyche on an emotional level.

To look at where the discourses on the EU migrant occur, I selected the following UK national newspapers: *The Sun*, the *Daily Mail* and the *Daily Telegraph* on the centre-right (arguing for Leave) and the *Daily Mirror* and *The Guardian* on the centre-left (arguing for Remain). Deacon *et al.* (2016) analysed all the English daily national newspaper titles. They found, in aggregate terms, 60 to 40 in favour of Leave, ahead of the UK's Brexit vote. By circulation, it rises to 80 to 20 for Leave. This vindicates the focus on the largest-circulation newspapers in the study: the largest-selling Murdoch-owned tabloid (*The Sun*); its direct centre-left rival (the *Daily Mirror*); the second largest-selling paper, dominating the middle market (the *Daily Mail*); the largest-selling broadsheet (the *Daily Telegraph*); and the main centre-left broadsheet (*The Guardian*). The term *EU migrant* was searched for in these newspapers in LexisNexis. The search was restricted to the main London editions only (discounting Scottish and Irish editions) because these were aimed at the English Eurosceptic audience, and to the main news (not business), to note if there was persuasion or indeed prejudice over the EU surfacing in what were supposed to be fact-based articles (Gifford 2016; Chalaby 1996). Anonymous editorials, as opposed to named columnists, were selected, to properly hear the collective voice of the newspaper, especially on the eve of the referendum, when the positioning on Brexit came to the fore. The dates chosen were Wednesday, 1 June 2016, and Friday, 3 June 2016, focusing on the middle and end of the working week.

The final date selected was 22 June 2016, on the eve of the referendum, when most newspapers included their final editorials, seeking to persuade readers to vote a certain way, although some did this slightly earlier.

The newspapers themselves could contribute to the 'circumstances in which objective facts are less influential in shaping public opinion than appeals to emotion and personal belief' (Oxford Dictionaries 2016, definition of 'post-truth') by possibly framing (Entman 1993, 2010) and triggering an emotional response with a paucity of supporting facts. For instance, migration and economy-related stories often reflect and sometimes amplify Euroscepticism (Springford 2013; Gifford 2016; Rowinski 2017). Mautner's (2008, 42) newspaper discourse methodology, was employed, as were argumentation theory (Reisigl and Wodak 2001) and conceptual metaphor theory (Lakoff and Johnson 1980; Musolff 2004). In linguistic analysis, the focus included lexis, intensification and mitigation, referential strategies and modality (Mautner 2008). Reisigl and Wodak (2001), in relation to discourse-historical analysis, refer to the 'intensification and mitigation' of discriminatory utterances. Mautner (2008) refers to the heightening of the sense of urgency and crisis, by the use of adjectives with negative connotations, as in '*soaring* violence' and '*rampant* immigration'. Mautner (2008) refers to 'ideologically-loaded keywords' surfacing in discourse. These can be 'banner words', signifying importance, or conversely 'stigma words', alerting readers to negativity. Patterns in the choice of words will be sought, especially those with a distinctive evaluative meaning. The discourse-historical approach incorporated into this chapter (Wodak 2001, 2004) tries to transcend the purely linguistic dimension of discourse, to systematically include the historical, political, sociological and psychological dimensions in the analysis and interpretation of a discursive event. In this sense the discourse-historical approach is context-dependent.

Reisigl and Wodak (2001) refer to 'topoi', in which argumentative strategies are more fully explored. Topoi can be described as parts of argumentation which belong to obligatory, either explicit or inferable premises. They are content-related warrants or conclusion rules, connecting the argument with the conclusion and justifying the transition from the former to the latter (Kienpointner 1992, 194). Similarly, if metaphors lead to conclusions that bind politicians and the people they are trying to influence, they must function like warrants in an argument. They must appear to give a valid justification for using particular premises in order to arrive at certain conclusions. Analysis of conceptualising metaphors was also included. Lakoff and Johnson (1980, 159) argue that 'metaphors play a central role in the construction of social and political reality'. This can, in certain instances, allow words from one domain to be used in another (Lakoff 1996, 63). Musolff (2004, 33–4) argues that unconscious conceptual frameworks are a form of argumentation-by-metaphor.

The notion of persuasive news (Rowinski 2016, 2017) is relevant. Britain played a pioneering role in developing fact-centred discourse (Chalaby 1996). Yet it can still be manipulative and comment-laden. I found British news on the EU littered with argumentation/metaphor. An attempt will be made to establish when there is a coarsening of UK newspaper discourse, *beyond* argumentation/metaphors, entering the realms of post-truth Eurosceptic emotive rhetoric, embedded in news and not just editorials.

Reisigl and Wodak (2001) note that persuasion can be double-edged. While both *überzeugen* and *überreden* (Kopperschmidt 1989, 116–21) can be translated as 'to persuade', *überzeugen* can also be translated as 'to convince'. Conversely, *überreden* denotes a particular, restricted consent, under conditions of suspended rationality. Here, forms of non-argumentative compulsion, such as emotionalisation, can compel approval by repressing rational and logical judgement and conclusion. This chimes with post-truth, and indeed the use of unmodalised declaratives (Mautner 2008), expressing the strongest form of affinity and commitment, with the speaker fully supporting the inherent truth in the assertion – even if it may be a lie and/or devoid of corroborating, supporting facts. Such occurrences will be deemed post-truth.

Reisigl and Wodak (2001, 265) argue that democratic legitimacy results from discourse 'performed under the condition of largely egalitarian reciprocity and located within the different public spheres of fields of political action, of a free, open and rational formation of public opinion about political problems and questions of shared interest'. In the case of post-truth Euroscepticism, that rational formation of opinion is possibly shrouded by the appeal to emotion.

The *EU migrant* in the national dailies

Deacon *et al.* (2016) catalogued how immigration was a key issue in the run-up to the vote, reflected in newspaper analysis for 1 June 2016. My LexisNexis *EU migrant* word search for 1 June 2016 returned three *Daily Mail* news stories with the term, one news story in the *Daily Telegraph* and five in *The Guardian*. The term did not surface in *The Sun* or the *Daily Mirror*.

Initial analysis of the *Daily Mail*'s coverage found collocations presenting the term *EU migrant* in specific contexts, after key Brexiteer cabinet members, Priti Patel, Boris Johnson and Michael Gove, revealed plans for an Australian-style immigration points system after Brexit. Groves (2016a) clarifies this for *Daily Mail* readers, in a piece headlined 'How the Tougher Rules Could Work'. In terms of the current points system for other immigrants, 'none of these rules can be applied to *EU migrants*' is then intensified to 'three quarters of *EU migrants* would fail to qualify if the points system was applied to them', and then intensified further still: 'Researchers said up to 94 per cent of *EU workers* currently employed in retail, hotels and restaurants would fail to meet existing entry requirements' (Groves 2016a). Similarly, Groves (2016b) writes in another 1 June piece: 'At present, Britain is powerless to stop *EU migrants* travelling here to work.' In the third *Daily Mail* piece on 1 June, Doyle (2016) writes: 'record numbers of *migrants* coming *from the EU*'; later in the piece, this is intensified to 'record number of jobless EU migrants' and 'widespread fears about the open door to *EU migrants*'. The reader is continuously reminded of the implications of continuing with the Freedom of Movement tenet of EU membership, the problem amplified further by the record numbers of *jobless migrants* coming.

While drawing on facts and some rational presentation of information, there is nevertheless an epistemic selection at work here. The counter-narrative, explaining how *EU migrants* are often highly skilled with few ever claiming benefits and many quickly finding work, is not presented (Springford 2013; Wadsworth *et al.* 2016; Rowinski 2017). Instead the negatively evaluative narrative of EU migrants cast as benefit tourists, acting as a drain on the state coffers, is drawn on.

The narrative that *EU migrants* in the UK are *benefit tourists* is misplaced (Wadsworth *et al.* 2016). David Cameron, ahead of the referendum, failed to renegotiate EU free movement rules on benefits. In terms of EU immigrant 'benefit tourism', 0.2 per cent claim unemployment benefit but have never worked in the UK; and 0.4 per cent are on unemployment benefit six months after arriving in the UK, rising to 0.8 per cent after a year (Springford 2013). The western Europeans and subsequent 2004 eastern European influx are better educated than the average Briton. More have finished secondary education and university degrees (Springford 2013; Sumption and Somerville 2010; Wadsworth *et al.* 2016). Springford's research (2013) shows that EU immigrants are net *contributors* to the treasury. The post-2004 employment rate is higher than that of British nationals, with 88 per cent in work, as opposed to 77 per cent for UK citizens.

It is apparent that collocations are not always obvious and longer phrases are needed to tease out meaning. Furthermore, the exact term *EU migrant* will not reveal all collocations that could prove pertinent to the focus here (e.g. *migrants from the EU, EU workers*). Furthermore, when it comes to establishing whether there is suspension of rational argument, replaced by a compulsion, drawing on emotion (post-truth), there is a requirement for wider meaning-making structures (Mautner 2008) embedded within the text. The *Daily Mail* (Doyle 2016) claimed in the headline: 'Migration Factor Boosts Brexit'. In this piece there was mention of *EU migrants*. However, it was in the wider reference to (EU) immigration that post-truth reared its head. The pattern in the discourse was reinforced by the introductory sentence: '*Public concern* about immigration has given a huge boost to the campaign to leave the EU, it emerged last night', and then again lower down: 'They [the opinion polls] showed huge swings to Leave in recent days as *immigration dominated the news*', and again later, in reference to the polls 'in which *immigration was the dominant issue*' (emphasis mine in newspaper quotations here and throughout).

Despite the facts relating to the opinion polls and the Australian-style immigration system proposed that day, the newspaper constructed unmodalised declaratives (Mautner 2008), stating the aforementioned as facts – without supporting evidence. The claim 'Migration Factor Boosts Brexit' is unsubstantiated. The emotive stigma words 'immigration'/'migration' (Mautner 2008) were repeated eight times in the Doyle article (2016), creating an inherent truth without factual corroboration. Here we enter the realms of compulsion/*überreden* (Reisigl and Wodak 2001) and post-truth rhetoric. The voice of the newspaper here is distinct from the politicians quoted. As Allen (2016) established, there is a tendency for UK journalists themselves to play the role of framing problems in the migration debate, rather than simply reporting on the words of others, such as politicians.

The notion is continuously presented that EU migration is having a direct impact on public services, including schools and hospitals, and on wages – without supporting evidence: a *post hoc, ergo propter hoc* fallacy (Reisigl and Wodak 2001). This is a case of mixing up a temporally chronological relationship with a causally consequential one. Reisigl and Wodak (2001, 73) argue: 'One can find an example of such a fallacious reasoning in the populist and very often racist or ethnicist argumentation that the increase in unemployment rates within a specific nation-state is the consequence of the growing number of immigrants.'

There is direct reference to *EU migrants* in this example from Doyle (2016): 'They [statistics showing record numbers of EU migrants entering the UK] *sparked widespread fears* about the open door to *EU migrants* and the impact on public services and wages in the UK.' Evidence supporting widespread fears and the impact is not offered, but this rapport with readers (Mautner 2008) reaffirms what they may *feel* is happening: post-truth. The ground is set by the use of a topos of and direct reference to fear (Reisigl and Wodak 2001), preceding the reference to public services. The topos is arguing: if you are worried about EU immigration, it is best to vote for Brexit.

Then we have the *Daily Mail* again in a piece headlined 'Immigration Revolution' (Groves 2016b: 'Migrants could settle here [under the Australian-style points system] only if they have skills needed by the economy. It would mean a ban on *jobless arrivals* from the EU.' As noted earlier, looking only for the specific term *EU migrant* is not to consider other related terms, which may be, say, more negatively evaluative or even ideologically loaded (Mautner 2008). The term *jobless arrival* is just such a term, offering up to the reader a series of presuppositions. This epistemic selection (Sismondo 2017) ignores the fact that such migrants do not remain *jobless* for very long (Springford 2013; Rowinski 2017; Wadsworth *et al.* 2016). These *jobless arrivals* conjure emotions and compel (Reisigl and Wodak 2001) and reaffirm readers in the way they feel – without supporting evidence: post-truth rhetoric. A rational discussion, presenting the counterarguments and indeed the evidence that *EU migrants* do not remain jobless and so are not a particular drain on the state, as being suggested, is not presented. Following media logic, the *Daily Mail* paraphrases a politician on the same page, reinforcing the message they wish to convey. From an ethnographic perspective (Rowinski 2016, 2017), journalists often get politicians to articulate the position the newspaper espouses, selecting quotes and politicians accordingly, as here. Embedded in the Groves piece (2016b) we find: 'In other developments in the Brexit debate: Former Treasury minister, Andrea Leadsom warns in the *Daily Mail* that George Osborne's national living wage is a "huge draw" for migrants that is fuelling "uncontrolled immigration" from within the EU.'

Mention of the term *EU migrant* also surfaces in the *Daily Telegraph* in a news story headlined 'Boris: Learn English if you want to move to UK' (Dominiczak and Swinford 2016). Although this time the sentiment is attributed to Gove and Johnson in heralding their points-based immigration proposal, and not presented as the voice of the newspaper, the *Daily Telegraph* nevertheless selected and framed their piece with an *argumentum ad verecundiam* (Reisigl and Wodak 2001, 72), an appeal to authority, to justify its positioning: 'Mr Johnson and Mr Gove warn that the scale of immigration is putting a "particular *strain*" on public services and that "class sizes will rise and waiting lists will lengthen" if Britain does not leave.' There is no evidence to support this emotive rhetoric. Yet it is presented categorically, albeit only including an unmodalised declarative at the start (Mautner 2008). Although the focus of this paper is the post-truth emotive rhetoric of newspapers rather than of politicians, newspapers do choose when to harness and utilise such political rhetoric for their own ends.

The term *EU migrant* did not surface again in *The Sun* or the *Daily Mirror* on 3 June. The term was prevalent in two *Daily Mail* news pieces, four in *The Guardian* and, again, only one in the *Daily Telegraph*. Although *The Sun* did not use the term, there was a piece built around quotes from the former Tory defence secretary Liam Fox. Fox referred to how if Britain remained in the EU it meant 'uncontrolled immigration'. He utilised a *post hoc, ergo propter hoc* fallacy in a piece in *The Sun* headlined: 'Fox: Vote Out to Get a House' (Hawkes 2016a), which served *The Sun*'s purpose and the politician's: Leave. Fox is quoted as saying: 'If we remain in the EU, if we have uncontrolled immigration, you will find it harder to get a home of your own. You will find it harder to see a GP, harder to get a school place, and you will see green spaces disappear.' This compels the reader to reach certain conclusions, devoid of substantiating facts – but ones they may feel or want to be true, hence post-truth, albeit articulated by the politician and not by the actual newspaper.

What has to be considered is that the term *EU migrant* can be substituted with more negatively evaluative terms, seeing an intensification in the discourse. It will be seen subsequently how the referential strategies used by newspapers (Mautner 2008) can move from relatively neutral terms, such as *EU migrant*, *EU national*, *EU citizen*, *EU student* or *EU worker*, to more emotive terms: *EU killers*, *EU convicts/criminals*, *EU rapists*.

The headline in the piece 'Poll Blunders Could Let EU Nationals Vote' (Slack and Stevens 2016), ahead of the EU referendum, is self-explanatory. The article refers to EU citizens and EU nationals, but it uses a quote from the Vote Leave chief executive, Matthew Elliott, to conjure a negative evaluation: 'There should be an urgent inquiry ... to discover who is responsible for illegally giving *EU migrants* the vote and undermining the foundation of our democratic process.'

In the *Daily Mail*, the focus under the headline 'Dave Learns What Voters Really Think on Migration' is on the then prime minister, David

Cameron, being quizzed on TV (Slack and Groves 2016). In the first part of a construction of reality that helps to create post-truth Eurosceptic emotive rhetoric, the second line of the article reads: 'In a bruising encounter, the Prime Minister was told that Britain's public services were sinking as a result of the never-ending stream of *EU migrants*.' Alison Hyde-Chadwick asked him: 'I think we're struggling. I think we're sinking. How do we deal with the increased demands on our public services given the never-ending, it feels *stream* of people arriving from Europe?' This is not to decry how Hyde-Chadwick feels (Kaltwasser 2014, 470). It is nevertheless unsubstantiated, post-truth emotive rhetoric, drawing a conclusion, without any rational argument in support. An interpretation would be that this has been fed by misinformation over decades (Gifford 2016; Garton Ash 2005; Rowinski 2017). Much as newspapers encourage politicians to concur with their agendas (and vice versa), so newspapers similarly know when to utilise a member of the public to construct a rapport with the readership (Mautner 2008), reflecting how the audience *feel*. The use of the analogical metaphor (Musolff 2004) conjured by the word *stream* in this context is to reinforce a negative evaluation of *EU migrants*; it conjures further, albeit in mitigated form (a stream not a river), Enoch Powell's infamous River of Blood speech, regarding the threats of immigration. Whether the member of the public was conscious of this is debatable. It is assumed that the *Daily Mail* was, in its usage of this banner word (Mautner 2008).

We then see an intensification in the *Daily Mail*'s headline 'A Dumping Ground for the EU's Criminals' (headline in the anonymous editorial), coupled with a news story headlined 'EU Killers and Rapists We've Failed to Deport' (Drury and Slack 2016a, 3 June). Around the issue of EU criminals held in the UK, we see clear evidence of persuasive news full of argumentation and metaphor, in the thrust to encourage people to consider voting Leave. The *Daily Mail*'s news story starts: 'Thousands of *violent thugs from the EU* are walking Britain's streets and clogging up our jails because the Government has failed to send them home.' This is to create an evaluative picture from the outset, denigrating and vilifying specific groups, linking them explicitly to their EU status. This simultaneously creates a topos of fear: they are a threat to the country – so if we leave the EU they will no longer be able to be. There is a process of intensification (Mautner 2008) reaffirming the danger of EU nationals in the second paragraph: 'The inquiry by MPs found the top three foreign nationalities inside our packed prisons are all now from inside the EU.' The intensification continues apace in the third paragraph: 'They include rapists, robbers, paedophiles and drug dealers.' The article then claims: 'More of those now living in the community after finishing their sentences, have successfully resisted deportation by using human rights legislation.' This remains unsubstantiated, though it is hoped the Home Affairs Committee report, which is the basis for the piece, does offer confirmation.

Both in this piece and the accompanying editorial headlined 'A Dumping Ground for the EU's Criminals', the failure to deport criminals is 'so dire that it casts doubt on the point of the UK remaining a member of the EU', and then in the editorial we find: 'No wonder the committee warns that the persistent failure to send these inmates back is "undermining confidence" in the UK's EU membership.' There is no clear attribution to the committee report. For that we have to go to the *Daily Telegraph*'s piece (Riley-Smith 2016) on this subject, where the committee is quoted directly: 'The clear inefficiencies demonstrated by this process will lead the public to question the point of the UK remaining a member of the EU.' Again the topos of fear (Reisigl and Wodak 2001) is extended to embrace this wider point, reinforced by the constructed rapport with the reader (Mautner 2008) reaffirming how the reader may *feel* about these issues, but without evidence to support it. It could be argued that the only reason this compulsion/*überreden* does not evidence post-truth emotive rhetoric at work in the pieces is because of the attribution of some 'facts' to the committee.

There were instances when news discourse was framed in such a way as to support populist political discourse, with the voice of the publication clearly heard. This was apparent with the pejorative use of *elite*. The *Daily Mail* (Stevens 2016) headlined with 'Now It's the EU Luvvies Who Are Telling Us What to Think'. *Luvvy* is a derogatory term for actors who are particularly effusive or affected. What should be noted is the prefix: *EU*. Some 140 of Europe's leading figures from the arts, science and sport had urged voters not to back Brexit. The article states: 'Organisers of the letter, which appeared in the Times Literary Supplement, claimed it was not designed to lecture British voters.' An interpretation could be that here we are not dealing with a phrase synonymous with *EU migrant*. Although *EU luvvies* is pejorative, it is not in the same caustic territory as *EU killers and rapists*.

The importance of context and not just the initial collocation is again apparent in a closer examination of the solitary instance in which the *Daily Telegraph* (Huggler 2016) mentioned the term *EU migrant*. This actually concerned the *EU's migrant* deal with Turkey, with the article focusing on that country's relationship with Germany and no mention of the UK at all. Again, one of the four articles on 3 June, when the term

EU migrant appeared in *The Guardian* (Smith and Kingsley 2016), can similarly be discounted, with the article focusing on the '*EU migrant* deal' between Greece and Turkey. In the remaining three *Guardian* news pieces (Asthana and Mason 2016a, 2016b; Mason 2016), the term *EU migrant* was attributed to Vote Leave and in all cases regarding the claiming of unemployment benefits.

The eve of the referendum and the intensification of post-truth

There was a further intensification of the negatively evaluative load of *EU migrant* just ahead of the vote: *The Sun* said, 'An estimated 152,000 *EU migrants* of school age came to Britain between 2000 and 2014' (Hawkes 2016b). Continuing this theme in the discourse under the headline 'Schools Could Face an Extra 570,000 Pupils from the EU', the *Daily Mail* (Slack and Martin 2016) said: 'The number of *EU migrants* applying for UK citizenship rocketed by 30 per cent', and the *Mail* (Drury and Slack 2016b) also referred to 'the publication of a report claiming that unskilled *EU migrants* cost each British family more than £200 a year'. Epistemic selection was evident here. The report was authored by the Economists for Brexit group. The *Daily Mail* (2016c) wrote in a piece on 22 June, headlined 'Undecided? Read this Essential Primer': 'More than three million *EU migrants* live in the UK, double the number in 2004.' And although mitigated somewhat, the negative evaluation also comes from the *Daily Mirror*, in its editorial on 22 June, which started: 'Tomorrow you have the chance to change the course of our country. How you vote will decide your future and that of your children, grandchildren and generations to come.' Lower down we find: 'After much consideration, in our view it is better for the people of this country if we stay in the EU.' In contemplating Leave, it said: 'We would be lumbered with the worst of all worlds, *having to accept EU migrants* but with no say at the top table.' As Buckledee (2018) argued, one of the key problems with the language of Remainers was a lack of unequivocal support, often qualifying it at the outset, as the *Daily Mirror* does here.

On the eve of the referendum, the *Daily Mail* flagged up its editorial on the front page, continuing inside. The unequivocal headline on 22 June read: 'If You Believe in Britain Vote Leave.' From the outset, the *Daily Mail* prepares to convince. The writer presents 'the most striking fact', that the Remainers 'have *failed* to articulate a single positive reason for staying in the EU'. This is Reisigl and Wodak's (2001, 70) notion of *überreden*. There is no attempt to justify, or indeed offer the reader an alternative reality. Initially the article focuses on economics, but soon the core focus becomes immigration (Deacon *et al.* 2016) and a topos of threat to the national interest, posed by immigration:

> We needn't look far for the explanation. For not only is the euro *destroying* livelihoods, but the madness that *is* the free movement of peoples *has* brought waves of migrants sweeping across Europe, *depressing* wages, *putting immense strain* on housing and public services, *undermining* our security against criminals and terrorists – and *making* communities fear for their traditional ways of life. (*Daily Mail*, 22 June 2016)

The persuasive force of the piece is heightened by harnessing a path-movement-journey metaphor (Musolff 2004, 60) and the use of *common sense* to help the public fully conceptualise the threat posed by '*waves* of migrants *sweeping* across Europe' akin to the *stream* of people that surfaced earlier. The section finishes with flag-waving banal nationalism (Billig 1995) for the *indigenous*, fearful for their 'traditional ways of life'. The emotive rhetoric comes to the fore, with an *argumentum ad populum*, popular fallacy, appealing to the emotions of the readers, with no substantiation offered for the 'destroying livelihoods', 'depressing wages' or 'undermining our security' caused by *EU migrants*. These are presented as unmodalised declaratives. Here post-truth rhetoric is at work, coupled with a *post hoc, ergo propter hoc* fallacy (Reisigl and Wodak 2001), as earlier.

The editorial attacks the then prime minister, David Cameron, over his 'second deception on migration – so obviously untrue that he even seems increasingly embarrassed to repeat it. This is his claim that the frankly pathetic "reforms" he secured during his humiliating tour of European capitals will have any impact on numbers.' This evaluative section is, however, utilised to attack 'Brussels bureaucracy': it is '*incapable* of meaningful reform' and it '*refuses* to listen to the British public's concerns' (this is articulated through an unmodalised declarative). There is no substantiation offered for the aforementioned EU positions. Post-truth emotive rhetoric is again prevalent. The editorial intensifies (Heer and Wodak 2008). We are again reminded of what was written at the outset. The writer presents 'the most striking fact', namely that the Remainers 'have *failed* to articulate a single positive reason for staying in the EU'. Reisigl and Wodak's (2001, 70) *überreden* resurfaces with an emotive post-truth appeal, clouding over the tenuousness of the 'facts' presented, and then again: 'No, if the Remainers have been unable to make a positive popular case for our membership, this is because the task *is* virtually impossible.' The lack of a 'single positive reason for staying in the EU' at the start is untrue and a further example of post-truth rhetoric. There is a relentless attempt by the *Daily Mail* to create fear around immigration. EU migrants to the UK tend to be young and skilled and with the highest employment rates of any EU country, paying in £22bn in British tax between 2001 and 2011 (Springford 2013). Britons in that period took out £624bn in benefits.

The *Daily Telegraph*'s editorial (2016, 20 June), headlined 'Vote Leave to Benefit from a World of Opportunity', employs a topos of history, referring back to its 1973 editorial, when Britain joined the EEC – but does not utilise EU migration to score any points. *The Sun*, in its 22 June editorial, 'Look Into His Eyes: Beleave in Britain', takes issue with Cameron's claim that he could reform the EU, making explicit to readers that it will 'NEVER reform'. Here we have *überreden*, imposing *The Sun*'s position on the reader while not offering another means of comprehending events: post-truth. In an unmodalised declarative, evaluative in tone, *The Sun* states at the outset that Cameron knew he could '*never* control immigration while in the EU. Yet he shamefully continued promising voters he could. Meanwhile mobs of illegal migrants force themselves aboard UK-bound lorries.' *Migrant* is used generically in this instance.

The *Daily Mirror*'s 22 June editorial, which starts, 'For the sake of our great nation's future', avoids argumentation but declares to readers that if we want to carry on trading with the EU, we will 'almost certainly have to accept freedom of movement', citing non-EU Norway and Switzerland as examples. The *Daily Mail* utilised argumentation to convince and persuade readers, often without substantiation. Instead the *Daily Mirror* counters such attempts: 'we are kidding ourselves' in thinking the UK could get preferential terms, instead 'being lumbered with the worst of all worlds, having to accept *EU migrants* but with no say at the top table', presenting the facts (Ashworth-Hayes 2016; BBC News 2016).

'*The Guardian* view on the EU referendum: keep connected and inclusive, not angry and isolated' (20 June 2016) is a direct challenge to the UK Eurosceptic press. The editorial describes the focus on immigration as often xenophobic, admits the EU's shortcomings and challenges the inward-looking approach of the Leave campaign. The piece challenges its readership in a way that sets up a binary between two concepts, forcing the reader, it could be argued, to accept how they *feel* about the former rather than the latter, countering the rapport (Mautner 2008) of the *Mail* and *Telegraph* with its own: 'Are we one member in a family of nations, or a country that prefers to keep itself to itself and bolt the door?' Yet there is room provided for the reader to rationally formulate a position, weighing the two up. The editorial picks up on how immigration became the central issue and the core conduit for Euroscepticism (Gifford 2016). It warns that the referendum risks 'descending into a plebiscite on whether immigrants are a good or a bad thing. To see what is at stake, just consider the dark forces that could so easily become emboldened by a narrow insistence on putting the indigenous first.' *The Guardian* refers to 'the most unrelenting, unbalanced and sometimes xenophobic press assault in history'. *The Guardian* also highlights the contradiction between Leave campaigners professing to be pro-immigration while 'fear-mongering' over possible Turkish accession. *The Guardian* argues that the EU is used as the 'whipping boy', much as Reisigl and Wodak (2001, 266) articulated it, for lots of ills, such as frozen wages and job insecurity.

Conclusions

In news stories, not only was there evidence of persuasive news (Rowinski 2016, 2017), in the form of argumentation, but also a suspension of rational argumentation, presenting emotive purported facts unequivocally, in the form of unmodalised declaratives (Mautner 2008). Closer inspection revealed there was no substantiation, but instead an appeal to how readers may have *felt* about issues such as immigration, which became a central focus. In terms of the linguistic means by which this was achieved, compulsion/*überreden* was effectively employed. Another way of understanding this is that such texts reaffirmed for readers what they wished to believe. Here there is at the very least the maintaining of a constructed sense of place, reaffirmed through the differentiation from the Other: Europe.

However, what should also be noted was that the specific term *EU migrant* only surfaced in a couple of stories. Yet when related terminology was used or indeed in articles touching on EU immigration, it was at that point that post-truth reared its head. There was indeed a correlation between the surfacing of immigration, as either a central focus or at least something mentioned in texts, and the prevalence of post-truth emotive Eurosceptic rhetoric. This is unsurprising given that immigration is one of the key drivers of Euroscepticism. Stories were often framed (Entman 1993, 2010) to facilitate the foregrounding of immigration, as apparent in this chapter, and this was even more prevalent when one looked beyond the term *EU migrant*. What was apparent was a theme in the discourse equating EU migration with a strain on public services and the benefits system – despite a complete lack of evidence to support this either from politicians or, most pertinently for this paper, from newspapers directly.

However, looking briefly at the research on a quantitative level, relatively few texts revealed post-truth emotive Eurosceptic rhetoric. It has to be considered that all the examples of post-truth over the days investigated are cited in this paper. For the rest, the journalists may have often been guilty of hyperbole and argumentation in news – but it rested on a substantiating fact, albeit brief, especially in *The Sun* and the *Daily Mail*. Nevertheless the coarseness of the discourse is very much apparent on the eve of the referendum in the editorials explored.

In conclusion, while newspapers are guilty of post-truth Eurosceptic emotive rhetoric surrounding the notion of the *EU migrant*, it is not on the scale feared and is akin to the coarseness found by Mautner (2008). Although the digital age may be impacting on how stories are written, the digital offerings of these newspapers are still working to the formulaic structures of news and editorials and not producing 'shouting' on the scale prevalent on social media such as Facebook and Twitter. This suggests the maintaining rather than escalation of a coarse media discourse, reaffirming England in relation to its Other, Europe.

The game-changer, as mentioned earlier, may be the 'circumstances', returning to the dictionary definition. The filter bubble of mediated digital content (Curtis 2016) may help to influence and entrench opinions, as Laybats and Tredinnick (2016, 4) argue. The difference is perhaps the scale on which this is now possible, amplified very quickly, so 'where information proliferates freely, inevitably, so also do untruths' (Laybats and Tredinnick, 2016, 4).

On social media, politicians and the public are circumventing the mainstream media. On the strength of this research, mainstream newspapers have not succumbed to 'shouting' yet (Coughlan 2017). But there is a danger they will, maybe by how they package their stories on Facebook and Twitter, compromising their role as gatekeeper in preserving the sanctity of facts, in the face of the seduction of how people *feel*, in this case, about *EU migrants*. The dangers for holding politicians to account are clear – and it falls to us, in turn, to help journalists to maintain their standards. At the time of writing, the EU was warning *EU migrants* in the UK to brace themselves for the worst and a no deal over Brexit. The media storm is perhaps only starting and, with it, a possible escalation of reasserting an English sense of place, as understood through a differentiation from EU migrants and that place, the EU – unless England and Britain row back and start to see EU migrants as fellow Europeans. That may mean Remain.

References

Allen, William L. 2016. *A Decade of Immigration in the British Press*. Oxford: Migration Observatory. Accessed 23 May 2019. https://migrationobservatory.ox.ac.uk/resources/reports/decade-immigration-british-press/.

Anderson, Peter J. and Tony Weymouth. 1999. *Insulting the Public? The British Press and the European Union*. London: Longman.

Ashworth-Hayes, Sam. 2016. 'We Won't Be in Single Market without Free Movement', *InFacts*, 6 April. Accessed 5 May 2020. https://infacts.org/mythbusts/uk-wont-single-market-without-free-movement/.

Asthana, Anushka and Rowena Mason. 2016a. 'EU Referendum: "Scaremongering" Cameron attacked by Michael Gove; Justice secretary agrees during acrimonious interview on Sky News to allow independent audit of leave side's £350m-a-week-to-Brussels claim', *The Guardian*, 3 June.

Asthana, Anushka and Rowena Mason. 2016b. 'EU Referendum: Michael Gove agrees to audit of Vote Leave £350m claim; Justice secretary defends claim about "real figure" sent to Brussels each week in follow-up to interview of David Cameron', *The Guardian*, 3 June.

Baudrillard, Jean. 1994. *Simulacra and Simulation*, translated by Sheila Faria Glaser. Ann Arbor: University of Michigan Press.

BBC News. 2016. 'Reality Check: Could There Be Free Trade without Free Movement?', *BBC News*, 27 June. Accessed 5 May 2020. www.bbc.co.uk/news/uk-politics-eu-referendum-36641383.

Billig, Michael. 1995. *Banal Nationalism*. London: Sage.

Buckledee, Steve. 2018. *The Language of Brexit: How Britain Talked Its Way Out of the European Union*. London: Bloomsbury Academic.

Calcutt, Andrew. 2016. 'The Surprising Origins of "Post-Truth" – and How It Was Spawned by the Liberal Left', *The Conversation*, 18 November. Accessed 5 May 2020. https://theconversation.com/the-surprising-origins-of-post-truth-and-how-it-was-spawned-by-the-liberal-left-68929.

Chalaby, Jean K. 1996. 'Journalism as an Anglo-American Invention: A Comparison of the Development of French and Anglo-American Journalism, 1830s–1920s', *European Journal of Communication* 11 (3): 303–26.

Coughlan, Sean. 2017. 'What Does Post-Truth Mean for a Philosopher?', *BBC News*, 12 January. Accessed 23 May 2019. www.bbc.co.uk/news/education-38557838.

Crace, John. 2016. 'Slapped Down: David Cameron Faces Hostility in TV Interrogation', *The Guardian*, 2 June. Accessed 5 May 2020. www.theguardian.com/politics/2016/jun/02/slapped-down-david-cameron-faces-hostility-in-tv-interrogation.

Curtis, Adam. 2016. *HyperNormalisation* [documentary film]. *BBC iPlayer*. https://www.bbc.co.uk/programmes/p04b183c.

Daily Mail. 2016a. 'Comment: A Dumping Ground for the EU's Criminals', *Daily Mail*, 3 June. Accessed 5 May 2020. www.dailymail.co.uk/debate/article-3623014/DAILY-MAIL-COMMENT-dumping-ground-EU-s-criminals.html.

Daily Mail. 2016b. 'Comment: If You Believe in Britain, Vote Leave: Lies, Greedy Elites and a Divided, Dying Europe – Why We Could Have a Great Future Outside a Broken EU', *Daily Mail*, 21 June. Accessed 5 May 2020. www.dailymail.co.uk/debate/article-3653385/Lies-greedy-elites-divided-dying-Europe-Britain-great-future-outside-broken-EU.html.

Daily Mail. 2016c. 'Undecided? Read this Essential Primer', 22 June.

Daily Mirror. 2016. 'Editorial: For the Sake of Our Great Nation's Future', *Daily Mirror*, 22 June.

Daily Telegraph. 2016. 'Opinion: Vote Leave to Benefit from a World of Opportunity', *Daily Telegraph*, 20 June. Accessed 5 May 2020. www.telegraph.co.uk/opinion/2016/06/20/vote-leave-to-benefit-from-a-world-of-opportunity/.

Deacon, David, Emily Harmer, John Downey, James Stanyer and Dominic Wring. 2016. *UK News Coverage of the 2016 EU Referendum* (Report 5). Loughborough: Loughborough University.

Diamanti, Ilvo and Fabio Bordignon. 2005. *Immigrazione e cittadinanza in Europa: Orientamenti e attagiamenti dei cittadini europei*. Urbino: Fondazione Nord Est.

Dominiczak, Peter and Steven Swinford. 2016. 'Boris: Learn English if You Want to Move to UK', *Daily Telegraph*, 1 June.

Doyle, Jack. 2016. 'Migration Factor Boosts Brexit', *Daily Mail*, 1 June.

Drury, Ian and James Slack. 2016a. 'EU Killers and Rapists We've Failed to Deport: UK's Inability to Expel Thousands of Foreign Criminals Undermines Case for the EU, Say MPs', *Daily Mail*, 3 June. Accessed 5 May 2020. www.dailymail.co.uk/news/article-3622924/EU-killers-rapists-ve-failed-deport-UK-s-inability-expel-thousands-foreign-criminals-undermines-case-EU-say-MPs.html.

Drury, Ian and James Slack. 2016b. 'Our Workers Paid Price of EU Dream Admits Red Len', *Daily Mail*, 21 June.

Economist, The. 2016. 'The Post-Truth World: Yes, I'd Lie to You', *The Economist*, 10 September. Accessed 6 May 2020. www.economist.com/briefing/2016/09/10/yes-id-lie-to-you.

Entman, Robert M. 1993. 'Framing: Toward Clarification of a Fractured Paradigm', *Journal of Communication* 43 (4): 51–58.

Entman, Robert M. 2010. 'Media Framing Biases and Political Power: Explaining Slant in News of Campaign 2008', *Journalism* 11 (4): 389–408.

Gaber, Ivor. 2011. 'Three Cheers for Subjectivity: Or the Crumbling of the Seven Pillars of Traditional Journalistic Wisdom'. In *The End of Journalism: News in the Twenty-First Century*, edited by Alec Charles and Gavin Stewart, 31–50. Oxford: Peter Lang.

Garton Ash, Timothy. 2005. *Free World: Why a Crisis of the West Reveals the Opportunity of Our Time*. London: Penguin.

Gifford, Chris. 2016. *The Making of Eurosceptic Britain*. 2nd ed. London: Routledge.

Groves, Jason. 2016a. 'How the Tougher Rules Could Work', *Daily Mail*, 1 June.

Groves, Jason. 2016b. 'Immigration Revolution!', *Daily Mail*, 1 June.

Hawkes, Steve. 2016a. 'Fox: Vote Out to Get a House', *The Sun*, 3 June.

Hawkes, Steve. 2016b. 'Schools All Full', *The Sun*, 22 June.

Heer, Hannes and Ruth Wodak. 2008. 'Introduction: Collective Memory, National Narratives and the Politics of the Past'. In *The Discursive Construction of History: Remembering the Wehrmacht's War of Annihilation*, edited by Hannes Heer, Walter Manoschek, Alexander Pollak and Ruth Wodak, 1–16. Basingstoke: Palgrave Macmillan.

Hope, Christopher. 2016. 'Facebook Farage Aims to Reach Parts Others Can't: UKIP Leader Takes His Leave Campaign North of London – and to Millions Watching Him Live on Social Media', *Daily Telegraph*, 3 June.

Huggler, Justin, 2016. 'German Vote on Genocide Enrages Turkey', *Daily Telegraph*, 3 June.

Ipsos MORI. 2015. *Perils of Perception 2015: A 33 Country Study*. Accessed 25 July 2020. https://www.ipsos.com/sites/default/files/2017-07/ipsos-perils-of-perception-charts-2015.pdf.

Kaltwasser, Cristóbal Rovira. 2014. 'The Responses of Populism to Dahl's Democratic Dilemmas', *Political Studies* 62 (3): 470–87.

Keyes, Ralph. 2004. *The Post-Truth Era: Dishonesty and Deception in Contemporary Life*. New York: St Martin's Press.

Kienpointner, M. 1992. *Alltagslogik: Struktur und Funktion von Argumentationsmustern*. Stuttgart Bad Cannstatt: Frommann-Holzboog.

Kopperschmidt, Josef. 1989. *Methodik der Argumentationsanalyse*. Stuttgart: Frommann-Holzboog.

Krasodomski-Jones, Alexander. 2016. *Demos*. Accessed 23 May 2019. https://demos.co.uk/research-area/casm/.

Kueng, Lucy. 2017. *Going Digital: A Roadmap for Organisational Transformation*. Oxford: Reuters Institute for the Study of Journalism, University of Oxford.

Lakoff, George. 1996. *Moral Politics: What Conservatives Know That Liberals Don't*. Chicago and London: University of Chicago Press.

Lakoff, George and Mark Johnson. 1980. *Metaphors We Live By*. Chicago: University of Chicago Press.

Laybats, Claire and Luke Tredinnick. 2016. 'Editorial: Post Truth, Information, and Emotion', *Business Information Review* 33 (4): 204–6.

Lewis, Helen. 2016. 'Post-Truth Politics', *Nieman Reports*, 18 November. Accessed 6 May 2020. https://niemanreports.org/articles/post-truth-politics/.

LexisNexis [online database]. Accessed 16 June 2020. https://www.lexisnexis.com/ap/academic/form_news_wires.asp

Mason, R. 2016. 'Iain Duncan Smith accuses PM of lying over EU immigration; Cameron's claim about negotiating EU deal over jobseeker's allowance is "clear attempt to deceive", says former Tory leader', *The Guardian*, 3 June.

Mautner, Gerlinde. 2008. 'Analyzing Newspapers, Magazines and Other Print Media'. In *Qualitative Discourse Analysis in the Social Sciences*, edited by Ruth Wodak and Michał Krzyżanowski, 30–53. Basingstoke: Palgrave Macmillan.

Moffitt, Benjamin and Simon Tormey. 2014. 'Rethinking Populism: Politics, Mediatisation and Political Style', *Political Studies* 62 (2): 381–97.

Morgan, David. 1995. 'British Media and European Union News: The Brussels News Beat and Its Problems', *European Journal of Communication* 10 (3): 321–43.

Musolff, Andreas. 2004. *Metaphor and Political Discourse: Analogical Reasoning in Debates about Europe*. Basingstoke: Palgrave Macmillan.

Newton-Dunn, Thomas. 2016. 'Stop EUr Waffling: Cam is Lambasted over Project Fear on Live TV: Telly Punters Pan "Prattling" PM: He's Let in 1.2m Migrants', *The Sun*, 3 June.

Oxford Dictionaries. 2016. 'Word of the Year 2016'. Accessed 1 February 2018. https://en.oxforddictionaries.com/word-of-the-year/word-of-the-year-2016.

Prado, C.G., ed. 2018. *America's Post-Truth Phenomenon: When Feelings and Opinions Trump Facts and Evidence*. Santa Barbara , CA: Praeger.

Reisigl, Martin and Ruth Wodak. 2001. *Discourse and Discrimination: Rhetorics of Racism and Antisemitism*. London: Routledge.

Riley-Smith, Ben. 2016. 'EU Convicts "Boost for Brexit"', *Daily Telegraph*, 3 June.

Romano, Angela. 2017. 'Asserting Journalistic Autonomy in the "Post-Truth" Era of "Alternative Facts": Lessons from Reporting on the Orations of a Populist Leader', *Asia Pacific Media Educator* 27 (1): 51–66.

Rowinski, Paul. 2016. 'Euroscepticism in the Berlusconi and Murdoch Press', *Journalism* 17 (8): 979–1000.

Rowinski, Paul. 2017. *Evolving Euroscepticisms in the British and Italian Press: Selling the Public Short*. Cham: Palgrave Macmillan.

Schickler, Jack. 2016. 'Voters Weren't Misled about "Common Market"', *InFacts*, 23 March. Accessed 6 May 2020. https://infacts.org/voters-werent-misled-about-common-market/.

Sismondo, Sergio. 2017. 'Editorial: Post-Truth?', *Social Studies of Science* 47 (1): 3–6.

Slack, Jack and John Groves. 2016. 'Dave Learns What Voters Really Think on Migration', *Daily Mail*, 3 June.

Slack, James and Daniel Martin. 2016. 'Schools Could Face an Extra 570,000 Pupils from the EU', *Daily Mail*, 22 June.

Slack, James and John Stevens. 2016. 'Poll Blunders Could Let EU Nationals Vote', *Daily Mail*, 3 June.

Smith, Helen and Patrick Kingsley. 2016. 'Calm as EU Migrant Deal Takes Symbolic First Step but True Test is to Come', *The Guardian*, 3 June.

Solon, O. 2018. 'George Soros: Facebook and Google a menace', *The Guardian*, 26 January.

Springford, John. 2013. *Is Immigration a Reason for Britain to Leave the EU?* London: Centre for European Reform.

Stevens, John. 2016. 'Now It's the EU Luvvies Who Are Telling Us What to Think', *Daily Mail*, 3 June.

Stevens, John and Jason Groves. 2016. 'Who Are You to Lecture Us, Mrs Merkel', *Daily Mail*, 3 June.

Strong, S.I. 2017. *Alternative Facts and the Post-Truth Society: Meeting the Challenge* (Legal Studies Research Paper 2017–4). University of Missouri.

Sumption, Madeleine and Will Somerville. 2010. *The UK's New Europeans: Progress and Challenges Five Years after Accession*. Manchester: Equality and Human Rights Commission.

Sun, The. 2016. 'Editorial: Look into His Eyes: Beleave in Britain', *The Sun*, 22 June.

Taggart, Paul and Szczerbiak, Aleks. 2004. 'Contemporary Euroscepticism in the Party Systems of the European Union Candidate States of Central and Eastern Europe', *European Journal of Political Research* 43: 1–27.

Wadsworth, Jonathan, Swati Dhingra, Gianmarco Ottaviano and John Van Reenen. 2016. *Brexit and the Impact of Immigration on the UK*. London: Centre for Economic Performance.

Wodak, Ruth. 2001. 'The Discourse-Historical Approach'. In *Methods of Critical Discourse Analysis*, edited by Ruth Wodak and Michael Meyer, 63–94. London: Sage.

Wodak, Ruth. 2004. 'Critical Discourse Analysis'. In *Qualitative Research Practice*, edited by Clive Seale, Giampietro Gobo, Jaber F. Gubrium and David Silverman, 97–213. London: Sage.

12
Rethinking the photographic studio as a politicised space

Caroline Molloy

Drawing from Crang, Dwyer and Jackson (2003), who argue that commodity culture provides an alternative way of advancing our understanding of contemporary transnationality, this chapter looks at the photographic studio embedded in a diasporic community in North London as a transnational space, a place in which hybrid identities are experimented with and existing rituals are reconfigured, retold and reimagined. I investigate how the photographic studio can be understood as a politicised space in which transcultural identities are experimented with and performed.[1]

Navigating my 'local'

The research focuses on my 'local', an area known as a 'Turkish' neighbourhood, based in and around North/North East London.[2] According to Yilmaz (2005), there has been a diasporic Turkish community in England since Ottoman times. He argues, however, that it was the political unrest in Cyprus in the 1950s and 1960s that saw a large migration of Turkish people move to London, and economic problems in the 1970s and 1980s that led to an influx of immigration from mainland Turkey.[3] He explains that Turkish migrants congregate in the same areas in London as other migrants from their hometown, conspicuously settling in Stoke Newington, Manor House and Green Lanes. This is an area I call home, and refer to in this chapter as my 'local'.[4]

I moved to London more than 20 years ago for career opportunities. For the first 10 years that I lived in London, I moved around frequently, living in 12 properties in four different areas.[5] My decisions about where to live were mostly governed by economics and a desire to be in close proximity to where I worked and studied. Ten years ago, I moved to a property in North London that was near where I worked at the time. I have remained in this property for a decade now, and call it home. During the short commute between home and work, from North to East London, I cycled through a number of different neighbourhoods. Although there were no physical borders to cross during the commute, the areas through which I travelled were different from each other, and often distinct in their identities. Examples of this are the many Turkish-owned late-night kebab houses on Stoke Newington High Street and along Green Lanes, which sit alongside the Turkish-owned hairdressers, beauticians, barbers, photographic studios and general stores. In addition, within the same vicinity on and around Ridley Road market, vibrant Afro-Caribbean fabrics are sold alongside Afro hair and beauty products, and fresh Caribbean vegetables and kosher butchers are found in Stamford Hill.

When reflecting on my 'local', I am reminded of Brah's writing about England. Discussing the intellectual surveying of landscape in post-war Britain in *Cartographies of Diaspora: Contesting Identities* (1996), she highlights the under-researched aspect of the 'diaspora space' of England. The place she writes of seems to capture the essence of my daily commute through London. She writes: 'In the diaspora space called "England" … African-Caribbean, Irish, Asian, Jewish and other diasporas intersect amongst themselves as well as with the entity constructed as "Englishness", thoroughly re-inscribing it in the process' (Brah 1996, 209).

We can understand that these intersections that Brah writes of arise through shared geographical locations. Despite there being no fixed boundaries to define and inscribe sociocultural geographic places in London, areas are often (although no longer exclusively) inhabited by people who originate from the same home country. I am curious about these patterns of diasporic intersection that flourish in the geographical locations through which I traverse, and am interested in how these cultural crossings become places of intercultural encounters. My working pattern and commute to work has since changed, but my interest in the surrounding areas remains constant. With a curiosity about the hybrid nature of my local as a starting point, I investigate my research site, the photography studio.

Thinking through the photographic studio as a research site

It may seem strange to argue that the photographic studio is a politicised space; however, if the services offered by the photographic studio and more broadly commercial photographic practices are examined, such as the marking of a milestone event or ritual by family and passport portraiture, the photographic studio seems an ideal place in which to observe and reflect on transcultural practices. Hall (2006), when writing about diasporic identities, alludes to the fluidity with which diasporic identities are formed. He writes: 'Diaspora identities are those which are constantly producing and reproducing themselves anew, through transformation and difference' (Hall 2006, 439). But where and how do these transformations take place? When writing about reimagining diasporic identities afresh, and thinking through practices of diaspora, Sigona *et al.* (2015) argue that transnational spaces are places in which transcultural practices take place. These are places of agency, they suggest, in which diasporic communities meet and reconfigure their identities. Sigona *et al.* identify churches and schools as transnational spaces. Could we consider additional spaces such as diasporic commercial photographic studios as transnational places? If the photographic studio and more broadly commercial photographic practices are places of self-recognition in which identities are experimented with and rituals are visually memorialised, could they also be understood as transnational places in which transcultural identities are imagined?

Postcolonial theory is a beneficial way of thinking through the photographic studio as a politicised space. To commence this analysis, we can refer to Mary Louise Pratt's (2008, 7) ideas around 'contact zones'. Pratt argues that 'contact zones' are social spaces in which different cultures meet, clash and grapple with each other. For example, we can consider London as a place in which cross-cultural exchanges simultaneously take place. In encountering each other, Pratt argues, traditional ideas of cultural practices evolve. Furthermore, Homi Bhabha's (1994) theory of the third space through which meaning is mobilised develops this idea further. He argues that the production of meaning requires the interaction of two things, in this case two cultures through a third space (1994, 36). Therefore, it can be reasoned that my research site, the photographic studios within the Turkish neighbourhood of London, can be conceptualised as that third space – a space in which Turkish and English culture meet and greet each other; a place in which, as discussed by Barthes (1981), the 'self' is experimented with and reconstructed, and wherein the photograph and photographic practices become evidence of cross-cultural identity formation.

Investigating my 'local' photographic studio

I stand on my local high street, and contemplate the photographs on display in the window of one of the commercial high street photography studios. This is an unusual photograph of a young boy aged seven or eight. He is wearing a formal white outfit, inclusive of fur-trimmed white cape and cap, embellished with silver trim, and holding a decorative sceptre. In contrast to the formality of the outfit, his pose is informal. He is seated on the ground and is smiling at the camera. His portrait has been digitally repositioned in front of a waterfall in post-production. To the viewer it appears that the boy is seated in front of the waterfall. For me this is a puzzling photograph, in which there is a disjuncture between the foreground and the background. It is unclear why the background of the portrait is a waterfall. It is a fascinating phantasmagorical photograph that raises many questions around transvisual representation. I am curious to know more about the motivation and construction of this photographic image. What is the significance of the background and what story is being told?

In the reflection of the photographic studio window on the surface of the glass, I see my own face staring back at me. I can feel the wind rushing past me and hear the noise of traffic behind me. I gaze beyond my own image and see the red buses and black cabs in motion, on the busy North London street behind me. This is where the research begins, in front of this glass-fronted photographic studio, which becomes one of my research sites. It is one of the five photographic studios that sit within a four-mile stretch on the A10 in North London.[6] There are four photographic studios located on Stoke Newington High Street, and a fifth can be found next to the large banqueting hall in Tottenham.[7] There are three additional photographic studios in the same area of London sited at different points on Green Lanes, a road which runs perpendicular to the A10. The studios serve the needs of the local community, which is historically, but not exclusively, a diasporic Turkish community. The photographic studios are almost entirely surrounded by other Turkish businesses. The local bank, hairdressers, travel agents and all of the restaurants, including the restaurant inside a former mosque, are Turkish. As one participant commented, this is London but it is really a little Turkish Town.

During the research, I observe photographic practices in and outside of the photographic studio. My interactions with each studio vary; they include some recorded in-depth interviews, on-site and location participant observation and online web-based research. Undertaking this research gives me the opportunity to observe and reflect on the photographic practices taking place. Initially, I believed the practices to be Turkish practices, but it soon became apparent that the rituals and portrait practices I observed and the photographs I examined were not precisely Turkish.[8] Indeed, the Turkish photographic practices had been influenced by practices seen in the geographical locale of North London. As an example of this, I refer to a conversation with one of my participants about an event we both attended.[9]

This event was a circumcision party she attended as part of the photography and video team and I as a participant-observer.[10] It was an all-day event that started off in the photographic studio with formal portraits of the celebrant boy, who was wearing a traditional Ottoman costume, with various family members.[11] As the day progressed, another team of photographers took over the evening session to document the formal sit-down meal/party, which included Turkish music and dancing, and the ceremony of pinning money onto the young boy. What interested me in terms of rituals were the 'in-between' practices that connect the formal events. After the studio portraits had been taken, the young boy and a few of his friends were driven around London in a limousine for the afternoon. After that, he rode a white horse into his formal dinner party, which included 500 guests.

So what is unusual about this? My assumption was that it was an unusual activity for the young boy, celebrating his circumcision ritual and dressed in his Ottoman regalia, to be driven around North London for the afternoon. This is a ritual we have seen many times as part of contemporary British 'hen party' practices. Through conversation with my participant, it became apparent that indeed the practice had been adopted from British hen party practices; however, it was not an unusual activity – in fact, this is now considered a common practice in Turkish communities in London. In adopting this practice, the influence of the geographical locale of North London can be seen. The boy riding the horse into his celebration party, on the other hand, I thought to be a common 'Turkish' practice in North London. This was not the case. My participant told me that, in the seven years she had been in London, she had never seen this practice. Further research revealed that it was a traditional cultural practice from the Turkish village where the family hosting the party had been born. What can be understood from reflecting on the conversation with my participant about these practices is that the family were trying to maintain their familial heritage and at the same time taking influences from the geographical locale of North London. The practices performed were neither exclusively English nor Turkish but a blending of the two cultures through developing transcultural practices.

The transvisual studio photograph

My second photograph is a studio portrait that is indicative of the many photographs I examined during the research. The photograph is a wedding portrait (see Figure 12.1). It is a transvisual photograph. The couple in the photograph are performing for the camera. They are wearing Western-style wedding outfits and enacting a couple 'in love'. It is a photograph that has been digitally montaged to create the narrative. For compositional reasons the couple appear twice in the photograph.[12] The background of the photograph is Tower Bridge, an easily recognisable London landmark, which is used allegorically. The photograph does not attempt to look realistic; its purpose is to send a symbolic message to the consumer of the photograph, the family back in Turkey, that the marriage took place in London. The linchpin of the photograph responsible for locating its cultural meaning is the digital background of Tower Bridge.

Figure 12.1 Transvisual studio wedding photograph. Created by Caroline Molloy. © Belda Productions.

If we understand the studio to be a place in which little theatres of the 'self', as Edwards (2004) suggests, are performed, it is logical to analyse the studio photograph to see how to speak of cultural practices. There has been extensive analysis of early studio photography, for example by Di Bello (2007), Edwards (2006), Flint (2015) and Linkman (1993), who discuss studio photography as a framework that reflects the class and cultural aspirations of the sitters in the images. To ground this research, Bourdieu's (1984) concept of the 'habitus' can be applied. He writes that our sense of place in the world is determined by our internalised structures and schemes of perception. Furthermore, these systems govern our aesthetic, social, economic and cultural tastes with which we identify. This he refers to as our 'habitus'. If the visual tropes in the studio photographs are then examined, the popularity and repetition of tropes in the images identify emblematic visual tropes that indicate cultural and social aspirations.

There is, however, limited analysis around digital studio photographic practices. The use of digital technologies has enabled a wider selection of backgrounds and *mises en scène* to add to and situate the meaning of the portrait. In doing this, there is more scope to expand the visual 'habitus' photograph. Rather than a radical break caused by digital technologies, digital photography has opened up imaginative ways in which to make studio portraits that blur the boundaries between the real and the symbolic, the imagined and the actual. Undeterred by the democratising effects of digital photography, studio photography still has a presence on the high street. However, there has been a skill shift in the making of a photographic portrait. The studio portrait is no longer limited by the physical space of the studio. The digital infrastructure enables the portrait likeness to be completed and given meaning on the computer. The wide availability of digital portrait backgrounds, props and *mises en scène* has enabled a fluidity in creating a contemporary studio portrait. With an increasingly broad range of online digital backgrounds and props available to add to the studio portrait, there are more opportunities to develop identities around the visual 'habitus' of the studio photograph. In fact, it can be argued that with a potentially limitless range available, the selection of the digital background and supporting props is more culturally specific than ever before. The visual 'habitus' of the photograph, whether in a historical analogue photograph or a digitally compiled photograph, remains integral to its reading.

Concluding comments

Using examples to support my theory, I have argued that the photographic studio, in my local, within its broadest sense, provides a suitable framework through which transcultural identities are explored. The photographic practices reflect the transcultural nature of photography and can be understood as a good indicator of the fluidity of cultural practices. I am conscious that this is reflexive research that is open-ended and ever-changing. In order to locate this perspective I draw from Massey (1994), who, when talking about the character of a place, describes it as a constructed articulation of social relations. There is fluidity in understanding this space and place that is associated with a specific historical point, which she calls an 'envelope of time'. This research, as an envelope of time, reflects my experience in contemporary North London photographic studios. However, I do not believe this is an isolated circumstance; it happens to be my local, which for me is an accessible place in which to carry out the research. I contend that it is a useful framework to look at the photographic studio as a politicised space, a transnational space in which transcultural identities can be transplanted to other established diasporic communities.

Notes

1. The content of this chapter is derived from my PhD research that looks at a broader scope of photography as a transnational practice, through which transcultural identities are formed. 'Transnational' and 'transcultural' are commonly misused terms. In order to follow the thread of this chapter, I qualify both. 'Transnational' can be understood as across nations. It commonly refers to a community of people who have migrated across borders for economic or political reasons. This could equally apply to a group of British expats living exclusively within a British community outside of Britain as it could to a group of political or economic migrants who have moved across borders. 'Transcultural' refers to cross-cultural activities/practices that have evolved through across-cultural exchanges of ideas and practices.
2. Although there is a visible sense of belonging to a diasporic Turkish community and an imagined cohesiveness of that community, it quickly becomes apparent that belonging to this 'Anglo-Turkish' community means something quite different to everyone I speak with. It is not a homogeneous community: many different identities with contradictory interests and divergent forms of identification shelter under the 'Anglo-Turkish' umbrella.
3. It should be noted that the use of the label 'Turkish' is overarching and can be misleading. It is a constructed term that infers a homogeneous group identity. In using the word 'Turkish', the multifaceted subtleties of cultural, ethnic, geographical, religious and national histories are often overlooked. For further reading around this, see Yilmaz (2005), who writes specifically about the Turkish diaspora in Britain.
4. I draw from Lippard's (1997) use of the word 'local'. She uses the word 'local' to refer to the pull of a place that operates within us, entwined with our personal memories, the known and the unknown.

5. I was brought up in North Hampshire and moved to London via the West Midlands. Neither of my parents is English (they are Irish and Welsh). They met in Wales and moved to southern England for work opportunities.
6. On this section of the A10, between Stoke Newington and Tottenham, the road changes name three times: Stoke Newington High Street becomes Stamford Hill and finally High Road.
7. Stamford Hill sits between Stoke Newington and Tottenham. This area is reputed to have the largest population of Hasidic Jews in Europe. There are no photographic studios on Stamford Hill.
8. As discussed in Note 2, the 'Anglo-Turkish' community is not a homogeneous one. Even in self-identifying as part of a diasporic Turkish community, my participants are in disagreement about what this means. They differ in self-recognition, simultaneously calling themselves Anglo-Turkish, London-Turkish/Kurdish-Turkish/Turkish-Londoners, and the London-ish community. During initial interactions everyone I spoke with identified as Turkish/Anglo-Turkish. Only through prolonged conversation did the complexities of individual identities start to emerge. This included participants who, to mention a few, distinguished themselves as Kurdish, Turkish Cypriots or Alevi Kurds as well as Turkish.
9. The interview discussed can be found at https://vimeo.com/230338763.
10. A circumcision party is commonly asynchronous to the actual circumcision ceremony. The circumcision ceremony was not documented by the photography studio.
11. There is no fixed age of circumcision for Muslim boys; the preferred age is around seven years old.
12. It seems to be common practice for the digital studio photographs to depict the sitter more than once in the same image. When questions were raised about this, there was no clear answer as to why this was the case beyond saying that it looked nice.

References

Barthes, Roland. 1981. *Camera Lucida: Reflections on Photography*, translated by Richard Howard. New York: Hill and Wang.
Bhabha, Homi K. 1994. *The Location of Culture*. London: Routledge.
Bourdieu, Pierre. 1984. *Distinction: A Social Critique of the Judgment of Taste*. London: Routledge & Kegan Paul.
Brah, Avtar. 1996. *Cartographies of Diaspora: Contesting Identities*. London: Routledge.
Crang, Philip, Claire Dwyer and Peter Jackson. 2003. 'Transnationalism and the Spaces of Commodity Culture', *Progress in Human Geography* 27 (4): 438–56.
Di Bello, Patrizia. 2007. *Women's Albums and Photography in Victorian England: Ladies, Mothers and Flirts*. Aldershot: Ashgate.
Edwards, Elizabeth. 2004. 'Little Theatres of Self: Thinking about the Social'. In *We Are the People: Postcards from the Collection of Tom Phillips*, 26–37. London: National Portrait Gallery.
Edwards, Steve. 2006. *The Making of English Photography: Allegories*. University Park: Pennsylvania State University Press.
Flint, Kate. 2015. 'Surround, Background, and the Overlooked', *Victorian Studies* 57 (3): 449–61.
Hall, Stuart. 2006. 'New Ethnicities'. In *The Post-Colonial Studies Reader*, edited by Bill Ashcroft, Gareth Griffiths and Helen Tiffin, 199–202. 2nd ed. London: Routledge.
Linkman, Audrey. 1993. *The Victorians: Photographic Portraits*. London: Tauris Parke Books.
Lippard, Lucy R. 1997. *The Lure of the Local: Senses of Place in a Multicentered Society*. New York: New Press.
Massey, Doreen. 1994. *Space, Place and Gender*. Minneapolis: University of Minnesota Press.
Pratt, Mary Louise. 2008. *Imperial Eyes: Travel Writing and Transculturation*. 2nd ed. New York London: Routledge.
Sigona, Nando, Alan Gamlen, Giulia Liberatore and Hélène Neveu Kringelbach, eds. 2015. *Diasporas Reimagined: Spaces, Practices and Belonging*. Oxford: Oxford Diasporas Programme.
Yilmaz, Ihsan. 2005. 'State, Law, Civil Society and Islam in Contemporary Turkey', *The Muslim World* 95 (3): 385–411.

13
Creative routine and dichotomies of space

Philip Miles

Do creative space and place matter when the thrill of creation is felt mainly within the self? Is an artist's or writer's room simply a physical location that bears little influence on the summoning of the muse, the flow of the routine and the satiation of invention? This chapter eschews analysis of wider geographical connection with places of creativity and opts instead to identify, expand and analyse the personal spaces of creativity, focusing on the creative locations of literary authors, fine artists and musicians, drawing out the potential influence of space on the creative routine and the ontological interstices involved in the technique of separating innovation and the mundane, routine everyday. I draw on existing ethnographic work undertaken over a three-year period, emerging in 2019 as a combined study of artists, writers and musicians experiencing the 'midlife' stage[1] and investing time and energies into the invention of novelty (Miles 2019). The study involved interviews and observations that were undertaken in art and recording studios, writing rooms, rehearsal spaces, exhibition venues, workshops buried deep in dense woodlands and a further cornucopia of random and exotic locations from non-league football grounds to huge kilns located in the Oxfordshire countryside. The purpose of the study was to uncover, observe and consider the artistic routines and influences of those engaged in the practice of creation and, essentially, how the meaning of the creative self was developed, maintained and exploited. The research also, crucially, considered spaces of creation – both specific-locational and metaphysical – and this segment of the wider criteria of the research provides our focus here.

Late modernism and empowerment

The research was undertaken within an analytical frame of the shifting, fluid contexts of sociological late modernity, namely understanding the actions of the individuals discussed as being situated in a time where old (grand) narratives of collective certainty have been gradually replaced by the driven sense of the individual, thus mindful of the associative risks involved in embracing a myriad of options, meanings and identities in contemporary life. The element of choice is therefore synonymous with an actor's decision to separate from a world that is multifarious in social, cultural and political contexts but still provides a certainty in that certainty is invested in a belief in the continued sense of variety. Art offers the chance to experience a chaotic uncertainty that elevates the possibility of creation above structural constraints such as age, time, ideology and social class. Art is otherwise largely dependent on space-time-place to achieve what Walter Benjamin (2008) would call 'aura', Mihaly Csikszentmihalyi (1996) would call 'flow' or, as Derek Attridge (2017) would attest, the amalgamation of 'idiocultural' familiarity resulting in the manipulation, exploitation and disruption of the oeuvre to ultimately extend the meaning and longevity of a particular narrative within art. The theme of distortion within the narrative of creative art is strong in late modern society,[2] and artists have the wherewithal to instigate such turbulence in the continuum almost at will.

With this form of uncertainty – and a challenging of hitherto omnipresent structural, reliable norms, values and mores – comes a crisis of familiarity, a sense of flux, a resigned acknowledgement of the need to remain in motion to somehow remain in focus with the shifting patterns of uncertain modern life. In 1984, discussing the emblematic shifting of literary convention, Patricia Waugh stated, without compunction, that *post*modernism[3] was a 'loss of belief in an external authoritative system of order that prompted modernism' (1984, 21). In many ways the simplicity of the statement belies its intensity in that it can be applied to something of a juxtaposition of the literary and the sociological, explaining a gradual drift in the representations and experiences of the social that embody the transition beyond the point where systems of order have *order* into a place where anything goes. However, the sociological late modern effectively stops shy of this place; we are arguably in a situation where the late modern is not quite 'post', retaining some semblance of order as we have known it, perhaps via an inbuilt desire to hang on just that little bit longer to certainty and not quite embrace the risks of complete absolution of such familiarities (Giddens 1990, 1991). Belief, therefore, is not completely lost at this stage. Society is still governed by a continued sense of the recognisable, all the time under pressure from the individualising thrust of contemporary life (and the commercial and media onus on uniqueness). This continued sense (and security) of the ordinary creates a tension in the binary between the reliable and the unique, arguably motivating a desire to transcend such anxious torsions and seek exciting gratification in the challenge of, individually or communally, inventing novelty.

Therefore, to define the late modern is a complex task, but the general ideas do transpose well onto debates on identity and culture in the following way. The generic thrust of variety, diversity and individualisation – embracing what Beck, Giddens and Lash, connecting with Patricia Waugh's assertion, have described as 'post traditional' (1994, 21) – features in contemporary lives via what Zygmunt Bauman (2000) explained as 'liquid' modernity. This involves capitalism as a shape-shifting phenomenon that exploits the perceived necessity of change and the simultaneous diminishing of the *Sicherheit* (security, certainty and safety) that maintains self-confidence in the individual (Bauman 1999, 17). This erosion results in the anxious scramble for empowerment as we seek to shape our individualised destinies, but it also arguably creates a desire to escape from the intricacies of such stratagems. The adoption of an alternative routine, existing simultaneously with the machinations of the real world, can provide this. However, the desire to escape from the Gordian 'everyday' is effectively reversed by artists who, if anything, see an anarchy of thinking as expounding an escape from the certainties of competitiveness in the real world. It is an interesting binary and one that sees the connection between the private physical spaces of certainty and the (ontological) mental spaces of creative disorder segueing to provide an antidote to the tedious, repetitive routines of everyday strategy. Creativity is witnessed as a rare, though unreliable, freedom and largely unconnected to a fixed location either physically or metaphysically.

Situating such freedom leads to a sense that available time (away from everyday matters) is diffused, effectively scattered around for the utility of multiple leisure, spent at will on a variety of pastimes from sports to family to non-stipendiary work (or, of course, the economic need to remain working). Thus, with contemporary late-modern freedom to fill time comes a pressure to fill it *well* and to eradicate the potential of boredom; we may seek to fill our time creatively, seeking effective satiation in the process. The desire to effectively blank out the risk (and insecurities) of modern life might come with the turn to entertainment via books and film, arts and music that offer an alternative, waking reality for people to indulge in the fantasy of possibilities. In addition, it is not surprising or unusual that some people turn to creativity themselves, seeking to *make* rather than to solely consume; this can be considered also as an escape from banal reality, but has the added incentive of haptic praxis, a proprioceptive encounter that has the promise of an antidote to entropy and the sense of achievement in producing something new (Witkin 2005, 57–72).

This, in other words, is not solely experiencing art but *authoring* art, doing it for a reason, actively seeking its emergence and being present at the commencement of the routine of reception. Being present is a moment of wonder, fascination and the sense of privilege and it is also situated in time-space, experienced '*in* the moment'. This is a moment that I call 'the mezzanine' – an in-between mental state and status where an individual – or group – is connecting knowledge with action and creating novelty in an instant, impossible to experience again, where everything that follows is simply a copy; a work of art is simply a rehearsed, revised and recited piece that can never be an exact copy of the original, having life that must be lived by others beyond the artist. This is what makes location, place, space and instance so contentious (and individualised) to the deliverance of novelty, of art and what makes it so personally endearing to its creator, so immune to entropy and so cathartic in its eventual emergence from the 'mezzanine condition'.[4] So, with this in mind, what role does the perception of place have in this routine for the people who 'make'?

Situating the creative: Places of invention and divestment

The research that spanned three years and numerous locations always tended to turn out the same conclusions in relation to the spaces of creation: namely, the lack of importance (if any) that creative people attached to their circumstances or, indeed, their physical location. Inspiration was seen as unattached to time-space or nostalgia; the principle of creation was drawn from the aspect of mood, sensuality and chance rather than a perceptible acknowledgement of origins, home, landscape or circumstance. That said, there *was* a tangible sense of pride and importance attached to the idea of order in their places of inspiration and, when visiting artistic people in their places of work, I was consequently struck by the sense of assiduous anticipation that I found in each place. It is perhaps forgivable to expect some kind of disorder in a space that is used to effectively assemble materials and ideas into palpable form, but I found little evidence of disarray; instead, I saw various phases of preparation. The interesting thing to emerge from such states of instigation was the sense of potential – it felt like a calm before a storm, but the storm, when it came, would leave no trace of damage. It was a curious, almost unnerving sense of expectancy.

From writers' rooms that were perfectly ordered – desks tidy, printer at arm's length, pens and pencils, papers and staplers, cables tied together and floor clear of clutter – to rehearsal studios with sofas and guitar stands out of walkways, designated zones for drums, guitars and vocals, space to move into, doors to drift out of, anterooms to loiter in for cigarettes, coffee and natter; all spaces were prepared for labour rather than to dream or to vacillate. The fine artists' studios were clean and logical, light (as you may expect) and inspirational (one in woodland that changes with the seasons outside), sparse and airy, almost waiting for ideas – and actions – to fill them. It was an interesting travelogue, yielding a sense that space matters, and that the geographic dynamics of town and country and the omnipresent – or oscillating – background noise or tranquil silence function equally as creative backdrops but rarely as sources of direct inspiration. In all but one location the spaces were highly personalised; these were individual, private zones that were unlikely to be penetrated by significant others or, for that matter, the outside world. They were places where television, the internet and mobile phones were banished to the boundaries. These were places of work – the realisation of an end-product was the central aim of entering the space. I realised that the creative muse was summoned via communality as well as solitariness, and the two categories of space were distinct.

Communal spaces

While 'the creative' revealed itself as a largely individualised, metaphysical process, in urban Derby I witnessed The Ruins – an alternative rock band with all the musicians involved experiencing life in their fifties – rehearsing and recording music in a small studio built onto the back of a modest suburban home in the city. Measuring approximately 11 feet by 15 feet, with a low ceiling and narrow window, this was a functional but welcoming place complete with corner sofa and low coffee tables that sat in contrast with banks of recording equipment, computer screens, drums and racks of guitars. This was where the band, in close proximity to one another, were able to rehearse music using what they called 'quiet rehearsal' or 'silent rehearsal', where headphones and electric instruments (including an electronic drum kit) were plugged into a mixing desk, leaving only the disembodied sound of strummed stringed instruments and the voice of the singer audible when I removed my headphones to sample the disconnection. In this space the band felt they could work with no time constraints, effectively and consciously exploiting the economic and domestic fruits of middle age that younger bands lack. The music could ebb and flow in intensity, stop, start, revise mid-flow, extend and peak and trough in intensity at will, always looking for the moment of 'aura' where the perfect version is transiently achieved, but always then 'covered' as the writing turns into rehearsal turns into recording turns into performance and the cycle is repeated over and over again in search of creative pique.

The importance of the location, the venue, the space of work is that the band are able to utilise their social and economic capital (Bourdieu 1993) and add another, non-Bourdieu, criterion – time capital. They have 'earned' the time to 'spend' the time accordingly and the studio provides a neutral, physical space in which to do this. The interesting observation at all times was that, despite being in each other's presence, the band were effectively detached from one another when in full musical flow – the headphones taking them away from the communal sound of the traditional rehearsal (where instruments and vocals are often indistinguishable from one another) and towards an individual concentration on technique and contribution through the channels of a mixing desk. It was an interesting distinction and one that immediately framed the contrast between the communal acoustics of, say, theatrical or orchestral rehearsal and a modern emphasis on individual, oscillating contributions.

The Ruins, however, divided their time between rehearsal/recording space and the stage, with the latter being an occasional foray into the exhibition of technique and expertise. Thus, these spaces differed in function: the studio provided a hub of escape but also of crucial simultaneous sociality and invention. It was here that the band could catch up with each other on a weekly basis, share experiences, opinions and plans and, ultimately, jam their music into discernible form, captured spontaneously and functioning organically. The band saw themselves as a studio project that required occasional stage exposure to somehow legitimise their labour. This, of course, gives extra credence to the idea that the space of production, where the ideas swirl and never stand still, is the crucial factor – more ontological than physical. In other words, the creation could be anywhere so long as the technology is in attendance.

There is also an interesting three-way split in defining the place of creativity: essentially the distinction between studio, stage, and the sublime, instantaneous and immediate sense of the spontaneous. Thus, to the band's keyboardist-guitarist, Miles, the creation of music is simply a nebulous stage; the place of creation is not just the studio but instead something diffuse, philosophical and fluid. It's 'an investment […] it's one of the most freeing places […] intuitive', he says, referring to the boundless sense of possibility, undetermined by time and place, existing 'anytime'. This is a view shared by his colleagues, but the importance of the physical space of the studio also assists in the development of art. Ian, the drummer (and the owner of the home studio), insists that having the equipment located in a fixed space means that songs are recalled – its value is 'not letting them be forgotten', he says, adding that a continuous venue also allows the band to loosen up, be themselves and, he laughs, be social and creative simultaneously in that 'you've missed it, you're ready for some action!'. The shift into a live performance setting creates a stark contrast, where nerves are created by the alien, the uncertain, the sense of expectancy and the fear of judgement (Ian says that 'It's like being told "well done" by a teacher'). This results in the effect that 'playing every six months […] causes the trouble with nerves,' he says, 'in the same way that if you fly too irregularly, your fear of flying rises!'

The place of creation for The Ruins, therefore, is based on comfort, familiarity, routine and sociality – to be sure, it could be anywhere, but being at Ian's house couldn't be better. He goes to his studio late at night to capture ideas in what he describes as 'quietness' after the family have retired to bed and the noise and bustle of his days are expelled. The studio is a location of thoughts, calm and solitary and almost meditative. He finds his mezzanine here, thoughts channelling into sound, somehow effortlessly translating, unforeseen and original but captured for posterity (and for the band). Thus, the place of creation is both a facility and transitive, conventional location for spontaneity and experimentation that is hermetically sealed in the moment from the community and culture of its geographical environs. It is a location that funnels and filters and captures, letting in no light, private and receptive to the vagaries of musical chaos and the resultant joy of unforeseen novelty. Places of creativity to The Ruins are places that are physical and transitory (the studio and the stage) but also involve the unpredictable and fluid notion of psychological flow: all of these issues are unrestrained by emotion, history/biography and nostalgia and are not determined by geography per se. It is simply a case where place is an invention of circumstance, mood and the relative spoils of middle age.

Solitary spaces

But artistic creation (or invention) is not always done in communal settings with omnipresent sociality and collective empathy in the pursuit of novelty. For most artists (arguably), the creative routine is solitary and can be viewed as being determined by a connection to physical place (i.e. the studio), environment (country and city, phases of external light, the seasons and weather, size and setting of room and so on) and the effect of life that bookends the creative phase (biography, occurrences, mood and so on). Fine art and the creation of literary text can be argued to be more determined by place than music, not least because of the perceptible lack of delegation of roles and arguably also due to the individuality of the whole process. While music is often created alone (as Ian speaks of above), it invariably becomes public via the input of other band members, its public recital and, of course, its sociality in reception and perception. Fine art and literary text also have elements of this supra-situating of meaning (including, of course, in editorial and peer reviewing), but are largely under the control of a single person engaged in a single haptic event. People tend not to write or paint in groups. While art and literature often become public through exhibition and publication, essentially (as Robin, an artist, described) giving life and character to art after the artefact's birth, the actual birth is usually mediated by one person, making the physical and mental location of conception important (i.e. facilities and desire).

However, the decision to create can often be facilitated by a casual offer, a prospect to separate oneself from the domestic location, family and other potential distractions, leading to new things via the accidental exposure to an awareness of hidden incentives. For Dominic, a fine artist located on the south coast of England, such a chance opportunity arose to utilise a wooden outhouse garden studio with wood stove and great light at a friend's house, just out of town. There, he set himself up as an artist for the first time. 'For six months I just went up there, carrying wood up there,' he says with an air of wistfulness. 'I'd light the fire every morning, used to heat my lunch up on the wood stove there and I just built up some materials, reading intensely some art books.' Such initial experimentation facilitated a separation of work space and home, using the garden studio as a place for formative preparation – almost a location that gave him the impetus to be an artist. However, he soon returned to the effective partitioning of his home, getting him closer to his family, the town, the dichotomy of stillness and movement, the contrasts of life and art. His time at his friend's studio was formative; it illustrates a location, but a location of thought rather than industrial output. This, if anything, is the commencement of aesthetic awareness, what Herbert Read would describe as a desire to create 'pleasing forms' that chime with an individual's sense of meaning: sensual, intuitive and individual (Read 2017 [1931], 17–20). This separation of thought-creation and the locational-innovative is crucial, as it essentially removes a situation from the flow of creativity, leaving 'place' as less *circumstance* and more *state of mind*.

This solitary space does, as we can see, eventually transmogrify into a more public space of creation – from garden studio to home and, thus, a place where others live. All of the artists I spoke to either lived with others who acknowledged their artistic processes and outputs, or actually worked alongside other creative people. For instance, Robin, an artist based in a variety of studio workshops in the Wytham Woods outside Oxford, worked with colleagues in the construction, and utility, of the Anagama (Bizen) Kiln Project, and has a partner who is also a working artist; Peter, another fine artist, worked within an artist's collective; The Ruins made use of a domestic abode as the location of their studio as well as relying on huge supportive input from family; and Dominic shared his studio with family by night, when it transformed into something of a sitting room. Only the writers that I spoke to separated their art from their domesticity in that, despite writing *at* home, it was not *of* home, but divorced from latent domesticity and the influences of the domestic (i.e. they were both working within the domestic space and working in parallel interrelationship with significant others). The principles of good writing are seen as distinct from the familial – critically individualised and jealously protected.

Thus, with the communal and solitary spaces of artistic creation seemingly detached from a sense of place itself (i.e. creation can happen anywhere, regardless), where can we best view the impact of creative space? It emerged, throughout the research, that routine and thought were best employed as a translator of how art is attached to place – but it is place itself that is best understood as an aim rather than a facility.

Elevating routine

Of course, art is developed in a variety of places and spaces, effectively creating an amalgamated location that merges physical environment and the metaphysical. Peter finds himself creating in an old barracks in urban Reading, with thick, white emulsion walls, formal in feel, separated into artistic silos, each room witnessing a different approach, different projects, different character; but each artistic venue that I visited was actually surprisingly similar in substance. Places, despite having a disorganised feel, were organised, usually with a significant artistic signifier of intent and labour at the centre (with Peter and Robin it was the large printing presses associated with their linocuts and woodcuts); as stated, each space had a preparatory feel, an anticipation of action and the sense of latent anxiety that floated, omnipresent, in relation to the expectancy (but not with guarantee attached) of artistic prosperity.

Thus, the location of artistic endeavour always felt – via music, art and the act of writing – like a site of routine and progression, variously anticipatory and reflective and having little to do with the outside world of urban Reading or rural Oxfordshire or, in other settings, suburbia, the south coast, the Wiltshire countryside vaguely reminiscent of an A. G. Street novel[5] or the thundering traffic of central London. The spaces are best understood as synchronic, full of temporal situational contrasts (a raging noise in the mind in concert with a tranquil peace; a thundering of heavy vehicles contrasting with the delicacy of a wood carving, a gentle caress of oil on canvas and so on). Place might figure in decisions to create: Peter noted that his decision to enter art school the first time round had been driven by a worship of Syd Barrett of Pink Floyd, his skill as an artist, his art school in Cambridge and Peter's proximity to that institution. However, the main decisions on places (or locations) of creation tend to be made based on functionality, utility and convenience. To Robin, the places are physical, but functional, emblematic of creation – such as the kilns in the woods that he has invested so much time in both creating and maintaining. They are, in turn, educational (such as the creative workshops in the lodge and the hut in the woods) and they are emancipatory – the freedom coming in the space to think, perhaps, more than do. Thinking, of course, can come without boundaries on all levels.

Robin is an anthropologist who converted from an original calling in geological sciences, and who is used to travel, exploring terrain as well as cultures, transient and attentive at once, analysing place and space for a variety of characteristics, largely 'off the verandah' (through immersion), as Malinowski (1961 [1922]) theorised. While the perception and understanding of place is not entirely dependent on the application of Weber's *Verstehen* principle[6] (empathetic understanding), it is nevertheless culturally detached, functionally separated for context and freedom to interpret. This, if anything, best summarises a central tenet of the mezzanine condition in that the space created in between is more productive and pure than the value-laden places and spaces 'on either side' of a value-free interpretative moment. Therefore, place is a concept that is best marginalised in both the conception and appreciation of art for the creator. Place is best left to the beholder, the 'reader'[7] who may apply mores, values and biography to create a new story of the art.

This idea came through with the greatest intensity when talking to Dominic, perhaps the most traditional of the creative artists that I spoke to in that he dedicated his time to the creation of what one may term paintings rather than woodcut and linocut prints or ceramics. Occasionally, the artist is forced into becoming an actor on both flanks of the mezzanine. To Dominic, his paintings were original and the end product of a deep, considered labour routine, but they were also his primary income source. In selling his paintings, Dominic was drawn into a naturally occurring combination of place, space and extended biographical exposure, being required to meet the public and explain his influences, and consequently being required to learn to recognise types of purchaser with an entrepreneurial eye and instinct and to exploit his connections to town, the sea vistas, its bohemia and its artistic community as a whole – he was selling himself as part of the story of the painting. He was, as he said, selling his presence as part of some future social capital to be exploited by the purchaser (i.e. as part of the narrative of dinner party stories about the painting, the artist, the thrill of the chase and the deal, and the resultant cachet of ownership).

Others interviewed throughout the research make reference to the shifting dynamic of place, transient, influential, sowing seeds of interest but acting as a distraction from the anxiety and adrenaline-fuelled metaphysical mezzanine. This distraction is often associated with movement or travel – Katherine Webb, who is now on to her seventh novel with a mainstream publisher, likened vacations to a deliberate discarding of the creative process, resulting in picking up threads when she gets back. Notably, she is clear that she begins her work in her head and, should she go away for a break, she has to 'gather it all up again, slowly [...] where it was going, the shape of it'. The holiday is a break from locations of work (creativity) but also a mental shift from the metaphysical anarchy of the mezzanine and towards an interim stability of an almost physical thought. Thus, place is divided three ways between the orderly certainty of routine (her desk, libraries, wandering in her garden in search of simultaneous escape and inspiration), the mezzanine condition of praxis (writing, flow, outputs) and the separate locations of certainty (expected originality of travels and so on).

Katherine is not alone. Annette, also an author, likens place both to a shifting sense of creative rhythm that is found when lying in the bath or out walking and to her own geographical origins and social class heritage, made diverse by university and metropolitan London. Neither attribute their creative muses to their places of abode or their places of childhood and so on. The creative sense of place is in sensing the certainty of uncertain flow – thus, the late-modern reflexive 'liquidity of risk' is not physical, biographical, familiar. It is, all the while, expected and the mezzanine is the embracing of the unexpected, the unforeseen and the uncapping of potential. Late modernism is, in effect, all about the unforeseen but expected. Travel is open-ended but framed. The mezzanine is without boundary; it is also, by definition, without location. Dominic talks of immersion when working with driftwood from the local beaches to create a kind of eco-art, therefore acting between the framing of the origins of the materials (the beach) and the immersion in what they become (the mezzanine). The place is important because he finds the wood there; the space is elevated beyond the place because the haptic and the mental are committed to the delivery of novelty.

The importance of time and space in locating creativity

Leonard Lutwack elegantly makes a distinction when considering place and its role in literary production and reception, distinguishing between what he acknowledges as real and symbolic places, setting, landscape and so on and the problem of representation (or the challenge) that comes from utilising location (Lutwack 1984, 28, Chs. 2–3). This conundrum can also be applied to an implied sense of influence that is noted upon the author of a work with reference – as it is here – to the physical locations of production. For instance, Derby does not appear in the output of The Ruins, either in lyrics, in some kind of adopted style (as, for example, in the Mersey Beat sound of Liverpool in the 1960s) or via some discernible effect on the individual members through biographical experience. If anything, the value of location of production is calculated via freedom (to produce without financial or time constraint) rather than embodied in geography and heritage. The rhetoric of place, as Lutwack would suggest, is measured via the experience of the author as well as the comprehension of narrative by the reader, recognising skilful time-shifting and the oscillation between interiors, exteriors, night, day, seasons and actions, both logical and illogical, in concert with environment.

Of course, all of these dynamics are arguably in play during reception but can be applied to the creation of art and, as we have seen, feature heavily in the routines of the artists I observed. Place, in other words, tended to be viewed as a combination of chance and physical space from which emanates novelty. In many ways, the structures of influence are akin to the structures of modernity in that they are reliable, unquestioned, omnipresent. In late modernism, such assurances are confused, blended, questioned and unreliable. Thus, place becomes more instantaneously understood as a state of mind rather than a series of settings that people may expect to be recognised by everyone. The writings in the postcolonial literary canon bear witness to this debatable sense of surety as a fine example. Symbolic place wins out; psychological space makes sense of the myriad of options available to create something and create meaning from it. The mezzanine becomes the situation of production, separated from the physical location, dispatching the need to attach to grand narratives, exploring the sense of the possible.

What is clear from the whole research process is that place is not perceived as an important dynamic for these artists when considered representative of geography. Art – and its creation – emerges from a place that is best understood metaphysically; that is, the place that matters most is the funnel of the mezzanine, the place where everything is in play, the location of a myriad of influences and possibilities. Therefore, while each artist declares something of a biography – and some, more than others, may choose to place a little emphasis on their geographical, economic and cultural origins as having a role in their development – the overall sense is that the villages, towns and cities that these creative people have emerged from do not connect to their outputs. These are not people who reflexively relate to location, who use location as a springboard in their creative routines. While the writers are almost duty-bound to situate their scenes (even via the potential extremities of literary modernism!), build their narratives and craft their form to serve such matters, the role of Hampshire or London in the production of text is negligible. It is the embodiment of a sociological late-modernist 'nod' to accept that the individual is at play in a liquid state of meaning and emblematic connectivity – the old rules of belonging no longer hold, and neither do the rules of production in the digital age. A sense of place, therefore, is about as opaque as the diminishing value of the grand narratives of social class, cultural connexions and notions of citizenship in an age of fluid uniqueness or the historical affiliations and determinants of politics, nationality or racial and gendered identities.[8] There are multiple levers available in the creation of novelty and these artists see no overt requirement to regress to determinisms of the past lest they frame the ideas too much and blunt the muse.

We need to be able to identify space not as a physical location, but as a liminal moment in time. The dichotomy of space is therefore the distinction between physical and mental in extremely transient form; thus it is not the separation of town and city or type of studio or whether a particular town is influential on a phase of Cowper's poetry or identifiable within a Hardy novel, or whether a popular music scene is a cultural chance occurrence or a commercially exploitable construct (Cecil 2009 [1929]; Williams 1972). It is, instead, a 'singularity'[9] of individual perception, isolated from everything apart from the normative perceived anxiety of eventual judgement. Thus, when considering creativity and place it is an incontrovertible observation that all art is dependent on the brush of the hand (to instrument, laptop keyboard, paintbrush or other object) in a precise moment rather than on the myriad biographical musings of the creator or, indeed, the immediate environs of the act itself. Sadly, of course, this takes some romance out of the observations of creation, but it also adds – conversely – an ontological chaos, a haptic chance and the idea that creation is something of a test of mental agility that is always a simple slip from disaster. This adds to the romance rather than diminishing it; it's just that we don't need to visit Hardy's Cottage at Higher Bockhampton, Monk's House, the Bunyan museum, the Dalí Theatre-Museum at Figueres or their ilk to fully understand the context of what we may perceive as affective genius – we can simply attempt to empathise with the excitement, adrenaline and anxiety of the potentially never-ending now.

Notes

1. Considered throughout the research as a somewhat arbitrary, purposive age range of 40–55 years.
2. For example, I consider T. S. Eliot's 'Tradition and the Individual Talent' to provide a central tenet of this argument (Kermode 1975, 37–44), as does Harold Bloom's *The Anxiety of Influence: A Theory of Poetry* (1973).
3. My emphasis. I wish to attend in this chapter to an idea of a 'pre-postmodernism', where individuals generically and subtly recognise the process of individualisation and their effective, conscious role in creating it via 'credentialisation' and the role of diversifying consumerist, somewhat globalised capitalism.
4. For more on this idea, see Miles (2019, Ch. 9).
5. One is always drawn to Street's *The Gentleman of the Party* (1936), but there are others, vaguely heard as echoes of their original pastoral locales, as much representations of a diminished past as a standard Thomas Hardy novel, continually 'situated' in the rural, though not timeless.
6. For an excellent discussion of Weber's *Verstehen* (understanding) concept, see Parkin (2002, 19–27).
7. See Iser (1974, 1978); also, Fowler (1991) is a masterful discussion of how the reader can utilise literature to adopt a resistance approach to the encompassing progress of late modernism.
8. This is not to say, however, that 'regionalism' is not occasionally experienced as a determining factor in the setting of cultural-artistic boundaries. That said, there are many other examples in the wider oeuvre, such as the Mersey poets being of Liverpool, but not writing much – if anything – about it.

9. Attridge (2017, 95) speaks of this idea in many phases, but it is best applied here as the manifestation of an author's collective 'idioculture' (the components of world view, values and so on) and a revelation of discovery coupled with an expectancy of reception – in other words, creation is a combination of satiation and separation anxiety that is autonomous of time-space and physical place but connected to a 'language' of cultural values, mores and norms.

References

Attridge, Derek. 2017. *The Singularity of Literature*. London: Routledge.
Bauman, Zygmunt. 1999. *In Search of Politics*. Cambridge: Polity Press.
Bauman, Zygmunt. 2000. *Liquid Modernity*. Cambridge: Polity Press.
Beck, Ulrich, Anthony Giddens and Scott Lash. 1994. *Reflexive Modernization: Politics, Tradition and Aesthetics in the Modern Social Order*. Cambridge: Polity Press.
Benjamin, Walter. 2008. *The Work of Art in the Age of Mechanical Reproduction*, translated by J.A. Underwood. London: Penguin.
Bloom, Harold. 1973. *The Anxiety of Influence: A Theory of Poetry*. New York: Oxford University Press.
Bourdieu, Pierre. 1993. *The Field of Cultural Production: Essays on Art and Literature*, edited by Randal Johnson. Cambridge: Polity Press.
Cecil, David. 2009. *The Stricken Deer; or The Life of Cowper*. London: Faber and Faber. First published in 1929.
Csikszentmihalyi, Mihaly. 1996. *Creativity: Flow and the Psychology of Discovery and Invention*. New York: Harper Perennial.
Fowler, Bridget. 1991. *The Alienated Reader: Women and Popular Romantic Literature in the Twentieth Century*. Hemel Hempstead: Harvester Wheatsheaf.
Giddens, Anthony. 1990. *The Consequences of Modernity*. Cambridge: Polity Press.
Giddens, Anthony. 1991. *Modernity and Self-Identity: Self and Society in the Late Modern Age*. Cambridge: Polity Press.
Iser, Wolfgang. 1974. *The Implied Reader: Patterns of Communication in Prose Fiction from Bunyan to Beckett*. Baltimore: Johns Hopkins University Press.
Iser, Wolfgang. 1978. *The Act of Reading: A Theory of Aesthetic Response*. Baltimore: Johns Hopkins University Press.
Kermode, Frank, ed. 1975. *Selected Prose of T.S. Eliot*. London: Faber and Faber.
Lutwack, Leonard. 1984. *The Role of Place in Literature*. Syracuse, NY: Syracuse University Press.
Malinowski, Bronislaw. 1961. *Argonauts of the Western Pacific*. New York: E.P. Dutton. First published in 1922.
Miles, Philip. 2019. *Midlife Creativity and Identity: Life into Art*. Bingley: Emerald Publishing.
Parkin, Frank. 2002. *Max Weber*. Rev. ed. London: Routledge.
Read, Herbert. 2017. *The Meaning of Art*. London: Faber and Faber. First published in 1931.
Street, A.G. 1936. *The Gentleman of the Party*. London: Faber and Faber.
Waugh, Patricia. 1984. *Metafiction: The Theory and Practice of Self-Conscious Fiction*. London: Routledge.
Williams, Merryn. 1972. *Thomas Hardy and Rural England*. London: Macmillan.
Witkin, Robert W. 2005. 'A "New" Paradigm for a Sociology of Aesthetics'. In *The Sociology of Art: Ways of Seeing*, edited by David Inglis and John Hughson, 57–72. Basingstoke: Palgrave Macmillan.

14
Doing things differently: Contested identity across Manchester's arts culture quarters

Peter Atkinson

I begin by noting the public face of the official arts and culture and how its images and myth are communicated through hegemonic channels of communication. Dave Haslam, a somewhat self-styled chronicler of Manchester, the 'pop cult' city, as he called it in his book *Manchester, England: The Story of the Pop Cult City* (2000), was the subject of a five-page article in *The Observer* newspaper (Sawyer 2018, 12–17). The feature had news value because it coincided with the release of his new book *Sonic Youth Slept On My Floor: Music, Manchester, and More: A Memoir* (2018), recollections of his time as a student, DJ and fanzine editor in Manchester in the 1980s. Haslam is one of several people who have been highly influential in composing the Manchester pop imaginary, the pop-cultural mythology that has been at the centre of Manchester's modern renaissance and branding. In the article, he features in a double-page colour picture leaning against a graffiti-covered wall, his head thrown back so his face is not visible, this effacement also being an indexical signifier of ecstasy. One of the comments from the public in response to the online version of the article accused the DJ and writer of 'Hoodwinking media mates' in London into writing about him – 'the media is truly eating itself here!', the respondent observes (Sawyer 2018). (Miranda Sawyer, who conducted the interview for *The Observer*, is from Manchester and, like Haslam, has a good university education. She started her career as a writer on the now defunct *Smash Hits* pop magazine.) On the website there are other negative comments regarding Haslam's authenticity (as a shaper of Manchester's late 1980s dance music scene), and about the claim that the 1980s Haçienda era 'made Manchester what it is' (Haslam, quoted in Sawyer 2018). Other comments cite the names of earlier local music venues (such as the Twisted Wheel) as being foundational to the development of the distinctive Manchester music scene. Here we see Manchester identities contested in the public sphere of national media.

The wall featured behind Haslam is in Manchester's Northern Quarter. This is significant to the argument being made here. The graffiti is a signifier of authentic urban street culture and hipness. There is much good-quality graffiti and street art in the city's Northern Quarter, which has, for some years, been understood as Manchester city centre's bohemian enclave, a jumble of independent shops, hip bars and eateries, small specialist music venues, cheap clothes shops and specialist record stores. If one were to pull the zoom lens back from this metonymic frame of the *Observer* photograph, the wider picture would reveal a city in the throes of extreme change. In other nearby areas of the city, cranes tower and the beige concrete cores and frameworks of high-rise buildings-in-progress reach for the sky. Manchester is experiencing substantial growth (Deloitte 2018). The rate of building in Manchester, particularly of high rises, is affecting the cultural environments in which the building is underway. I argue that the very space of the Manchester city core and immediate periphery's cultural environment is being contested, but in different ways. Rapid change is creating different cultural dynamics across the city centre and its immediate periphery. One of the central cultural differentials is between the 'official' arts culture provision and the effect that new building (and ownership of land and property) has on smaller arts and cultural service producers, bodies and organisations. It could be argued that we are seeing Manchester go the same way as New York and London, cities in which the unique and creative features that made them desirable places to be are being forced out by investment in property development by large corporations (see Jeremiah Moss's blog *Vanishing New York* [Moss n.d.] – a similar thing is happening in Manchester). In order to develop this argument, I briefly recall the history of Manchester's modern rebirth as a 'creative' city.

Selling the city

Jacobs notes, paraphrasing Fredric Jameson, that the way in which culture has been appropriated and set to work as the fuel for the now semiotic motor of capital accumulation is the defining feature of late capitalism (Jacobs 1998, 254). New regimes of representation and image-making regulate the transformation from the industrial to the semiotic society, the effect being most apparent in cities, where there is a condensation of consumptive practice, and where 'desire is paramount' (Jacobs 1998, 254). There are many problems with this in terms of inclusion, which is selective. However, what is being discussed here is the creation of a city image for (the implied place) 'Manchester' (see Atkinson 2015, 72–3), and how that image prioritises, privileges and promotes certain aspects and even areas of the city, as well as selected officials, partners, users and investors. Other players, social actors and artists in the city are either already excluded, or are increasingly being persuaded to leave the city centre in order to pursue their various activities. Contested identities are thus emerging in Manchester city centre; different parties have different priorities and are doing things differently.

The celebrity Granada television presenter and record label owner Anthony (Tony) Wilson once proclaimed that 'This is Manchester, I believe we do things differently here' (Wilson 2002, 29). Such sayings, along with the images and texts associated with Wilson, have become a part of Manchester's post-Thatcher-era image-building, its branding. This modern cultural history informs perceptions of the city and influences practice, investment and cultural development, as briefly considered below with some theories of urban development. The increased prevalence of the spectacle and processes of aestheticisation are part of the self-conscious exploitation of cultural capital in urban transformation, Jacobs (1998) contends. She continues:

> Many types of urban change are taken into this ostensibly new cultural logic of city development: events-led planning, gentrification, the process of selling a city image, the expansion of sites of consumption, and even the rise of urban design as the new planning common sense. This transformation in the way in which urban development and change is understood to operate is regularly linked to the always voracious, but now more cleverly stylish, penetration of capital into the everyday lives of city dwellers. Relatedly, these processes of aestheticization and spectacularization are linked to the more complete grounding of capital accumulation in the sphere of consumption. (Jacobs 1998, 252)

Capital accumulation is at the core of city image-building. For Hospers, a city's image is influenced, positively, by the extent to which it is known, and loved (2008, 363). Cities strive to be recognised as being 'creative' as this encourages visiting, participation and investment. Such potential participants in the city's activities, culture and economy use whatever knowledge they may happen to possess, Hospers argues, to shape a view of the city. He continues:

> That knowledge is always selective and is formed out of experiences from the past and by outside sources, by information gleaned from the media, for instance. Using this perception, people construct for themselves an image of reality. The view we have of the world is therefore always coloured. And the image we have of a particular human settlement is also formed in this way. [...] That image is of major importance for the choices people make when deciding on where to work, live or spend their free time. Such decisions are not made on the basis of the objective characteristics of an area but on the subjective grounds such as the perception people have of the area. (Hospers 2008, 363)

The image of a city therefore determines whether people (who are privileged enough to be able to make such choices) use or participate in that city's activities, society and culture.

Manchester's image began to be transformed from around the start of the 1980s, and the roots of the transformation were in the mid-1970s phenomenon of 'punk rock'. At the heart of this construction of the popular culture myth was the Manchester music culture, germinated – we are informed in a range of popular publications, documentaries and feature films, as outlined below – in what Tony Wilson called 'another dawn of high pop art' (Wilson 2002, 32). For Wilson (see also Nolan 2016) this dawn was marked as the London group The Sex Pistols performed a cover of the song 'Stepping Stone' (by the sub-Beatles US pop group The Monkees) at a poorly attended gig at the Lesser Free Trade Hall on 4 June 1976. From this point on, Manchester began building its credible image as England's second city for the twenty-first century.

Bottà, using a tripartite grouping of representation, materiality and branding, observes how these resulted in a broadening of the significance of popular music in the urban environment of three cities, including Manchester (2008, 285–6). He writes of 'the cultural sensibility' of a few musicians, photographers, independent producers and entrepreneurs becoming an instrument to 're-imagine the city, its built landscape and its culture' (2008, 289–90). A batch of bands from Greater Manchester began to gain the attention of the national rock press and specialist radio programmes such as John Peel, following the 1976 event. The most prominent of these, arguably, were Joy Division (formerly Warsaw),

Buzzcocks, The Fall and, in 1983, The Smiths. As I have noted elsewhere, the focus of rock media upon these bands suggested a homogeneous 'Manchester' scene, characterised by a bleak, realist aesthetic (Atkinson 2015, 76). Black and white photographs of Joy Division by Kevin Cummins for a January 1979 *New Musical Express* cover shoot framed what *The Telegraph* quite recently referred to as 'the bleak intensity of the band's image' (Lachno 2014). Gatenby and Gill describe these as 'Un-Rock & Roll' pictures (2011, 67) having connotations of a bleak Eastern Europe which reflects the influence of David Bowie's 'Berlin period' on the band. The suicide of Joy Division's Ian Curtis in May 1980, and the poignancy and pathos of their single *Love Will Tear Us Apart* in that moment, as it achieved chart success, embedded the myth of 'Manchester' as an alternative music city distanced from London's hegemony.

Thus the stage was set for 'Manchester', the implied place, to distinguish itself as 'not London', the trope 'we do things differently' expressing a cherished otherness, an otherness which has proved to be highly marketable in an era when London has become increasingly inaccessible. The cultural mythology of Tony Wilson, Factory Records and 'Madchester' developed from this foundational myth. The narrative of this reimagining of the city is reproduced extensively. It is evident in several documentaries and two key feature films – *24 Hour Party People* (Winterbottom 2002; a story mainly about Anthony Wilson and his Manchester enterprise Factory Records) and *Control* (Corbijn 2007; a biopic of Joy Division's Ian Curtis). It is also evident in a range of media including a wide range of books, images and tourist giftware. Factory Records iconography prevails in these, and the yellow of Peter Saville's safety sign black-and-yellow-stripes graphic has now been opportunistically incorporated into Manchester's re-emphasis of its worker bee motif as a badge of communal self-assertion and solidarity in the aftermath of the May 2017 Manchester Arena atrocity.

Witts (2018) observes the processes involved in rebranding Manchester. Building on the mythology of its having a unique, quirky music scene, and needing to define and promote a 'distinctive, reborn cultural character for the Millennium, Manchester's elite political networks started to construct a modern history for the city'. They centred it 'on their entrepreneurial selves, opening the civic biography in 1996', the year a bomb destroyed a large part of the city centre. Physical rebuilding allowed the renaissance story to be 'predicated on urban renewal', he argues, including 'lifestyle manifestations such as the gay village …, the bohemian Northern Quarter redeveloped by property entrepreneurs Urban Splash, and the promotion of the city by the

Manchester Independents action group and others as a centre of popular culture' (Witts 2018, 24).

Cultural quarters

Manchester's 'pop cult' city image-making has become a part of the official arts culture of the city as, in Bottà's (2008) scheme, the tripartite relationship between popular music, representation and materiality shapes both representation of and the materiality of the city. Thus, a new city piazza is named 'Tony Wilson Place'. A proposed new multi-million-pound performance arts space to house the Manchester International Festival is to be called the Factory. As I note elsewhere (Atkinson 2017), the historical events, cultural productions, practices and venues – new and old – involved in the rebirth of Manchester's cultural character are all centred in a very small geographical area of the city. For example, the multi-million-pound Factory will be built near the former site of the famous Granada, and later ITV, Studios in what will be called St John's Quarter, adjacent to the Museum of Science and Industry. This is a five-minute walk from the aforementioned Free Trade Hall (built on the site of the Peterloo massacre). It is only another minute or so's walk from there to Central Library and Albert Square. Then a two-minute walk takes one to the Manchester Art Gallery. It is only a short walk from there to the Bridgewater Hall concert hall, and also to the site where the Haçienda once stood (now replaced by luxury apartments, which retain its name). A further one-minute walk leads you to the arts centre HOME – situated in Tony Wilson Place. Castlefield Gallery and the Ritz and Gorilla music venues are close by, as is the rebranded, and expensive, Refuge (formerly the Palace Hotel), which hosts the *Louder Than Words* music literature festival. Refuge, nearly next to the site of the demolished BBC Manchester, now replaced by a multi-million-pound development, is on Oxford Road, which leads down to the universities, and the Whitworth art gallery.

This area, I suggest, represents the legitimised, and increasingly commodified, official arts and cultural provision in the environment of the south of the city core, around Albert Peter's Square, down Quay Street to St Johns, to Castlefield, and down to Oxford Road. This has organically grown as a cultural quarter as the result of the geographical interrelation of key cultural institutions: museums, art galleries, libraries, broadcasting institutions, a conference centre, theatres, music venues and an arts cinema. The modern mythology of Manchester pop culture and of the Wilsonian 'we do things differently' was founded here and now supports commodification of the area and a proliferation of high-rise building, gentrification and an influx of retail chain outlets. This is the area where the first dense development of high-rise buildings is in progress. Two towers of the four-tower cluster of 'Deansgate Square' (marketed as a 'ground-breaking development bringing new levels of style and sophistication to the heart of Manchester') are nearly completed, rising near the existing Beetham tower, and it is proposed that they will be joined by another 51-storey block. Apex Tower reaches upwards opposite the Haçienda apartments (and blocks light from the historic Deansgate Locks). More light will be blocked if a proposed 40-storey block is built straight opposite. More high-rise developments are planned in the southern and south-western city core as a part of the new St John's Quarter. These developments are contentious and, indeed, are actively condemned and contended by urban activists in the city.

I conclude that, in this official cultural zone, commodification of arts and culture and gentrification are leading to selective usage and consumption, and pricing now proves prohibitive for many people. The independent media site *The Meteor* has recently signalled the lack of affordable housing being made available in many of these new blocks, along with statistics of the percentage of developments which have evaded meeting a set quota of such. Meanwhile, the arrival of retail chain outlets around the key official arts institutions, such as Manchester Art Gallery and HOME, arguably serves to make the environment they inhabit more bland. This may nullify the stimulating effects these arts institutions inspire as one walks out into a retail-centric street that essentially could be anywhere. Thus, there is contested identity in this area between the need for affordable (and social) housing and the creation of thousands of luxury flats. There is also contestation between the cultural impact of inspirational arts facilities and the commercialised surroundings, colonised by national and international retail outlets. They are the only businesses who can afford to pay the premium rents and rates demanded of the properties in the immediate vicinity of these cultural institutions.

Contested identities are also evident in central Manchester. The environmental and cultural tension between the unofficial culture of Manchester's Northern Quarter, and the officially sanctioned, commodified and gentrified culture of the south, south-west and, increasingly, the west of the city, illustrates this. The Northern Quarter, which is immediately adjacent to the city centre to the north-east, was, until recently, considered to be bohemian, having been a community made up of artists, cultural providers and mainly independent retailers. Residential development is creeping into this area too, particularly in neighbouring Ancoats, but, at present at least, it tends to be somewhat less intrusive, more low-rise and lower density than in other parts of the city. In a number of streets in the Northern Quarter, small independent retailers have an enduring and diverse presence. There appears to be a lesser presence of chain retail outlets and the area still retains a creative ambience. This is reflected in the creative artwork that adorns some of the buildings in the area (see Figure 14.1) and is, I suggest, why the London-based *Observer* had Haslam photographed there, with the intention of glossing the manufactured brand image of 'Manchester' that he represents as an authentic one, reflected in a creative, hip street culture.

Rising rents and the threat of property development in the Northern Quarter are increasingly forcing arts providers who lack funding, and independent retailers, out of the area, however. Although still encompassing more artistic, creative and commercial diversity than the 'official' cultural quarter, it is undergoing significant change as independents are leaving and the area is increasingly making appeal to the 'hipster' market. Sandor (2018) asks if the Northern Quarter is in danger of becoming 'just another Shoreditch' as she compares what is happening there with the self-conscious commercialisation of the London area as an over-priced hipster resort and habitat. Acknowledging that the same patterns recur in culturally and economically buoyant cities, where artists, creatives and independent shops are attracted by cheap rents in run-down inner-city areas, Sandor laments that gentrification is 'inevitable', and that artists 'will always be nomads moving from one area of a city to another until they're priced out and move on to another city where the process starts again' (2018). She notes that while new bars and restaurants are opening, arts organisations and related businesses are moving out, or shutting because of rising rents. This is a trend, and she names one grassroots innovation organisation which has been persuaded to move from the Northern Quarter. They have joined an open design studio and workshop space close to Victoria station which is supported by a property development consortium (Sandor 2018).

Emery (2018) notes, in a *Frieze.com* report, that Manchester's property boom 'backdrops the continuing displacement of the cities' [Manchester's and Salford's] artists, as studios continue to be razed by developers to make way for luxury accommodation'. In 2017 the long-established Rogue Artists' Studios relocated from the city centre because of redevelopment plans. The Studios had been home to more than 100 artists in the Grade II-listed Crusader Mill at Ancoats, slightly east of the

Figure 14.1 Street art near Oldham Street, Northern Quarter, Manchester. © John van Aitken.

Northern Quarter. The property was sold to developers who worked with Manchester City Council and Arts Council England to relocate Rogue to a former Victorian school in Openshaw, East Manchester. There were mixed views amongst the Rogue artists about the move. Palmer (2017) notes that Rogue's co-director of the time, Martin Nash, considered that the organisation had 'forged a unique model' in order to secure its future. Other artists, however, resented the move away from the city-centre community and the additional travel involved in getting to the new studios. Emery (2018) noted that Manchester City Council were evidently taking 'the same approach to artists' studios that they do to affordable housing: it does not need to be within the city centre itself, that is increasingly reserved for the privileged few'.

Two former Rogue studio holders – Hilary Jack and Lucy Harvey – have meanwhile founded Paradise Works, in Salford, but close to Manchester city centre, and which opened in October 2017. Emery observes that:

> With a culture-friendly developer on board in Urban Splash, as well as support from Salford City Council, Jack and Harvey are aiming to provide some stability for the group of artists that now call Paradise Works home, giving them an opportunity to think long-term and make work without having to worry about the looming threat of eviction. Whether Paradise Works can sustain this intention remains to be seen. Ultimately it is reliant on long-term support from Urban Splash, but feelings are nonetheless positive about the future. (Emery 2018)

Paradise Works describes itself as 'an artist run initiative providing studios & project space to a community of proactive, intergenerational, contemporary artists'. The copy on their website continues:

> Paradise Works is currently home to 28 artists working across sculpture, installation, painting, drawing, design, film, audio, performance, photography & curation. Our outlook is local, national and international, and we believe artists hold a vital role in the development of a vibrant and diverse city. Paradise Works aims to create a sustainable urban model for artist-led activity in the growing arts ecology across the Salford & Manchester border. (Paradise Works n.d.)

At the a-n artnews assembly, Salford, in May 2018, the issue of artists' expulsion from Manchester city centre was discussed along with concern about the future of Paradise Works. The relationship with co-funder Urban Splash is rather ambiguous for, as one attendee observed, that company's 'Irwell Riverside' development is moving ever closer to Paradise Works, and there was speculation at the assembly about what the picture will be in even a year's time. The Development Manager of Salford City Council participated in the afternoon discussion and it was suggested that a mechanism was required to join up the planning work he is involved with, and the nuts and bolts of physical infrastructure, with wider policy agendas, including Salford's nascent Culture Strategy. Kerry Harker, founder and Director of the East Leeds Project, who attended the meeting, felt that the problem, 'as ever', is what is 'happening at the strategic level and with the tiny few who end up making the policy' (pers. comm., 25 May 2018). Many artists in the North are scrabbling for every crumb from the table – Manchester, or I should say, certain parts of the city, merely represents a microcosm of this. Again, we see contested identity in Manchester–Salford within a small geographical area. Artists feel that they should have a place in communities; property developers prioritise profit but, in some cases, are supporting artists and groups because they see the benefits in promoting arts and culture in the physical areas they are developing.

Conclusion

It has been seen that Manchester has been rebranded from the Thatcher era onwards. The resultant mythology of the 'pop cult' city provides an imaginary for a creative city which is at the hub of the 'southern North' agglomeration of creative clusters (Atkinson 2018; Hughes and Atkinson 2018). This place-knowledge has been cultivated by capital, and the imaginary that has been thereby fostered drives investment, promotes tourism and persuades people to perceive, use and consume 'Manchester' in certain ways. City-centre Manchester is an arena of, and for, spectacles, as festivals, exhibitions and arts events populate the yearly calendar, as the city hosts major music and sporting events, as its resident broadcasting and digital institutions promote their brands, and as a host of charities produce spectacles in the pursuit of their causes. Manchester has developed greatly from the city that was the focus of so much social-realist imagery in films, TV series and popular music texts. One of the key aspects of the city's development during these years is that people now live in the city centre.

Property development is fomenting great change in the city. It is not the purpose of this chapter to comment on the logistics of these developments, how they are financed and how planning permission is granted. Such comment could be produced by those who have expertise in this particular area. However, I have observed some of the cultural impact of development in the city. Property development has resulted in a series of contested identities becoming apparent in the city core and its immediate periphery, the principal one being affordability and the need for development to serve the community, and not just narrow interests. Tony Wilson's phrase 'This is Manchester, I believe we do things differently here' provided one of the key images of the city's promotion as a centre of popular culture. His statement was a strong assertion of provincial community against the metropolitan hegemony. As the cranes tower above the city, and the patchwork of industrial heritage and steel and glass renewal constantly changes below, there are conflicting identities at many levels, as illustrated here. In this evolving, changing environment, Wilson's famous phrase might be adapted to, 'this is Manchester, everyone's doing things differently here'.

References

Atkinson, Peter. 2015. 'The Sons and Heirs of Something Particular: The Smiths' Manchester Aesthetic, 1982–1987'. In *Regional Aesthetics: Mapping UK Media Cultures*, edited by Ieuan Franklin, Hugh Chignell and Kristin Skoog, 71–89. Basingstoke: Palgrave Macmillan.

Atkinson, Peter. 2017. 'Producing Habitus: ITV Soap Operas and the "Northern Powerhouse"'. In *Heading North: The North of England in Film and Television*, edited by Ewa Mazierska, 151–71. Cham: Palgrave Macmillan.

Atkinson, Peter. 2018. '"Manchester" and the Southern North Creative Cluster'. Paper presented at the Investigating Regional Creative Clusters symposium, Watershed, Bristol, 6 March 2018.

Bottà, Giacomo. 2008. 'Urban Creativity and Popular Music in Europe since the 1970s: Representation, Materiality, and Branding'. In *Creative Urban Milieus: Historical Perspectives on Culture, Economy, and the City*, edited by Martina Heßler and Clemens Zimmermann, 285–308. Frankfurt am Main: Campus Verlag.

Corbijn, Anton. 2007. *Control* [film]. London: Momentum Pictures.

Deloitte. 2018. 'Manchester Crane Survey 2018: Living for the City'. Accessed 24 July 2018. https://www2.deloitte.com/uk/en/pages/real-estate/articles/manchester-crane-survey.html.

Emery, Tom. 2018. 'In Manchester and Salford, Sustainable Artist-Run Spaces Power Forward', *Frieze*, 4 April. Accessed 5 April 2018. https://frieze.com/article/manchester-and-salford-sustainable-artist-run-spaces-power-forward.

Gatenby, Phill and Craig Gill. 2011. *The Manchester Musical History Tour*. Manchester: Empire Publications.

Haslam, Dave. 2000. *Manchester, England: The Story of the Pop Cult City*. London: Fourth Estate.

Haslam, Dave. 2018. *Sonic Youth Slept on My Floor: Music, Manchester, and More: A Memoir*. London: Constable.

Hospers, Gert-Jan. 2008. 'What is the City but the People? Creative Cities beyond the Hype'. In *Creative Urban Milieus: Historical Perspectives on Culture, Economy, and the City*, edited by Martina Heßler and Clemens Zimmermann, 353–75. Frankfurt am Main: Campus Verlag.

Hughes, Alan and Peter Atkinson. 2018. 'England's North–South Divide is History – but the Nation's Rifts are Deepening', *The Conversation*, 1 July. Accessed 26 April 2019. https://theconversation.com/englands-north-south-divide-is-history-but-the-nations-rifts-are-deepening-99044.

Jacobs, Jane M. 1998. 'Staging Difference: Aestheticization and the Politics of Difference in Contemporary Cities'. In *Cities of Difference*, edited by Ruth Fincher and Jane M. Jacobs, 252–78. New York: Guilford Press.

Lachno, James. 2014. 'Kevin Cummins Q&A: "I Saved Joy Division from Being Bon Jovi"', *The Telegraph*, 7 June. Accessed 14 February 2018. www.telegraph.co.uk/culture/photography/10882054/Kevin-Cummins-QandA-I-saved-Joy-Division-from-being-Bon-Jovi.html.

Moss, Jeremiah. n.d. *Vanishing New York* blog. Accessed 26 April 2019. vanishingnewyork.blogspot.com.

Nolan, David. 2016. *I Swear I Was There: Sex Pistols, Manchester and the Gig that Changed the World*. London: Music Press Books.

Palmer, Stephen. 2017. 'New Home for Manchester's Rogue Artists' Studios Provides "Long-Term Security"', *a-n News*, 22 August. Accessed 23 July 2018. www.a-n.co.uk/news/new-home-for-manchesters-rogue-artists-studios/.

Paradise Works. n.d. 'Paradise Works'. Accessed 26 July 2018. www.paradise-works.com.

Sandor, Andrea. 2018. 'Is Northern Quarter in Danger of Becoming Just Another Shoreditch?', *Manchester Confidential*, 10 July. Accessed 24 July 2018. https://confidentials.com/manchester/is-northern-quarter-in-danger-of-becoming-shoreditch.

Sawyer, Miranda. 2018. 'Dave Haslam: "That Music Changed Lives. It Made Manchester What It Is"', *The Observer*, 13 May. Accessed 24 April 2019. www.theguardian.com/music/2018/may/13/dave-haslam-memoir-manchester-hacienda-sonic-youth-miranda-sawyer.

Wilson, Tony. 2002. *24 Hour Party People: What the Sleeve Notes Never Tell You*. London: Channel 4 Books.

Winterbottom, Michael. 2002. *24 Hour Party People* [film]. London: Film4, Revolution Films, Baby Cow Productions, UK Film Council, The Film Consortium.

Witts, Richard. 2018. 'Manpool, the Musical: Harmony and Counterpoint on the Lancashire Plain'. In *Sounds Northern: Popular Music, Culture and Place in England's North*, edited by Ewa Mazierska, 17–36. Sheffield: Equinox Publishing.

15
First, second and third: Exploring Soja's Thirdspace theory in relation to everyday arts and culture for young people

Steph Meskell-Brocken

'Place-making' has become a recent 'buzz-term' within the UK arts and cultural sector as a way of describing the implantation of arts activity into communities that are perceived to be 'socially excluded', 'deprived' or any other such deficit-loaded term. This has been highlighted by Gilmore, who said, 'current arts policy aims to address and rebalance arts participation patterns on the basis of geography' (2013, 88), as exemplified by the Creative People and Places programme, which works specifically within areas that have been designated as having low participation. This sort of project activity aims to demonstrate that participation in arts and cultural activity can in some way serve to build community and, by extension, a sense of place. However, throughout much of the literature around the Creative People and Places programme, there are gaps in understanding that appear to be 'hiding in plain sight'. In Boiling and Thurman's report, the following statement is made with relation to 'Places and spaces':

> It is self-evident that arts events happening in non-arts spaces are likely to reach non-arts audiences. People can stumble across experiences incidentally; programming in places that people are already familiar with and comfortable in can remove one of the risk factors of arts going for the first time; presenting work in unusual or iconic spaces, which have a particular place in the history and memory of local people can be a powerful draw; and 'taking the

unusual to the usual' can help residents re-imagine their local area in new and surprising ways. (Boiling and Thurman n.d. [c. 2018], 9)

The central conceit of this statement is that all arts programming in non-arts spaces will engage new audiences who regard the non-arts space as more familiar or comfortable than the arts space. What this fails to consider, however, is 'what if it has the exact opposite effect?' What if, in fact, bringing the arts activity or event into the space that has value for an individual disrupts the relationship that they have with that space and causes a disconnect for that individual which makes them far less likely to engage? This possibility is a particular risk when developing work for young people. In 2014 I conducted some research with young people with whom I was working at a large, recently built youth club in Lancashire. I was employed as an arts worker, tasked with delivering six hours of drama activity in the youth club per week. One of the key findings from this research was the level of negotiation that was needed to encourage young people to take part in something with a degree of structure and outcome in a setting that is connected, for them, with relaxing, chatting with friends and directionless activity.

In making reference to the heading 'Places and spaces' used in the report, I am aware of the importance of defining and delineating these terms which are so often used in tandem or as synonyms. In the context of this chapter, my understanding of the terms follows de Certeau's system of definition, which states that Space 'is a practiced place […] i.e.: a place constituted by a system of signs' and Place 'is the order (of whatever kind) in accordance with which elements are distributed in relationships of coexistence' (1984, 117). Using this definition, place becomes a more concrete notion of stability, whereas space is that which is constructed through action.

I contend in this chapter that Soja's Thirdspace theory can shed light on this vacant space in discourse and that his theories can aid in a movement that seeks to go beyond the deficit or 'problem' model into a removal of binary barriers between concepts, forms and ideas. His ideas are not alien within the current discourse. In his book *Thirdspace: Journeys to Los Angeles and Other Real-and-Imagined Places* (1996), Soja suggests that space and spatiality have been neglected in previous thinking on the subject of 'being' in favour of an overt focus on 'Historicality' and 'Sociality' (p. 71). He suggests that when this has occurred, 'Spatiality tends to be peripheralized into the background as a reflection, container, stage, environment, or external constraint upon human behaviour and social action' (p. 71). In the current move towards consideration of the importance and interconnectedness of socially engaged art practices and the spaces and places in which they reside and create, this seems to be precisely what artists, policy-makers and academics alike are beginning to attempt and theorise. I argue that the theories of Soja are not only relevant in the analysis of this current work but also form a useful and forward-looking way in which to begin to see space and place through different eyes and with potential for new and exciting methods of place-making.

In this chapter I explore Soja's theory of 'Thirdspace' in detail and then move on to address some current thinking around the status of the 'young person' and how such thinking can shed light on their inclusion or otherwise in place-based discourses. After that I will take a look at some of the recent work that has been undertaken within the Understanding Everyday Participation project which has attempted to usefully problematise notions of place, participation and deficit models of thinking in arts policy discourse. I will finally move on to making some suggestions as to the ways in which Soja's work can help in understandings of space and place with relation to arts and cultural programmes with children and young people.

Soja's Thirdspace theory

Edward Soja developed his notion of 'Thirdspace' in his 1996 book *Thirdspace: Journeys to Los Angeles and Other Real-and-Imagined Places* as a response to and evolution of the work of Henri Lefebvre, a Marxist philosopher and sociologist. In particular, Soja takes his inspiration from Lefebvre's *The Production of Space*, stating his intention to 'purposefully reappropriate' (1996, 53) his work. Soja's own theorisation of the idea of 'Thirdspace' moves through a process in the book by which he interrogates Lefebvre's work, interprets it and reinterprets it, making for a challenging concept to make sense of. However, this is not by accident. As Soja highlights in commentary on *The Production of Space*, Lefebvre himself reorders and reprioritises aspects of his work as an attempt to avoid 'systems' (p. 64, fn) and demonstrate one of the key tenets of 'thirding', the creation of 'an expanding chain of heuristic disruptions, strengthening defences against totalising closure and all "permanent constructions"' (p. 61).

The first term that Soja introduces his reader to is 'the Aleph', a concept taken by Lefebvre from a short story by Jorge Luis Borges. The

Aleph is compared to eternity in spatial terms, 'one of the points in space that contains all other points' (Borges, cited in Soja 1996, 55). However, despite the assertion that *'everything* comes together in Thirdspace' (p. 56), the concept is neither as simple nor as complex as a totality. He moves on to describe the process of 'thirding' through the second chapter, focusing initially on what he refers to as 'social space'.

Soja begins his argument by presenting several triads that he has borrowed from Lefebvre, the first of which is 'the *physical*-nature, the Cosmos; secondly, the *mental,* including logical and formal abstractions; and thirdly, the *social*' (Lefebvre 1991, 11–12, cited in Soja 1996, 62). The second of these triads is described as 'Spatial Practice (perceived space); Representations of Space (conceived space); and Spaces of Representation (lived space)' (1996, 65). Despite this focus on triads, however, he guards against the temptation of creating any form of 'holy trinity'-style construction and instead suggests that the process of 'thirding' is designed to 'not stop at three [...] but to build further, to move on, to continuously expand the production of knowledge beyond what is presently known' (1996, 61).

Soja underlines throughout this chapter that the aspect of the triad that he (and Lefebvre) are primarily concerned with is that of 'social space'. Soja contests that social space can be seen, as can the physical and mental space, as 'simultaneously real and imagined, concrete and abstract, material and metaphorical' (p. 65). It is here that the core of the notion of Thirdspace can be found. Thirdspace asks the interpreter to move beyond binaries and, in fact, as Soja follows up, not just 'beyond the binary but beyond the third term as well' (p. 65). The choice to 'third' is not a rejection of either of the possible binaries presented in the interpretation of space, more an acceptance of them, a way of seeing them as inherently interconnected and a suggestion of what interpretation may develop from the initial perception. Following on from the delineation and description of social space, Soja moves on to digging deeper into Lefebvre's second triad regarding spatial practice, representations of space and spaces of representation. Within these descriptions, his concepts of Firstspace, Secondspace and Thirdspace become clearer and more thoroughly elucidated.

Firstspace, Soja posits, relates to Lefebvre's 'Spatial Practice'. This is the material understanding of space, the way in which individuals interact with that space and the methods through which that space is produced, constructed and reconstructed. He states, 'spatial practice, as the process of producing the material form of social spatiality, is thus presented as both medium and outcome of human activity, behaviour and experience' (p. 66). He also describes this as 'perceived space' (p. 66), that which can be seen within measurable and quantifiable constraints. Secondspace, he goes on to describe, relates to Representations of Space and is identified as the space as seen through the eyes of those who interact with it. This is termed as 'conceived' space (p. 67) and is the space of designers, planners, urbanists and so on, and also, importantly for this piece of work, artists. Secondspace is conceptualised as a custodian space not only of knowledge and signs but also of 'utopian thought and vision' (p. 67).

Finally, Thirdspace, related to the concept of spaces of representation, reaffirms the previous points around coexistence and development of its companion spaces. Soja states that this space is seen by Lefebvre 'both as distinct from the other two spaces and encompassing them' (p. 67). This space is referred to as that which is 'directly *lived*' (p. 67) and inhabited by those who aim to decipher and 'actively transform the worlds we live in' (p. 67). It is unsurprising given this description that he also specifically mentions artists along with specific mentions of 'imagination' (p. 68), suggesting that Thirdspace is also a space of reimagining and recreation. He is keen also to underline the significance of the political within the conception of Thirdspace, suggesting that 'combining the real and imagined, things and thought on equal terms, or at least not privileging one over the other *a priori*, these lived spaces of representation are thus the terrain for the generation of "counterspaces"' (p. 68).

This suggests that within Thirdspace lies the potential not only for reimaginings of existing structures but a more radical movement within the process of 'thirding' towards spaces and conceptions of spaces that recognise and attempt to break with existing power structures and dynamics.

Young people and place-making

At this point I wish to reflect back on the material that I have presented thus far with relation to Soja's theory of Thirdspace and suggest how this may be relevant to the question of young people's participation in arts and cultural activity related to place-making. I see the relevance of Soja's theory as twofold. In the first instance, seeing and interpreting space is a vital element in engaging any community in arts work and place-making. Through analysing conceptions of space through the lens of First, Second and Thirdspace, doors can be opened and practices dissected in ways that enable the researcher and/or practitioner to develop a different understanding of the ways in which young people interact with and perceive space. This understanding in turn can enable models of practice to develop which are responsive to these perceptions. LeftCoast, a Creative People and Places project working in Blackpool and the Fylde, have developed as part of their programme several spaces that aim to connect notions of the historicality and sociality of spaces that hold relevance to Blackpool with the production of contemporary art. One of these is the 'Art Bed and Breakfast'. The project is described on the website thus:

> A B&B will be a traditional Blackpool Bed and Breakfast re-imagined by artists for 21st Century. Its central mission is to support arts, culture, training and development opportunities for local communities and creatives whilst still performing as a highly attractive hotel for staying guests. [...] We will commission as many aspects of the re-creation of the hotel as possible from artists – integrating it into the physical space and day-to-day operations – and once open we will invest in a continual programme of new commissions, public engagement, learning and talent development. (Art B&B 2017)

This project demonstrates the foregrounding of the Thirdspace notion of pulling together the threads of material and representative and pushing forward to create something that is both recognisable and new as a form. However, there is no direct connection here to the engagement of children and young people.

The political notion of Thirdspace and its significance as a place where space and place can be reimagined and power hierarchies challenged is also of significance to work that seeks to emancipate communities and encourage deeper engagement in their own spaces and places through art work and creativity. Additionally, I believe that the notion of 'thirding' is a concept that transcends the conceptualisation of space alone and can be applied across the arts and the many sectors that arts work intersects with. As arts organisations and practitioners are increasingly required to collaborate across sectors and, some may argue, instrumentalise their work, to view this form of practice through a Thirdspace perspective offers a way of transcending the separation of disciplines and practices and, therefore, enabling the creation of new space for practice. Often the difficulty in articulating examples of this form of practice is in discovering projects where the relationships between the arts and 'other' disciplines or areas are non-hierarchical. The 'lead organisation' tends to be whoever is in receipt of the funding that has enabled the project to take place. The Manchester young people's mental health charity 42nd Street, however, have been pioneering in the development of projects that synthesise the arts into their existing service delivery. In 2016, 42nd Street transformed a building next door to their existing base in Ancoats, Manchester, into the Horsfall, a space that fuses an awareness of heritage via the connection to the Ancoats Art Museum of the nineteenth century, with participatory art projects, professional art commissions and exhibitions, and the provision of mental health services for children and young people (42nd Street n.d.). Within the Horsfall, neither of these elements takes precedence over the other: it is not a gallery with a young people's programme, nor is it a youth service with an arts programme, rather it exists as a Thirdspace.

I now wish to take some time to address the importance of placing children and young people at the centre of this discourse around space/place and participation. Naturally, much of the impetus for asserting the importance of this focus is led by my own experiences and beliefs. However, if the concept of audience development is truly at the centre of place-making art practices (as suggested by Gilmore 2013, 89), then I believe that as future audiences and cultural producers, this work begins with young people.

It is important to note at the outset that the categorisation of a 'young person' is regularly debated and in flux; however, for the purposes of this chapter, I am referring to the 5–18 age bracket. Verhellen conceptualised young people as 'becomings' or 'not-yets [...] not yet knowing, not yet competent, and not yet being' (2000, 33). This notion is supported and developed by Garratt and Piper, who suggest that young people find themselves in a process of 'othering' (2008, 490) by adults. This sense of the young person as 'the other' is also supported by Osler and Starkey, who have suggested that youth is 'portrayed as threatening yet politically apathetic' (2003, 245), a dichotomous description that helps to highlight the contested status of youth. This is echoed by Garratt and Piper, who pinpoint a discursive no-win situation that young people may find themselves in, 'damned as a rebellious teenager if they have an opinion, and damned as apathetic if they do not' (2008, 490).

Garratt and Piper suggest that the young person is often seen as a force that needs to be controlled, and dangerous (2008, 483). In fact, as suggested by Mycock (2011), there is a viewpoint that strong opinions, free time and an absence of the experience (or weariness) of adulthood, when coupled with a modicum of received political knowledge, have the potential to be a lethal combination for the ruling classes if young people decided that they wished to stand up for or against a particular political issue. These two perspectives present a conflicting vision of the young person as, on the one hand, powerless and lacking in value, and, on the other, dangerous and powerful. The evidence provided by these writers suggests that there is a conflict at play between perceptions of young people politically and the emancipatory goals of those developing arts projects.

Jans makes use of the terminology 'writing one's own biography' (2004, 29) to conceptualise the way in which children and young people negotiate their path through adolescence. This analogy helps to demonstrate the young person playing an active role in creating their own future at the same time as emphasising the importance of the present moment to the young person. Jans makes it clear that, in today's society, the writing of one's own biography is not an exclusively individual practice. He suggests that young people are able to 'borrow examples, alternatives, values and norms from social practices' (2004, 29), foregrounding the idea that young people must be viewed within their own social context, as part of communities, networks and groups including both their peers and adults. Jans suggests that in order to support this 'writing' process, practitioners and policy-makers must start from the point that children and young people are 'fundamentally influenced by the same economic, political and social powers that constitute the context of adults' lives' (2004, 28). In this context Jans can be interpreted as suggesting that practices within society that are deemed to have an impact on the adult population must also be recognised as impacting young people.

With Jans's assertion in mind, the most recent piece of research into young people's participation in arts and cultural activities demonstrates another conspicuous gap. The Culture and Sport Evidence (CASE) programme set out to gather information from young people about their levels of participation in arts, culture and sports activities, connecting this with health and well-being. In this particular set of surveys, young people aged 10 to 15 years were surveyed, with over-16s being asked to take the adult version. This survey, although yielding useful data around levels of participation and their connection to the well-being agenda, does not bring a geographical perspective to the analysis of participation (Gilmore 2013, 87–8). Also lacking a geographical perspective is the Taking Part Survey, an annual survey undertaken by the Department for Culture, Media and Sport that looks at participation in arts, museums and galleries, heritage, libraries, archives and sport. Equally, in data-heavy reports on the Creative People and Places programme, where geography is key, children and young people are left off the agenda. There is a clear disconnect in the way in which space and place is being applied to an understanding of young people's participation in arts and culture.

Everyday participation, community and space

Additional supporting evidence can be found in the Understanding Everyday Participation (UEP) project. This study aims to address the deficit model of thinking that dominates discourse around arts and cultural participation through a consideration of the 'everyday participation' taking place in communities throughout England (Gilmore 2013; Jancovich 2017; Miles and Gibson 2016). It also states one of its aims as to investigate 'the relationship between space, place and participation' (Schaefer, Edwards and Milling 2017, 47). Schaefer, Edwards and Milling state that within the current agenda and discourse, 'cultural participation is posited to have an impact (only and always positively) via the regeneration of economically deprived, (typically) urban areas experiencing high levels of "social exclusion"' (2017, 48). This statement places arts and cultural participation squarely at the centre of the discourse around space, place and place-making. They go on to suggest that this positioning is led by the aforementioned deficit model and the 'geography of lack' (Rose 1997, 8).

Jancovich's (2017) study of the participation agenda identified multiple studies that have taken place highlighting a dissonance between what cultural policy-makers and those engaged in work within arts and culture aspire towards in terms of participation and engagement, and what is actually happening in practice (p. 108). Key to this dissonance is a sense of understanding the barriers between individuals and their participation. Jancovich states that whereas practical barriers have certainly been shown to be an issue in participation, psychological barriers have been identified as more of an issue than those classed as practical, as observed by Bunting *et al.* (2008, 7–8). Jancovich goes on to list these psychological barriers as a 'feeling of exclusion or lack of interest in the arts on offer' (2017, 108).

Jancovich (2017) also found that artists and those working as current arts professionals more commonly noted the importance of visiting cultural institutions such as theatres or galleries as stepping stones on their path of engagement with the arts, than any participatory activity (p. 113). This contrasted with members of the public who were interviewed and were more likely to make mention of 'everyday culture such as drawing and playing music at home, as evidence of a cultured childhood' (p. 113). Both this specific mention of space through the words of the interviewed professionals and the mentions of psychological barriers point towards evidence, not just of the significance of space, but of the importance of an understanding of space that includes both the physical and the psychological. Thirdspace, therefore, can help to provide an understanding of the issue of *Schwellenangst* or 'fear of the threshold' that is described here, demonstrating a sense of the power that space and place can hold over the arts participant in conjunction with notions of cultural capital.

Rose's work on community arts projects has been influential in informing the discourse around notions of space within the Understanding Everyday Participation project. Her work develops a conceptualisation of space that relates notions of space and place to community and, by extension, identity. She states that because of the nature of identity as conflicting and intersecting, 'spaces, places and landscapes become meaningful in the context of power-ridden social relations, and [...] dominant forms of spatiality can be contested' (1997, 2). Power is the key theme within Rose's conceptualisation of space, with her work located specifically in Edinburgh and analysing the conflict between the inner city, seen as powerful, holding important investment and the locus of cultural capital, and the outer limits of the city, its suburbs, estates and 'communities' at the 'margins' (pp. 4–9). She also suggests that policy-makers have perhaps used arts projects in attempts to encourage development of cultural capital within these marginal spaces (driven by arts workers from the centre) but also to drive individuals to become part of the central locus (p. 9), in a movement comparable with neoliberal 'trickle-down economics' (Andreou 2014) which advocates tax reductions (for this read greater investment) for the wealthy and big business (for this read large cultural institutions). She argues, 'to imagine "community" through the same spatiality as that through which power produces its margins is only to reproduce that marginalization' (Rose 1997, 13).

However, Rose (1997) also speaks of a kind of community that can be created through projects that are led by the creation of connections and networks between people. She writes:

> The body politic of the other 'community' is thus understood as a kind of organism. But this discursive analogy does not work to naturalize a time-less 'community' of unchanging and pure identity; just the opposite. What is naturalized in this discourse is an 'other' community of unstable 'flux'. (Rose 1997, 10)

This notion of 'flux' and a sense of organic growth is reminiscent of the fluid and ever-developing idea of Thirdspace. The description of the 'other' community also connects with language used around young people that has been referenced earlier. The E17 Art Trail, having developed from a small element of a music festival into an arts festival in its own right, demonstrates some of the tenets of Rose's notion of 'community' projects. The trail is open access, enabling anyone to submit a piece in a wide range of artforms, as organiser Laura Kerry has highlighted:

> When we first began we imagined it as a visual arts trail but every conceivable art form has been programmed in the E17 Art Trail over the years: from bell-ringing to live tattooing, floristry, crochet, spoken word and to creative industries creating, for instance, bespoke furniture. (Laura Kerry, interview by Weedon, Chapter 4 in this book)

The team behind the trail use a mixed model of engagement to offer open-access opportunities for local people and professional artists to take up, whilst also offering support and 'creative spark' to communities who may not respond to an open call. Morag McGuire expresses this as: 'At the heart of the E17 Art Trail is the invitation to be involved and in some communities and neighbourhoods we take more time to make sure that the invitation reaches everyone and offer some support for neighbours to co-produce something' (interview by Weedon, Chapter 4 in this book). Kerry and McGuire also highlight that the Art Trail has served as a pivot point for the further development of arts and cultural stock within their borough. Kerry states:

> The cultural landscape now is so dramatically different. We have regular designer markets and pop-up maker spaces and music festivals. This year [2018] we have seen two festivals of theatre in the last four months, there are window galleries year round, we have a theatre pub, many artist studio complexes and many more are planned, other art trails were established in the borough and numerous others are being developed. New creative businesses selling the work of local makers are opening where the business rates are lower, creating districts with distinct personalities. Other types of business employ local creatives to paint murals, design their branding, shop fronts and interiors. There are local culture publications: we have this amazing monthly magazine, *The E List*, which features artists, local creative heroes, and supports their

business enterprise. [...] So that we now have, in 2019, Waltham Forest as the first London Borough of Culture. (Laura Kerry, interview by Weedon, Chapter 4 in this book)

This stock will go on to develop further cultural capital that has been generated from within the borough, helping to achieve the breaking down of the patterns of development that Rose has identified as reproducing marginalisation (Rose 1997, 13).

Evaluation reports from the aforementioned Creative People and Places programme have been wide-ranging in their attempts to distil the qualities that have made for successful and unsuccessful place-based engagement work. To return to the quotation from Boiling and Thurman's (n.d. [c. 2018]) report that was cited at the start of the chapter, it is clear that, in referencing 'risk factors' (p. 9), there is a sense of the significance of the psychological barriers that Jancovich (2017) speaks of, along with an impetus to foreground space, if not with connection to young people. However, in order for the level of success that is suggested within the quotation to occur, it is necessary that the presence of the arts and cultural activity or event within that space is not there to rewrite the purpose or significance of that space, and that instead it coexists with that connotation or perhaps even interacts with it. This demonstrates a potential example of the creation of Thirdspace for an arts audience through the process of acknowledging and situating the Firstspace and Secondspace of such locations and the action of thirding through the generation of new connotation, memory and significance.

The world of site-specificity in art and performance has much to say about this interaction of the old and new in art spaces. Kaye (2000) discusses the work of the Welsh performance company Brith Gof in his study of site-specific art and performance. Brith Gof present socially engaged performances in 'socially and politically charged sites' (p. 52). Kaye describes how 'the guiding metaphor for the construction of Brith Gof's work in these places has been the coexistence of distinct "architectures" inhabiting one another and the site itself without resolution into a synthetic whole' (p. 53). The use of the architectural metaphor helps in articulating the notion of seeing a multitude of meanings, connotations and relevances within a space without overwriting or rewriting. This enables a process whereby an audience member or participant is able to perceive existing spatial connotations alongside new meanings in a non-hierarchical way.

Both Gilmore (2013) and Rose (1997) address the movement and situation of capital between spaces and places. Rose's (1997) consideration of space and its relationship to power suggests that the presence of arts and cultural activity within particular areas, often big city centres, points towards a sense of situated power within those places. Rose's suggestion is that the draw of investment from councils or external bodies leads to a convergence of cultural and economic capital that creates a central body of power. This 'trickle-down' approach demonstrates a clear sense of hierarchy as well as a ripple effect motion that sees power, capital and investment feeding from the interior to the exterior.

Gilmore (2013) highlights the importance of 'mobile capital' (p. 89) in the cultural geography of creative towns and cities, connecting notions of tourism and the transient with regard to the drive for members of the public to come and visit a place for its cultural stock, as well as alluding to some of the forms of cultural activity that are often employed in such 'place-making' projects, referencing Harvie (2011). Soja's (1996) assertion of the political and emancipatory potential of Thirdspace suggests that such hierarchies of interior–exterior and central–marginal, which are also binaries, can be transcended through thirding. To consider place through the lens of Thirdspace removes the privileging of forms of capital and opens out the potential for a more democratic view of participation that embraces the 'everyday'.

Conclusion: Suggestions for a 'thirding' approach

The narrative around the engagement of children and young people remains one that is missing in the discourse of space, place and culture. It is my contention that a 'thirding' approach can be employed to start to bring children and young people into this conversation. In the first instance, the very notion of 'thirding-as-othering' is built upon the foundations of a removal of hierarchy and a reinterpretation 'of the relationship between the colonizer and the colonized, the center and the periphery' (Soja 1996, 126). Taking the lead from Verhellen (2000), Garratt and Piper (2008) and Spivak (1988), and making the assumption that young people within conventional practices are seen as incomplete, other or 'the unnamed subject' (Spivak 1988, 274), then Soja's insistence that narratives and metanarratives can coexist and be equally critiqued within a postcolonial framework is relevant. Soja contests that Thirdspace enables the amplification of 'other' voices along with a coexistence of histories, geographies, development and progress, and social justice (p. 126). The Thirdspace, therefore, is perhaps the space for the young person's voice. The individual seen as 'becoming' or 'in between' is perhaps the most equipped to embody the notions of synthesis that are inherent to the process of 'thirding'.

Indeed, if the sector is to be able to see the impact of space and place on cultural participation and its associated aims of emancipation, empowerment and so on, then it must be through a lens that is inclusive rather than exclusive – capable of embracing the social, the historic, the physical, the mental and the emotional, and of transcending the binaries and separations between fields. In order for this to happen, research must investigate the impact that place-based initiatives are having on young people's participation, as well as addressing the question of how young people feel their lives and their participation are affected by notions of space. This is undoubtedly a huge 'can of worms' to open and requires a multidisciplinary approach involving not just the arts and cultural sector but also education, youth work and sports development. However, I believe this approach, supported by the work of Soja, could be of enormous use in supporting the body of knowledge in this area and helping to fill a conspicuous gap.

References

42nd Street. n.d. 'The Horsfall'. Accessed 29 April 2019. http://42ndstreet.org.uk/horsfall/.

Andreou, Alex. 2014. 'Trickle-Down Economics is the Greatest Broken Promise of Our Lifetime', *The Guardian*, 20 January. Accessed 29 April 2019. www.theguardian.com/commentisfree/2014/jan/20/trickle-down-economics-broken-promise-richest-85.

Art B&B. 2017. 'Art Bed and Breakfast: A Pioneering Platform for Experiencing Contemporary Art within a Traditional Bed and Breakfast Re-Imagined for the 21st Century in Blackpool'. Accessed 29 April 2019. www.abandb.co.uk/about-test/.

Boiling, Sarah and Clare Thurman. n.d. [c. 2018]. *Mapping and Analysis of Engagement Approaches across the Creative People and Places Programme*. Creative People and Places. Accessed 6 May 2020. www.culturehive.co.uk/wp-content/uploads/2018/08/Mapping_and_analysis_of_engagement_approaches.pdf.

Bunting, Catherine, Tak Wing Chan, John Goldthorpe, Emily Keaney and Anni Oskala. 2008. *From Indifference to Enthusiasm: Patterns of Arts Attendance in England*. London: Arts Council England.

Certeau, Michel de. 1984. *The Practice of Everyday Life*, translated by Steven Rendall. Berkeley: University of California Press.

Garratt, Dean and Heather Piper. 2008. 'Citizenship Education in England and Wales: Theoretical Critique and Practical Considerations', *Teachers and Teaching: Theory and Practice* 14 (5/6): 481–96.

Gilmore, Abigail. 2013. 'Cold Spots, Crap Towns and Cultural Deserts: The Role of Place and Geography in Cultural Participation and Creative Place-Making', *Cultural Trends* 22 (2): 86–96.

Harvie, Jen. 2011. '"Social Mobility": Cultural Policy, Art Practices, Gentrification and Social Housing'. Paper presented at the Performance Research Group, Public Investments, 2011/12, Kings College, London, 24 October 2011.

Jancovich, Leila. 2017. 'The Participation Myth', *International Journal of Cultural Policy* 23 (1): 107–21.

Jans, Marc. 2004. 'Children as Citizens: Towards a Contemporary Notion of Child Participation', *Childhood* 11 (1): 27–44.
Kaye, Nick. 2000. *Site-Specific Art: Performance, Place and Documentation*. London: Routledge.
Lefebvre, Henri. 1991. *The Production of Space*, translated by Donald Nicholson-Smith. Oxford: Blackwell.
Miles, Andrew and Lisanne Gibson. 2016. 'Editorial: Everyday Participation and Cultural Value', *Cultural Trends* 25 (3): 151–57.
Mycock, Andrew. 2011. 'Young People and Citizenship after the London Riots'. Paper presented at the Department of Social Sciences, University of Chester.
Osler, Audrey and Hugh Starkey. 2003. 'Learning for Cosmopolitan Citizenship: Theoretical Debates and Young People's Experiences', *Educational Review* 55 (3): 243–54.
Rose, Gillian. 1997. 'Spatialities of "Community", Power and Change: The Imagined Geographies of Community Arts Projects', *Cultural Studies* 11 (1): 1–16.
Schaefer, Kerrie, Delyth Edwards and Jane Milling. 2017. 'Performing Moretonhampstead: Rurality, Participation and Cultural Value', *Cultural Trends* 26 (1): 47–57.
Soja, Edward W. 1996. *Thirdspace: Journeys to Los Angeles and Other Real-and-Imagined Places*. Cambridge, MA: Blackwell.
Spivak, Gayatri Chakravorty. 1988. 'Can the Subaltern Speak?'. In *Marxism and the Interpretation of Culture*, edited by Cary Nelson and Lawrence Grossberg, 271–313. Urbana: University of Illinois Press.
Verhellen, Eugène. 2000. 'Children's Rights and Education'. In *Citizenship and Democracy in Schools: Diversity, Identity, Equality*, edited by Audrey Osler, 33–43. Stoke-on-Trent: Trentham Books.

16
A sense of play: (Re)animating place through recreational distance running
Kieran Holland

While the popularity of recreational distance running has risen, culturally and academically (Samson *et al.* 2017; Tan 2018a), reflections on how this practice contributes to the construction of place are rare. This chapter examines how running creates a sense of place. It does this by studying three artistic explorations of running: NVA's *Speed of Light* (2012), Kai Syng Tan's *Hand-in-Hand* (2016) and All The Queens Men's *Fun Run* (2017). Arguing that artistic explorations of habitual and somatic practice draw greater attention to the place-making potential of an activity, the chapter explains how these three performances gesture towards existing ways in which running events create a heightened, inclusive, supportive and healing sense of place. It also highlights how these performances draw attention to potential ways in which running organisations can develop a sense of place by drawing on existing associations between health, success and running. As such, the discussions in this chapter offer place-makers and running organisations alternative ways to play with the structures and connotations of running to further develop an individual and collective sense of place.

Running

From its earliest origins, the act of running has influenced how we think about place.[1] Yet reflections on the unique place-making ability of running are relatively rare.[2] Currently, the ways in which we encounter and consider running are often through discourses of health and well-being. Research continues to highlight that running can help you physically get fitter, notice positive differences in your body image and improve your mental well-being (Bourdieu and Giorgi 2010; Shipway and Holloway 2010, 2016; Stevinson, Wiltshire and Hickson 2015). Running magazines such as *Runner's World*, running clubs and race-related organisations also advertise how running can make a healthy difference to your lifestyle. For example, while I was participating in the Bournemouth Marathon (7 October 2018) a recorded loop continuously reminded me that by running in this event I was 'making a seriously positive difference to myself and the people I cared about'. Whilst these health-related messages are important to underline, stressing these benefits too much risks drawing our attention away from the additional effects of running.[3] As Julie Cidell notes, running is a 'fruitful area of study' (2016, 93). Its variety of events offers 'a number of avenues for further research' to explore the different effects of running (p. 93).

Place-making can be one such avenue of research. Running has the potential to be a substantial place-making activity. It is an international mass participatory activity which brings individuals across the world to a specific place.[4] Arriving at these locations, individuals are given the opportunity to participate in a range of different performances which can inform their own perceptions of place. Running clubs, get active initiatives, such as Couch to 5k (C25K), and weekly local running events, such as Parkrun, bring individuals together and give people the opportunity to build a community together in a specific place (see Stevinson, Wiltshire and Hickson 2015). Race (5 km, 10 km, half-marathons, marathons) and non-race events (Tough Mudder, Rough Runner, Secret London Runs) also bring people together. They create opportunities for people to work together and get to know one another in places they habitually or rarely engage in. They also provide entertainment to masses of runners and spectators and aesthetically alter the places these people inhabit.[5] In short, the structures of running events give people a range of opportunities to alter or develop their sense of place. Thus, by studying these structures closely, we can better understand the ways in which this activity influences perceptions of place.

This chapter considers the structures and performances of running to understand its place-making potential. It does this by exploring artistic running performances.[6] Arguing that performance practices draw attention to the place-making dimensions of any activity (cf. Mackey 2007a, 2007b, 2016; Mackey and Cole 2013), I discuss how artistic performance practice involving running can offer substantial insights into how this physical activity influences an individual and collective sense of place. Analysing the documentation of three different artistic performances which develop place (*Speed of Light* 2012, *Fun Run* 2017, *Hand-in-Hand* 2016), I convey how, through interplay with landscape, participation and intimacy, each of these works draws attention to the range of ways in which running can alter and adapt our sense of place.

Before offering this analysis, it is important to explain what place is and how our sense of it is continually developed. Therefore, the next section will offer a definition of the concept of place. It outlines how our sense of place is constructed through iterative and temporal performance(s), and explains that to understand this construction of place, we need to be able to critically distance ourselves from these performances to interpret them. Identifying that artists subvert us from reality and make our daily structures perceptible, I argue that reflecting on artists' work can draw attention to the existing ways in which habitual activity influences our sense of place and can further show us the place-making potential of any activity.

Understanding place through performance

The common usage of 'place' is for a location or a point on the map. But it can also be considered as a critical concept which teaches us how our interpretations of a 'place' are continually influenced by social, economic and political constructs in space (Harvey 1996, 293–9, 316–19; Thomson 2004; Kyle and Chick 2007; Grey and O'Toole 2020). Place can be discussed in relation to experiential encounters (Casey 1993; Relph 2009; Merleau-Ponty 2012; Seamon 2014), and the stories we hear and see also contribute to our conception of place (Massey 1994, 2005; Harvey 1996, 293–4). For Edward Casey each embodied response to people, animals and the environment alters the way we perceive place (1993, 43–70). Getting out of the chair to read a book only to find it is no longer in the room, being harassed by the dog whilst attempting to read, and experiencing people rush into the secluded reading room to get the dog: all these can alter the way we consider the place we are in (Casey 1993, 47–8). This means that whatever we conceive as place today is likely to be different tomorrow. Therefore, when we discuss the place-making potential of any activity we need to identify suitable ways of exploring the evolving nature of place.

Researchers have identified that studying performances in a place offers a useful way of understanding the development of place (Sheller and Urry 2004; Coleman and Crang 2002; Hill and Paris 2006). This is because our performed actions within a framed space continually influence our perception of place. For example, walking through the centre of Paris and going into the Louvre and up the Eiffel Tower may give us a historic, positive sense of place, causing us to see Paris as a city of culture. Yet walking along the outskirts of Paris and seeing the homeless on the street may create a sense of anguish and instil in us a sense that this place is a place of poverty. Given this adaptative nature of a sense of place, the challenge for researchers lies in finding ways to analyse these temporal performances in the context they occurred in.

To discuss how place is developed by performance, researchers continually seek to critically distance themselves from the performances they study in order to perceive their place-making potential clearly. For example, researchers have used the step-aside techniques of participant observation, interviews and historical documents to understand how volunteering on lifeboats, playing in the playground or listening to and reading the media develop a perception of place (Harvey 1996; Thomson 2004; Grey and O'Toole 2020). However, they have rarely turned to the creative arts, where somatic practice is widely used for its theoretical insights to understand how place is made and developed through iterative and temporal bodily acts, such as in dance (cf. Olsen 2014). This is surprising given that creative arts also offer a way of enhancing an audience's understanding of place, by subverting the habitual ways they engage in place (Mackey and Cole 2013; Mackey 2016). According to Sally Mackey, watching or participating in creative work can create 'a greater engagement with place' for audiences and performers (Mackey and Cole 2013, 51). By being involved in performance, it can enable audiences to connect more with the place they are in, and it can also create thicker connections to place that were previously distant or non-existent (Mackey 2016).[7]

Additionally, watching creative performances also offers the opportunity for audiences to understand existing ways in which their daily acts influence their experiences, such as their sense of place. Lois Keidan (2006) briefly refers to this revealing potential of performance, in an exploration of how creative arts (referred to by Keidan as Live Art) engage with place: 'Live Art can offer a place, a context and a process in which audiences can become involved or immersed in the creation of artworks and in which the experiences of the neglected, the marginalized, the disenfranchised or the disembodied can be made visible, sometimes for the first time' (p. 14). In other words, by being involved in a performance, even by watching it, art can reveal experiences in place that we were unaware of.[8] This means that creative arts also have the potential to creatively make us aware of how our actions develop a sense of place. Thus, whilst participating in or viewing creative arts can reveal the existing ways in which performances develop our sense of place, studying artistic performance has the potential to give us a glimpse into how reframing these actions can transform our sense of place.

Given these insights, examining artistic work appears to offer two unique opportunities for researchers to understand the development of place. Firstly, reflecting on artistic work enables researchers to understand the existing place-making effects of the performance itself. Secondly, analysing the effects of artists' performances should also draw attention to the potential ways in which playing with this activity can develop an understanding of place. In the context of this chapter, this means that, by understanding how artistic explorations develop a sense of place through the practice of running, I will be able to gesture to the potential and existing ways in which running influences an understanding of place.

Developing this idea, the rest of this chapter will now explore how the effects of artistic explorations of running reveal more about this physical activity's place-making potential. Drawing on documentation and participant accounts of three recent running performances which connect to place – *Speed of Light* (2012), *Fun Run* (2017) and *Hand-in-Hand* (2016) – the next sections show that playful experimentations with running highlight how this physical activity already reanimates place in relation to landscape, community, history and intimacy. It will also explain how running can further transform a sense of place by playing with its health connotations.

Performing environment and sensing place in NVA's *Speed of Light* (2012)

NVA's performances *Speed of Light* are a collection of site-responsive artworks, which use running and exoskeleton suits to transform participant and spectator perception of landscape and space (Edensor and Lorimer 2015; NVA 2018a, 2018b, 2018c). To date, the performances have taken place in Edinburgh (2012), Yokohoma (2012), Ruhr (2013) and Salford (2013), with each responding to running and landscape in different ways. For example, in the Edinburgh edition runners and walkers remove themselves from the city and explore the rural environment of Arthur's Seat and its surrounding hills together (Gardner 2012; Edensor and Lorimer 2015; NVA 2018b). Fitted with light-emitting technology, an exoskeleton costume for the runners and a staff for the walkers, both runners and walkers contribute to the visual choreography and display of the landscape (Edensor and Lorimer 2015). In other versions of the performance, which focus on town or city environments, walkers are not included in the formation of light patterns. In Salford Quays, only the runners are illuminated by the exoskeleton suits. This is to ensure that only the runners create patterns and draw attention to darkened parts of the city. Spectators' roles remain fixed on viewing and interpreting this spectacle rather than participating in it (NVA 2018c).

Despite these differences, each iteration of *Speed of Light* consistently played with the dynamics between running and landscape in each performance (NVA 2018a). Therefore, due to the constraints of this chapter, I will reflect on how staging the mobile body playfully in light, in the Edinburgh iteration of this performance, creates a greater awareness of how running has place-making potential.

In the Edinburgh version of *Speed of Light*, audience members and runners were separated and given different roles in the performance. Audience members were tasked with walking up Arthur's Seat to view the spectacle produced by mass runners. They were also asked to leave behind the top part of their light-emitting staff, which began to sonically resonate at the top of the hill to act as a beacon for other walkers climbing to the 251-m summit (Gardner 2012). Runners, equipped with a head torch and an exoskeleton suit, moved around the surrounding landscape and performed set choreographies in response to the environment (Edensor and Lorimer 2015, 2). In these ways, both walkers and runners were given a visual or embodied experience of running. It is by reflecting on these alternative views and experiences that I want to explore how playing with the structures of running in *Speed of Light* developed both groups of participants' awareness of the place.

Through play with light and the mobile body, NVA's *Speed of Light* showed that any form of night running can transform and heighten an awareness of environments we habitually engage with. Reflecting on the experience of running in the dark in this event, Hayden Lorimer notes that the light was too poor to draw on advance knowledge of the terrain, causing runners to feel their way around the landscape (Edensor and Lorimer 2015, 7). Runners struggled to see and had to draw on other senses. This heightened their awareness of balance as well as the feel and texture underfoot, allowing Lorimer and other runners to gain a 'more intense' feeling of discovery about the landscape (Edensor and Lorimer 2015, 9). In other words, it caused their perception of place to alter. Runners' visually dominant perception of place became a multi-sensual embodied relationship of place, one where each foot stroke and leap through the air brought a new awareness of, and responsiveness to, their connection with the landscape (Edensor and Lorimer 2015, 9–11).

Whilst this was the effect for the runners, the visual choreography witnessed by the walkers also indicated how acts of seeing runners can reanimate and emphasise places we are situated in. For Tim Edensor, seeing the runners enact different-shaped patterns highlighted the topography of the landscape (Edensor and Lorimer 2015, 13). Paths and the edges of Salisbury Crags were revealed by the different ways participants occupied the environment (Edensor and Lorimer 2015, 13). The act of runners coming together also drew attention to the transformative potential that mass-running bodies have for our sense of place. Instead of seeing bodies in motion on a hill, the coming together of runners changed the dynamics of the landscape. Participants lost sight of the running bodies and instead encountered images of 'fireflies, a child's kaleidoscope' and 'extra-terrestrial visitation' (Edensor and Lorimer 2015, 13). The runners physically altered the audiences' perceptions of place, transforming it, in some cases, into another world.

Thus, by playing with participants' (runners' and walkers') awareness of light, darkness and sense of mobility in landscape, NVA's *Speed of Light* revealed some of the place-making potential that running already offers. Firstly, by reframing night running in a performance setting and getting participants to rely on additional senses to vision, the performance emphasised that running already develops our sense of place, by literally developing our embodied senses. Secondly, the performance highlighted how the spectacle of running can physically transform the way people visually perceive place. Witnessing the activity enabled spectators to identify the boundaries of landscape and see the ways runners transform place. It also enabled spectators to come together and be aware of how each individual journey becomes a collection of journeys within place. As such, by building on existing structures of night running, the performance hinted towards the ways in which running events, that take place in the dark, can transform a landscape and physically alter visual and experiential perceptions of place. Building on these structures further, the performance also hinted at the idea that running can bring people together to relationally and cohesively develop a sense of place together: an idea which I will now explore in relation to All The Queens Men's *Fun Run* (2017).

Re-creating a communal place through running: *Fun Run*

Fun Run is a performance event that takes the structure of a marathon running event (26.2 miles of movement and witnessing) staged over a long period of time, in this case five hours (All The Queens Men 2018). Originally shown at the Next Wave Festival in Melbourne (2010), the production has been performed in Sydney (2013), South Korea (2015) and Finland (2015), and recently returned to Melbourne (2017). I want to focus on the most recent production of this performance (Melbourne 2017), to discuss how the performance enriches our collective engagement with place and reveals the potential of running as a socially cohesive place-making event.

The beginning of this performance drew attention to how the themes connected with a marathon are already a creative medium for getting people to invest in one another's stories of place. The performance begins with the grand spectacle of Tristan Meecham (director of All The Queens Men and representing Pheidippides in this performance), paraded outside the Melbourne Arts Centre in a chariot by his dance troupe/Athenian Army 'the Haus Da Fun Run', bringing in crowds of spectators.[9] After announcing himself to the crowd and reaching the stage, Meecham tells the audience the story of the marathon, the story of Pheidippides. Pheidippides, we are told, is a Greek messenger sent from the battle of Marathon to Athens to announce the defeat of the Persians (Meecham in Arts Centre Melbourne 2017). After running the whole way and successfully delivering this message, Pheidippides collapses, exhausted from this mammoth effort, and dies. This performance, according to Meecham, is Pheidippides' story (Arts Centre Melbourne 2017; All The Queens Men 2018). By sharing this story, the audience is made aware of how the narrative of running connects to place. It is an action which connects people and places through a narrative of success and celebration at the cost of a person's body – a dimension which all marathons share.

Whilst this has the potential of making the performance of a marathon and its connotations bleak, this performance highlights that these readings can be avoided through the constant celebratory acts that the duration of a marathon enables. During the 'marathon' event for spectators and performers alike, this five-hour performance invited 24 diverse community groups, ranging from sports trainers to dancers, to perform, centre stage, in front of Meecham (Arts Centre Melbourne

2017). By staging a variety of community performances, the event celebrated the rich variety of culture already on offer within this place. It offered people the opportunity to encounter and learn more about local stories and communities. It connected people usually disconnected from one another and helped establish an inclusive sense of place (cf. Arts Centre Melbourne 2017). This is a dimension which already exists in running events.[10]

This image of a collective community was further created through group flash mobs. Every hour of Meecham's five-hour run, the Athenian Army, his performance troupe which at these stages also included community members who had been taught the dance prior to the event, initiated a flash mob with the crowd to get people engaged in the performance (Arts Centre Melbourne 2017). Spectators were invited to participate in the spectacle of the event and encouraged to move together in any capacity they could in order to become part of the communal experience. Any contribution was seen as helpful, and every single body was seen as an important component in the development of place. Here, reflecting on the performance alludes to how encouraging audience participation at running events can help ensure spectators also develop a communal sense of place.

The death of Pheidippides offered the final way of bringing people together and also drew attention to why the narrative of a marathon creates a celebratory sense of place, instead of a negative one. At the end of the performance, Meecham (representing Pheidippides) completes the marathon, steps off the treadmill and collapses, crawling slowly to the front of the stage (Arts Centre Melbourne 2017). The crowd goes silent, unaware of whether Meecham is performing or is genuinely in trouble. After a few seconds, Meecham springs up, bows to the audience and blows kisses to them to show he is fine and signal that it is time to continue celebrating what they have accomplished together. The silence is broken with cheering, and footage shows snippets of spectators hugging, crying and saying goodbye to the people they have shared the five-hour journey with (Arts Centre Melbourne 2017). Thus, even the finish of a marathon, which can be painful and exhausting for runners, is highlighted as offering the opportunity to extend and develop connections between people established through the event.

Overall, reflecting on All The Queens Men's *Fun Run* highlights that running can act as a hive to draw together a diverse range of people and get them to take part in a cultural celebration of place. It shows that the durational structure of a marathon offers a great opportunity to get people to share passions, invest in the sport and form bonds with other members of the community, as they all celebrate and contribute to the stories of success and triumph created during a marathon, as well as by the event's history. Thus, by using the allure of the event, its durational structure and the running events' history of inviting community performers to support runners and entertain spectators, *Fun Run* draws attention to how running events already create an intimate, relational and inclusive sense of place.

Whilst reflecting on *Fun Run* therefore highlights how marathon events offer unique place-making opportunities due to their lengthy structures, running can also develop our sense of place due to its already existing metaphors of kindness and health. Turning to Kai Syng Tan's *Hand-in-Hand* in the next section, I will explain how studying this performance highlights how running organisations can reframe health discourse to develop a sense of place.

Intimacy and creating a place of change: *Hand-in-Hand*

While the other artists I have discussed have used running sporadically in their work, Kai Syng Tan's *Mains Dans La Main/Hand-in-Hand* (2016) represents an ongoing dialogue between Tan and running. Tan is the director of Run! Run! Run!, an international organisation designed to explore running across the arts and humanities (Tan 2018a, 2019). The collective work of Tan and other members of the organisation aims to explore 'how [running's] physical processes can be mobilised as metaphor, methodology, and material to enable us to reimagine ourselves and the world around us' (Tan in Cianetti 2016, 93; cf. Tan 2017, 2018a, 2018b). Whilst this means that a range of Tan's work can be analysed to indicate the ways running creates a sense of place, I will draw on *Hand-in-Hand* to articulate how running alone together can alter the way we consider place.

Hand-in-Hand, a running/walking/mobile performance, 'is a participatory artwork that asks: amidst a volatile and hostile reality [Brexit, war], how could image-makers, researchers and "ordinary citizens" invent everyday poetic/political/playful interventions to celebrate difference[?]' (Tan in Cianetti 2016, 100). Staged in two locations, as part of the Fête des Tuiles (Festival of Tiles) in the Cours de la Libération-et-du-Général-de-Gaulle in Grenoble, and at the Culture Shots Festival (in the park opposite the Whitworth Art Gallery in Manchester), Tan's answer comes from tying people's hands together with red ribbon and getting them to renegotiate a place, hand in hand, whilst running, walking or skateboarding over a distance of 1 m, 10 km or 100 km (Tan 2017, 60; 2019).

Physically tying people together with red ribbon had several intentions in this performance. Firstly, the use of ribbon encouraged participants to run together and share individual stories. It brought people together in place and opened up the opportunity for people to physically and mentally develop a bond with one another. Being tied together, over various distances, gave participants the opportunity to talk to one another and learn about their individual hopes and dreams whilst moving together (Tan 2017, 2018b). It physically created a space where participants could share their stories with people willing to listen to them. In this way, Tan's work altered a possibly 'hostile, volatile' or individualistic reality of place and moulded it into an inclusive place for all participants.

Tying people together also enabled participants to become more perceptive about others in the place they inhabited. Participants said they had become aware of each other's rhythmic patterns, such as breathing, allowing them to monitor the effect one person's pace had on the other (Tan 2017, 2018b). Due to this, they began to care for each other and attempted to look after one another, by altering their paces. In other words, as well as being physically attached, participants also became emotionally attached to one another in the temporal place they occupied (Tan 2017, 2018b). Thus, while the act of tying people together allowed participants to become more perceptive of other people's performances, it also enabled them to create intimate and deep bonds with each other within a place. In short, it altered their sense of place.

While the ribbons worn by the participants gave runners the opportunity to alter their sense of place, the red ribbons were also used to symbolically show how the health connotations of running can alter and heal individuals' and collectives' negative and restrictive perceptions about place. For Tan, the red bands in the performance piece were representative of the tags that refugees in Cardiff have to wear to receive food rations (2017, 62). This meant that, as an identifying mechanism, the bands could create a negative association with place as they mark people as different and isolate them from other people within a specific place. However, instead of seeing red bands as negative, Tan relied on the connection of bands with blind running to invoke the messages of hope, trust and enjoyment that blind runners experience when moving through space with their guide (Tan 2017, 62; Cianetti 2016, 100). In this way, Tan planned on using the positive connotations of running to 'subvert the "handcuffs" that ostracise the migrants' (Tan in Cianetti 2016, 100–101).

She aimed to remove these handcuffs and build a new experience, a new inclusive sense of place in the world for those who felt excluded from it. As such, Tan relied on and drew attention to the transformative potential running has because of its health connotations, and by playing with this metaphor Tan drew attention to how this healing dimension of running is part of its place-making ability.

It is difficult to know if these messages came across in the performance – even Tan is unclear whether the performance achieved these effects (Tan 2017; Tan in Cianetti 2016). Nonetheless, reflecting on the intentions in this work signals how running can be an empowering place-making activity. Running brings individuals together. It gives us the opportunity to talk to one another, get to know each other and care for one another (without being tied up). With its connotations of health, it also presents the opportunity to metaphorically heal negative perceptions within a place/about a place and give individuals a positive, supportive and inclusive sense of place. As Tan's work highlighted, running is rich with health-related messages and these messages can be used and altered in events to tackle a wide range of problems within a local or global sense of place.

Furthermore, by tying people together to get people to work together in place, Tan's work also highlights playful ways in which events can encourage participants to experience inclusivity and support in running, at times when the activity may come across as too individual. Therefore, reflecting on *Hand-in-Hand* draws attention to creative ways organisers can encourage collaboration and inclusivity to develop a supportive sense of place.

Conclusion

The development of a sense of place is formed through iterative and temporal performance(s) within it, and running is one such practice. However, it can be difficult to understand the place-making ability of any activity whilst we are immersed in it, unless we can find a way to critically step back and assess our performances. This chapter has argued that studying artistic explorations of running offers a significant way of stepping back and understanding how events alter and transform our sense of place. This, as I explained, is because artists frequently play with the pre-existing structures already on offer in activities. Therefore, reflecting on artists' performances can draw our attention to the place-making dimensions of an activity that we may have overlooked.

Examining *Speed of Light* showed that running, especially night running, can produce new sensual explorations of landscape for both runner and spectator. Exploring *Fun Run* and *Hand-in-Hand* highlighted how running brings people together. It creates a mass celebration of diversity and community. Analysing *Hand-in-Hand* also signalled that the health connotations surrounding running can be used to alter negative perceptions of place. As such, these artistic explorations showed that running already creates a sense of place because, regardless of the size or type of event, running encourages masses of individuals to interact in a positive, supportive, celebratory and caring manner.

Furthermore, reflecting on these artistic practices also showed that, by playing with existing structures and representations of running, organisations can take advantage of the place-making ability of running and enhance it. *Hand-in-Hand* used the already prevalent health connotations of running and built on these metaphors to change the unhealthy way we perceive the place we are in. Cancer charities similarly do this with the *Race for Life*, changing a place of suffering and disease into a place of survival, celebration and success (cf. King 2006). Yet more running organisations may find using pre-existing connotations of running useful to continue altering the way we perceive the places we are in. To do this, turning to artistic work can offer a great opportunity for identifying these connotations and help organisers understand the possible effects these experimentations can have.

Overall, the lesson for local authorities, planners and sports organisations is that running already offers us events which bring people together and develop a positive, supportive, inclusive sense of place. Artistic work exemplifies this. Yet if we continue to study artistic work, organisers and place-makers alike may find that the unique and alternative ways in which artists stage running can be implemented and mapped onto their existing designs and structures of running events to improve and create an inclusive, healthy and supportive sense of place.

Notes

1. For the ancient Egyptians (2650 BC), running was seen as an essential way of (re)animating place to control or alter the opinions of people within a king's domain. Upon their first ascending to the throne, Egyptian kings would run across their domain to symbolically prove they were fit enough to rule the kingdom (Sears 2015, 14). By succeeding in completing the act of running, the king would be accepted amongst his subjects, whilst place would be interpreted as safe, secure and protected by a strong and athletic ruler (Sears 2015, 14–17). If this endurance task was failed, place would be seen as hostile and dangerous. The king's weak and feeble attempt to cross the distance symbolised the weak structure of a kingdom. This meant that rulers in nearby provinces would see the place(s) the king ruled over as vulnerable,

enabling them to assault these places in order to claim it under a new authority. In short, warfare allowed them to force people to reperceive who ruled over their place (Sears 2015, 14–17). Thus, while the outcome of the run could drastically alter people's experience of place, this Egyptian ritual highlights an important dimension of running and place. As a performance and spectacle, the physical activity offers an exciting and unique way of altering the way we consider place.

2. The term 'place' is dominantly used in the sense of physical backdrop in running research. Place is depicted as a location. It is described briefly or not at all to give a reader a sense of where the researcher is. Exceptions to this are Bale (2004), Sheehan (2006), Lorimer (2012), Cook, Shaw and Simpson (2016) and Hanold (2016). Investigating placelessness and running, John Bale notes that, whilst running tracks are designed to be replicable and placeless, each event creates its own unique performance conditions (such as wind resistance), meaning that every event can influence the way runners consider place (2004, 9–37). Rebecca Sheehan's (2006) exploration of the Crescent City Classic 10k in New Orleans and Maylon Hanold's (2016) application of Lefebvre's concepts of representations of space, spatial practice and spatial representation to ultra-marathon running have explored how running creates temporal and freeing senses of place during events. For Sheehan (2006) and Hanold (2016), running creates a space for people to explore new places playfully. It also provides them with the opportunity to encounter and experience new modes of running that go against the grain of personal competition and speed (Sheehan 2006, 254–8; Hanold 2016, 185–8). For example, whilst attending the New Orleans Classic 10k, Sheehan found that runners use the event to perform and play with their perceptions of the place they are in. They dress up in drag to conform with gender and identity play situated in the cultural climate of New Orleans (p. 254). They also enter the race halfway in, walk slowly in groups, and drink at each pub along the course to play with the alcohol-consuming image of New Orleans (pp. 255–8). Lorimer (2012) and Cook, Shaw and Simpson (2016) have also built on the idea that running builds a meaningful connection to place. For Lorimer, running brings a deeper sensual connection to place, one which makes us more acutely aware of the differences in its terrain. For Cook, Shaw and Simpson, running provides individuals with an opportunity to escape from mundane and even claustrophobic places associated with office and home life, and also allows them to explore new open places in a town or city that people rarely engage with (pp. 743–54). They also observe that running continually brings us into a shared space, one where we have to learn how to deal with the challenges of navigating with and around non-runners (pp. 757–62). As such, they point out that running does more than develop a runner's sense of place; it also influences a pedestrian's perceptions of place.

3. There is an extensive amount of research which explores aspects of running beyond its connections to health and well-being. Researchers have described runners' experiences of running alone or with groups (Allen-Collinson and Hockey 2007, 2015; Koski 2015; Griffin and Phoenix 2016). They have discussed how repetitive acts of running can produce a social identity (Shipway and Jones 2007, 2008; Robinson, Patterson and Axelsen 2014; Ronkainen et al. 2018). They have traced the global history of running (Krise and Squires 1982; Gotaas 2009; Sears 2015), documented and discussed the different ways running events are staged (Herrick 2015; Cidell 2016) and also highlighted how listening to audio performances alters and influences an individual's experience of running (Darby 2014). Although these studies have explored a range of meanings for running, it is important that we continue to investigate running differently in order to expand our knowledge about this activity.

4. For example, on 22 April 2018, 41,003 runners from around the world participated in the London Marathon, whilst thousands of spectators gathered in the city to watch the event (Virgin Money London Marathon 2018).

5. Walking around London can appear visually and aurally different during the London Marathon. During the marathon, navigation alters and is restricted by barriers and road closures. Noise levels increase, and the city appears to shrink as thousands of spectators pack themselves across 26.2 miles of a staged route to cheer on and celebrate mass acts of running.

6. This may come across as surprising to the reader, as investigating running events directly also offers an opportunity to understand the place-making potential of this physical activity. Whilst this is true, as I will argue, studying artistic explorations of running offers an alternative and, perhaps, more effective way of understanding what running does and can do to our sense of

place. As Andrew Filmer notes, 'artists are playing an important but underacknowledged role in exploring the experiential and expressive dimensions of running' (2020, 30–31). Therefore, by discussing how artists' explorations of running help us to consider the place-making potential of running, I hope to join Filmer in emphasising the important role artists have in drawing attention to additional dimensions of running that are rarely recognised in our current health- and achievement-oriented view of sport.

7. Reflecting on the *place* project conducted in Oldham, Greater Manchester (2012–13), Mackey (2016) discusses a range of ways in which her applied theatre workshops improved migrant participant connections with a place they may have felt estranged from. Participants drew images of pleasure onto lighting gels that they were able to see each time they passed the window of the Oldham Theatre Workshop building (p. 118). Continually passing these gels helped some of them feel connected to the place they were in (pp. 118–19). Another way performance reframed their sense of place was by carrying out a devised choreography in a familiar place, Oldham Indoor Market (pp. 119–20). Carrying out these actions gave them new memories of the market, subverting the way in which they originally viewed place (pp. 118–20).

8. This revealing mechanism of performance has long been credited with the doubling effect of theatre. By reframing daily acts on stage, artistic works double and imitate reality. They create a critical distance between reality and audience which allows people to re-view habitual actions as if seen for the first time (Aggerholm 2013; Jirásek and Kohe 2015, 262). In this way, by distorting reality, artistic engagements present the mechanics, qualities and hidden dynamics of performance in front of an audience to help spectators reflect on the variety of effects that daily actions can produce (Aggerholm 2013; Jirásek and Kohe 2015, 262). Therefore, if researchers need to understand the place-making effects of different performances by critically distancing themselves from them, studying how these performances are reframed in artistic explorations offers a substantial way of understanding how any activity can potentially develop our sense of place.

9. At this point, the army is made up of members of All The Queens Men performance troupe and, in this performance, a team of professional dancers from indigenous dance groups who had previously worked with Bec Reid (co-founder of All The Queens Men; cf. Reid in Arts Centre Melbourne 2017). As the performance continues and the flash mobs happen, the Athenian Army grows, with members of the community becoming part of this supportive troupe through flash mobs.

10. Across events I have spectated at during my PhD research, I have noticed that marathons, half-marathons and 10-km events all invite different community groups, such as silver bands and charities, and even athletic celebrities, to perform alongside the running event to entertain and bring people together. Reflecting on the effects of community performance in *Fun Run* can offer organisers a way of understanding how their additional community performers create an inclusive and celebratory sense of place.

References

Aggerholm, Kenneth. 2013. 'Express Yourself: The Value of Theatricality in Soccer', *Journal of the Philosophy of Sport* 40 (2): 205–24.

Allen-Collinson, Jacquelyn and John Hockey. 2007. '"Working Out" Identity: Distance Runners and the Management of Disrupted Identity', *Leisure Studies* 26 (4): 381–98.

Allen-Collinson, Jacquelyn and John Hockey. 2015. 'From a Certain Point of View: Sensory Phenomenological Envisionings of Running Space and Place', *Journal of Contemporary Ethnography* 44 (1): 63–83.

All The Queens Men. 2018. 'Fun Run'. Accessed 7 May 2018. http://allthequeensmen.net/projects/fun-run/.

Arts Centre Melbourne. 2017. 'Fun Run | 2017', YouTube video, 1 August. https://youtu.be/N0qNUkDCKh4.

Bale, John. 2004. *Running Cultures: Racing in Time and Space*. London: Frank Cass.

Bourdieu, Alison and Barbro Giorgi. 2010. 'The Experience of Self-Discovery and Mental Change in Female Novice Athletes in Connection to Marathon Running', *Journal of Phenomenological Psychology* 41 (2): 234–67.

Casey, Edward S. 1993. *Getting Back into Place: Toward a Renewed Understanding of the Place-World*. Bloomington: Indiana University Press.

Cianetti, Alessandra. 2016. 'Interviews: Live Art, Crossings, Europe (October 2016–February 2017): Kai Syng Tan – October 2016'. In *Performing Borders: A Study Room Guide on Physical and Conceptual Borders within Live Art*, by Alessandra Cianetti, 92–107. London: Live Art Development Agency.

Cidell, Julie. 2016. 'Time and Space to Run: The Mobilities and Immobilities of Road Races'. In *Event Mobilities: Politics, Place and Performance*, edited by Kevin Hannam, Mary Mostafanezhad and Jillian Rickly, 82–94. London and New York: Routledge.

Coleman, Simon and Mike Crang, eds. 2002. *Tourism: Between Place and Performance*. New York: Berghahn Books.

Cook, Simon, Jon Shaw and Paul Simpson. 2016. 'Jography: Exploring Meanings, Experiences and Spatialities of Recreational Road-Running', *Mobilities* 11 (5): 744–69.

Cresswell, Tim. 2015. *Place: An Introduction*. 2nd ed. Chichester: Wiley-Blackwell.

Darby, Kris. 2014. 'Our Encore: Running from the Zombie 2.0', *Studies in Theatre and Performance* 34 (3): 229–35.

Edensor, Tim and Hayden Lorimer. 2015. '"Landscapism" at the Speed of Light: Darkness and Illumination in Motion', *Geografiska Annaler: Series B, Human Geography* 97 (1): 1–16.

Filmer, Andrew. 2020. 'Endurance Running as Gesture in Contemporary Theatre and Performance', *Contemporary Theatre Review* 30 (1): 28–45.

Gardner, Lyn. 2012. 'Speed of Light – Edinburgh Festival Review', *The Guardian*, 10 August. Accessed 5 May 2018. www.theguardian.com/stage/2012/aug/10/speed-of-light-arthurs-seat-review.

Gotaas, Thor. 2009. *Running a Global History*. Translated by Peter Graves. London: Reaktion Books.

Grey, Christopher and Michelle O'Toole. 2020. 'The Placing of Identity and the Identification of Place: "Place-Identity" in Community Lifeboating', *Journal of Management Inquiry* 29 (2): 206–19.

Griffin, Meredith and Cassandra Phoenix. 2016. 'Becoming a Runner: Big, Middle and Small Stories about Physical Activity Participation in Later Life', *Sport, Education and Society* 21 (1): 11–27.

Hanold, Maylon. 2016. 'Ultrarunning: Space, Place, and Social Experience'. In *Endurance Running: A Socio-Cultural Examination*, edited by William Bridel, Pirkko Markula and Jim Denison, 181–95. London: Routledge.

Harvey, David. 1996. *Justice, Nature and the Geography of Difference*. Malden, MA: Blackwell.

Herrick, Clare. 2015. 'Comparative Urban Research and Mass Participation Running Events: Methodological Reflections', *Qualitative Research* 15 (3): 296–313.

Hill, Leslie and Helen Paris, eds. 2006. *Performance and Place*. Basingstoke: Palgrave Macmillan.

Jirásek, Ivo and Geoffery Zain Kohe. 2015. 'Readjusting Our Sporting Sites/Sight: Sportification and the Theatricality of Social Life', *Sport, Ethics and Philosophy* 9 (3): 257–70.

Keidan, Lois. 2006. 'This Must Be the Place: Thoughts on Place, Placelessness and Live Art since the 1980s'. In *Performance and Place*, edited by Leslie Hill and Helen Paris, 8–16. Basingstoke: Palgrave Macmillan.

King, Samantha. 2006. *Pink Ribbons, Inc.: Breast Cancer and the Politics of Philanthropy*. Minneapolis: University of Minnesota Press.

Koski, Tapio. 2015. *The Phenomenology and the Philosophy of Running: The Multiple Dimensions of Long-Distance Running*. Cham: Springer.

Krise, Raymond and Bill Squires. 1982. *Fast Tracks: The History of Distance Running*. Brattleboro, VT: The Stephen Greene Press.

Kyle, Gerard and Garry Chick. 2007. 'The Social Construction of a Sense of Place', *Leisure Sciences* 29 (3): 209–25.

Lorimer, Hayden. 2012. 'Surfaces and Slopes', *Performance Research* 17 (2): 83–86.

Mackey, Sally. 2007a. 'Performance, Place and Allotments: Feast or Famine?', *Contemporary Theatre Review* 17 (2): 181–91.

Mackey, Sally. 2007b. 'Transient Roots: Performance, Place and Exterritorials', *Performance Research* 12 (2): 75–78.

Mackey, Sally. 2016. 'Performing Location: Place and Applied Theatre'. In *Critical Perspectives on Applied Theatre*, edited by Jenny Hughes and Helen Nicholson, 107–26. Cambridge: Cambridge University Press.

Mackey, Sally and Sarah Cole. 2013. 'Cuckoos in the Nest: Performing Place, Artists and Excess', *Applied Theatre Research* 1 (1): 43–61.

Massey, Doreen. 1994. *Space, Place and Gender*. Cambridge: Polity Press.

Massey, Doreen. 2005. *For Space*. London: SAGE Publications.
Merleau-Ponty, Maurice. 2012. *Phenomenology of Perception*, translated by Donald A. Landes. London: Routledge.
NVA. 2018a. 'Speed of Light'. Accessed 5 May 2018. http://nva.org.uk/artwork/speed-light/.
NVA. 2018b. 'Speed of Light Edinburgh'. Accessed 5 May 2018. http://nva.org.uk/artwork/speed-light-edinburgh/.
NVA. 2018c. 'Speed of Light Salford'. Accessed 5 May 2018. http://nva.org.uk/artwork/speed-light-salford/.
Olsen, Andrea. 2014. *The Place of Dance: A Somatic Guide to Dancing and Dance Making*. Middletown, CT: Wesleyan University Press.
Relph, Edward. 2009. 'A Pragmatic Sense of Place', *Environmental and Architectural Phenomenology* 20 (3): 24–31.
Robinson, Robert, Ian Patterson and Megan Axelsen. 2014. 'The "Loneliness of the Long-Distance Runner" No More', *Journal of Leisure Research* 46 (4): 375–94.
Ronkainen, Norra, Amanda Shuman, Ting Ding, Shilun You and Lin Xu. 2018. 'Running Fever: Understanding Runner Identities in Shanghai Through Turning Point Narratives', *Leisure Studies* 37 (2): 211–22.
Samson, Ashley, Duncan Simpson, Cindra Kamphoff and Adrienne Langlier. 2017. 'Think Aloud: An Examination of Distance Runners' Thought Processes', *International Journal of Sport and Exercise Psychology* 15 (2): 176–89.
Seamon, David. 2014. 'Place Attachment and Phenomenology: The Synergistic Dynamism of Place'. In *Place Attachment: Advances in Theory, Methods and Applications*, edited by Lynne C. Manzo and Patrick Devine-Wright, 11–22. London: Routledge.
Sears, Edward. 2015. *Running Through The Ages*. 2nd ed. Jefferson, NC: McFarland.
Sheehan, Rebecca. 2006. 'Running in Place', *Tourist Studies* 6 (3): 245–65.
Sheller, Mimi and John Urry. 2004. *Tourism Mobilities: Places to Play, Places in Play*. London: Routledge.
Shipway, Richard and Immy Holloway. 2010. 'Running Free: Embracing a Healthy Lifestyle through Distance Running', *Perspectives in Public Health* 130 (6): 270–76.
Shipway, Richard and Immy Holloway. 2016. 'Health and the Running Body: Notes from an Ethnography', *International Review for the Sociology of Sport* 51 (1): 78–96.
Shipway, Richard and Ian Jones. 2007. 'Running Away from Home: Understanding Visitor Experience and Behaviour at Sport Tourism Events', *International Journal of Tourism Research*, 9, 373–83.
Shipway, Richard and Ian Jones. 2008. 'The Great Suburban Everest: An 'Insiders' Perspective on Experiences at the 2007 Flora London Marathon', *Journal of Sport & Tourism*, 13, 61–77.
Stevinson, Clare, Gareth Wiltshire and Mary Hickson. 2015. 'Facilitating Participation in Health-Enhancing Physical Activity: A Qualitative Study of Parkrun', *International Journal of Behavioral Medicine* 22 (2): 170–77.
Tan, Kai Syng. 2017. 'Hand-in-Hand: Activating the Body in Motion to Re-Connect with Ourselves and Others amidst a World in Motion and Commotion'. In *Chronotopies: Lecture et écriture des mondes en mouvement (Chronotopics: Readings and Writings on a World in Movement)*, edited by Luc Gwiazdzinski, Guillaume Drevon and Oliver Klein, 59–69. Grenoble: Elya Editions.
Tan, Kai Syng. 2018a. 'About RUN! RUN! RUN!'. Accessed 9 May 2018. http://kaisyngtan.com/project-type/about-run-run-run/.
Tan, Kai Syng. 2018b. 'Hand-in-Hand (Grenoble Festival, Whitworth Art Gallery, KCL Medical Education Workshop)'. Accessed 9 May 2018. http://kaisyngtan.com/portfolio/handinhand/.
Tan, Kai Syng. 2019. 'An Exploration of Running as Metaphor, Methodology, Material through the RUN! RUN! RUN! Biennale #r3fest 2016', *Sport in Society* 22 (5): 829–45.
Thomson, Sarah. 2004. 'Just Another Classroom? Observations of Primary School Playgrounds'. In *Sites of Sport: Space, Place, Experience*, edited by Patricia Vertinsky and John Bale, 73–84. London: Routledge.
Virgin Money London Marathon. 2018. 'Record Finish as Largest London Marathon Displays Its Spirit'. Accessed 13 May 2018. www.virginmoneylondonmarathon.com/en-gb/news-media/latest-news/item/record-finish-as-largest-london-marathon-displays-its-spirit/.

17
Shiftless Shuffle from Luton: An interview with Perry Louis

Jane Carr

Background

Styles of dancing collectively known as UK or 'underground' (or now 'old skool') jazz dancing have perhaps been rather neglected in terms of studies of twentieth-century British dance. Yet during the late 1970s and early 1980s, many young people developed expertise as dancers in styles of jazz dancing that proliferated in a network of clubs stretching from Canvey Island in Essex in the south, to London, then up to the big northern cities such as Leeds and Manchester and further on into Scotland (Cotgrove 2009). I have previously considered the marginal or 'underground' status of this so-called 'lost dance' in relation to how the styles of jazz dancing and associated dance practices fell outside of the dominant discourses of British dance of this era. Where more 'mainstream' dance took place in established dance venues, UK jazz dancing developed within club-orientated youth subcultures with roots in both Black British and working-class cultures (Carr 2018). Moreover, UK jazz dancing broke many of the dance conventions of the time. In the wider field of British dance of the 1970s and 1980s, the boundaries between social and theatre dancing and between dancing of the African diaspora and Western theatre dance forms were more clearly defined than they are in the early decades of the twenty-first century. In contrast, while jazz dancing took place in social spaces, many dancers displayed the virtuosity and performance skills associated with theatre dance, and while many dancers drew upon dance skills gained from their immersion in their diasporic heritage, their dance moves drew upon numerous other influences (Carr 2012).

UK jazz dancing developed at a time when the British children of post-Second World War immigrants from Africa and the Caribbean ventured out from their immediate family circle to find entertainment. Racist attitudes to immigrants from previous British colonies meant that not all clubs welcomed Black youths, but there were venues with a more open attitude and whose DJs' collections of music included imports featuring Caribbean and African-American musicians. In part this dancing developed in response to those DJs who pioneered the playing of fusions of jazz with funk, Latin and rock music (Cotgrove 2009). Jamaican ska and 'shuffling' dance moves may have been particular influences on some early jazz scenes in the UK, but jazz dancing may also have previously developed within African-Caribbean communities who brought the dancing to the UK (Nurse, cited in Carr 2012, 232; Edwards, cited in Cotgrove 2009, 257).

Paul Gilroy describes how, in Britain in the 1950s and 1960s, African and African-Caribbean immigrants shared in the development of an expressive culture through a range of social events and dancing to records imported from America, Africa, Latin America and the Caribbean (Gilroy 2002). According to the DJ Seymour Nurse (2012), in the 1960s there was a thriving scene of house parties and underground clubs at which a wide range of music was played for dancing, including imported jazz records. Nurse understands the jazz scene as growing out of these 'blues' parties. However, as a younger generation ventured out to clubs, new styles of jazz dancing developed that became known collectively as UK jazz.

There was not one single style of UK jazz; rather, different styles were associated with 'scenes' that developed in particular cities focused around dancing in clubs. According to the DJ Mark Cotgrove (Snowboy), by the late 1970s there were three key styles: contemporary (or ballet) style jazz, jazz funk and fusion (Cotgrove 2009, 40–41). This latter style, which Louis and members of the dance group IDJ practised, developed out of jazz funk in clubs around the London area. This style, which developed in the 1980s, emphasised fast rhythmic footwork punctuated with drops to the floor and turns. It was more grounded and had a stronger dynamic quality than the more 'balletic' jazz styles still danced in the northern clubs at this time. However, the different styles influenced one another as dancers from one city travelled to another to test their dance skills elsewhere. The dancing was also influenced by film and television. While Nurse (2006) emphasises the influence of the American TV show *Soul Train* on the London scene, Cotgrove (2009) and Lewis (cited in Carr 2012), who started dancing in Leeds, also refer to dance sequences in televised musicals and ballet and the actions in martial arts films. Some dancers, including Edward Lynch, one of the members of the Leeds-based Phoenix Dance Company and RJC, were also influenced by the 'contemporary' dance that was taught at school (Cotgrove 2009).

Jazz dancing was often competitive. Jazz dancers took part in challenges in which dancers competed against one another, dancing within a circle. This practice developed from African diasporic traditions which many young people would have experienced through family and community gatherings. However, these challenges took on a new intensity in the club scene. Those dancers who in their local club might compete against one another would band together to travel to another city to take part in 'all dayers' at which groups of dancers representing areas from all over the UK would challenge or 'battle' each other. These events fostered strong local bonds and pride in belonging to a particular area: for many of the dancers, being part of a particular jazz dance scene was a route to gaining a sense of belonging along with an opportunity to achieve recognition.

The sense of status that young people could gain through their dancing was particularly important in the late 1970s and early 1980s. Job opportunities were limited, particularly within Black communities due to Black youths being disproportionately affected by unemployment (Brown and Gay 1985). With time to spare, young people could and did spend time and energy practising dancing. The ability to copy, and even improve upon, the moves of another dancer was one way to demonstrate superior skills – so there was an incentive for dancers to develop their range of steps and styles (Lewis, cited in Carr 2012). Moreover, the best dancers could gain employment, and professionally organised dance groups emerged: Brothers in Jazz, Bubble and Squeak, Expansions, Foot Patrol, IDJ, the Jazz Defektors (who also became established as a pop group), Mahogany and the Untouchable Force appeared as guest acts in clubs or theatre shows or in pop videos and film.

Dance challenges featuring dancers from across the country not only contributed to the influence of local styles upon each other but also created the sense of belonging to a broader UK jazz 'scene'. While many of the dance influences were from outside the UK, the dancers understood their dancing as uniquely British. Drawing upon Stuart Hall's notion of 'new ethnicities' (Hall 1992), I have argued previously that UK jazz dancing provided opportunities for young people to negotiate their embodiment of new British identities in ways that recognised their diasporic heritage (Carr 2017). At the time, the dancers were primarily concerned with developing their style and skill to enhance their position in the jazz scene. Yet viewed as a 'field' of cultural activity, this scene provided the space for young people to establish new styles of 'being' and a sense of belonging even when elsewhere in Britain young people of a diasporic heritage were often faced with hostile racism.

UK jazz dancing can be understood as embodying interrelationships between people and place that are of significance to the changing social context of postcolonial Britain. As someone interested in the history of this dancing, I was excited to discover that Perry Louis, one of the key proponents of jazz dancing and music, is keeping the tradition alive in Luton. He works as a DJ in London and internationally, and his 'Shiftless Shuffle' club nights continue to keep the tradition alive. The following interview, conducted on 17 July 2018, was an invaluable opportunity to gain an insight into Louis's experiences as a dancer and DJ. Thanks to a career that has taken him to many different countries, Louis has a sense of the place of UK jazz in a global context. The highlight of his career, as he explained as we began the interview, has been 'getting the untapped and unnamed style of my dance and music recognised on a global platform'. It is evident that his continued concern to raise the profile of UK jazz is a focus of his current activities. In addition to providing details about the music and dancing that he remembers, Louis also reveals how through jazz dancing he gained a sense of belonging. As a dancer he experienced being recognised as belonging to Luton, his birthplace, and that also provided a quasi-North London identity when he travelled to cities elsewhere in the UK. Yet he also has a sense of being part of a broader community of jazz enthusiasts. Perhaps in contrast to concepts of communities as 'imagined' (Anderson 1991), Perry reveals how a sense of belonging can be established through music and dance.[1]

Interview

JC *Perhaps we should start at the beginning – how did you and your family come to be in Luton and what was life like there when you were young?*

PL My parents wanted a different life to the one they'd led in St Lucia. They believed that moving to England would be better for them, and for their children, as we would have more opportunities. My godmother, who was one of the first people to settle in Luton in the late 1950s, told my parents to come and arranged their passage, and they went to live with her to begin with. I was born in Luton in 1961 and my life was exciting and happy, as I was sheltered from the real world – so to speak – until I started school. Then, I had to learn how to communicate with others and also to fit in, mix with other kids and be accepted. Until then, I hadn't realised that I was 'different'. I remember always being inquisitive and seeking adventure. I think I'm still like that now.

JC *What are your earliest memories of the music and dance when you were growing up in Luton?*

PL We had music all round us really. My godfather – Dad's best friend – and my cousins always played music when we went to visit and likewise, we played music when people came round to our house. My parents always played music in the house so for me it was natural to listen to music and of course, we always danced when we played music; and if we weren't dancing ourselves, we watched our parents, cousins and aunties dance – music and dance always went together.

JC *Can you remember the kind of music being played and the moves that went with it?*

PL Going back to the late 1960s and early 1970s, the music which was staple at the time was reggae or some people would say it was ska. But there was also merengue – which at that time was early folk music from the Caribbean with connotations of salsa, and also soul – even early country ... which was kind of weird. It was definitely [music for] social dance where the parents were dancing together – you know, jive or salsa. The youngsters were trying to dance on their own: at that age you didn't want to dance with a girl so you were dancing on your own, trying to create something that was related to the music. But sometimes your parents would grab you and dance with you so you were learning how to dance – with other people of the opposite sex.

JC *And the music? Was it on records? Where did they come from?*

PL It was on records. There were outlets. My uncle and godfather got music [that was] imported. Sometimes they went over to the Caribbean, but there were specialist shops in London where you could pick up some of the latest tunes. If people were coming over from the Caribbean they might have brought a record over so it kept you up to date with what was going on in the Caribbean. And, as a social thing, when everyone got together it was reminiscent of being what at that time they called 'back home'... and mixing it with some of the music that 'works'. At that time it might have been something like Chuck Berry, a kind of bluesy rock and roll, but [this was] mixed in with the merengue [and] with the reggae ... Being in the UK there were influences coming in from the States ... but it was just music for us.

My godfather and uncle were developing their own sounds. So if there was a party they'd supply the music. They were on a mission to bring the latest sounds from the States and Caribbean and what was happening – like Blue Beat and Island Records – on UK labels playing Caribbean music.

JC *Tell me more about the music and dance scene in Luton and Dunstable that you experienced while growing up.*

PL The music and dance scene in Luton that I experienced was special. When I grew up, there was a strong youth club culture, in fact, I lived opposite a youth club where I used to watch people go to a Friday disco night. It was called Beechwood Club. I remember sneaking into the club when I was about 11 or 12 which really got me interested in going out. Also, my cousins would sometimes go there and we were quite close. Being my inquisitive self, I learned about other disco sessions, as they were called at the time, and started to find a way to go to some, where I met other people and made friends. That led to me getting to know specific tunes, record shops, fashion and going out – and there was always somewhere to go. Before long, I was getting recognised by people, which was very exciting! I went to some under-18 clubs, but also to places such as California Ballroom, Sands, Hatters, Didoz, Youth House, Chanley, Halyards, the Barn, St Joseph's, St Augustine's, Caesar's, Pink Elephant and quite a few more. It was a very healthy scene.

JC *What kind of music was being played and how did people dance when there was no older family around?*

PL Those days (1972–73) you were listening to Ike and Tina Turner, chart-related music, soul music from the States – George McCrae *Rock Your Baby*, Donna Summer – which was a very early disco sound – and the Average White Band which was a funky soul. People were dancing more on their own. There was an energy to their dancing and because of that energy and how [their dancing] related to the music they were getting noticed. I can remember when you were dancing to *Rock Your Baby* you were taking one step forward and one step side, like a rocking motion that went with that style of music.

JC *You had your family environment, which was Caribbean-orientated, but then you went out clubbing with more young people and there was an American influence. So when you were dancing in the clubs were you drawing on some of your Caribbean-influenced moves and bringing them into the American disco style?*

PL There was a completely different disco style but remember we were very, very young so the influences we had were the social family environment in which we were listening to music and maybe some soul would come into that. When you went to the youth club they were playing the music of the day but if you had one of the DJs trying to make a name for themselves they would create their own sound, maybe bringing in soul music and progressive music together with chart music. So you had two things going on and from there it started to focus more on soul and disco ... at that period all the music kind of went together ...

The connection was what you understood dance to be. When you went to a family gathering you danced a certain way but when you went out and tried to dance the same as at family gatherings it didn't quite fit so you started to develop your own style to belong to the music that you were hearing and the social environment that you were going to and belonging to. So you started to adjust ... and that's kind of what happened. But some of the older people had a thing that they were developing. Because you were younger you didn't know quite what that was because you weren't privy to those kind of clubs yet.

JC *How and when did you start to become aware of a broader jazz dance scene in London and the rest of the UK?*

PL I started to become aware of a broader club scene when dancers would come to places such as California Ballroom [Dunstable]. Me and my friends would challenge the dancers who had a different style of dancing and by talking to some of them, I found out they came from London and Leicester. Some of the older dancers also came from Luton and they told me where else to go out, either in London or other towns. Back then, it wasn't a jazz dance scene, however – jazz was starting to be played in the clubs alongside disco, funk and soul. My style of dance and my energy suited the faster, harder, jazzier rhythms, so I decided to explore different clubs and go to London. And that was when I got a rude awakening. The music I was hearing was so different, more rhythmical, harder-edged, and the dancers blew my mind. That was when I realised I wanted to be part of that movement and that scene, which I found was a deep music scene that was also spreading.

JC *Why? Can you give more detail regarding the music and the style or names of dancers you remember?*

PL This period was a strong influence [on UK jazz]. It was the music first of all. You were hearing groups such as Cameo, the Fat Back Band, Kool and the Gang. These guys were jazz-influenced, making groove music.[2] (This was before they had commercial success when their music changed.) The dancing then was influenced by dancers like 'Mohammed' – an East London guy whose style of dance was completely different to things you could ever imagine, Paul 'Trouble' Anderson who ruled the underground style, Trevor Shakes, Ian Baptiste, even people who went on contemporary dance [courses], Stuart Thomas and Little John: they had their own particular style that was groove-based but contemporary. They were creating this whole new style of dance that was so different to what was going around in Luton and I dare say the rest of the country.

JC *Can you try and explain this new dance style?*

PL That's very hard because this was the first time I was seeing it. It was very sophisticated because there was a 'groove' to it. These dancers were in control of the dance that they were doing. It was very rhythmical and it wasn't based on just one step but an amalgamation of steps. But it flowed. And at the same time they were doing spins and grooving while dragging their feet. It went with the music. Then they would stop right on the beat and then they'd start again. There was a definite style to it and a definite 'coolness' to the actual groove and they were always in control – they always knew what they were doing – and yet it just seemed to be 'way out there'.

JC *I have seen clips of IDJ dancing later – was this similar to their style?*

PL No, it was different to that. More disco funky and a little bit slower. It wasn't jazzy – that came later, where disco met groove met jazz.

JC *Can you explain how you identified with dancers from both Luton and London?*

PL When I started going to London I went on my own and was in the background trying to learn to dance and also learn about the music. Luton had its own style, which started to be influenced by the London scene, as – like me – some of the Luton dancers were going to London clubs and studying the style. So when they danced in a Luton club, they stood out. Since I was one of them, I'd be dancing with them, recognising their style influences. It was like being part of a secret society, as none of us were letting on where we'd learned that different, harder style. Dancing in those days was very competitive, and I wanted to be one of the 'faces' in Luton.

JC *How did you get involved with IDJ?*

PL I was probably the first person Jerry Barry asked to dance for IDJ [around 1983] as I went to incredible jazz dance clubs, such as Jaffas, Electric Ballroom, Spats and Jazzi Funk Club, and learned to dance with the best dancers I had ever seen. I was also very competitive, which helped me to become a 'face' on the dance floor. Anyway, I was asked to join IDJ but turned them down, as I was, at that time, a middle-distance runner for Luton and was winning races and Luton were doing well in the leagues. Also, as the clubs were getting smaller and smaller, I decided to concentrate on athletics and try to run for England. Sadly, I got myself a hamstring injury and wasn't really good enough so had to take a break, during which I ended up meeting up with old friends who invited me to come out to a club session. Feeling a bit down, I said yes and in the club they were playing jazz. Plus, Jerry Barry who started [IDJ] was there and asked me if I was still dancing. I said I hadn't been but that I was thinking of coming back out to see if I could find my feet again. I remember people treating him like a star and asking who I was and I also remember one of his dancers jumping in front of me and ripping up the floor whilst giving me a look that said 'so what are you going to do about that?' I laughed and said ok but by the time I got on the floor he had gone. I told Jerry that I'd be back, to which he replied that if I found my feet again, we would talk. He ended up inviting me to a rehearsal where I met up with the very guy who'd ripped up the floor as well as dancers who I'd been teaching to jazz dance. I was in shock when Jerry told the guy he'd probably got off lightly and so after that, I started dancing with IDJ. That was in 1988–89.

JC *How would you describe their style of dancing?*

PL Jerry came from the groove-based scene. He was going into jazz funk clubs or what we called boogie clubs or really funk groove clubs. He had the style passed down from dancers like Paul 'Trouble' Anderson and Trevor Shakes who had a different style of dance. Because the music was getting jazzier, Jerry was working together with Paul Anderson on that style of dance that became recognised as fusion. It was a fusion of jazz funk, funk and groove but we were doing it to jazz music. Back then it was called jazz, footing, stepping or fusion. These days, we call it UK dancefloor jazz. Still to this day, not many people actually 'get' the style. The London style (which some people call fusion) came from jazz, funk and a groove bass but it was fast, high-energy and stylish, as well as athletic. It was a more footwork-based style and faster because of the music. The music dictated the rhythm and speed of the dance. It looked fast because of the energy we were dancing with and the speed of the music we were dancing to. You either danced on the beat or you double-timed the dance to fit the jazz. The good dancers made it look effortless ...

If you could do it properly, you got noticed. And I love it ... It is still evolving and has many different influences but mainly, you have got to have some funk to do the London fusion style properly. If you just came in learning jazz without that background, if you didn't understand what happened before, you didn't get the complexities of the rhythm.

JC *How would you describe its significance for you?*

PL For me, its significance is that it gave me a purpose and a life. The music, the dance, the culture is a lifestyle which I have lived and am still living.

JC *I notice that Seymour Nurse considers jazz as part of 'West Indian' culture but Irven Lewis reports how his crowd were quite 'mixed' – although generally poor. How would you describe the jazz scene in terms of the diversity of those participating? Did this vary according to location?*

PL The jazz dance scene I experienced was a mixed culture, and it helped a lot of people come together from all cultures and walks of life who would never have met otherwise. It is like Notting Hill Carnival, full of West Indians but absorbing anyone who wants to accept it. The dynamic of the crowd changed depending on where you went to. And yes, a lot of us were poor, as we got into the scene before we started work at the age of 15 or 16. So some of us got jobs such as paper rounds or working in shops so that we could go out and spend our last £1.50 to go to London to a club and dance all afternoon. The diverse group of people were brought together because of the music, and some of the dancers from East London had hard living conditions but dancing took them away from that for a bit. It also depended on which DJ you were following but people were drawn in from all different types of background: middle class, working class, poor, better off, Black, White, Indian. It was very special and it was a lifestyle, not just a recreational activity.

JC *Was jazz dancing and music important to your sense of identity and belonging?*

PL Hugely. I belonged to a special club that was not for everybody, and it gave me a huge sense of pride – still does. Belonging to the scene gave me a sense of comfort which enabled me to go to places and meet very special people including my heroes of music and dance. And being recognised as one of 'the Dancers' was amazing.

It did give me a sense of identity. Although I went to jazz funk, rare groove and funk clubs, it was only when I started dancing to jazz that everything seemed to 'fit'. My energy, the way I was dancing, the way that I was able to be creative to the music – it really fitted. That's where I felt more at home and got recognised for what I was doing and met people who were leading that style like Jerry Barry who formed IDJ, Keith Haines who started a group called Afro Block, and Philip Octane. They were really leading that style of dance, especially in London. There were others but they were the ones I remember. And when you are talking about bands there was a group called PAZ, led by Dick Crouch, who was making jazz dance music at the time for that 'scene' and Tiny Maria. I got to work with both of them in later life … These were early heroes that were special to me.

JC *How did you get to be a jazz music DJ? Did this change or develop your understanding of jazz?*

PL I started buying music from the late 1970s. I was buying jazz funk – things like T-Connection *Do What You Wanna Do*. I was also buying little bits of reggae 'cos of early influences. I was looking for specialist jazz tracks, for example the Ivan Chandler Quintet *Final Approach*, Lonnie Smith *Straight to the Point* … They were the 'jazz dance royalty tracks' that were hard to find as you never knew what they were but you were looking for them. I was also buying disco and funk.

I thought these styles of music would always be around so didn't really think about DJing, but I do remember hearing about the DJs and their collections and thought it would be really cool to be part of that! So when I started to talk to the DJs I found that in fact, I had a lot of the music and knew quite a bit about it. And I also recognised that because I was always on the dance floor, I could develop different angles of playing.

Of course, I had to learn my craft and get accepted as a DJ, as they were two different worlds. So I decided to look into it and see if I could get involved; not because I wanted to be a DJ but because I wanted to be able to show that dancers had knowledge which we could expand and share to encourage others. This enabled me to shape and develop my dancing, as I was listening to lots of different styles of jazz with different rhythm patterns. And that meant I could experiment more and challenge myself and my dancing, which helped me to be more creative. It was a whole new exciting world.

As a DJ I had to learn to put music together. There were such influential DJs playing great music. If you were going to do it, you didn't want to be the same. You had to learn or try and formulate a way that people would gravitate to. Anyone can play records but you've got to play them in a way that keeps the audience engaged and keep the dancers engaged and then work the floor because people get tired and energy levels go up and down so you have to work a way to keep it flowing and working. So I went out to try to create something that was about the dance floor but not about being a connoisseur DJ playing the latest tunes. I wanted to create something specifically for the dance floor whether it was jazz funk, jazz or funk.

I knew a lot of DJs who were prominent at the time. I was travelling to specialist sessions with Gilles Peterson, Snowboy, Patrick Forge, Sylvester, Simon Mansell. I followed Paul 'Trouble' Anderson, Paul Murphy, Colin Parnell, Bob Jones, Chris Hill and Cleveland Anderson. I was going to all the best places and associating with top DJs so to call myself a DJ I had to have something special for them to say: 'OK. He understands. He's got something.' That took a long time to formulate.

JC *When and why did you start JazzCotech?*

PL I started JazzCotech because in the early 1990s, there were so many people who were talking about jazz dance and what it was and who should represent it. I had danced with IDJ as well as being a solo dancer, and knew other dancers who said they wanted to dance in a group. So I decided that I wanted to create something that would represent the scene, the music, the culture and the diversity of dancers, i.e. boys, girls, Black, White, Indian, Asian – plus non-dancers who just loved the music and wanted a chance to be taught. I also wanted the dance style to be recognised as an art form and stop the negativity that surrounded the jazz dancers who had somehow got themselves a reputation for being arrogant and rude and just interested in themselves, not the music. So I decided to take on that task and form a jazz dance collective that would be diverse and totally inclusive, made up of people who loved the music and wanted to dance. That was in 1992. I didn't just invite existing 'known', top dancers into the group – if I could see something in someone, that special something, that feel for the music, I would encourage them. I got quite a bit of stick for doing that but I didn't care – for me, jazz dance has always been for everyone and if someone shows me the right attitude, the hunger to learn and the feel for the music, I don't care who they are.

JC *I notice lots of people in Luton know you and often make the effort to say hello. What do you think you have contributed to Luton?*

PL I'm proud of being a Lutonian and I wanted Luton people to say: 'OK, there goes Perry Louis, one of our own'... I think I have managed to change some people's perception of Luton, by inviting them in, either to perform here or watch a performance here. And I think I have enriched the cultural diversity of Luton, by running events that appeal to a wide range of audiences and artists from different cultural backgrounds. I'd like to think I've done Luton proud.

JC *And how are you are aiming to establish a means of celebrating and 'safeguarding' this heritage back in Luton?*

PL I want to create a musical footprint that links the present to the past. Things happen at such a fast rate it's easy to lose your culture and sense of where you come from. It's important to recognise the history and background so we can move forward. Otherwise that sense of belonging can be lost.

Notes

1. The importance of interactions situated in the world of lived experience is well understood within the field of community arts. For example, the benefit of such interactions is core to the values of community dance (Houston 2008).
2. Groove music, for Perry Louis, is defined by its funky back beat which stimulates the dancer to perform with more varied phrasing.

References

Anderson, Benedict. 1991. *Imagined Communities: Reflections on the Origin and Spread of Nationalism*. Rev. ed. London: Verso.
Brown, Colin and Pat Gay. 1985. *Racial Discrimination: 17 Years after the Act*. London: Policy Studies Institute.
Carr, Jane. 2012. 'Re-Remembering the (Almost) Lost Jazz Dances of 1980s Britain', *Dance Chronicle* 35 (3): 315–37.
Carr, Jane. 2017. 'Researching British (Underground) Jazz Dancing 1979–1990'. In *British Dance: Black Routes*, edited by Christy Adair and Ramsay Burt, 35–54. London: Routledge.
Carr, Jane. 2018. 'Battling under Britannia's Shadow: UK Jazz Dancing in the 1970s and 1980s'. In *Narratives in Black British Dance: Embodied Practices*, edited by Adesola Akinleye, 217–33. Cham: Palgrave Macmillan.
Cotgrove, Mark. 2009. *From Jazz Funk and Fusion to Acid Jazz: The History of the UK Jazz Dance Scene*. London: Chaser Publications.
Gilroy, Paul. 2002. *There Ain't No Black in the Union Jack: The Cultural Politics of Race and Nation*. London and New York: Routledge. (First published 1987.)
Hall, Stuart. 1992. 'New Ethnicities'. In *Stuart Hall: Critical Dialogues in Cultural Studies*, edited by David Morley and Kuan-Hsing Chen, 442–451. London and New York: Routledge. (First published 1989.)
Houston, Sara. 2008. 'Dance in the Community'. In *An Introduction to Community Dance Practice*, edited by Diane Amans, 11–16. Basingstoke: Palgrave Macmillan.
Nurse, Seymour. 2006. 'Seymour Nurse's "Jazzifunk" Club Jazz History/Music Chart'. Accessed 29 April 2019. www.thebottomend.co.uk/Seymour_Nurses_Jazzifunk_Club_Jazz_Chart.php.
Nurse, Seymour. 2012. 'Harris Berlin'. Accessed 13 June 2020. www.thebottomend.co.uk/Harris_Berlin.php.

Afterword

Tamara Ashley and Alexis Weedon

As this book went into production, the Covid-19 pandemic broke out across the world. Travel was restricted and our geographical sense of place focused on the local: our neighbourhood, our street, our house, our room. We had to renegotiate distinctions as places for work and domestic living, schooling and relaxation overlapped.

We are in the final stages of publication in July 2020 with little time to reflect on the past few months, but as editors, we wanted to acknowledge the profound and astonishing changes that have been brought by the pandemic. The lockdown affected each one of us in different ways, and as co-editors, we offer a short dialogue on our experiences of lockdown that are redefining our sense of place.

AW Tamara, can you describe how the lockdown affected you?

TA Immediately, I was affected by the loss of contact and touch in my daily work. My work involves building a sense of place through touch – human-to-human contact through movement and dance. My body is a place that holds and witnesses these intersections of communication, touch, movement and learning. Daily, this work remakes me, defines my sense of place, refines my intelligence, relating, being and community building with others. Lockdown took dance out of the studio into the bedroom, from skin-to-skin contact to screen-to-screen contact. The screen-to-screen interaction lacks tactility, a key part of my usual everyday practice. When I am teaching, I find myself reaching into the screen – my body expands and reaches in reaction to what I observe and what I want to feel, which is the reciprocal kinaesthetic exchange that characterises dancing in a room together.

AW What immediately affected me was the change in our house as we had to fit four people in to work alongside each other. Our previously shared areas changed function, and functions were layered within rooms. Our boundaries between work and relaxation, between screens and real life, online appointments and domestic rhythms, even work days and holidays all had to be renegotiated. We developed a routine and focused on meeting at two points in the day: for a lunch-hour walk and an evening meal. We found that in the neighbourhood, the farmers re-marked footpaths, installed signs to protect land use and diverted walkers away from animals and buildings. The village's communal playgrounds, parks and sports grounds closed and we sought to find alternative walking routes from home to add variety. It was a swift and profound change in our family's – and other citizens' – freedom of movement.

I also noticed that there was an equally swift change in language. The leisurely turnover of terms between generations (e.g. *meh*, *bloomers*) or over a decade cycle (e.g. *firehose tweets*) was replaced by rapid redefinitions: *contactless* was no longer waving your bankcard over the shop's machine reader, it meant stepping back when the delivery van driver left a package at your door. Social distancing was no longer being in the online virtual world Second Life, it meant waving in a friendly manner as you crossed the road to avoid someone, giving them two metres' distance. Lockdown was not a prison term, it meant staying at home and keeping safe.

I felt that the language was heavy and restrictive: it could have been more positive if we had said 'touch-free', implying a freedom not to touch, or 'distant socialising', implying that our social chats were just happening at a distance, or 'sequestering', as this was, more or less, the effect on our lives.

TA Yes, I agree that the language has been very affective. During lockdown, my body and mind search for the wisdom and knowing that I used to encounter daily through moving with others, in shared space, touch, energy and contact. These practices based on sharing movement together shift in this extended period of isolation, and I feel how the language is defining us, even as I resist the definitions. I move by myself. I walk in nature. I listen and open my senses to the somatic relational learning in each moment. Movement can shift the mind and body, give new senses of place. By myself, the changes are subtle and gradual. I miss aligning energies with others, where the absorption gives presence and new organisation for all of us. I find new ways to experience tactility. I find self-sounding is like a superhighway to change. I resonate my body through tones and pitch; the vibrations expand, open, soothe and reorganise. I chant every day and then improvise in my body, moving the voice like a limb, like a wave and a self-hug. It changes inner and outer configurations.

AW Yes, I am missing colleagues and friends whose contact gives me energy. I began to spin other threads by saying hello to neighbours, keeping an eye open for the more vulnerable, becoming part of the village in a way I have not been before. As I went for my daily walk, I saw how the community was coming together creatively: artwork appeared in front gardens in praise and support of the National Health Service workers, a stream beside the recreation ground became a fairy dell decorated with handicrafts from painted travellers' stones to dream catchers, and hand-coloured rainbows appeared in front windows or chalked on the pavement as a symbol

Examples from the outpouring of community art during lockdown in Toddington, Bedfordshire, April 2020. © Alexis Weedon.

of hope. One resident had set up an 'interactive' trail around the village, with challenges from drawing and quizzes to throwing balled socks through complicated hoops and down runs. These were unscripted and unsolicited offerings – evidence that in times of crisis when people need support, they turn to arts practice to come together and generate a sense of community.

TA As an artist, I felt very compelled to create and participate in the sense-making of this time. I started generating short dance films to try to explore some of these new experiences, while also providing some inspiration and starting points to students whom I am mentoring in choreographic projects. Students started to generate site-sensitive responses to isolation and lockdown. Moving filmic portraits of dancers in isolation emerged. The weather during the spring was dry and sunny, and many projects were filmed outside, drawing dancers closer to nature. There were also some poignant representations of

Still from the film *Corona Spring* by Tamara Ashley.

the pressure of confinement and lack of social contact. My own work conceptualises the space inside in black and white, and the outdoor space in vibrant colour; with person-to-person contact reduced, I perceive nature as more resonant and alive. In lockdown, there is the possibility to dance in the smaller spaces inside or in the vast expanses of the fields that I can visit on my daily walk. In June, after 14 weeks of lockdown, I was walking in Fen Drayton nature reserve and the damsel flies swarmed me in iridescent blue clouds. After weeks without touch, it was like an embrace from nature, an oxytocin hit.

Zoom emerged as a performance platform where the tessellated screen is harnessed incredibly creatively by performing artists. Gestures are passed through the screen to create choreographic continuity, and musicians harmonise across geography to play together in the virtual space. Seeing into the intimate spaces of artists, their living rooms, bedrooms and kitchens, while simultaneously

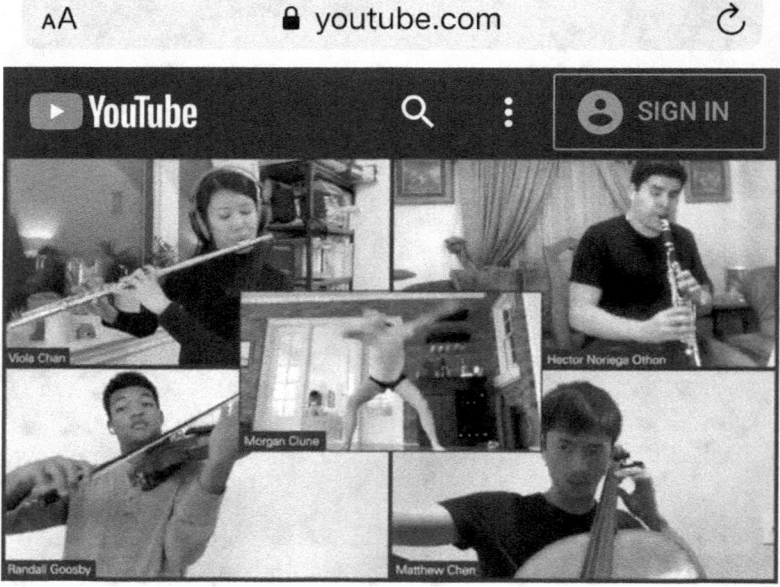

Bolero: screenshot by Tamara Ashley.

appreciating the resonance of ensemble, is very moving. My favourite example was the Juilliard School's rendition of *Bolero*, which enabled collaboration between the school's dance, drama and music students with cameos by some of their famous teachers, such as Laura Linney and Yo-Yo Ma.

AW I wonder how much of this we will remember? I am sure we will hear of how we all lived in the virtual world – teleworking, socialising on apps and switching on the free streamed offerings of opera, musicals and plays from closed theatres – but if anything, it has taught us that the virtual environment is draining and does not energise us in the way that connecting with the life experience of others does. I have sought out the live and communal in my teaching and my exercise classes, where the living of others connects with, informs and enriches our own. I have found that my sense of place is rooted in the ecosystem which we develop around us and which comprises our living conditions, our closest family and friends, our street and the connections maintained through precarious forms of telecommunication. I have needed to counteract the creep of lethargy which can come from restricted movement with other sources of vital energy, and so have had shared theatre and film evenings with friends, exchanged notes on growing plants and walked the country footpaths around me.

TA The arts and culture offer during lockdown has been generous. Companies and organisations have offered streaming shows and free classes for practitioners. It has been possible to watch full-length plays, contemporary dance shows and musicals, while also being able to participate in classes with leading practitioners in various global performing arts centres. Access to information not normally available unless one travels has been a positive aspect of being an artist in lockdown, and sharing time and space with artists across time zones has enabled shared connections on the experience of the pandemic from diverse geographic locations. Archives of work created during the pandemic have been established. For example, my second film, *Oxytocin*, is archived on the website http://www.timeofpandemic.co.uk.

Meanwhile, at the time of writing in July 2020, theatres, studios and many galleries are closed, posing a real long-term threat to the survival of the sector, and many of the artists involved in the shows we have enjoyed watching at home on the laptop are out of work. The future is uncertain and the pandemic is not over. The resilient and creative nature of artists, which allows them not only to adapt to new conditions but also to express the meaning of collective experiences, has been very evident since March 2020, but as access to theatres and rehearsal studios remains limited, the sense of place of the theatre itself is under revision and will affect the performing arts for a long time to come.

In our Introduction to this book, we said that our 'sense of belonging to place is fragmented, disrupted and under continual redefinition'. We have experienced, during the course of the book's production, one significant shift which has confirmed, in a startling way, our comment that the 'bringing together of communities in a place is increasingly important in creating a sense of connection, *well-being* and understanding'.

Index

Abbott, Andy 78
Abrahams, Roger D. 139
adaptation(s) xv, 20, 162–4, 177–8, 181–2
aesthetic(s) xi, 8, 14, 103, 113, 141–5, 147–8, 153, 156–7, 209, 220, 229, 231, 256
Alencar, Daniel 148–50
'Aleph' concept 242–3
Allen, William L. 190
Alsop, Will 87
Anderson, Benedict 275
Anderson, Eric 51
Anderson, Paul 279, 281, 283
Anderson, Peter J. 184
Andersson, Jan-Erik 87
Angel of the North 87
apps, use of xv, 46–8, 52–3, 291
Arnstein, Sherry R. 37–9
Art Bed and Breakfast (AB&B) project 245
art work 5, 66, 244–5
  in non-arts spaces 240–1
Artillery (organisation) 6, 61
artistic endeavour, xxi
  location of 221
artists: origins of 224
  role of 4–5, 9, 14, 84–5, 95–6
Arts Action Group 36–40
Arts and Humanities Research Council 3
Arts Council 20, 26–7, 29, 30, 76, 79, 82, 84, 93–4, 96, 116–18, 142–3, 147, 235
'artwashing' 10, 94
Ashley, Tamara xi
  co-editor, co-author of Introduction and Afterword
Atkinson, Peter xi, 10
  author of Chapter 14
Attridge, Derek 213, 226
audience development 26, 50–1, 60, 80–1, 246, 251
audiences for theatre 23, 26
Aujla, Imogen xi, 7, 121
  co-author of Chapter 8
Ayckbourn, Alan 20
Azubuine, Oz 74

BAME people 76, 152
Barlow, Peppy 30
Barr Beacon 44–9, 52–4
Barrett, Syd 221
Barry, Jerry 280–2
Barthes, Roland 114, 205–6
Bat Yam 10
Battle for the Winds 145–8

Baudrillard, Jean 185
Bauman, Zygmunt 214
Bazalgette, Sir Peter 8
Beam (arts charity) archive 84–96
Beck, Ulrich 214
Bedfordshire University 9, 73, 78, 82, 120
belonging, feeling of 1, 99, 110, 224, 274–8, 282, 284, 292; *see also* sense of place
Benjamin, Walter 213
Berger, John 103
Berlin 7
Bhabha, Homi 205
'Bieguni' 163
Birmingham 88, 94, 117, 128
Blunt, Alison 110–11
Bobadilla, Natalia 6, 10
bodies as places 13–14, 109, 155, 169, 261
bodily experience 164–5, 169, 181, 260
Boiling, Sarah 240–1, 251
Bolsonaro, Jair 157
Bordignon, Fabio 186
Borges, Jorge Luis 242–3
Bottà, Giacomo 230, 232
Bourdieu, Pierre 9, 209
Bournemouth Marathon 256
Brah, Avtar 204
Bramble, Forbes 29
Brazil 150–2, 155–7
Brexit 90, 264; *see also* newspaper coverage
'bricolage' 147
Brith Gof (performance company) 251
British Broadcasting Corporation (BBC) xi, 51–2, 197, 232
British Railways 92–3
Brown, Basil 25–6
Bruns, Axel 50
Buckledee, Steve 195
Bündchen, Gisele 151–2
Bunting, Catherine 248
busking 143

Calcutt, Andrew 185
Cambridge and Cambridge University xiii, 9–10, 26, 221
Cameron, David 189, 192–3, 196–7
Campkin, Ben 9
career patterns xvi, 7, 74–5, 105, 118–19, 121–9, 132, 227, 275
carnival 139–48, 151, 156, 281
Carr, Jane xi–xii, 13, 73–4, 275–84
  author of Chapter 17
Casey, Edward 257

293

Cecchetto, Fátima 153
Certeau, Michel de 162, 241
Chambers, Iain 109
Cheeseman, Peter 21–2
Cheng, Julia 81
Chipperfield, David 90
Cidell, Julie 25
City of Culture programme 3–4, 78, 80, 258
civic arts 1, 90, 94
civic development 3, 229
Clarke, Gill 118, 125, 127
colonisation 173
Commission for Architecture and the Built Environment 95–6
community interest companies (CICs) xv, 6, 35, 61, 76
community involvement 2–3, 6, 37, 162, 250
competitions 6, 142, 145, 148, 157
Connected Communities project 3–5
constructivist research 19, 119
Control (film) 231
Cooper, Mary 30
co-production 5–6, 39, 68, 95
Cording, Alastair 30
Cosgrove, Mark 273–4
cosmopolitanism 6
Coult, Tony 20, 31
Covid-19 pandemic 286–92
'craftivism' 11
Crang, Philip 203
creative cities 2
creative class model 2, 8, 10, 147
creative industries 8–9, 57, 80, 250
Creative People and Places programme 76, 82, 240, 245, 247, 251
creativity 2, 13, 212–15
 artistic 219–23
 spaces of xvii, 6–7, 215–21, 66, 147, 158, 212, 218, 220, 222, 225, 245
Crenshaw, Kimberlé 12
Cresswell, Tim 139
Croft, Jennifer 162–3, 177
Croose, Jonathan xii, 10
 author of Chapter 9
Crossick, Geoffrey 90
Crouch, Dick 282
cultural capital 141, 229, 249–52
cultural leadership 82
cultural policy and cultural politics 140, 142, 147
cultural practice 3, 12, 92, 139–41, 183, 209–10
cultural workers 9, 13, 116
culture: power of 1, 6
 role of 1–2
Culture and Local Development (OECD, 2018) 1–2
Culture and Sport Evidence (CASE) programme 247
cultured childhood 248–9
Cummins, Kevin 231
Curtis, Adam 185
Curtis, Ian 231
Cutting, Ivan xii
 author of Chapter 1
Czikszentmihalyi, Mihaly 213

dancers and dance artists 7, 116–34; *see also* jazz dancing
Darwent, Charles 89
Deacon, David 186, 188
Dean, Roger T. 99–100, 110
deficit model of cultural participation 248
degeneration 8
democratisation of culture 70, 142, 152, 155, 157–8, 209
Department for Culture, Media and Sport (DCMS) 2, 247
Derrida, Jacques 180
devolution 5
Diamanti, Ilvo 186
diasporas 204–6, 210
digital technology 12–13, 199, 209
disc jockeying 282–3
discourse analysis 12
discourse-historical approach 187
diversity 6, 77, 125, 141, 149, 151, 155–7, 214, 234, 267, 281, 284
Dobbs, Rachel 38
Dobrowodzka, Anna 178
documentary theatre 21–3
Douglas, Noel 74
Dowling, Robyn 110–11
Doyle, Jack 191
dual careers 7; *see also* career patterns
Duchamp, Marcel 179
Durham University 9
Dwyer, Claire 203

East Anglia xii, 19–22, 25–6, 30, 32
Eastern Angles theatre company 19–33
Eastside Projects 94
Eco, Umberto 165–6, 177
Edensor, Tim 141, 158, 261
Edinburgh 5, 12, 249, 259–60
Edwards, Elizabeth 209
Edwards, Delyth 248
Efford 35–43
Elliott, Michael 192
Elsaesser, Thomas 178–9
embedding of artists in place-making 96
Emery, Tom 234, 236
Emson, Kenny 28–9
English language 172
E17 Art Trail 6, 56–70, 250–1
ethnography 99–100, 140, 191, 212
Euroscepticism 183–8, 193, 198–9
Evans, George Ewart 23
Evans, Graeme 147
everyday life information seeking (ELIS) 12
Exeter 20, 40, 82, 146, 159
exoskeleton costumes 259–60
expenditure cuts 2

'familial gaze' 104–7
family photographs 98–110, 113, 205, 208
 'reading' of 103–4, 207
family relationships xviii, 29, 104–6, 114, 130, 167, 214, 218–20, 274–8, 287, 291
 myth and *lived reality* of 104, 273
Farrell Review (2014) 91
Farrer, Rachel xii, 7, 121, 125, 129
 co-author of Chapter 8
favelas 152–6

film-making 5, 98–9, 112–15, 172
Finding Temeraire 162–3, 172–3, 177–9
fine art 219
Firstspace concept 243–4, 251
Flaubert, Gustave 172–3
Flintoff, Beth 33
Florida, Richard 8
'flux' 249–50
Ford, Sam 51
Forkert, Kirsten 7–8
42nd Street (charity) 245–6
Fox, J. 158
Fox, Liam 192
Franks, Alan 31
freelancing 116–18, 121, 131
Freshwater, Helen 86
Freud, Sigmund 164–5
friends and family members, support from 130; *see also* family relationships
Fun Run event (2017) 255–64, 267
funding sources xviii, 6–9, 20, 35–7, 41, 49, 53–4, 60, 63, 65, 69, 74–8, 93, 95, 117, 122, 124–5, 143–4, 147, 155, 157, 245

Gansel, Mireille 176
Garratt, Dean 246, 252
Garrett, Bradley L. 13
Gatenby, Phil 231
Gehl, Jan 90
gentrification 2, 93, 149, 154, 229, 233–4
Georgiou, Myria 12
Giaccardi, Elisa 51
Gibson, Rachel 125
Giddens, Anthony 11–12, 214
Gifford, Chris 184
Gil, Gilberto 155
Gilbert, Helen 150–1
Gill, Craig 231
Gilmore, Abigail 240, 251–2
Gilroy, Paul 273
Godber, John 20
Gogol, Nikolai 20
Goldman, Tony 6
Goransson, Marie 6, 10
Gormley, Anthony 87
Gove, Michael 189–92
Gramsci, Antonio 172–3
graphic design 85
Grayling, A. C. 185
Green, Joshua 51
Gresswell, Sophie 78, 81
Grillo, Moriam 80–1
Groves, Jason 191
Gruenewald, David 13
Guy, Kenneth L. 108

'habitus' 209
'hacking' 5
Haines, Keith 282
Hall, Stuart 205, 284
Hambleton, Robin 10
Hand-in-Hand event (2016) 255–9, 264–7
Hanem, Kuchuk 172
Harker, Kerry xii, 86, 237
    author of Chapter 6
'Harnessing' conference (2019) 82
Harrison, John 32

Harvey, David 139–40, 146, 148
Harvey, Lucy 236
Harvie, Jen 252
Haslam, Dave 227–8, 234
Haynes, Sarah 11
health connotations of running 256, 259, 265, 267
Henderson, Graham 91–2
'heritage', use of the word 32
Heritage Lottery Fund 28, 32, 44, 49, 52
Heseltine, Michael 29
higher education institutions 96; *see also* universities
high-profile practitioners 123–5, 128
high-rise buildings 228, 233
Hirsch, Marianne 101, 104, 106
holidays 222, 287
Holland, Andrew 30
Holland, Kieran xiii, 12
    author of Chapter 16
The Holy Inquisition 171
home, concept of 110–12
Horwood, Joel 31–2
Hospers, Gert-Jan 229–30
Hunter, Victoria 4
Hyde-Chadwick, Alison 193

identity, establishment of xvii, xxi, 12–14, 25, 28, 90, 95, 107, 121, 127–8, 139, 141–57, 173, 206, 233, 237, 249, 282
images: of places 1, 229–30
    still and *moving* 113
immersion in artistic activity 223
inclusion and inclusivity 94, 229, 253
Independent Dance (organisation) 117–18
Independent Dance Review Report 129
innovation 2, 9, 67, 177, 212, 234
intersectionality 12, 178
'iterative cyclic web' model (Smith and Dean) 99–100, 110

Jack, Hilary 236
Jackson, David xiii, 11, 107–15
    author of Chapter 7
Jackson, Peter 139–40, 203
Jackson, Vincenza (Tina) 107
Jacobs, Jane 3, 228–9
Jakobson, Roman 166
Jameson, Fredric 228
Jancovich, Leila 248, 251
Jans, Marc 242
Jaray, Tess 87–91, 94–5
jazz dancing 73–4, 272–5, 278–84
    styles of 273, 283
Jellicoe, Ann 29
Jenkins, Henry 50–1
Johnson, Boris 189–92
Johnson, Mark 187
Jones, Hannah 38
Jones, Phil 7, 9
jouissance 164–5, 168–71, 176, 181
Joy Division 230–1
Judd, Ian 92
Juilliard School of Music 291

Kahne, Juliet 2
Kapoor, Anish 87

INDEX   **295**

Kaszynska, Patrycja 90
Kaye, Nick 251
Keidan, Lois 258
Kenny, Mike 20
Kerr, Andy 88
Kerry, Laura 56–70, 250–1
Khan, Amadu Wurie 5–6
Khan, Sadiq 6, 64
Khanna, Ranjana 175
Kong, Lily 7
Kristeva, Julia 170–2, 177
Kuhn, Annette 98, 101–3, 113

Lacan, Jacques 165, 170, 180
'ladder of participation' 37–9
Lakoff, George 187
Lash, Scott 214
'late modern', definition of 213–14
Layard, Antonia 4
Laybats, Claire 185, 199
Lea T 153
Leadson, Andrea 191
Lee-French, Segun 31
Lefebvre, Henri 242–4
LeftCoast project 245
Lewis, Helen 185
Lia Rodrigues dance company 154–5
A Light Wave 92
'liquid' modernity (Bauman) 214
literary texts, creation of 219, 222, 224
'Live Art' (Keidan) 258
live performance 218
Liverpool 11
localism 5–6, 13
London 7–12, 56, 119–20, 126–30, 140, 203–6, 221–4, 231, 234, 272
Long, Paul 7, 9
Lorimer, Hayden 260
Louis, Perry 73–4, 273, 275–84
Lovell, Vivien 94
Lummertz, Vinicius 148–9
Luther, Martin 171
Luton xix–xx, 73–81, 275–80, 284
Lutwack, Leonard 223
Lydon, Mike 10
Lynch, Edward 274

MacColl, Ewan 21–2
McGuire, Morag 56–70, 250
Mach, David 87
Mackey, Sally 258
Makuwe, Stanley 162–3, 172–80
Malinowski, Bronisław 221
Malta 99
managerialism 8
Manchester 227–38, 245–6, 264, 272
    cultural zone 232–4
    housing provision 233–6
    Northern Quarter 228, 231–5
    property development in 237–8
Manifesto for the Arts in Place 91–2
marathon running 256, 262–4
marginalisation 251
Marseilles 6, 10
Marten, Maria 33
Massey, Doreen 140, 148, 157–8, 210
Matthews, Peter 51

Mautner, Gerlinde 187, 199
measurement of results 8
Mediterranean image 107–10
Meecham, Tristan 262–3
Meirelles, Fernando 151
Melbourne 262–3
Melhuish, Clare 9
Mellander, Charlotta 8
memory and memory work 11, 98, 100–3, 109–10, 112–13, 240, 251
Merleau-Ponty, Maurice 13
Meskell-Brocken, Steph xiii
    author of Chapter 15
'mezzanine condition' 215, 218, 221–4
Miami 6
Miles, Malcolm 158
Miles, Philip xiii, 11
    author of Chapter 13
Milling, Jane 4, 248
mobile phones 47, 52, 216
modernity 11
Mollett, Nicole 77, 79
Molloy, Caroline xiii, 12, 204
    author of Chapter 12
Monteiro, Simone 153
Morgan, David 184
Morgan, Luke 87
Motta, Wallis 12
Mould, Oli 6–11
Moving Tides procession 146–8
Mujeri, Charmaine 178
multidisciplinarity 10–14, 253
multimedia 52
Murphy, David 74–80
Museum of London 52
music, creation of 216–19
Musolff, Andreas 188
Mycock, Andrew 246
Myerscough, Morag 87
mystery plays 21

Nancy, Jean-Luc 114
Nash, Martin 235
Nathan, Max 4–5
National Trust 26, 32
neoliberalism 2, 149, 156–7
networking 59, 77, 122, 126–30
new urbanist principles 2
new writing for the theatre 30–1
New York City 3, 10, 228
newspaper coverage of Brexit referendum 186–200
Nietzsche, Friedrich 185
The Northern Way 85, 87, 91
Nurse, Seymour 273, 281
Nutt, Michaela 80

Oakley, Kate 7–9
Octane, Philip 282
Olympic Games 140–57
One Dance UK 117
1000 Swifts event 58, 68
open-access opportunities 250
Organisation for Economic Co-operation and Development (OECD) 1
Osborne, George 191
Osler, Audrey 246

'otherness' 11–12, 107, 231
Oxford Dictionaries 183–4

Pahl, Kate 5
painting 88–9, 139, 219, 222, 236
Palmer, Stephen 235
Paradise Works initiative 236
Paris 258
Parker, Charles 21–2
participatory design 3
partnering with a place 4
Pasmore, Victor 94
Patel, Priti 189
Payne, Emma-Rose xiv
    co-author of Chapter 5
pedestrianisation 89
Peel, John 230
peer review 219
peer support 116, 129
Pendle 94
People Making Places programme 93
Perry, Beth 7, 9
Peterborough 26–33
Peterlee 94
Pheidippides 262–3
Phillips, Martin 5–6
photographic studios: as politicised spaces 203–10
    as research sites 205–7, 210
photography, importance of 101–2
Pichault, François 6, 10
Pinsky, Michael 87
Piotrowska, Agnieszka xiv, 11–12, 171–2
    author of Chapter 10
Piper, Heather 246, 252
place: attractions of 8
    as a concept 221–2
    definition of 241, 257
    of origin 111
    as a state of mind 224
    understood through performance 257–9
place-based arts practice 139–45, 157–8, 253
place-identity 140–3
place-making 1–13, 51, 85–6, 88, 95, 240–8, 252
    arts-based 7–10, 141, 157
    case studies of 5–7
    first use of the term 3
    local, regional and *national* 146, 148
    participation in 4, 96
    potential for 255–61, 266–7
    processes of 139–40, 149
    state-funded 140–2
    sustainability of 95
    and young people 244–8
'placelessness' 2
'placeness' 162
The Planner 88
planning 3, 6, 14
Plensa, Jaume 87
Plymouth *see* Efford
Polizzotti, Mark 176, 180
polyphonic dialogue 6
Pool, Steve 5
populism 186, 194
portfolio careers 121
postcolonial theory 205, 224

postmodernism 185, 213
post-truth 183–200
    intensification of 195–8
Potsdamer Platz 3
Powell, Enoch 193
Powell, Robert 87
Pratt, Mary Louise 205
Prescott, John 87
Preston 94
Priestley, J. B. 92
Pritchard, Stephen 2
Project for Public Spaces (PPS) 3
protest action 141
psychoanalysis 164–5, 168–9
psychological barriers to participation 248, 251
public art 85–96
    origins of 94
Public Arts (organisation) 88, 91–3
    change of name to Beam (2007) 95
public–private partnerships 3, 149
public spaces 88, 94, 147, 158

quality of life 1
Quick, Charles 92–3

Race for Life 267
Raising the Barr project 44–54
Ramsay, Tony 29–31
Read, Herbert 220
regeneration projects xx, xxi, 3–5, 9–10, 35–42, 73, 93, 94, 141–3, 147, 149, 157, 248
regional development agencies 84, 87, 95–6
Reisigl, Martin 187–90, 196, 198
relativism 185
Relph, E. 145
research methods 120–1
research participants, pseudonyms and backgrounds of 133–4
Rigby, Robert 30
Rio de Janeiro 141–2, 145, 148–52, 156
Roberts, Julia 12
Roche, Jenny 125
Rogue Artists' Studios, Manchester 234–6
Rose, Gillian 249–52
Rousseff, Dilma 152
routine, artistic 212, 220–3
Rowinski, Paul xiv, 12
    author of Chapter 11
The Ruins (rock band) 216–20, 223
running 255–67
    organisations for 255, 267
Rushdie, Salman 177

Said, Edward 172–4
Salford 236–7, 259–60
Sandifolo, Eddi 178
Sandor, Andrea 234
Saville, Peter 231
Sawyer, Miranda 227–8
Schaefer, Kerrie 248
Schneider Alcure, Adriana 152
Schwellenangst 249
Secondspace concept 244, 251
Seeger, Peggy 21–2
self-employment 116–19, 132
selling yourself as an artist 222

sense of place 1–4, 11–14, 19–20, 26, 30, 33, 53, 114–18, 123–5, 130–2, 162–3, 178, 181, 183–5, 198–9, 220, 223–4, 240, 255–9, 265–6
The Sex Pistols 230
sexual satisfaction 165
Shakespeare, William 20
Shand, Rory xiv–xv, 5
   co-author of Chapter 2
Sigona, Nando 205
Singapore 7
Sismondo, Sergio 185
site-specificity 251
Situations (organisation) 95
slavery 151
Sloane, Alexia 81
small-scale venues 90
Smith, Fran 84
Smith, Hazel 99–100, 110
social capital theory 2, 217, 222
social distancing 287
social justice 155, 252
social media 5, 46–7, 50–3, 58, 185, 199
social networks 130, 132, 139, 142
social space 3, 205, 243
Soja, Edward W. 241–4, 252
solitary creativity 219–20
space: conceptualisation of 249
   and place 251–3
   understood as a liminal moment of time 224
Speare, Simon 81
Speed, Chris 5–6
Speed of Light event (2012) 255–61, 267
Spivak, Gayatri 172–3, 252
'spreadable media' 51
Stam, Robert 177
Starkey, Hugh 246
state funding 9, 140–2, 157
Stolarick, Kevin 8
Storey, Gayle 74–5, 81
studios 216–18
success, perceptions of 123–8
Sultan, Irving 105–6
Sultan, Larry 104–7, 114
Sutton Hoo treasure 25–6
Swift, Charles 28–9
'symbolic landscapes' 139–41

Take A Part (TAP) organisation 35–43
Taking Part Survey 247
Tambling, Pauline 125
Tan, Kai Syng 264–6
Temer, Michel 152
Teresa of Ávila, St 162, 170–2, 177
TestBeds project 73–83
Theatre in Education (TIE) 20
'thirding' 242–5, 251–3
Thirdspace theory 241–6, 249–53
Thomas, Wyndham 28–9
Thurman, Clare 240–1, 251
Tilley, Christopher 140
time capital 217
Titchner, Mark 80
Todd, Jane Marie 164
Toffler, Alvin 50
Tokarczuk, Olga 162–3, 166–70, 174, 176, 179

tokenism 39
topoi 187
transcultural identities 210; *see also* identity
transferable skills 123
translation 165–6, 176–81
transmedia stories and strategy xv, 44, 51–3
travel psychology 167–8
Tredinnick, Luke 185, 199
'trickle-down' theory 249, 252
Trump, Donald 185
Turino, Celio 155, 157
Turkish community in Britain 203–4, 207–9
24 Hour Party People (film) 231

Understanding Everyday Participation (UEP) project 242, 248
United Kingdom government's white paper on culture 2
universities: partnership with towns 79–82
   projects led by 9–10
unpaid work 122
urban regeneration *see* regeneration projects

Vargas, Eliane 153
Verhellen, Eugène 246, 252
vernacular practices 51, 140–51, 145, 147–8, 154–5, 157–8
Voices from the Favela 153

Wakefield 88–95
   cathedral precinct 88–91, 94–5
   The Hepworth 90
   Westgate station 92–3
Wakeford, Tom 4
Walla, Nala 13
Walthamstow and Waltham Forest 6, 56–9, 63–4, 68
Warner, Marina 176–7, 180
Warwick Commission (2015) 9
Watson, Kate 74
Waugh, Patricia 213–14
Way, Charlie 20, 31
Webb, Katherine 222
Weedon, Alexis xv, 6, 56–70, 250–1
   co-editor, co-author of Introduction and Afterword, author of Chapter 4 and co-author of Chapter 5
Weiss, Peter 21
'Welcome to the North' 87, 91
Weymouth 141–5, 156
Weymouth, Tony 184
Whyte, William H. 3
Wicks, Sanna xv, 5
   author of Chapter 3
Wide, Kim xv, 5
   co-author of Chapter 2
William Morris Gallery 63, 69
Williamson, Kirsty 12
Wilson, Alva 78
Wilson, Richard 87
Wilson, Tony 229–33, 238
Wings of Desire (film) 3
Witts, Richard 231
Wodak, Ruth 187–90, 196, 198
Woods, Richard 87
Word of the Year 183
words, nature of 163

work places and work spaces 216, 219–21
working conditions 116, 118, 121
world heritage sites 144, 146, 159
The Wuffings 25–7, 30

'yarn bombing' 11
Year of Culture programme 76, 79
Yilmaz, Ihsan 203

young people 244–8, 252–3, 275
    definition and characteristics of 246–7
    participation in cultural activities 247–8, 253

Zimbabwe 12
Zoom platform 290
Zupančič, Alenka 165, 168

www.ingramcontent.com/pod-product-compliance
Lightning Source LLC
LaVergne TN
LVHW011446180426
R19332200001B/R193322PG836100LVX00002B/3